MEXICO

Also by Kate Simon

A RENAISSANCE TAPESTRY:
The Gonzaga of Mantua

A WIDER WORLD:
Portraits in an Adolescence

BRONX PRIMITIVE:
Portraits in a Childhood

NEW YORK:
Places and Pleasures

NEW YORK
(with Andreas Feininger)

FIFTH AVENUE:
A Very Social History

ITALY:
The Places in Between

ROME:
Places and Pleasures

KATE SIMON'S PARIS

KATE SIMON'S LONDON

ENGLAND'S GREEN AND PLEASANT LAND

KATE SIMON

MEXICO

Places and Pleasures

FOURTH EDITION

HARPER & ROW, PUBLISHERS, NEW YORK

Cambridge, Philadelphia, San Francisco, London,

Mexico City, São Paulo, Singapore, Sydney

MEXICO (Fourth Edition). Copyright © 1962, 1963, 1971, 1979, 1988 by Kate Simon. All rights reserved. Printed in the United States of America. No part of this book may be used or reproduced in any manner whatsoever without written permission except in the case of brief quotations embodied in critical articles and reviews. For information address Harper & Row, Publishers, Inc., 10 E. 53rd Street, New York, N.Y. 10022. Published simultaneously in Canada by Fitzhenry & Whiteside Ltd., Toronto.

First PERENNIAL LIBRARY edition published 1988.

Designed by Ruth Bornschlegel

Indexed by Auralie Logan

Library of Congress Cataloging-in-Publication Data

Simon, Kate.
    Mexico, places and pleasures.

    Includes index.
    1. Mexico—Description and travel—1981–
—Guide-books.   I. Title.
F1209.S5   1988   917.2'04834   88-45061
ISBN 0-06-055130-5
ISBN 0-06-096291-7 (Perennial Library: pbk.)

88 89 90 91 92 CC/FG 10 9 8 7 6 5 4 3 2 1

Contents

Preface

Elsewhere in this book is mentioned its subjectivity, a distillate of one particular set of leanings conditioned by one particular complex of experiences that have been accepted and rejected. It is also a selective book, again a matter of personal tastes and judgments, and the fact that Mexico, like every other country, stumbles here and there into dry dullness.

The scheme, in general, is to indicate only lightly the ways of thick towels and "Cielito Lindo" and to follow more carefully other paths, which, though they are also reaching for the glories and profit of tourism, are just beginning to shout their wares; paths not yet crammed with hotels like surrealist dreams nor their color entirely translated into comfort. The time is almost here; but hacking out jungle roads, establishing smooth routes of transportation, teaching primitive peoples the harm in tiny *animales* they can't see and haven't the water to wash off are not accomplishments of tomorrow morning. Therefore, some of the trips described are not along enameled paths of absolute comfort; but none is especially difficult for the curious, the open, the patient person.

As introduction to the country there are essays on the textures of Mexican life—nonexpert and with too much respect and affection to say, always, "How pretty! How quaint!" With the essays and a number of vignettes as frames, various areas are pictured, for pleasure in remembrance and with the hope of drawing a reader into the aura of that pleasure. Then, having responded to its spirit, the reader is given specific notes dealing with its matter: hotels, restaurants, shops, and markets, and a grab bag of practical advice.

This book would have been possible, but a much less pleasant job, were it not for the presence of friends in Mexico who waited at the end of long craggy roads with hot showers, festive tables, fresh clothing, good conversation, and enthusiasm: Esther and Al Freedman, Fannie and the late Al Paperno, Reva and Leonard Brooks, David and Judy Frenkel, Lini di Vries. And to all the Rosas, Juans, Marías, Benitos, and Lupes who tried to help, I am grateful.

MEXICO

Introduction

In a world which is becoming homogenized with fearsome rapidity, Mexico is still a wonderful confusion and melding of disparate facts, eras, art, sociology, and mental climates. It is a country, in spite of present financial desperation, busily constructing dams, pulling roads out of the jungle, building and peopling seaside resorts, and in the process bringing to light its majestic antiquities. Its aesthetic sense is highly developed—anyone with hands can shape a lovely object—yet it prefers plastic crudities. The government has banned billboards from its dramatic roads but disregards the maddening, incessant yammer of radio commercials and deforms hills, palm trees, rocks, fences, and storefronts with the face and name of its next president, although there is no contest and no need for electioneering in a one-party country. Politicians sound large strophes to *revolución* while the government grows more stolidly U.S.-capitalist in style. Mexico speaks innumerable Indian languages, including a strange vocabulary of whistling, and prides itself on its very careful Spanish. Some of its people are chic worldlings; many of their compatriots still move in the dark of superstition and witchcraft. The tropics dance, sing, catch fish and fruit as it drops off the trees, and sleep away the rainy season; an hour's ride upward into the hills enters an atmosphere of seriousness, hard work, and inwardness. Modern factories pour their smoke over huts of adobe and thatch and minimal company housing. And where the sun shone clear, there are skies that are brown blankets of smog. Glittering, grandly ornamented skyscrapers loom over lame, blind Colonial palaces. The unyielding highlands are abandoned and their people join the squatter colonies on the edges of big cities. Much of Mexico is rural and little of it is bucolic; at one moment it is a garbage dump, at another moment it is the Garden of Eden. This kaleidoscope finds other facets in a geography which is a tight crumbling of volcanic peaks, high wild forests, stretches of aridity out of dense, ebullient tropics, long green valleys with white-gold beaches at their feet, bitter cactus and tumbling, profligate bougainvillaea, and mountains like screams of fury, like heaps of satin, like unshaved cheeks, like prehistoric hides.

And there is no other place so near the United States which displays such a brilliant variety of indigenous peoples: Tehuanas (Zapotec ladies from the state of Oaxaca) who travel in great convoys, dimming everything else in their wake; small, slender Totonac ladies in lacy bridal white; the white comforter matrons of Mayan villages; the capable Tarascan woman who spins as she briskly walks her remote paths; the shrewd, poised merchants of Mitla; the Mixe woman in her long, striped homespun skirt, a painted tray of zeppelin-sized pineapples balanced on her head. The cities, too, are happily different. Oaxaca is a gentle, mellow aristocrat; Guanajuato is anachronistic, strong, and proud; Morelia is a bluestocking and Jalapa is trying to be one; Veracruz is a slaphappy extrovert and Las Casas peers suspiciously from under dropped lids.

A guidebook is a driven talker who tells you more than you want to know and less; there is always some monumental fact which is torturingly not there. A book of travels is more peculiar; it lures and seduces, and having eased you into the boudoir, abandons you. A travel-cum-guidebook is most peculiar, giving too much or too little, cajoling to improbable and even impossible places and—final indignity—stamping its own eccentric tastes on a country and a reader. Travel- and guidebooks are also pathological liars. A nineteenth-century wanderer doing Europe could depend on finding Sicily in the same immutable Greek-Saracen-Norman torpor described by eighteenth-century travelers. Now, having carefully arranged his itinerary to be in Agrigento in almond-blossom time (on instructions from a guidebook published three months before), the modern tourist finds that the blossoming trees have been trampled to fertilize a new hotel. In the frenzied improvements going on in many parts of the world to meet "tourist tastes"—usually meaning American—what *is* will not be tomorrow morning, the latest information is obsolete before it is printed, and there seems to be no solution. The more traveling, the more changes; the more guidebooks, the more errors; the more revisions—an idiot dog chasing his tail.

The subjective travel-guidebook, such as this one, can move even further away from verity. Filtered through one set of tastes, the selective vision of one pair of eyes, the responses of one particular temperament, a place can become—to other temperaments, tastes, and eyes—almost a fiction. One person can know the ride to Palenque in a two-passenger plane as a transmigration into bird, a supreme sensation; another will recall it as a terrified time of frenzied bead-telling, supplications to the Virgin, and palsied, ceaseless signs of the cross. The hope here is that tastes of writer and reader meet at some points, that the whole endeavor may become something more than a bundle of delusions and disappointment over places omitted or treated lightly. Here again the question of taste enters, in addition to the fact that some areas of Mexico (the north, for instance) are intrinsically less interesting than others and that some, like Acapulco, have postured so long and loudly that additional information isn't merely that; it is the thousandth repetition.

Mexico is not always the easiest country to travel in even on the deep-grooved, somnambulist tourist routes. It is never indifferent, so you cannot be. It is vulnerable (though Nicaragua calls it the "Colossus to the North") and you find yourself vulnerable. Enchantment and exasperation are inseparable twins here and sometimes the whole stretch between El Paso and Las Casas seems to be a suburb of Behind the Looking-Glass. The degree of a traveler's pleasure in Mexico is a question of his own responses; here, as elsewhere, being a contented tourist requires some of the ingredients of a contented marriage—a willingness to be pleased and pleasing, sustained interest, openness, acceptance, and some self-knowledge. Can you go naked of prejudices, interested in rather than disturbed by modes of life that are not your accustomed patterns? Can you delight in a mountain town which explodes its greenery into copper crags and not be bothered by the absence of the very best mattresses? Must you have trustworthy spigots, constant hot water, phones that click to immediate attention, and electric power which is always powerful? Have you the poise and stamina to ride a second-class rural bus with chickens, turkeys, sacks of onion, bundles of *yerbabuena* (mint), Indian babies like ripe plums and their not too meticulous gentle young mothers whose faces have the sparse perfection of archaic sculpture? In other words, should you limit yourself to the cushioned charms of Mexico City's internationalism, Cuernavaca's sophistication, and Acapulco's hand-fed ease or are you equipped for the mulchy, overripe villages of the tropics and a jeep ride through a tunnel of jungle brush to see a Mayan temple which looks as if it might have been built by ancient Greeks?

The careful traveler to Mexico goes equipped with some knowledge of its complex past, the astonishments of its geography, its imposing archaeology, its riches in crafts, and an invisible valise full of relaxed, accepting attitudes. There have been a few rare birds who journeyed the fast U-turn to Mexico City—a quick look around and back home. For most others it's been an immortal, if troubled, love affair.

Bon voyage and don't forget your raincoat (the one with the air vents); take woolens for the highlands and cottons for the tropics; leave time for the unexpected; and try to be as courteous, gentle, and tolerant with the Mexican as he will be with you. Even if he is wearing a cracked straw hat and torn pants, he is still the fruit of several sophisticated cultures—Indian and European—which did mighty deeds while we were crawling on all fours. Except when tequila overtakes him, he is humane, generous, resourceful, quick-witted, and to be respected as a citizen of the only country which, in spite of the Conquest and through a bloody history, valiantly held on to its great Indian heritage and continues to. The only "reservations" in Mexico are a few ghettos of expatriate *norteamericanos*.

MEXICAN HOURS

6:40 *A train due to leave at 7:00* A.M. *sits in the Mexico City station accepting salesmen, children with grandmothers, eccentric travelers, rural farmers—red-eyed and drained by a bibulous visit to the big city—assorted blanket bundles crammed with clothing, giant-size bottles of Coca-Cola, bananas, and small breads.*

6:50 *A boy comes through collecting coins for disabled railroad workers; everyone gives him something. Hard on his heels comes a vendor of nylon sweaters, hoping the morning's chill will induce purchases. No one buys, but several women, dressed in thin cotton* rebozos *(shawls), look yearningly at his armful of bright warmth.*

7:00 *Trays of* pan dulce *(sweet rolls) and* gelatinas *(stiff, sweetened gelatin structures) are brought aboard, paid for, and consumed hungrily along with gulps of cola by a few. The others curl up for more sleep.*

7:05 *Walking and talking briskly, a wristwatch salesman flashes his glittering laden forearm at the assemblage of eaters and sleepers, nervously aware of how little time he has to negotiate a sale and hop off should the train begin to move. The train sits, quiescent.*

7:10 *Beyond the sea wall of Veracruz, the wife of a launch owner slips her brown, soft bulk over the side of the boat and takes an oily, refreshing swim in the Gulf.*

7:12 *Burning toast floats its threatening smell through a modern kitchen in Guadalajara. The frightened new Indian maid bursts into tears over the cruelty of the cursed máquina and runs for water to pour over it.*

7:15 *The train snorts and whoops warnings of imminent departure. The man vending bread and rolls pays no attention.*

7:20 *The train moves out slowly and everyone congratulates himself and his neighbor on its "punctuality" and the social progress this connotes.*

7:22 *The train stops. Someone who can read neither signs nor tickets should be on another train. He is put off.*

7:35 *Having started again, the train pauses for a local stop at Tacuba. The bread and sweater men get off and are replaced by another collector of alms, a salesman of oilcloth table covers, a woman with a basket of bananas and oranges to sell. A minstrel with a high, cracked voice and an inept guitar leads (by means of a belt-to-belt string) a boy, a blind deaf-mute. Everyone in the train gives something.*

8:30 *A large American car pulls up to the doorway of a private school in Mexico City. Two little girls in neat, moist braids, small bits of gold in their ears, blue jumpers neatly pressed and white blouses freshly starched, emerge from the back, open the front door, and ceremoniously kiss the hand of papa, who has been driving, in farewell and homage.*

9:00 *The train stops at a rural station, just beyond a set of one-room huts whose tin roofs are anchored by rocks. A severe-looking man in glasses leaps aboard, uncovers his large basket, and brings out of it chunks of barbecued pork encased in glistening warm fat. Behind him trails his round daughter,* carrying hot tortillas for wrapping around the meat. By this time the sleepy torpor of most of the passengers has lifted, the cold clouds of early mountain day have risen in the sky, much sweet soda pop has been consumed; the assemblage is ready to eat and talk.

9:30 *Three large Tehuanas of Juchitán, each a Roman legion, scornfully move into a bus and conquer it, sapping color and life from the other passengers, insignificant backgrounds to their splendor. In a few hours they will take over Oaxaca with their confident presence, their sweeping skirts, their high lacy headdresses, and their chains and bangles of old twenty- and fifty-dollar gold pieces (U.S.).*

Mexico City: The Beginning

A sleek, black Mercedes-Benz (*the* arriviste symbol in Mexico City) sweeps down one of the rose-bordered avenues which leads to the center of town. In it sits a woman dressed in *haute* style—a fine Italian suit, heavy pearls in her ears, heavy gold on her wrists, and on her head a Paris kerchief which covers the imperfect hairdo she is taking to her *salon de belleza* for repairs. A maid emerges from a new apartment house resplendent with glass and mosaics, to take a pair of shoes for repair to the shoemaker whose shop is a strip of grass under a corner tree. Down the next street come two burros, ambling along the edge of a torrent of traffic, laden with carbon and wood in sacks of handmade rope mesh, and led by an Indian father and son who have walked miles to sell fuel to the *ricos*. Ten blocks from the radiance of jewelry and French imports, a family of ragpickers— grandmother (or mother; poor women age fast everywhere) and two children, pecking like hungry chickens—pick up cigarette papers, an old newspaper, discards from the cans of an apartment building. Two carts casually roll among the dashing bullets of highly polished European cars, conversing amicably as they go. One is a fanfare of tall plume-like brushes and the heaped shine of tin pots; the other carries brilliant snacks: cucumbers cut and spread like huge water lilies, their delicate color enhanced with a sprinkle of sienna-red chile powder; slices of coconut make a picket fence around chunks of Tamayo-pink watermelon.

Standing in the doorway of a central hotel, one can sometimes hear the whistle of the public baths, announcing the triumph of hot water. On the roofs of modern apartment houses maids slap and beat the laundry on stone slabs, gossiping the hours away as they used to in their *pueblitos* in Oaxaca, as did their mothers before them. One of the new prosperous market areas, which sports French cheese, "New

York"–style salamis, Italian shoes, and a resplendent supermarket, is inhabited also by an elderly gentleman who tethers his magnificent game rooster—high-arched red and gold feathers, long spurs and high comb, and the same proud *hidalgo* air as his owner—to a tree, for airing and viewing the larger world. Nimbly threading his way in front of charging buses or hanging on to their backs, a boy on a bicycle balances a hundred rolls in the enormous brim of his straw hat, a skill becoming rare but still occasionally visible.

Rarely does one hear the pat and slap of tortilla-making any more. (If the quiet Indian woman had a voice, the rhythmic, soft *clap-clap* was it.) Now and then, however, the patter comes out of a restaurant or house whose owners won't have anything to do with the machine-made variety stamped out in the local *tortillería*. If one listens carefully, through the roar of buses, through the blast of horns and the screech of brakes, through the bleat of doormen's whistles, one can still hear the pipes of Pan of the itinerant knife grinder; the high, sweet flute of the *camote* (sweet potato) vendor; the tin whistle of the mailman; the small, timid wail of the night watchman.

Clever modern monoliths, whose fathers were Mies van der Rohes and whose mothers were Toltecs, press in the cheeks of a few remaining fat-faced turn-of-the-century houses, curled and sashed with turrets, porticos, pillars, and stained glass. Slums like open sewers lose their tenants to light, airy housing projects, and fill up again from the endless, silent march of the rural poor, cramming the already immense, bursting city. It is estimated that if there is no halt to the migration or the population explosion which rivals and threatens to surpass India's, the city will hold 30,000,000 people by the year 2000. In spite of propaganda that stresses unemployment and lack of housing, they keep coming.

New shops glitter at the sides of soft, old, lopsided churches. The students studying in the brilliant virtuosity of University City have recently come from schools which had been Jesuit monasteries, founded by the *conquistadores* and still in use. A new house may have to pick its way around still another Aztec temple.

From the heights of one of the newer of the city's upper-class developments of flowered roadways, strong iron fences, immense bright rooms, and generous sweeps of terrace, one can look down into a squatters' settlement neatly hidden in a gorge. The ragged children and skinny dogs play around the clothes, spread to dry on patches of dirt and grass, while the women spend their days washing threadbare blankets and faded shirts in stone troughs under a modern highway. The children rarely come out of their small worlds; the men have gone or will. Only the dogs wander, and the women who catch glimpses of the upper-class world on their trips for water from the garage taps of their modern neighbors.

In another neighborhood, two boys, one wielding bull's horns, the other the *muleta* (the bullfighter's red cloth) and sword, spend endless hours practicing the passes and turns of the *torero*. They see themselves in white and gold suits, stained with bull's blood; they hear *olés* and fanfares of tribute music; they can touch the moist, rough triumphal ears and tail; they can feel themselves carried around and around the arena on the shoulders of adoring fans. (Bullfighting or "futbol" championships are the dreams and passions of the poor boy. They speak to him of glory, conquests, and impossible wealth in much the same way that prize basketball lures our slum boys.)

Until, or unless, we reach the stage of a universal, classless society, all big cities will have their economic contrasts, easily available to anyone who cares to look. Like New York, London, Paris, Rome (even the fine museum which is Florence has its slum areas), Mexico has its layers. Its special excitement is not so much in the carefully boxed-off contrasts one is accustomed to in other cities, but in the shiftings and blendings. The city is working very hard—sometimes foolishly, sometimes wisely, and too often shaken by earthquakes—to create a well-ordered metropolis out of its sprawling, amoeboid shape; but the Mexican, who has survived a variety of conquests, won't yet be conquered by enclosures, particularly if the results threaten to be cold and monotonous. If the benches and the dry little grass plots and the lolling, watching, talking, eating humanity are wiped out of the Zócalo (the main plaza), to be replaced by a gray concrete stretch, barren and irritated, he does his resting and visiting in the yard of the cathedral. If the fly-by-night vendors of tricks and trinkets are chased from the arcades of the great square, they move to other streets and then quietly seep back. If the beggars are taken from the eye of the tourist in the popular centers, they ring doorbells in outlying areas, or catch a benefactor at a red light. If his favorite dance hall and saloon is closed down at the shameful hour of midnight, the Mexican finds a joint which doesn't close until the early hours and whose best whisky is, as the Mexicans say, that which is wrung out of the bar rag. A Mexican can be docile, but a truly regimented Mexican is a contradiction in terms.

Add to the whirling, colorful contrasts old, curved female fountains, new direct male fountains; statuary that is loud and aggressive and statuary that is painted spaghetti; parks and plazas of old, green beauty or sternly cemented; boulevards of dahlias of incredible size and color topped by tall, broad trees; a populace of chic, smooth, vital, swift-moving people and slow, passive, uncertain people; the smells of exhaust and perfume; the smell of frying tacos and the rancid-oil smell of poverty; the abundance of flowers and fruits which make the city a huge cornucopia, and the spare bodies which sell them. And add the possibly odd effects of its altitude—7,349 feet—(plus, unfortunately, industrial smog) which may depress a visitor into an utter loathing of all the city's blandishments or exhilarate him to the unselective, uncritical love of a happy drunk.

MEXICO CITY'S WANDERERS

Under the stentorian splendors of this city of twenty million inhabitants, there is the shimmering, soft bass of its wanderers. They are not particularly noticeable in the slum areas of the city: the streets around the Tepito market, Peralvillo, around the Merced, some parts of Tacubaya, Vallejo. There they might be country cousins come for reasons of sociability or despair, but not conspicuously different from the city's poor except when they come in brilliant regional costumes. It is in the more prosperous, residential areas that they look strange and moving, among the big, secretive houses of Polanco, of the Lomas, and the well-protected Pedregal. Along these streets may trot a girl no older than fourteen, her feet bare and dirty, her uncombed hair pulled back and tied in a string, her wild, narrow, dark face thrust forward, pulled by an invisible rope of urgency. She walks a little, then trots some more, making sure not to disturb the baby she has bundled in her *rebozo.* Her stained long white skirt and shirt are not local; she has probably walked from the mountains of Puebla or Oaxaca. A few tortillas were her food. She is still too shy and country-proud to beg.

Where is she going? She doesn't know. Once, she had heard of cousins who lived in Mexico City and, assuming it was a pueblo a little larger than her own, she thinks she might find them by walking through all the streets. Maybe she thinks she can find the father of the child, but born and early trained to certain wisdoms, she doubts that any help would come of such an encounter, if it happened. Possibly, she hopes that someone will stop her and ask if she wants a job as a domestic. ("A girl from the country" is a universal bargain.) With no training—not even comprehension of the simplest facts of city kitchens—and burdened by a baby, she won't earn much for a day that starts at six and ends whenever the household goes to bed. The baby will lie in a box or nest of rags in a cold room on the roof and learn early to contain its hunger and discomfort until the mother can give it a moment. She might, on the other hand, have the great good fortune of being accosted by a refulgently stylish lady who will put the child in an institution, buy the girl a ravishingly shiny pink satin dress and a lipstick, and introduce her to gentlemen who always wear shoes. In time she might, in a fatalistic, absent-minded way, accumulate a few more children, whom she will teach to beg along with her, to look as ragged and piercingly sad as they really are.

Wanderers are not often that dour and often make a lively ribbon which stitches up the sunny streets. A country family—several adults and a covey of children—make their way by second-class bus, trucks, and foot to some relative with a household job in the city. Papa or uncle wants a job, or to borrow money; or they want to show the children the big city; or they miss the niece or daughter who works in an apartment house with her own room and toilet, which they can't quite believe in. They move in with her, sleeping on the floors, and she is delighted to have them. A Mexican housewife will permit it, sometimes, depending on how devoted she is to her maid (the Mexican maid can be confidante, mother, and daughter); the American housewife, intimidated by years of scant and expensive help in her own country, permits it almost always, not knowing quite what else to do and because such strong family feeling moves her. If she lives in a large house with service entrances and maids' quarters far removed from the main rooms, the mistress may not know the family is there at all for some days; country cousins are very quiet and eat little.

Once in a while an enterprising group of village potters will decide to bypass the middleman. Equipped with a stack of tortillas, a few oranges, and fewer pesos, they tie the two dozen pots in ingenious arrangements around their bodies and set off on the big business venture. Unabashed, unembarrassed (and this may be a true measure of Mexican democracy), they ring gilded doorbells, stop lacquered ladies in the streets, and when they are tired, lie down on the grass which separates the traffic lanes of the upper-class avenues and go off to sleep in the sun that shines on them and on the Lancias driven by the young bloods.

The streets almost constantly flow demonstrations and pilgrimages. Toward the end of January, for instance, an immense pilgrimage gathers at Toluca and walks—it takes about two days—into the city, to pay homage to the Virgin of Guadalupe. The thousands of women and children start first, and then comes the endless contingent of men and older boys, carrying wreaths and wax flowers to be placed at the shrine. The handsome Paseo de las Palmas becomes strewn with orange peels as the pilgrims walk and eat. On the grass divider, under the carefully kept row of palms which gives the avenue its name, sit the old men, sandals at their sides, cooling their worn leathery feet. Women set up taco stands, equipped with the braziers, tin griddles, tortillas, and shreds of chicken brought all the way from Toluca. Others carry one wooden box, two bottles of tequila, a few limes, and a bag of salt; they set up minuscule *cantinas.* The Paseo, for the day of the pilgrims' passing, might be the Plaza Merced, but no one minds. Every resident of the dignified neighborhood—even though his car might be held up on its way downtown—considers that an important part of his Mexico and wouldn't have it changed, orange peel, battered grass, broken tequila bottles, and all.

There is a group of roamers who might be called the "sometimes" wanderers: a peddler of *serapes* who works one particular neighborhood sporadically, only when he is absolutely broke; an itinerant shoe repairman who carries tools, shoe forms of various sizes, bits of leather, shoeshine cans, and rags—all in a shapeless cloth sack. He sets himself up on a front lawn, under a broad tree, and arranges all his tools, nails, bits, and pieces in a semicircle around him and proceeds to work on the household shoes, observed by an entranced audience of neighborhood children. (Just possibly Mexican children are so dexterous because an important part of their learning and entertainments—at home, in the streets, in small open shops—is watching the magic of making and mending.)

The parade is thick some days, thin others, but it never wholly stops, except for one inexplicable phenomenon, the immobile man. He will stand on a corner, dreamy, apathetic. He is not waiting for a bus or a friend, nor looking at anything in particular; he isn't restless or impatient. Maybe he is just taking the air or the sun or waiting for life to pour a treasure over his head. One can't ask; it would be foolish, sacrilegious to disturb such monumental calm. One might as well ask a tree what it's doing there.

A NIGHT OF COUNTRY QUIET

Mexico City has comparatively few mopeds or motorcycles; those who can afford to buy them stretch the mouth of the family purse wider and buy a lustrous car with great black sides and glories of chromium. Those who can't, take taxis, or *peseros,* the community cabs—much cheaper; the working class uses buses on weekdays and taxis on Sundays. The paucity of motorized wheels may also have to do with the fact that a Mexican girl doesn't care much for the unlady-like, sportive, wind-and-rain-in-the-hair experience that the back seat of a Honda affords; nor does her mother think she should clasp the waist of a boy, even if it means her life, during a wild ride that allows no space for a *dueña.*

This accounts, in part, for the fact that Mexico City is considerably quieter to sleep in than Rome, Florence, Paris, or almost any European city you can mention, the stillness broken rarely except by the whistle, reminiscent of the ancient, flutelike *chirimía,* blown by the street watchmen to signal that all is clear. (Actually, according to some Mexicans, this is a plaintive appeal to troublemakers to please go away and not be troublesome.) But an auto horn does get stuck, sometimes an occasional street fight rips through the quiet, or the clash and crash of two inimical windshields. Toward dawn, house-maids and cleaning boys emerge, swishing thunderous large rags down the halls, and into corners, loudly and cheerfully recounting and re-recounting yesterday's pleasures and disasters, filling the cor-ridors, your rooms, your bed, your ears, with their obtrusive lives. If your hotel has a court, it will soon be invaded by the tortilla women, the gardener, the milkman, houseboys who whistle, houseboys who play guitars.

You remain cheerful and philosophic—when in Rome, etc.—but trying to enjoy your breakfast, you decide that a smaller city will be sleepier. You proceed to Puebla, heavily studded with churches. The bells start early and go on into breakfast, filling the narrow streets with reminders of God and mortality. On to Oaxaca. Not quite so religious, but it, too, has an abundance of churches, all proud of their bells and eager to outdo each other in a daily contest of holiness and vigor. Veracruz? It is a lively port town, full of sailors, stevedores, fishermen, musicians, and women who keep very informal hours.

Cuernavaca is where people go to rest; you do too. One inn is crowded with North American remittance men and women who drink the amorphous days and nights away. They fall against furniture, slam doors, and break bottles and growl at each other. Another inn is lovely and quiet, with placid gardens and a nice, peaceable, aged clientele, sober to moribund. The lights are out at ten, the gate locked, the long-delayed balm of sleep floats softly down and around you. Across the street, a birthday party gathers and mounts to the crashing crescendo of "Mañanitas" sung in all its full, long versions, from two in the morning until four. This wakes the turkeys, who rattle in shrill alarm; the roosters go into their loud, mindless turn; irritable dogs answer back; a burro brays in annoyance. Peace washes in at about five, a spread of blank canvas which is waiting for the violent, clashing colors of blatting exhausts and irate mothers, which reawaken the turkeys, the roosters, the dogs, the burros; the brilliant day, dimly viewed through gritty eyeballs, has started.

Entonces, deeper into the country, into a small town with one *cantina* and one church, fronted, for security and ancient, unrelinquishable habit, by a magnificently coiled stone serpent. Having realized that the domestic animals around won't respect your hours, you decide to respect theirs; you go to bed very early in the small, whitewashed, one-bulb room of the local inn. But it is Saturday night. The *cantina,* a frail shack dimly lit by a few weak bulbs, houses a jukebox which battens on the night air and grows into a behemoth devouring the night. Dawn is announced by the sound of guns which follows the inevitable Saturday night scraping of barbed egos and the inevitable duels of *machismo* (page 50). Someone pulls the church bells to disperse the contest of masculinity, and since it is Sunday, the bell (the puller is drunk, too) goes on ringing after the last drunk has fallen, dead or alive, under the nearest tree.

Maybe the lazy, soporific, perfumed, heavy-aired tropics will make a cocoon of sleep, so the leaden-legged trek continues to an obscure beach hamlet in the tropics. Beds are hot. (Middle-class houses in the tropics keep one mainly for a show of conspicuous consumption and childbirth.) So, one asks that a hammock be slung from the deeply embedded hooks in the walls. Once in the hammock, pushing away from the floor lightly with one foot, one is back, very far back, in the rocking of infancy. (Maybe a whole lifetime of being rocked makes the Mexican of the tropics much lighter, gayer, more poised and friendly than his mountain compatriot.) The gentle rocking, the balmy air, the fragrance of night-blooming vines, the absence of thick mattress and heavy, humid sheets combine exquisitely; the body sinks into the weightless cradle, the eyelids droop like heavy satin.

A restless stallion roars and neighs and gallops wildly in his enclosure, screaming imprisoned protest. A neighboring burro laughs at him in penetrating, obscene, shocking, macabre shrieks. An impatient rooster decides it is time for the hens to awaken; they do. The pigs begin to splash and grunt, the ducks quarrel. It is all a lightweight nightmare, "Old MacDonald" gone mad.

After a tortured century, the tattered quiet gathers itself together. Then, at five-thirty, a group of ambitious workmen saunter by, exchanging full-day noise and jokes. They stop nearby and stay to chop bricks with resounding trowels, splash streams of water into sand pits, drop pails and bits of steel for a new addition to your inn.

This can go on and on, through a long string of exhausted variations, but there is no point, nor hardly a moral, except: learn to siesta, or catnap, like the Mexican on the "typical" bookend; or carry a large supply of efficient sleeping pills—or go back to the comparative quiet of the big city.

HOTELS

A night's shelter in Mexico can take a dazzling variety of shapes and color, from *mesones,* which echo the classic Arab inn (a ring of stalls which house burros and produce while owners and guardians sleep fitfully in the court), to crystal palaces encrusted with mosaics, murals, and reliefs translated from raw primitive tombs to marble halls. At both ends, the scale reflects two large facts of Mexico's economic life: its populace of wanderers with a little something to sell and its dependency on tourism as a major source of national income. In between are the inns, which cater to a rising middle class, housing it in simple, comfortable rooms off abundant gardens, or huge vaults of rooms in great turn-of-the-century hotels which have slipped downward through the years, nothing left in them but grand tattered lobbies and multitudinous brass beds. Or, bare white-washed walls around a bed, a wooden chair, a wall hook, and one naked light bulb, obviously the creation of an ambitious smalltownsman who is supplying a need but won't offer frills, mainly because he doesn't know what they are.

It is quite possible that Mexico City has *mesones,* well hidden beyond the range of the tourists' senses, but the rest of the hotel variety and variations within that variety extend eager availability from several parts of the city. The following listing moves downward from high life to basic use in a scale of commensurate prices not intended to be exhaustive, but rather to give you some idea of what you might expect to find and how it might suit your travel budget. Also, it is a good thing to remember that Mexico lost several hotels—some still in the rebuilding—during the earthquake of 1986.

To remember and be lured by: the peso was valued at 1500 to the dollar in the summer of 1987. Therefore hotel rates and those of restaurants will probably be one-third of American and European prices. "Expensive" will not actually mean that in terms of the dollar. An example—$50 a night for a single, $70 for a double, and less for package deals.

Two warnings before you embark on a tour of hotels: No matter what the category of your hotel, you may find the service sincere, charming, and odd, and you will usually find too few hangers. (The word is *"ganchos."*) Also, some of the "moderates" don't accept credit cards or personal checks.

The following is a list beginning with the most distinguished and moving through several categories.

Camino Real On Mariano Escobedo. A starkly modern city that holds ten restaurants, one of them of very *haute* French cuisine, another an all-day and all-night coffee shop; pools, convention auditoria, and a large collection of shops; 700 rooms, golf greens, tennis courts. Even if you have no interest in staying or eating, walk through the hotel. Some people find it cold and oversimplified as architecture. Some admire the endless white textured walls studded with boxes of color, the huge vermilion Calder, a sudden corner of grand seats designed for the repose of kings, and the huge basin, part of the main-floor décor, whose waters are kept agitated and splashing like a storm at sea. Expensive.

El Presidente Chapultepec Off the Reforma, a short distance from the Anthropological Museum (Campos Eliseos 218, Polanco). A clever, colorful study in creating an illusion of broad spaces, although it is actually two tall building slabs set in a narrow area. Even if you can't afford it, look around and have lunch on one of the oddly placed balconies. Expensive.

Maria Isabel Sheraton Paseo de la Reforma 325, near the Independence Monument. Large, reputable, and near shopping centers. Expensive. In the process of being expanded and refurbished.

Holiday Inn In the Zona Rosa. Promised for early 1978, the hotel is certainly, at this reading, ready for guests.

El Presidente Zona Rosa, Hamburgo 135. Exuberant in design and décor; what might be called "Mexican fantasy modern"—black marble, gold, turns and twists, indoor waterfalls, and a jazzy American-style bar, with good music. Moderate.

To live in the shine and curves of art nouveau, of shirred French curtains and chinoiserie, stuffed birds on immortal branches in cages bound in stained glass, apply to the **Gran Hotel,** on the Zócalo, a reformed department store of turn-of-the-century splendor. Moderate.

Del Prado Juárez 70. A government-built hostelry, whose grill restaurant spreads an unusually generous buffet. The street-level arcade is a fine oasis with shops to browse in, coffee and snack places open quite late, and last, but not least, the mordant "Dream of Sunday Afternoon at the Alameda" mural by Diego Rivera in the lobby. Moderate.

Aristos Paseo de la Reforma 276, off the Zona Rosa. Offers restaurants, late bars, and a popular nightclub. Expensive.

Monte Cassino Génova 56. In the almost deluxe category, but much calmer and more modest without self-effacement or too much hoopla.

Del Paseo Paseo de la Reforma 208. Views of the Paseo as it threads its way through the park, décor on an attractively human scale, and breakfast or lunch near a pool (upstairs).

Del Angel Río Lerma and Reforma. Has a good restaurant and views.

International Havre Havre 21 in the Zona Rosa.

Reforma Paseo de la Reforma, at Paris. One of the first of Mexico City's "tourist" hotels and a lively, livable hotel until it was damaged in 1986. Check to find out if its old ebullience has returned.

Cristóbal Colón Colón 27 (just off upper end of Alameda). Well appointed, careful, and nicely situated between new and old Mexico City.

Some recently built residential hotels (most with kitchenettes), sitting in the middle of a dense tourist area, the Zona Rosa, where Spanish is hardly necessary and probably will soon be obsolete, ask comparatively little for doubles and less for long stays.

Golden Suites Londres 115, for one. Or, the Michel Angelo Suites, on the other side of the Reforma, the very new Don Mario Hotel, at Londres 223, Hotel Suites on Hamburgo 9, Suites Orleans at Hamburgo 67, and a good number in the process of construction.

Hotel Ritz Madero 30. Newly refurbished in an area that has become a pleasant series of pedestrian malls. Good location, between the Zócalo and the cathedral, the old Sanborn's, and the Bellas Artes.
And find out if the **Prince,** Luis Moya 12, is still solid and maintains its good dining room.

Majestic Madero 73, on the Zócalo. Once a great hotel for the rural gentry on their annual city visit, now having a revival. The city is moving away from it, but the rooms are still splendidly large and turn-of-the-century. Its roof garden has many uses—for eating, resting, viewing—and will be referred to in the sections on walks and restaurants.

Cortés Avenida Hidalgo 85. The Cortés holds on tenaciously to its Colonial ecclesiastical façade and fountained inner court, which can be a delight when the sun shines. The goldfish dart around the fountain, the potted flowers stand high, and the happy tourists chatter gaily over the bottomless pots of coffee. But when the rain pelts down and the only refuge is one's room—authentically dour Colonial—it isn't quite the same golden bird cage. In any case, the Cortés is a good place for people traveling alone; its limited size and patio life make for easy sociability. Also, it has a devoted repeat clientele and a few addicts who stay for months at a time, so reservations must be made well in advance.

Luma   Orizaba 16. Well located for proximity to shopping and fine restaurants. The suites are of a companionable size and decorated in tactful modern, neither impressive nor uncomfortable.

Beverly   Insurgentes, at Nueva York 301. A bit away from the center, in a main street which offers buses and taxis and which conveniently leads in one direction to a bull ring. Brightened often by a theatrical-intellectual crush of clientele around its outdoor pool.

Montejo   Paseo de la Reforma 240. Superbly placed on the rim of the great boulevard, it has been heaving out its heavy furniture and discouraged mustiness, refurbishing its roof for *dolce far niente* sunning and drinking and, generally, making itself a happier member of the hotel community. Should have recovered from the earthquake. Moderate.

Four homes away from home for Americans who live elsewhere in Mexico and come to Mexico City for shopping or to take a Spanishless visitor off a plane are: the **Geneve** (pronounced Henova), with an evocative old section and a "new" section, almost elderly by now, connected by a wondrous, ornate glass gallery and with a central location in the Zona Rosa; the **Seville**, near Sullivan, smaller and more gregarious; the **Bristol**, off the Reforma at Panuco and Sena, larger and quite dignified; and El **Regente**, on Paris, a block from the Paseo de la Reforma, nicely furnished and well mannered. All inexpensive.

Once upon a time the carefree who made no prior reservations found themselves at the **Geneve**, a bit eccentric, careless and stuffed with odd, old furniture. As the **Calinda Geneve** (Londres 130) it has improved its image, but not to dullness, yet. Moderate low.

Gin   (pronounced Heen) Eufrates 3, near Rhin. On a small street, not in the center but nearby. A *gemütlich* little hotel whose bar gives forth good jazz once in a while.

Meurice   Marsella 28. This is of another, older type of *gemütlichkeit*, more like a European pension, where as much French and German are spoken as English and Spanish.

Suites Emperador   Cuauhtémoc 604. This is farther out and seriously worth considering. Fine for someone with a car and the confidence to use it in D.F., although the street is a big one and commonly cruised by taxis. Suites are available for the cost of singles in better-known hotels; the restaurant is decent and inexpensive.

MODEST

This category includes small hotels, decent and clean, which offer the basic amenities at low prices.

Regente   On Paris near the Reforma.

Hotel Emporio   With a dazzling psychedelic lobby at 124 Paseo de la Reforma.

Arizona   Gómez Farias 20.

Compostela   Sullivan and Serapio Rendon. The **Sevilla,** on the same corner.

At the meeting of Mariscal and R. Alcazar, across from the Academy San Carlos, two small, inexpensive hotels—the **Imperial** and the **Carlton.** Also not far from the Reforma and in the same category, **Hotel New York** on Calle Edison.

Casa Gonzales   69 Rio Sena. A pre-Revolution mansion of stained glass, family portraits, amiability, and generous breakfasts. You may have other meals there (not on Sunday) or wander out.

A good number of hotels now ask for a deposit that covers a stay of a few days and add a 15% tax to your bill. Also to keep in mind: one of your favorites may have been severely damaged in the earthquake. Check on the condition of its health before you reserve.

WALKS, RIDES, AND MARKETS

These walks are designed to give you a look at various parts of the multi-toned city: the new, the old; the city of the walkers in worn sandals, the Cadillac-borne, and the middle class, who ride the *peseros.* You will need curiosity, mainly, although sturdy shoes, a good map, a receptive eye, and an understanding which tempers harsh judgments help immensely.

The walks are geographically short, usually skirting damaged areas or those still shaky, but each can take most of a day—or little enough time to be combined with others or parts of others, depending on individual interests and pace. Their brevity was dictated by the altitude (which depletes some people quickly), by the exigencies of tourist time, and by the fact that the multiplicity of sounds, smells, and sights crowded into old neighborhoods by time and history can best be sensed and absorbed within a compass which isn't too demanding.

Points of departure mentioned are likely to be those places and avenues with which you will become familiar most quickly and to which you can find your way back most surely. (Although Mexicans are voluble, enthusiastic misdirectors—it is very impolite to say, "I don't know"—you can safely ask for the Alameda or the Zócalo or Palacio de Bellas Artes.) For a rough idea of the geography of the city, mark out a crossroads which runs east and west along Madero-Juárez and north-south along the many-named Serdán-San Juan de Letrán-Niño Perdido, etc. Very close to the crossing point you will find the Alameda (a small rectangle on your map), and directly east of it, the improbable Bellas Artes palace. A few blocks east of this confection sits the immeasurably old Zócalo, holding in its lap the cathedral, resting *its* feet on Aztec palaces. The shops in which maids buy their trousseaus and grooms their shoes, the immense markets, the streets of Colonial mansions battered and worn into slums, the old schools which flash the lightning and thunder of murals, and the government buildings are in an arc north, east, and south of the Zócalo.

You will shop, or at least window-shop, along the east-west line of Madero and Juárez and, possibly, find some of your entertainment along the north-south line. Just plain eating can be done in many parts of the city; dining and glossier shopping are done in the Niza-Londres-Hamburgo area, the Zona Rosa, which lies south of the Reforma, west of Insurgentes, and is distinguished by streets named after European cities—Estrasburgo, Varsovia, Estocolmo, for instance, along with the others of greater glow. Various *colonias* mentioned (these should be marked on your map, in slightly heavier type than the street names) can be located by their relationship to Chapultepec Park, a big, jagged patch which engulfs the Paseo de la Reforma on its western stretch. Polanco is directly north of the park's widest area; Barrilaco is directly west of that; Lomas Chapultepec, southwest of Barrilaco. The name of a *colonia,* incidentally, is a handy thing to know; they are rarely extensive—not like our vast, vague big-city divisions—and limit themselves to one type of street name, so that hearing a street name that is a river, for instance, you will direct your eye to the area marked "Cuauhtémoc." (This is not an entirely logical arrangement: it would be more reasonable for the *colonia* to be named "Nile" or "Amazon," but that isn't the way it works.) Anzures, Morales, and Polanco gather in the poets, playwrights, and philosophers; Roma and Roma Sur take care of Mexican cities, and so forth.

Here and there, Insurgentes is referred to. It is a long north-south street which, most uncharacteristically, does not change its name except for adding "Sur" as it runs southward from Paseo de la Reforma; "Norte" on its northward swing. It cuts across the Paseo de la Reforma, skirts the Zona Rosa, and roars on, thriving and bus-laden.

There is no advice one can give to obviate a foreigner's confusion over the many names one street will carry—history is long and its archives filled with many splendid men worth commemorating. For instance, put your pencil on Hidalgo, which makes the northern border of the Alameda, and see what happens to it in its progress east and west; or San Juan de Letrán in its journey north and south, as it meets and leaves Madero. Wherever necessary, in locating points of interest, a street will be related to its most common or central name.

Note: Demolition and reconstruction are going on at a frenzied rate, abolishing or hiding antiquities. Much remains, but you may have to search carefully.

SATURDAY MORNING WALK *(Merced market)*

The Merced market area, which stretches through many streets, is frequently mentioned as being on the site of *the* great Aztec market, when the city's name was Tenochtitlán, or Mexica, as purists say. That may or may not be precisely so. There was a market on or near the Plaza Santiago Tlaltelolco described by Bernal Díaz del Castillo in awed tones, high above the drone of his usual, stolid, soldierly prose.

> Each kind of merchandise was kept by itself and had its fixed place marked out. Let us begin with the dealers of gold, silver and precious stones, feathers, mantles and embroidered goods. Then there were other wares consisting of Indian slaves both men and women. . . . In another part there were skins of tigers and lions, of otters and jackals, deer and other animals and badgers and mountain cats, some tanned and others untanned, and other classes of merchandise.
>
> Let us go on and speak of those who sold beans and sage and other vegetables and herbs in another part, and of those who sold fowls, cocks with wattles, rabbits, hares, deer, mallards, young dogs and other things of that sort in their part of the market, and let us mention the fruiterers, and the women who cooked food, dough and tripe in their own part of the market; then every sort of pottery made in a thousand different forms from great water jars to little jugs.

And he goes on to enumerate in fascinated detail types of foods, materials, ointments, sweets, breaking off impatiently with, "But why do I waste so many words in recounting what they sell in that great market?—for I shall never finish if I tell it all in detail." He can't stop, however, and after a breath, takes us on to salt, knives, fish, bread, and metals, finishing his account reluctantly with, "I could wish that I had finished telling of all such things which were sold there, but they are so numerous and of such different quality and the great market place with its surrounding arcade was so crowded with people, that one would not have been able to see and inquire about it all in two days." (Elsewhere he speaks of the market as much broader and larger than the one in Salamanca.)

The great markets of Mexico City have had their faces lifted and scrubbed, pulled out of the colorful dirt and disorder they fell into after the Conquest, but in essence they haven't changed much from the days when they first overwhelmed the provincial *conquistador*.

Up to thirty years ago—when a municipal typhoon of house

cleaning struck the city—tomatoes, onions, bananas, mangoes, chiles, babies, garbage, mud, and smells spilled like a burst dam through the whole district, filling the side streets, mounting the sidewalks, pushing into storefronts and the edges of the small plazas. There were areas where no break could be seen—no difference between gutter and sidewalk, between one mound of merchandise and another. To navigate one had to step carefully in the minute void between María's heap of bananas and Juana's elderly tomatoes, and stride accurately over Rosa's avocados. The innumerable dark-*rebozoed* women bent over their wares spread on the ground, the thick hum of thousands of hushed voices, the moist babies lying among the fruits, the stench of hot, crowded humanity, of discarded leaves and rotting pulps festering in the sun was what Mexicans call, in matters of art, "strong." (American women, fresh from white refrigerators and plastic-coated vegetables, had been known to turn faint at the assault of dark sights and smells and the potential threat of raw, unretouched humanity.) The fount and center of this flood was a covered market—very imperfectly covered, but it did have a roof. It housed, among other tidbits, stalls of medicinal herbs—which helped obscure the smell of tamped-down garbage, the soft rug for the earth floor—and such novelties as rat poison, advertised by a tall Mephistopheles who enjoyed swinging a dead rat. Once in a while, someone brightened the dim shed with red nylon stockings, totally unstretchable and unwashable, five pesos the pair. In spite of the sour details, the dirty old Merced was a brilliant place, exciting and wary, a tough old gaudy sloven with a quick tongue.

Now the Merced is clean and controlled, designed mainly for wholesale and retail food selling, although its outer sections contain much of practically everything else. The food center (enter on General Anaya) is of simple imaginative design, whose clouds of color float outward in soft, large billowy shapes of green, yellow, terracotta, red, and orange.

The section for chiles is a many-colored world: dark, long purple-red chiles, already dried; sweet green and sweet red, plump and shining moistly; long, thin dark-green; delicate, round spring-green; minute green and red chiles which have the innocent look of beads that a child might string and which bite with the sting of red ants. Fronting the chiles are the onions, perfectly shaped, washed, and peeled to disclose the luminous silk of their inner layers. Avocados, like chiles, come in assorted sizes and colors: little purple ones like ripe figs; long, pimpled greens and purples; large, round, solid, and glossy like well-fed ecclesiastics.

Look for the flattened yellow mango, in the shape of a Persian leaf design; the mamey, a pointed fruit of dusty cocoa brown covering bright terra-cotta flesh around a smooth, precisely turned pit; the almost globular watermelons into which doors are cut to reveal their deep red-pink flesh and the rhythmic set of their small black seeds. (It is easy to see why the watermelon is to Mexican painters what the apple was to Cézanne.) Examine diseased corn encased by a dusty black-and-white fungus, a local delicacy—and near relative of penicillin, the market women say.

Except for beans and grains, nothing is poured out of its sack and allowed to become the shapelessly heaped victim of gravity and haste. A Mexican vendor will place four small avocados in a tight square, delicately place three others above them in a superimposed triangle, two above that, and one at the peak. Their shapes are awkward, but the vendor makes the arrangements patiently and tenderly, as if she were the trainer of young acrobats or an inept dog act.

Outside of this Ceres' chamber, across the street from where you entered, is the street of Santa Escuela. Follow it past the shops which hold boxes and cans of cheap, outrageously colored candy, past the wholesale banana stalls, past the small restaurants of oilcloth-covered tables and hard, crude chairs whose supply of the ubiquitous and essential chile sauce is held by huge stone bowls of dark volcanic material in the same shape as the sacrificial bowls of the Aztecs.

Start watching for an opening, on the left-hand side of Santa Escuela, which leads into a labyrinth of stalls, paths, and wire cages. The walk between the stalls is very narrow, its center worn down into a shallow trench and crowded with women seated on the floor, holding on to live chickens. On one side is a counter of already slaughtered fowl. The vendor has spread a newspaper over them and is fast asleep on her pillow of dead chickens. Above and back stretches a network of wire cages restraining a dark jungle of weeds. These are the medicinal-herb collections whose proprietors function like the old-fashioned pharmacist, eager to design a cure once a diagnosis is made, and not too proud to make a diagnosis if asked. (Here it would be of value to speak Spanish or to go with someone who can translate, to get the full benefit of the drama and science hidden in the barks and weeds.)

She may still be there, one hopes, the aging *curandera* with a serious, intelligent face, slightly pock-marked. Her eyes are small and quick, and although the pupil of one of them is a bit off-center, she has none of the vague, underwater look such people often have. As dedicated to her work and herbs as any rural witch doctor, she is sufficiently worldly to give trained city doctors their due, and repeats, eagerly, that she would like to analyze for them the infusions she knows are efficacious, through her own applications of them and the centuries-old knowledge and experience she has inherited. (When told that physicians have been studying her branch of medicine and have found much of it valuable, she appears skeptical and a bit angry, not especially pleased at news of the invasion she thought she wanted.) Having finished with a general discussion, she launches into specifics. Her brother-in-law had an unknown disease which swelled his leg hideously. He went on the usual medical searches with no results except the threat of amputation; gangrene had set in. Then (deep breath and long significant pause) he came to her, pleading that she help him. She said (here her face takes on an expression of hurt pride and sternness) that she would not and could not interfere with the work of the doctors, and as long as he was going to them, she couldn't help. He pleaded (she folds her hands in prayer, then wrings them to repeat his desperation) and promised to put himself into her more skillful hands. Immediately she went to work with (another momentous pause while she pulls out a strip of reddish bark covered with nodules) a tea made of this bark. He drank rivers of it while she wrapped the leg—malevolent purples, reds, and blues, gaudy as a peacock, to hear her describe it; the veins swollen and tormented as if little moles were running through them—in cloths soaked in the same infusion. Now, she says triumphantly, he is on crutches, the leg still intact and its owner pleased enough to be offering, at that very moment, thanks to the Virgin of the Remedies.

After a rest, a pause for your words of wonder and praise, she will go on to demonstrate other medicinal magics; the same anti-gangrene bark produces a sap which, when applied to cuts, gathers the flesh together quickly and leaves no scar tissue, no matter how deep the gash. A fuzzy moss, the color and texture of teddy-bear fur, is absolutely guaranteed to remove excess fat from the kidneys and restore their perfect functioning. Something like ginger root clears away dark thoughts; a dusty gray leaf does remarkable things for children and on, and on, as long as you have the time and attention span.

Having made courtly thanks and farewells—she considers herself a member of a highly skilled profession and not a vendor—go back to Santa Escuela and follow it northward until it meets Corregidora. Turn left on this street, easing your way the best you can through the shopping, carrying, talking, eating, drifting mobs. Remember to glance up occasionally for a look at whatever saint may still live in the niche of an old building, or to see the fortress-style detail on some of the ancient roofs, and whenever you can, snoop into the courts which were once the carriage entrances of lordly houses. Barber-shops—always crowded because being shaved and shined is a major male occupation and entertainment—jostle *puestos* (stalls) of tacos and *chicharrón* (cracklings), and both are squeezed by large shops plastered with urgent, hand-lettered signs: "Cheap!"—"Big sale!"—"Take it away!"—"Take advantage!"—"Profit right now!" What there is to take away at great profit right now is blue enamel spoons and frail tin pots, crude knives, cheap shoes, elderly hardware, small cheap quantities of almost anything; a few centavos' worth of spice, a few meters of sewing thread wrapped on a stem of paper.

As you proceed on Corregidora, you will notice signs of *Baños* (public baths) and *Excusados* (public toilets) common in this area. No one will stop you from looking in, if you're curious; whether you'll want to use them is a matter of your condition and theirs. Watch for an ancient, narrow alley on the left, the Callejón de Manzanares. It is not lively, or pretty, or gay, or, for some of us, believable. One cannot actually go into the houses; the doors of the inner alleys are kept closed to strangers and will swing back on your nose, sharply and justly, if you try to push a door in. The main alley itself, the smells, the dirt, the dimness, the half-naked babies wandering bare-foot in the dust, the women selling fifth-grade vegetables, the tacos filled with minute dried fish at a few centavos, should be enough.

Out of short and bitter Manzanares, like a shout of relief and pleasure, bursts the Plaza Merced. The plaza is sunshine, roses, and people on the grass. A girl in a pink dress and apron, probably a maid on her day off, sits by her young man and watches him, pleased and awed, while he reads in a worn volume of verse. He glances at her now and then, smiles, and goes back to his reading, while she sits and silently admires as long as he wants her to. Three men from the country, with thick rebellious thrusts of coal-black Indian hair, pass a bottle of mescal solemnly around their triangle; conversation is desultory while they await the brilliant, inner monologue of the alcohol. An Indian woman, probably from distant hills to judge from her dress, nurses her baby, and very decorously, with the help of some covering cloths, changes its wet rag for a dry one. She croons at the rag-bound, cherry-eyed baby and dandles it with smooth, small movements. There is little play or gaiety in Indian women from the mountains, but they sometimes glow with a pale, bashful light. Nearby sits a lady clochard surrounded by bundles of her possessions; fat and proud, she lolls and drinks regally under her private tree.

Two children, examining and exchanging blades of grass, suddenly leap up to follow a bird vendor, calling to the blue, green, and yellow birds of the tower of cages he carries on his back. A family from the local Lower Depths picnics on its tortillas and bananas. The women and children drink Pepsi-Cola while papa takes his refreshment in the local *pulquería,* where life grows foggier and easier as the Saturday hours float away on the sour odor of pulque. The hurdy-gurdy man, almost the last of his tribe, walks a maze through the park, sagely lingering before lovers and passing the drinkers by. His music is hardly that, but the approximate, light, tinny tunes are proper echoes for the gay, cheap earrings of the girls, the large pink roses on the bushes, the gaudy birds, and the thin finery of the families on the grass.

Rambling back through Uruguay, possibly, look for the Calle Tabaqueros. It is a small, low set of deep shops with little order (except in the owner's mind) that concentrates on baskets and brooms, some souvenirs, and piles on piles of regional hats, particularly the big Pancho Villa type. Look also for a place that sells canes shaped of rough boughs and bargain, with the knowledge that you will never work your way down to the prices paid by the market people, for whom this street is a wholesale source.

All of this may have been enough for one Saturday morning. Make your way back to the Zócalo, a short distance northwestward, have a look at the coats of arms in its arcades, then lunch at **Prendes, El Danubio,** or the **Hotel Majestic** roof. Or, open the basket in which you've dropped the mamey, the mangoes, or the sweet, plum-like *zapotes* you bought in the Merced market and eat them in any plaza.

TOY MARKET *(Combine with Merced walk)*

If medicinal herbs don't interest you, go from the main section of the Merced market to the outer departments, the flower stalls near the attractive fountains, and running off the Calle Cabaña, the alleys of pots and pans, china, baskets, and bird cages arranged on shallow, shaded stalls. The cataracts of baskets are not as varied as those you will find in the basket section of the San Juan market, on López, but they are cheaper, and the atmosphere less self-conscious and forced.

At one end of these alleys is an avenue of stone benches, for a rest, and if you like, conversation: advice from passers-by; reassurance about the price and durability of a purchase; "Where in the United States do you come from?" followed by, "Maybe you know my brother in San Diego?" Since this is a secluded, quiet part of the market (except on weekends), the children of the stall owners play in the alleys as if they were the backyards of their homes, which in a sense is so. The little girls fold their thin arms across their meager chests and talk solemnly for hours, while the boys improvise horses out of long poles and gallop them—three on a horse—fast, all six legs perfectly coordinated.

Unless you really know someone's brother in San Diego (in which case you will not be able to leave the market for some hours), follow Calle Cabaña southward a block or two toward Fray Servando Teresa de Mier, a dignified and saintly name which hardly prepares one for the fact that its street is run by the most headlong, furious buses in Mexico. Make your way, very carefully, across the avenue to a group of small, joined buildings, rather like a stretched accordion, which constitute one of the prettiest and calmest markets in the city. Under the childish triangles of connected roof, market women from the older suburbs buy *ollas* as large as bathtubs, bags full of plastic baby bottles for dolls, minute pink Ferris wheels, and bright-banded wooden tops, to resell for a few centavos.

In the tiny central plaza of the market sit the bird-food women, surrounded by willowy grasses and pink berries. (How much can they sell, how much can they earn?) Among them is a boy asleep on a yellow mound of grasses, like a young peasant in a Breughel painting. Armadillo skins, snakeskins, bark, seeds, grasses, flowers, and amulets of brown seeds hung on a red-beaded string to ensure against ulcers and "bad airs" of the night hang protectively over his sleeping head.

A slender, black kid stands tethered nearby. He may be for sale, but no one offers to sell him and he remains petted, well fed, and abundantly loved. Farther back, much deeper in the shade, sit the chickens, squabs, and turkeys made somnolent by the calm air and the soft light. And still farther back is the outdoor café which serves the market people—and anyone else. The waitresses are shy and awkward with strangers, but they try their inept, valiant best; the tables are umbrella-shaded and kept well wiped; and the smells of tacos, *chiles rellenos* (stuffed peppers), and the magnificent Mexican soups, ambrosial. If you feel safer with Nescafé, you can have it served in a large tumbler holding a blue-enameled spoon for mixing. Off to one side of the café are public baths and toilets, here called *Sanitorios.* A few pesos buy an entrance ticket, a length of paper, and a glimpse of the baths, an experience you may not want to miss at so cheap a price.

The pottery is better elsewhere (although a good piece can be found here with persistent searching); the toys have little distinction except their low price; the herbs and amulets will be of questionable efficacy for you, since you don't believe in them; you will hardly be buying a kid or a squab; the toilet in your hotel is more comfortable, the outdoor cafés more elegant elsewhere; but the bucolic appeal of the place, its very unimpressive wares, its unenterprising sales-women, its simple-minded color make it a delightful oasis in the turbulent, roaring market area.

THE CATHEDRAL VILLAGE *(Late Saturday morning in the course of any walk near the Zócalo)*

The big cathedral on the Zócalo, encrusted with history and various styles of architecture, conducts a lively trade in baptisms and confirmations, clearly indicating the sections for each, rather like government offices. The vast space of the cathedral allows room for long, winding lines and the constant movements of parents briskly conducting children in and out. The busy efficiency is interesting to watch, but the major attraction is the little girls in their best clothing and most awed expressions. The round, dark, tropical-fruit faces lit by small golden hoop earrings are almost lost in clouds of stiff net, bits of lace, and crisscrossing of ribbons on their dresses, often made by mothers whose dressmaking is less skill than act of homage: the harder the work, the more elaborate the decorations, the more pleasing to God and the Virgin will the child be. The result is a display of children and infants who look like the fanciest of *Bon Voyage* baskets.

A less devout show goes on outside the church. At its portals sit the vendors of rosaries, religious medals, chromos and booklets (some in English), including an evocative apologia for the Inquisition. Farther out, but still in the yard, one can buy plastic balls on strings, small, neat portions of *gelatina,* cookies, candies, balloons—the sort of thing one finds in a neighborhood plaza on a holiday or the Alameda on Sundays. Boys match coins next to a family of imperturbable Indians in from the country, eating their picnic lunch on the sacred earth of the churchyard.

In another part of the yard, a dancer with a Mayan profile, dressed in the plumed headband and short fringed skirt vaguely suggestive of mural "Aztec," stamps, turns, taps, jingles, and sweats for a playful, hard-boiled audience, which comments, "I wonder where in the Lomas [a prosperous *colonia*] his house is." "Is he dancing for the greater glory of God or the peso?" Only the children and the Indians drop coins into the basket placed suggestively near the dancer.

A ten-minute subway ride from the monumental show-off station of Insurgentes brings you to the station of Pino Suárez, with its own vestiges of pyramid, in the old city. You emerge to a few large buildings, signs pointing to the City Museum, a glimpse of the ancient church of San Miguel dressed in a pretty little fountained park, and shops and shops, some of them dress shops—one named for Liza Minnelli—and, approaching Mesones, seas of shoes.

Pino Suárez presents a tablet that commemorates the meeting here of Cortés and Moctezuma on November 8, 1519. Nearby, still on Pino Suárez, is the antique Hospital de Jesús Nazareno, whose old, old arches and beamed ceiling (one may look in) are concealed by decrepit, broken-windowed modernism, which may not matter too much since the strength of the hospital is its twenty-four-hour emergency service, essential in an area of guns and knives flashing in *cantinas.* A telling contrast is the magnificent Colonial building of the City Museum at the far corner of Pino Suárez and El Salvador.

You might do well now to turn left on Venustiano Carranza for a venerable department store, the Palacio de Hierro (the "Iron Palace," which tells its style and period). The Palacio de Hierro has kept the shine of its art-nouveau mosaics on exterior walls and has modernized its interior without destroying the grace of arches and ironwork balconies hanging below a glorious, high ceiling of art-nouveau jungle in stained glass. Another apogee of this style stood at the corner of the Zócalo and the street of the 20th of September. That store was transformed as the Gran Hotel, an incandescence of gilded chinoiserie, huge, lustrous chandeliers, curvaceous metal work and stained glass. One hopes they are still in their indigenous places, having resisted the drive uptown-ward, chic-ward.

Madero was for decades a busy, crowded shopping street that marched briskly from Sanborn's House of Tiles to the Zócalo. It is still a crowded shopping street, its pace made gentler and more aristo-cratic by the change of dusty, unattractive side streets like Palma, Mofolinia, and Gante into appealing pedestrian malls with boxes of greenery and curly iron benches taken from a disused elderly park, and by the shop façades looking more pleased with themselves.

At Cinco de Mayo and the western edge of the Zócalo stands the imposing Monte de Piedad, of restrained baroque. Reputedly this was the site of Moctezuma's palace. Later, in Colonial times, it was the palace of newer god-kings, the Viceroys sent to rule by the Spanish Crown. Now the National Pawnshop, it displays carefully labeled typewriters, earrings, enamel kitchen tables, radios, watches, antiques, and "antiques" in its endless row of beehives. Visitors are lured by stories of mounds of viceregal jewels sold at the price of glass. In actual experience they may have been there yesterday or will be there tomorrow, but never today. Whether you find treasure or not, it is worth a visit, if only to see how big, variegated, open, busy, and democratic a government pawnshop can be, as opposed to the shame-faced stores which hide in our obscure neighborhoods.

From the Monte de Piedad walk north on the Zócalo side (this should be Brasil) two blocks to Donceles, and right one block to Argentina. Near the corner, you will find the convent and church of La Enseñanza. The convent is now a government building and the church is pressed and shadowed by larger, newer buildings; not enough, though, to dim the eighteenth-century liveliness of its ba-roque façade. The interior has an exuberant altar, white and gold choir screens, and encrustations of tile, added at various times. In the glitter of white and gold above, there appear ribbons of *M*'s—possi-bly the insignia of Maximilian? Because Mexico has so many churches with too much history and because the lack of interest in Maximilian is thorough, the possibility cannot be sure fact, but the gold and white, the neo-classic Empire floridities seem appropriate to the man and his time.

Walk a bit north and south, not too far from the Zócalo, on

Argentina. If you haven't already done so, look into the gun shops and the bookstores, some of which sell embroidery patterns rarely available in the States. (These might make unusual, inexpensive, lightweight gifts for demon needlewomen.) Argentina is a busy and crowded street, one of the major arteries stemming from the ancient, throbbing square. Order a soft drink or a beer in one of the many places open to the street and watch part of the Mexican world go by.

Just west of Argentina, at Luis González Obregón 23, is the Colegio Nacional, which presents lectures and courses in adult education and publishes learned works. Its renovated inner courtyard is a beautifully proportioned, graceful, open room quite unlike the large imperious courtyards innate to much Colonial architecture.

Continue the short distance westward to Brasil, where the old Plaza of Santo Domingo opens itself to view. (It has been renamed officially the "Plaza del 23 de Mayo" but the name is as little used as "Avenue of the Americas" by New Yorkers.) On the north side, at Venezuela, stands the Church of Santo Domingo, which was built to supplant the first Dominican establishment, begun in the sixteenth century and flooded out some two hundred years later. In spite of revolutions and overzealous improvements, it is still an impressive building in baroque style, obviously worthy of its early job of housing the Inquisition. In front of the fine church there sits an iron man, a turn-of-the-century intellectual, frail and frozen in dark metal, typical of the European and Mexican monument art of its time.

In another part of the square sits his counterpart (in period) and opposite (in size and power), the indomitable Corregidora, Doña Josefa Ortiz de Domínguez. This heroine of Mexico was extraordinarily valiant in the revolution of 1810. A grateful government has done her an endlessly repeated disservice for her valor. Her statue, life-size and literal to the comb in her hair, repeats the cliché of the angry, tight-lipped woman who appears on billions of coins. She looks like the irascible mother-in-law of the comics, capable of quelling a son-in-law or an army with the lightning of her glance. Granted that public statuary is often peculiar, that Mexican park statuary is richly peculiar, La Corregidora is still unique in the category.

The house she faces, and in which she was purportedly born, is worth entering to see the pillars in the courtyard, to admire the double, curved stairway and the huge studded door which closed off from the world that secluded castle, the Colonial residence.

The Plaza of Santo Domingo used to be referred to as "The Square of the Scribes." It still is, although the scribes who labored under the *portales* have given way to typist-correspondents who read, and explain, official documents for those who can't or don't trust themselves to. Most of the scribes use more or less modern office typewriters; a few use an old, graceful machine whose keyboard is a series of graduated metal arches which quiver like dragonfly wings. On a chair at the side of the scribe sit his clients, bent toward him in worried concentration, their intense eyes drawing magic from the flying keys, willing the writer to wisdom and strength in their behalf.

Nearer the sun, right under the arches, are the small stands which bear rudimentary presses not too much improved from Gutenberg's original. Surprisingly, they serve, and serve well, spewing out birth announcements, advertisements, and notices of union meetings at a gallant rate.

LORETO, SAN ILDEFONSO

When you are somewhere in the vicinity of the Paseo de la Reforma, where most *peseros* (group cabs) do their rattling, take one to the Zócalo (eastward), the end of the commonest *pesero* line. In all likelihood you will have to cross the vast square, no more difficult than crossing the Place de la Concorde or Times Square if all its traffic lights were out of order. Unless it has become a pedestrian mall, which is happening to a number of streets in a number of Mexican cities, attach yourself to a group of fleet, local citizens, until you have reached the far end of the cathedral and the front of the National Palace, the low wide buildings on the east side of the square.

Walk north one block and then eastward on Guatemala, glancing at the serious well-stocked bookshops which supply the academic life still clustered in this area despite the existence of the stunning (in several senses of the word) University City on the outskirts. Look in at the food stalls, some just big enough to hold two rickety tables and a drink freezer. They give off the usual, disproportionately large, magnificent odors, and may still display on their front counters a neat gargoyle row of flayed and barbecued heads of kid, staring out accusingly at the indifferent world. On Guatemala, too, there is a fine-herb shop whose windows are heaped with small mounds and boxes of supremely confident curatives, explicitly labeled "for the liver"; "for menstrual trouble"; "for bed-wetting"; "for debility in men"; and "for cancer." Something of a medical center, seemingly, Guatemala also houses a meeker shop of homeopathic medicines.

Continuing on Guatemala, one soon comes to the Calle Loreto, which leads into the Plaza Loreto. It is an amiable plaza with a lovely fountain surrounded by barefoot black-thatched babies pattering around in the sun and spray. In one corner an itinerant storyteller-comedian, clown-painted face topped by a cheap, wild wig, is talking his heart out, frantically fast and loud, trying to impress a crowd which can afford him only a few pesos. They are attentive and sober-faced (the highlands poor usually take their pleasures solemnly, with curiosity, rather than joy) and watch as they might in a zoo, while the entertainer charges on, the sweat pouring off his face, his thin body bent in eagerness, feet restless, hands and arms moving in complement to his intense, mobile face. The crowd remains unmoved.

In another corner, someone has mounted a bench and is making a speech. Passionately, violently, with the same fervor and gestures as the hard working storyteller, he demands that prices be lowered and wages raised. His listeners, a mob of four, are as impassive as the funny man's audience. Unheeding of both are the women with their market baskets resting on the benches, the old men reading any day's paper, the boys strolling slowly through the plaza on their way home from school, stopping to play now and then.

On the north end of the square stands the Loreto church, Palladian-domed and extraordinarily naked for a Mexican church, lacking the plateresque or Churrigueresque pasta which boils on the façades of most Mexican churches. It is a cool neo-classic French lady of a church, a touch déclassé because she lurches forward drunkenly, like many old buildings in the city. Diagonally across, on the east side of the square, is the busy neighborhood church, officially called Santa Teresa, although the locals may call it *La Señora de Loreto* or *El Señor de la Salud* as well. Its ceiling is high and bare, its images simple, declarative statements, but it is a hive of activity. The front gate does a brisk trade in blatant chromos and small silver replicas of legs, hearts, lungs, and eyes which, if pinned on the Virgin's skirt, will restore that ailing member to health. Among the vendors a twisted knot of beggars acknowledge coins with "God will pay you" or "God will pay you more"—a phrase which seems to carry a faint note of rebuke. At the side of the church a long line of women carrying small pails, soft-drink bottles, tequila bottles, beer bottles wait for an allowance of holy water to take back to their sick or to put on the family altars.

Having sat on a bench under the trees (if they have escaped an anti-tree campaign) and watched the flow of life around you, go to the southern end of the square (Justo Sierra) and walk right, to Argentina. On Argentina, at 21-A, behind an inconspicuous slot of an entrance, there is a dark, small wax museum—if it hasn't disappeared in an earthquake gulch—which asks a timid entrance fee. The figures are, naturally, mainly historical: the indomitable hero, Juárez, portrayed as usual, as a man who never smiled, and possibly, was never smiled at. This seems to be true also of such disparate personalities as the cultivated, music-loving Father Hidalgo; the poor country priest of tremendous vision, Morelos; the peasant rebel, Zapata—all consistently portrayed with Byronic frowns covering stormy thoughts, a stereotype which makes them look surprisingly alike. It is a relief to turn to the tableau of the gentle, sweet-faced Victorian intellectuals who wrote Mexico's national anthem. The climax of the dumb show is the starved figure of a skeletal woman with a white-green face and disheveled black hair staring at the "White Death" (tuberculosis) from a brass bed. Even Maria Callas, at her thinnest and most histrionic, couldn't touch this fourth-act Violetta for pathos and terror.

In contrasting and abundant health the sturdy young Cuauhtémoc stands near the exit, resplendent in dusty gold cloth and musty feathers. He was the defender of the city during its last days of arson, pillage, siege, and final devastation by Cortés and his forces. He was a valiant young man—particularly in contrast to his uncle, the vacillating, complex Moctezuma—and he had, at one time, for that reason, become the cult hero of a small group of supernationalists for whom he stood as a vaguely fascist ideal of warrior strength, of an aristocracy of ancient blood and the concomitant right to hate all non-Mexicans, and selected Mexicans as well.

The next block one meets should be San Ildefonso. A turn right (east) brings into view, almost immediately, the National Preparatory School. It was, in the sixteenth century, the Jesuit Seminary of San Ildefonso, rebuilt in the Spanish baroque splendor of its present style in the mid-eighteenth century. It houses, besides many boys on the stairways and in the classrooms, the work of an impressive roll call of Mexican muralists: a superb set of Orozcos, a group by Rivera, some by Charlot, and others by Leal. And, if it hasn't been whisked away, a richly carved choir stall which once belonged to a seventeenth-century monastery.

A good time to go, if you can, is about noon, when the early session lets out and the boys studying English (*Prepa* covers senior high school and junior college studies, roughly) will, for the practice and the sheer pleasure of exerting amiability, show you—sometimes in unwieldy droves—around the courtyard and the murals.

Continuing on San Ildefonso (trying to imagine the great Aztec palaces and temples which once stood here), have a look at some of the small printing plants and scholastic bookshops embedded in cavelike rooms lit by one bulb. To us this indicates poverty and may actually be the reason for such paucity of light in such paucity of space. It might also indicate a common Mexican characteristic: the ability to accept and adjust to discomfort and adversity, and an active pride in such stoicism.

At the corner of San Ildefonso and Carmen stands the early seventeenth-century church and convent (used in its meaning of a "gathering place" rather than "nunnery") of San Pedro and San Pablo, now a public building, massive and dour, and proud.

Continue on Carmen southward, to where it becomes Correo Mayor, the street of the main postal depot at some distant time, and now the central street of inexpensive yard goods sold *por mayor* and *por menor,* wholesale and retail. The street, not particularly stimulating except for comparison shopping in yard goods, sometimes wears boutonnieres of Indian women—girls, in our terms—and their babies, selling a few avocados or figs. They are not so much interested in sales as in sociability; most of them are pretty and extraordinarily gay for Indian women. Their scrutiny of passers-by is unusually open, their talk unusually voluble, their laughter quite free.

At the juncture of Carmen with Correo Mayor, turn left (east) toward Jesús María. Like the rest of the neighborhood, this street has been long abused by poverty and decay but still carries some vestiges of its noble Colonial past. As you approach the street of the Corregidora, you will stumble on the shapeless old Plaza of the Granary (Plaza Alhóndiga), where you may still see an antique coat of arms emblazoning a broken archway, a thickness of overconfident Spanish wall sheltering a heap of tin braziers.

One block north of Corregidora is the Calle Soledad. Follow it right (eastward) through its seas and forests of inexpensive shoes until it empties into the Plaza Soledad, importantly occupied by the church of that name. The church is rather Italianate baroque, its surface cut into by square columns and a few clumsily sculptured large figures in niches. They are primitive and crude and appear crippled but are infinitely more appealing than the Virgen de La Soledad, whom they surround. Usually, the Lady of the Solitudes is sweet-faced and aristocratic in a stiff wide dress of deep blue, reminiscent of Infantas in Spanish paintings, with a gentle, well-born look. To get back to *this* Virgin: she appears rigid and punitive, as hard and angular as a pyramid, and one wonders about her appeal, which is obviously wide and deep. Beneath the figure, from a carved plaque, comes her harsh voice: *"Nadie pase este lugar sin que afirme con su vida que María fué conceptuada sin la culpa original."* ("No one may enter this place without avowing with his life that Mary was conceived without original sin.") And that's that, except for thieves—Catholics or freethinkers—whom this Virgin is expected to protect, maybe because she looks mightier than any police sergeant.

ALAMEDA *(Incorporate with a Bellas Artes visit, the Pinacoteca Virreinal, or shopping along Juárez)*

Walk slowly through the damaged but peaceable little park which breathes of age and no longer betrays its role as auto-da-fé site for the Inquisition. Two working girls on their lunch hour listen intently to Shostakovich's *Leningrad Symphony* piped out to them by the local classical music station. Young couples lash themselves together in close intimacy. On Sundays the balloon sellers are out with their ingeniously shaped octopi and clowns, which mesmerize the little boys polished up for the day in baseball jackets and stiff denims, new and bought big enough to fit three and four years hence. The professional photographer is out—or half out, his upper half hidden by the black cloth which shrouds his elderly camera. Sitting patiently through his instructions and adjustments is the prototype of countless Mexican paintings: a dark, round-faced little girl with huge black eyes, waiting and passive. In another part of the park an itinerant clown gestures frantically at his stolid audience. Elsewhere, a group of boys try out their guitars and voices on the coveys of pretty quail clattering by in tight blue jeans and the highest of heels.

Having crossed the park in a meandering diagonal, you should be on Avenida Hidalgo. If you haven't done so before, look in at the courtyard of the Hotel Cortés or have a beer and then wander down Hidalgo, toward the Bellas Artes again. The contrast with Juárez doesn't have to be pointed out when you observe the clothing of a boy who is selling tamales out of a clock sack; the bewildered, joyous-eyed Huicholes in their brilliantly embroidered suits, dirty with the long voyage from home, come to sell the woolen symbols now popular with tourists. On one side of a church that leans forward and to the side, there was for centuries a hospital for women; now, on the other, buildings bannered with signs: "Doctor X. Infirmities of Women," "Dr. Y. Diseases of the Blood." Old-timers say that this was once one of the red-light districts, that the church was the church of the prostitutes, that the hospital was theirs and they took their troubles and diseases to the local doctors. The church steps are still crowded with working-class women, eating and gossiping. The antique hospital has been replaced by a crafts showcase and the rest of the square prettied up with old lamps and benches and a fountain in Colonial style.

Before you leave this neighborhood, for the shining life of Juárez, walk a few blocks northeast for a look at the Plaza de la Concepción, a worn-out beauty holding some remarkable old houses and a fine church. A block or two away, there is a simple market in which one may still find *metates,* the slanted, legged stones on which corn for tortillas is ground into *masa.* Neither pretty nor handleable as souvenir, the *metate* is one of Mexico's truly impressive antiques. It is old enough to have appeared, close to its present shape, under the ancient lava flow which covered the Pedregal area thousands of years ago.

Should you reach Insurgentes Norte and Carpio, on your left you will find the old park of the section of Santa María, once a proud *hidalgo* neighborhood with only a few of its old houses left to prove its former splendors. Once-handsome trees are now dry and sparse, and the manicured little plots of French formal garden quite gone. Why should you bother, then? Because, in the middle of the park (if earthquake and reconstruction have spared it) sits one of the most glorious bandstands in Mexico, a country devoted to bandstands. Someone mortally stricken by the great mosque in Córdoba and the Alhambra in Granada was apparently responsible for the design, which repeats the Arabic arches of the great prototypes in miniature, and imitations of Arabic mosaics on the metal pillars. A far flight from Spain (one of the characteristics of Mexican art and architecture is that it rarely sustains the effort of slavish copying) is the wooden, slatted ceiling, radiating out in a functional cone, and the iron grill-work, more Porfirio Díaz than Moor.

RODRIGUEZ AND TEPITO MARKETS

The Rodríguez market is a basic-cost market, which the central areas of the Merced and San Juan are not. It is bordered by a street devoted to the making of funerary wreaths, it is the market to which much of Mexico goes before Christmas for the figures and miniature palm trees of its crèches, and for the *piñatas* the children will break. It leads a mundane life most of the year and becomes an enchantress in December.

A cab driver will know the market; if possible, have him drop you at the Callejón de Girón, the street of the flower-wreath and cross makers. The big, deep stores are completely open to the street, so that you can watch the consummate skill and dexterity with which gladiolas, daisies, camellias, and purple ribbons become transformed into designs much too lively for death.

One of the evocative meetings of extremes so common and stimulating in Mexico also distinguishes this street: one side lives in somber, fragrant dignity, the other surrounds itself with slapdash bits of pottery, toys, and figurines of primitive color and design. (Look through these carefully if you have the time and inclination. Sometimes, the clay animal whistles of a type that go back to pre-Conquest days, and are now becoming rare, find their way in among the novelties.) The light odor of leaves and flowers is countered by the bolder smells of frying meat, beans, and chiles in the *puestos* near the pottery; the concentrated quiet of the flower craftsmen finds its opposite in a two-saxophones-and-a-drum trio—market serenaders whose sad, slow tune has no buoyancy but great volume. (Is it actually true that Mexicans are a musical people, or do they simply like noise?)

The interior of the market before Christmas is a Mexican Disney production. Every bit of space over the stalls is hung with *piñatas,* flowers, flames, globes, stars, harps, torches, girl rabbits, boy rabbits, huge purple carrots, immense pink roses, elephants with pink ears, elephants with blue ears, clowns, ships, birds, fish, lambs, a Santa Claus, and a magnificent bronze abstraction with white streamers—all echoes of the ancient craft of decorative paper work which goes far back into Mexico's history. One can buy wise men on donkeys, pretty Marys, Christ babies in the Spanish style—sad old faces and droopy eyes—and zoos full of tiny animals (to add to the hominess of the crèche, they often come in families of mama, papa, and two young) for as little as a few cents apiece.

The Tepito market deals in things secondhand, third, or twelfth, or the product of very petty theft, or broken remains still usable to people who live on discards. The market and the streets around it are full of color and flavor, the color and flavor of marginal living, sometimes too strong for the sheltered, for those to whom poverty is an accusing finger.

Forewarned, walk north on Girón to the Plaza del Estudiante. Its formal walks are dusty and orange-peeled, the fountain is not very watery, the bird-cage bandstand seems to rest uneasily on its heavy concrete base, and its neo-classic lady statue had for some time a wire lasso around her neck. This may have been the act of an outraged aesthete or one of the local boys now sitting in the jail at the side of the square. (It is discernible from other official buildings by the line of women carrying packages of food and babies, waiting to see the imprisoned men.)

Continue northward along Florida (at the east side of the plaza), a street of *vecindades* whose alley doors are usually kept closed except on holidays, when the local children run in and out, leaving glimpses of cutout paper banners with which they decorate the yards. Florida will lead into the Plaza de Fray Bartolomé de Las Casas, an enclave of small leather shops. One or two can afford the luxury of whole hides, but the rest seem to be involved in making strips out of pieces, heaping them into mounds which billow in even rows back and back into dimness, the cutters and heapers taking only a few moments off to watch the women gathered at the public laundry troughs, a short distance off.

The market spreads north of the plaza, the first two buildings limited to inexpensive food and objects, odd assortments of used radios, records, bottles, coils of wire, and boxes of nails. Outside the main buildings, look for the tables which may hold a monstrous race of naked dolls, all victims of the same error; the red of their lips floats into their left cheeks. It is on the stands on Las Toltecas, though, where the most improbable things turn up: "Señores" and "Damas" plaques stolen from public toilets, faucets, bits of dentures, boxes of dried-out mascara, halves of pliers, and jars of antique pomades. Examining, selecting in this miscellany of rusty unconsidered trifles, are the people who do their Christmas shopping here, careful and hesitant about whether to spend their few pesos on one half of a small plastic truck or will it be the cracked head of a doll?

The building behind these stalls is less a melange: a vast robust market of secondhand clothing—maybe stolen, maybe not—where it is fun to watch the vigorous, persuasive selling which persuades everyone but grandma. She takes her time, feeling, measuring, judging, bargaining, while her assorted numerous brood stands respectfully by.

Now might be the time to pick up a cab at the Plaza de Fray Bartolomé de Las Casas for the return to good restaurants and first-hand shops or a siesta. Tip the driver a bit extra. The streets he will traverse from here to the center are narrow and clotted with traffic all day, and he will have earned little in a half hour of crawling progress.

For the inexhaustible there is another possibility in this area—not a very short walk or terribly long—the Plaza of Santiago Tlaltelolco (you will have noticed by now the common practice of giving a place both its Spanish and Indian names), a vital and bloody site in the conquest of the city, the place of the great market which Díaz described with such amazement, the place of the oldest temple—from which Cuauhtémoc signaled surrounding towns for help against the Spaniards—the site of the earliest college. It was from here that Cortés and his Indian cohorts retreated and heard on the way "the sound of trumpets from the great Cue [temple] which from its heights dominates the city, and also a drum, a most dismal sound indeed it was, like an instrument of demons, as it resounded so that one could hear it two leagues off, and with it many small tambourines and shell trumpets, horns, whistles. At that moment, as we afterward learned, they were offering the hearts of ten of our comrades and much blood to the idols." Elsewhere, Díaz stressed the cannibalism that went on at the Cue of Tlaltelolco.

Now it is a faded, not much used, old square with tall, tired trees and what has been described as "its flaking brown barracks walls" turned to a bilious ocher on the angry government building which hunts down foreign cars whose papers are not in order. Off a corner of the square is a church almost as old as the Conquest, whose base covers what might have been the great Cue.

Sitting in the exhausted square, knowing something of its past, among the uncommunicative office buildings and the decayed church is hardly a picture-postcard experience, yet deeply evocative to anyone with a sense of history and a taste for somber colors.

LA LAGUNILLA *(Late Sunday morning)*

The "little lake" is a sea of market comparable to the Merced in size, ebbing and flowing in an area which starts about a half mile north of the downtown Sanborn's. (Around Paraguay, reaching north to Libertad, Santa María Redonda and Comonfort vaguely its west-east borders.) Allende cuts through the market area and still has a few antique shops that cherish a treasure or two of Colonial art—a *santo* (the image of a saint), a chest of drawers. Most of the market, however, is market—food, kitchenware, good, inexpensive clothing, and like all Mexican markets, lively and full of surprises. One walks indifferently through gilded crosses and inexpensive rosaries and comes on a beautiful collection of crystal beads from Czechoslovakia; an ordinary market street gives way to an outdoor knitting factory, countless needles flashing and dipping in the sun.

The star of Lagunilla is its Sunday morning market, a flea market whose proprietors can spot an American while he is still sitting in Sanborn's (even fair-haired Mexicans have a hard time driving a good bargain) and where the prices soar to Zona Rosa levels. Quick to learn what is selling uptown, Lagunilla has imitations at various levels of excellence to offer you cheaper, and it isn't a bad idea to make some comparisons if you have the time. It takes a sharp eye, stubbornness, and a dogged tenacity to come away with a bargain, but the effort is part of the reward. Among a thousand nondescript pieces of jewelry you may spot a hand-worked Victorian brooch; among dozens of plaster saints made yesterday, there may be an old, wooden *santo;* among the sex magazines and manuals of electricity you may find a sixteenth-century treatise on mathematics in Latin; among piles of nondescript crockery, an exquisite French dish. The actual purchasing is an exhausting set of departures and returns, of prices offered, prices rejected, and lectures on the rarity of your choice, the sophistication of your taste, and how hard it is for an honest man to make a living in Mexico. Keep your wallet safely tucked away, don't expect too much, take time to watch the boys at the used-magazine stalls, and if you are near, make a gesture of homage to Mexican humor, toward an alley off Comonfort. It was a street of "the pupils of schools of bad education" and is called Organo.

PLAZA OF THE THREE CULTURES

North of the Zócalo and Lagunilla market, modern rebuilding gathers in a Colonial church and an important Aztec site. A hospital, a social security building, a spacious playground, and fresh working-class housing border the bases of pyramids and Aztec walls and, accompanied by more gentle structures—fountains and trees—the dark-red church built early in the Conquest, its interior modernized but its massive wooden doors still intact. A handsomely engraved plaque tells in Nahua that the last local ruler was Cuauhtemoctzin (1515) and another, near the church, informs that here Tlaltelolco, probably a warrior chieftain, fell in 1521 to the might of Cortés. "This was not," continues the engraved legend, "triumph or defeat. It was the sad birth of the Mestizo people, the Mexico of today."

If you have the time and curiosity, take a short stroll through this changing neighborhood, with the new and vestiges of the elderly to show. The railroad station is good-looking functional modern, neighbored across the street by the anachronistic Museo del Chopo, its best exhibition the structure itself, built in imitation of the Eiffel Tower and British railroad stations of the time of Edward VII. The confection of delicate towers, glass held in metal embroidery, archlets somewhat Italianate and very Belle Epoque, is one of the most beguiling of its type and time, and quite bewildered in its angular setting.

POLANCO, CONDESA, CUAUHTÉMOC

By now you may have seen, via streets and markets, a fair number of the city's lumpen, working class, lower-middle-class people and places. If you've been to University City, you undoubtedly sampled the luxurious fantasy which is the Pedregal area. For more exhaustive coverage, if you are interested, you might try other middle-class areas: one fairly new and Europeanized, with a faint touch of Westchester; one old and indigenous; one newer yet equally indigenous.

Have a taxi take you to the market of Polanco, or if you can find a *pesero* that goes as far as Petroleos, get out there (you can't miss it, a large, heroic monument celebrating the return of the oil industry to Mexico), and walk right on Molière. Stay close to the map; a number of streets tangle at the monument. Molière will soon lead you into President Masaryk and, clinging to the Czech statesman, design a set of loops along any streets whose names may appeal, for their exoticism or your gratitude for literary pleasures. Try the combination of Ibsen, Goldsmith, and Poe, for instance; or, a bit east, Tennyson, Eugenio Sue, and Aristoteles. They will show you well-kept houses, some of them opulent, on green lawns sporting British prams and jungle gyms imported from the States, amid an increasing number of glassy apartment houses. The dogs—quite unlike the yellow, lean curs that are the scavengers of rural and slum Mexico—are as carefully clipped and polished as the starched children. Their mistresses, sleek and cleverly dressed, tap out confidence with their Italian heels while they chatter with their friends in French, German, Yiddish, Italian, Japanese, and, frequently, Spanish.

At some point find the street of Oscar Wilde, which runs diagonally southward between Masaryk and Emilio Castelar. Follow it to Castelar, which is fronted by a manicured strip of park named for Abraham Lincoln, who stands there surrounded by a little pond, strict rounds of flowers, and a Chinese clock tower. Here you might watch the neighborhood children being aired before you plunge into the market, which sells strong garlicky sausages on the avenue of Oscar Wilde and household paints on the street of Virgilio. The market streets form a daisy design, petals spraying from a center which holds the supermarket, the stalls of vegetables and flowers, and if it has held on in an area that is swelling and modernizing rapidly, a fish place whose proprietress does all her scaling, deboning, cutting, and scraping with a large machete wielded with astonishing artfulness, while she keeps up animated conversations with two or three customers at a time.

The foreign flavor of the neighborhood, if you've missed it before, becomes strongly evident in the food shops: a bakery that sells genuine American honeybuns at genuine American prices, a shop which produces very authentic kosher-style pickles among other Jewish delicacies; shops of Spanish mountain ham and French pâtés, of Italian sweaters and high-style pocketbooks, and spotted through the area, pleasant little outdoor cafés. Around and among them, a strong base tone under lighter colors, is the unquenchable native flavor. A burro carrying a crude platform loaded with firewood crops at a bit of grass under a tree, exactly as if he were in Mexico. Tortilla vendors sit outside the supermarket calling out the freshness and tastiness of their handiwork. Two men and a marimba set themselves outside a restaurant of *chiles rellenos* and *quesadillas* and add to the busy air the hollow, clacking resonance of an old waltz.

Progress in Polanco is a shopping arcade that displays a little of everything, including arts and crafts. It starts at the street of witty Oscar Wilde and ends at imaginative Jules Verne. Progress is also the costly gift shops on Masaryk and Hegel, the good-looking new tourism building across the street, and the well-designed modern houses on Hegel.

It is fairly easy to get a taxi in the market, on Castelar, or on Masaryk. Take one to the eastern end of Chapultepec Park, where the avenues of Chapultepec, Tacubaya, and Veracruz meet, and walk some of the streets between the latter two avenues; these are the old *colonia* Condesa. A few streets not far from your starting point— Melgar, Matehuala, Pachuca, Mazatlán, and the alleys that run among them—should give you the rather retiring old-fashioned flavor of the area. Although there are new buildings here, one feels the hush emanating from the still, old, solid houses, eminently respectable and very private, like certain parts of Brooklyn Heights. And like that area, Condesa has an air of subdued Bohemia with a touch of studio in the houses on Melgar and, on Matehuala, a remarkable row of Vie Bohème (well-fed style) houses. The large windows are almost floor length, separated by heavy window boxes full of richly colored flowers; ivy and vines cover the rest of the walls, the green mat varied only by blue-walled stairwells. Neither very new nor very old, these houses are distinctly particular and special, once enhanced by their "Private" street sign.

Directly across the Paseo de la Reforma from the splendors of the Zona Rosa is the *colonia* of rivers—Eufrates, Tamesis (Thames), Tiber, Mississippi. Very near the tourist centers, increasingly invaded by new hotels and restaurants, it still retains a remotely residential flavor. Among the meticulously kept private houses and larger apartment houses there is an unusual number of furnished apartments in houses less strictly cared for; not poor or neglected, just casual. The apartments are often equipped with bright, light furnishings of thirties modern, heavily biased toward large blond bars, pink rayon drapes, and curly lampshades. It is said that these apartments, easy to get to and inconspicuous at the same time, are often *casas chicas*, the houses of a man's second and even third family. Not all of Cuauhtémoc is illegitimate, by any means, and most of the houses are fiercely respectable, but it might entertain you to walk through the ambience (no overt dramatics or sin visible) of one of the pillars of Mexico's social structure.

SUBWAY

It is still largely true, what they say about Mexico City's subway; it is light and quiet and clean, the signs attractively designed and clearly coordinated, the stations serene and occasionally splendid. For those who cannot read, each stop has a gay, traditional symbol: a bell for Insurgentes, a cricket for Chapultepec, the ship *Pinta* for Isabel la Católica, etc.

Planned like the Paris Metro (and called that in Mexico), it has mechanized gates that close—rather than whip as they do in Paris—automatically to hold back the late and impetuous from crashing into a closing door or knocking down emerging passengers, the "correspondences" for connecting lines are well planned and graphically indicated. The going has been slow. Like Rome, Mexico has met, been impeded by, and decided to circumvent archaeological treasures. But on the surface they have moved quickly and made each station a monument to progress and taste, occasionally art. Go to the Insurgentes Station, then look around at the large sunken plaza that gives room to shops, garden patches, and play areas. Entering or leaving the station proper one follows a long wall of creamy yellow stone carved in the graceful, orderly glyphs of the Mayans, a wall that might be Palenque. Another wall repeats the gay, wide-eyed, lively angels carved in innumerable churches by Indians centuries ago from drawings and models given them by the church fathers. Accompanied by Mozart, whose symphonies are sometimes piped in, platform space is enlivened by photo murals of fields of flowers and pretty girls, of bold strong machinery and its sturdy attendants, or old photographs or prints of national heroes. In order to avoid at least one of the famous subway difficulties, there are few, if any, toilets in the stations and some stations have policemen to watch for suspicious lingerers, whom they put on the next train or order back into the street.

The system is civilized, and well schemed, but it has two faults. A ticket costs three times the price of the cheapest bus ride. Consequently, the poor must still use up long periods of uncomfortable time on the most worn—with screeching brakes—vehicles and ride the subway, back and forth and back and forth, for Sunday outings only. And more effectively than skyscrapers, glittering hotels and icy office buildings, luxurious shops and sheer ballooning size, the Metro has given the Mexican face that big-city look, the look of "rushing for the subway." It has created silent, determined, purposeful crowds (most un-Mexican) that lean in the slanting, driven pace innate to subway catchers. Sauntering, a contented pace, is leaving the city; the scowling, concentrated subway face has, beyond any other development, finally made a metropolis of Mexico City.

The scattering of grimy old bus stations has been replaced by two well-built, well-lit, well-organized bus terminals: Terminal del Norte for northbound buses and Terminal del Sur for those going to the south. Destinations and times are clearly marked, and, like the airport, the terminals provide booths for taxi or minibus tickets, fairly priced, that will take you to any part of Mexico City.

A good way to see a Mexican neighborhood in transition is to take a bus along Insurgentes Sur from its meeting with Liverpool. It is a long, middle-class shopping street and trying for better with boutiques, airlines offices, office buildings, and a few good restaurants among its many. The street it was only a few decades ago—a road through the near suburbs—is still witnessed, though, by the fanciful turn-of-the-century houses and their small gardens in the side streets.

MEXICAN HOURS

9:45 *The milkman guides his burro through the restless alleys of Jalapa, stopping now and then to pour milk into proffered pitchers, tequila bottles, and Coke bottles, from the graceful tin cans tied on the burro. The household maid, gesturing with her tequila bottle, and the milkman with his milk-can cover engage in an animated discussion of his mother-in-law's illness, rife with swellings, blood, consolations, sympathy, advice, and good wishes.*

10:00 *In one of the lovely hyacinth-filled canals outside of Villahermosa, two little brown boys tease the passive, flower-chewing cows as they paddle around in their shallow dugout.*

10:30 *A tall, spare, very dark woman with piercing eyes of deep amber, who is dressed in the wrapped coarse skirt and square woolen* huipil *of a colder climate, strides through the dusty hot streets of Tehuantepec, carrying a large live armadillo. She offers to sell it to an American couple. The American woman explains that her home and kitchen are too far away for cooking armadillo. Indian woman: "Take it home, then, on the bus." American: "I live farther away than a bus can take me." The Indian woman looks skeptical: there can be no place farther off than the reach of the local bus. But she keeps trying: "Armadillo meat is very good for men; it keeps them young, it keeps them strong." Leering delicately, she goes into particulars, adding that armadillo skin is powerful medicine for various ailments. American woman: "I know and I'm very grateful to you, but it is impossible for me to buy an armadillo today. Maybe another day." The vendor, who has disregarded the man altogether (a common habit of the area), turns to the husband: "You have not a good wife; she will look neither to your health nor your pleasure." She turns and walks away.*

11:00 *In Sanborn's, in the café of the Calle López in Mexico City, in the Parroquia Café in Veracruz, under the* portales *of Oaxaca, in coffeehouses of Monterrey, of Mérida, and even taciturn Puebla, dark-suited, correct businessmen gather—for the first of many coffee breaks of the day—to discuss and possibly cure the world of its intransigent stupidity.*

11:20 *For the third time this morning, a tourist is stopped and asked what time it is. He tries to figure why; there are clocks around. Can't they tell time? Why, since Mexican time is a shapeless wispy thing of no importance, is everyone so anxious about it? He begins to realize that time has nothing to do with it; the asker wants a closer look at an American watch, at American clothing, at an American face, and the entertainment of eliciting an answer in bad Spanish which he will imitate wickedly well later on.*

11:30 *The news vendors gather on Bucareli Street in Mexico City to get their papers, to talk, to eat tacos and chile-dusted cucumbers from the bright stands which crowd the street for one ebullient half hour and then are gone.*

11:35 *The train passes a mountainside monumentally scratched with the name of a political candidate:* Viva Fulano *(roughly, "Hurray for Joe Doakes"), repeated in horizontal and vertical furrows in the green. After the large, monotonous shouts, a devout disgusted soul has carved out a correction:* Viva Cristo!

"MACHISMO"

Machismo is a scourge of Mexico—a killer, a root and flower of poverty, and one of its great sports, indoors and outdoors. It is the relentless reflex, the unremitting watchfulness to prove oneself a man; always and in all circumstances, one must be a *macho*. It is an attitude that shadows the atmosphere of Mexico much as the thick, low clouds shadow the mountaintops.

Born of Indian pride and fatalism, of the strangled anger of the many years of Conquest and rigid class distinctions, of strong latent homosexuality (overtly practiced among some Indians in centuries past, and still), of the adoration of blood and death common to Aztecs and Spaniards, of the aristocratic stance of the Spanish *hidalgo*—at one extreme, the boldness of the *conquistadores* and at the other, the noble madness of Don Quixote—*machismo* has its heroic aspects, its gestures of greatness. Father Hidalgo, one of Mexico's immortal heroes in its struggle for independence, scratched a message of thanks to his jailer on the wall of the cell he occupied just before he was executed. Morelos, as monumental a figure in the same cause, refused an opportunity to escape from his cell before he was killed. Both were men of immense stature; in any place or time, they might have made their symbolic, identifying gestures, but since they were Mexican, one suspects a touch of *machismo*.

Machismo is the defiance and narcissism of the bullfight, the *torero* a flash of lustrous splendor, arched like a jeweled saber, dancing a *pavana* with the dark bulk of death. He twists and dizzies the snorting mass, then turns his disdainful back on it and walks away slowly. His is the outrageous show of courage and insane romanticism the lesser *macho* yearns toward. ("*Olé*" is breathed with each beautiful, dangerous cape pass, but when the *torero* makes his circle of the ring after the death of the bull, the shout is "*Macho!*") The male flamenco dancer is another of the portraits of *machismo*. Like the *torero*'s, his tight suit is outer skin for the taut, vain body, tensed like a bow; his face is distant and noble, distorted in a very private pain, the frustration and anger he hammers out of his furious heels. His is a terrible beauty and passion, as he violently and impotently protests the heavy clays of life that keep him from high, iridescent flight. *Torero* and *bailador*, pushing out of the ordinary dimension of the timid, human act and the pallid, human sensation, are reaching for the larger-than-life-size of *machismo*.

The lesser portraits are compounds of Don Juan, Superman, Robin Hood, and Buffalo Bill, and the much-admired bold, big-time crook—the governor who steals the funds needed for the new capital building and safely disappears; the high official who lifts, as if it were pounds of butter out of a refrigerator, gold bricks out of the national treasury.

At its darkest, *machismo* is a prolific destroyer, accounting in large part for an extraordinary homicide rate. Among the poor and uneducated a show of excessive strength is often the result of terrible debilities and guilts: not being able to find a job or hold one; the children implanted on weak compliance and then abandoned; the distraught, hungry women who must feed the children; the beatings given and taken; a future that doesn't exist and a past that dare not be looked at. If the man drinks, and he often does, the women, the children, the regrets, the angers float in a dark phantasmagoria through his melting brain, and to dispel them, he takes out his gun—his male strength—and kills. Having been an abandoner, he translates himself into the abandoned. (The lyrics of Mexican songs often sung by men show an interesting emphasis: "I am abandoned by a woman and God," "I suffer terribly from the absence of a cruel woman"—and so on in the same self-pitying and self-mortifying strain.) The saloon and the fellowship of *compadres*—a close and complex relationship of godfatherhood, which, less formally, stands for "palship" also—are his rock of Gibraltar and his church. Here he is safe—but never quite enough—and the drunker he becomes, the more touchy and open to insult; challenging, looking for trouble, eager to prove himself. The actual triggering incident can be idiotically simple. One man asks a stranger to drink with him in friendship, throwing a chummy arm over the newcomer's reluctant shoulder. The stranger says, "No, thanks, not now." After some cajoling, the arm-hugging tighter, the alcoholic breath closer and stronger, repeated offers and bids for friendship, the stranger still refuses; and the guilt-anger, the inferiority break through! "Aren't I good enough for you? If we're too low class for you around here why don't you drink in the tourist *cantinas?* So I *am* dirty and I *am* drunk, but I'm a hell of a lot more man than you!" Out comes the gun or knife. In rural areas, the odd man who won't drink with the locals—and doesn't have the sense to say that the doctor forbade him to drink and that he has come to the *cantina* for a little companionship only— may be driven out of the saloon and stoned to death as he runs. A drunken *macho* is belligerent about every threat of superiority; he will kill the nondrinker because he himself is a sot, he will shoot at a car because he doesn't have one, fire a hovel which contains a bed superior to the straw mat on which he sleeps.

The complex aspects of *machismo's* sexuality make for contempt and mistreatment—if not downright brutality—toward their women, for a social life that is lived exclusively with men, and for devoted friendships that often demand the sacrifices and fidelities of love. One shares with his *compa'* a floor to sleep on, a mug of pulque, a lottery win, and even a woman—if she is not of the neighborhood or the vast interlocking tribes of illegitimacies and plural families that link poor Mexicans.

Machismo has, of course, lighter colors than the red of blood and the black of death. A man bumps into a woman on the street. Instead of saying, "Excuse me," he says, "How nice!" Or let us take, for instance, the *macho* as the driver of a car. He cannot confess to being any less skillful than the greatest driver; nor be outdone by a better or newer or larger car, or the demands of the machine itself, or traffic regulations, or pedestrians. The less his real confidence, the greater his audacity; and like his hero, the *torero* who strives for the largest close-up of death, the driver finds his proofs in skimming fenders and fanning skirts as he makes a tight, screaming turn on two wheels. As often as not the fear of fear induces prodigious feats of driving. There is hardly a remote mountain village which doesn't count as its life line a rattling truck, held together by will power and improvisations of repair, which flies up and around unpaved mountain roads strewn with boulders in dry weather and mud slicks in the rainy season, either hazard capable of thrusting driver and truck into a gorge 3,000 feet deep. A good deal of this is accomplished on the wings of *machismo*.

As an outdoor game, *machismo* has the charm of being playable anywhere, anytime. It may be played standing on a street, reading a newspaper with just enough antennae out, swaying and groping freely, to sense an approaching female. It may be played while frankly standing and staring, or strolling, or getting one's shoes shined, or lifting a load of onions off a truck, or repairing a telephone line, or plastering a wall. Home base is ubiquitous. The game is, in essence, extremely simple, with room for ascending spirals of virtuosity. The lazy or inept satisfy themselves with a complimentary comment, as a woman goes by, which sounds like a cross between a hiss and a kiss. The "flower throwing" of a busy man may consist only of one descriptive word—*guapa,* for a handsome woman; *güera,* to a fair one; and *chula,* to cover the meanings of "cutie." The more versatile and ambitious apply magnificent flourishes: "Rush to my mother! Tell her I'm cured! Tell her to stop making appointments with all those doctors who can't find out what's wrong with me! All I needed right along was this balm, this beauty, and now I've found her!"

As an indoor sport, *machismo* has its preposterous appeal, too. It can be observed at the counters which carry magazines from the States, where, during the interminably long coffee breaks that Mexican businessmen take, a group of properly dark-suited, middle-aged men can be found slowly and carefully, with the dedicated concentration of scientists, examining sex and fashion magazines for pictures of the fair, long-legged beauties of the North. Even a magazine of knitting instructions might do, as long as the sweaters on the models are sufficiently *pegado*—pasted on. Even if he is only casually interested, the Mexican male cannot pass up an opportunity to flex his *macho* muscle.

When there is no opportunity in the present, one talks of his glorious, heroic past, as a taxi driver recently did to a passenger. He had the litheness of a bullfighter and the thunderous face of a pirate, and could hardly wait to begin as the door of the cab closed.

"You know, lady, I used to be a volcano of love, a storm of passion. I stole money from my father, a famous *torero,* to spend on love. Not on women—although they profited—but as offerings on the altar of love. Perfumes, imported from France! Gardens full of flowers! Serenades—I played the guitar and sang, and I hired another guitarist and two fiddlers. Presents—gold, silver, diamonds—shining mountains of presents. How do you like such a life? What do you think of it?"

"Very interesting, very romantic. But shouldn't we have turned at that last street?"

"I was once so in love with a girl that I couldn't breathe. My blood turned thick and black with torment. I was in church one Sunday; she was in another part of the church. I couldn't go to her and I was consumed, burning like a torch, with anguish. The priest was talking about hell. And I, a youth of sixteen—only sixteen, mind you—shouted, 'Hell is here, not later; it is here, in this church where I am racked with love which is not requited.' How do you like that, hmm?"

"Fascinating. Very brave."

"The priest came down from the pulpit and walked slowly toward me, his eyes piercing me. 'You don't know what love is—you are not old enough—and you must not desecrate this church with your foul talk of the tortures of fleshly love.' 'If it's foul, why did God make it? Answer me that. God made man and God made man to love!' He pointed me out of the church and I went. But that was pretty strong for a young boy, don't you think?"

"Very."

"I went to the University of Guanajuato, but I never took my degree. I was writing poems, magnificent, beautiful, emotional poems; and they were printed. They were all about love; there is nothing else to write poetry about."

Having throbbed and intoned a number of indifferent quatrains, he asked again, "How do such poetry and such a life strike you?"

"Very beautiful, very emotional. And do you still write poetry and lead such a life?"

"Why, of course. Always, always, always, I will love women and love loving them and will be a devoted slave of love. And I'll kill anyone who stands in my way. I have, you know."

The last phrase was added, as a lucky afterthought, to complete the composition, the ideal self-portrait of the great *macho*. Obviously, most of the autobiography was invented—including a mother who was, of course, a famous opera star—but why shouldn't a man invent a bigger life than has been given him?

Mexico City: The Middle

TO EAT OR NOT TO EAT

As any traveler knows, Mexico did not invent the twisted innards and physiological excesses known as *turista,* or Moctezuma's Revenge. The sacred groves of French culinary miracles (see George Orwell, *Down and Out in London and Paris*) and those lilting, fruit-hung *trattorias* in Italy—not to mention restaurants of the Near and Far East and the United States—can attack outraged entrails as vigorously as a Mexican *torta* can.

Not everyone who goes to Mexico is invaded or needs to be, yet the fear hangs over travelers like a black omen, and the more suggestible begin to feel the internal knotting before they claim their luggage at the airport, creating a visceral atmosphere which welcomes almost any bug. There are several simple rules to remember: Don't be afraid, light caution will do; stay away from uncooked greens—and reds and yellows; peel your own fruit; avoid milk products, unless you can be sure that they are pasteurized. Break the rules, if you are so inclined, in the good restaurants of Mexico City and in the *posadas* run by and for Americans and Europeans in Cuernavaca. Elsewhere, hang on to the safeties. (This includes Acapulco, especially with the delicacies offered by beach vendors.)

Outside of Mexico City, eating is dictated by conditions other than habits of cleanliness. Coastal towns are expert at judging and cooking seafood and less familiar with meat, which may not be in large or fresh supply. Therefore, the choice is easy. When and where in doubt, remember that soups are good (garlic soup with an egg in it, for instance), breads are full of flavor and integrity, everyone can produce a couple of eggs or a chicken. *Carne asada*—a thin broiled filet surrounded by tortilla variations and beans—is safe and available almost everywhere.

If none of this appeals to you, buy some bread at the *panadería;* a can of tuna *(atún)* or *sardinas* at the grocery; tomatoes, onion, fruit, and peanuts in the market (it is assumed that you will be carrying an all-purpose knife and a can opener if you're driving through rural areas); and settle down to an al fresco lunch in the plaza.

You have heard—possibly too vehemently and often—that the water is unsafe. It is. But the beer is as good as the water is bad; the soda pop is dazzling and oversweet, but there is always Pepsi or Coke or canned fruit juices or bottled water. (Ask for *agua pura* or *Tehuacán* or *agua embotellada.*) The famous antique, pulque, is not easy to like; doctored with fruit juice it isn't impossible. Mexican wines are improving, though hardly choice, and worth a try. As for stronger drink, remember that American and British whiskies are quite expensive, that tequila is cheap and rough, mescal is cheaper and rougher, and Mexican rums are good and inexpensive, as are Mexican versions of Scotch, vodka, and gin, when you can find them.

Mexican "cuisine" is really of two kinds: Spanish usages with strong touches of French, plus a bit of U.S., and vaguely "Continental" echoes found in the big cities; the indigenous soups, greens, *frijoles,* fruits, chiles, and the omnipresent tortilla, which is about as old as corn and the absolutely basic staple of Mexican life. The corn kernels are soaked in water with limestone, then ground into *masa,* patted into flat, round disks, and baked on a griddle. The musical days when Mexican women spent most of their time slapping and shaping dozens of tortillas for the family's daily meals are about gone except in very primitive areas. Every town now has its mill for grinding the *masa* and a machine for stamping out the disks. Like many things Mexican, the tortilla is ingenious: it serves as a scoop or spoon, as a plate, and having functioned also as a napkin, is eaten. It can become a taco, a *tostada,* an enchilada, a *quesadilla,* a *gordita,* a *panucho,* a *pelliscada,* a *papadzul* (described as they appear in other pages of this book), to mention a common few; it can be folded, rolled, toasted, fried, stuffed, or shredded, and cooked with sauces; Puebla makes them small; Tehuantepec makes them large; the north makes them of wheat; Yucatán fills them with squash seeds. One can go on, but this may already be more than you care to know about tortillas, except that you should try them in their various guises, not risky if you can see them hot and freshly made.

The visitor soon hears about the glories of *mole,* turkey or chicken covered with a very complex sauce of chocolate, chile, and a dozen other ingredients. Obviously, it is a thing to respect, but no non-Mexican has been known to develop a passion for it and a number of Mexicans look at it the way we do the Thanksgiving turkey (*mole* is a feast dish also)—an essential part of the stage set but not necessarily lovable. Not to be confused with *mole* at all is *guacamole*—a mash of avocado, onion, tomato, a bit of garlic and chile—a delicious heap that should accompany every order of chicken tacos. Chile and its violence can be handled. If you suspect that a dish may be too spicy, ask that it be made *suave*—although a sophisticated waiter will, after one lightning glance at you, instruct the cook with one word: *turista.*

Keep in mind that Mexicans are not great cooks, but they are much nicer as a rule than the French; that Oaxaca won't feed you as well as Bologna might, but that it is a much gentler city; and that you didn't, after all, go to Mexico to search out its three-star restaurants. That would have been a serious mistake.

If, in spite of intelligent caution, you should be attacked by intestinal pests, take (unless you are allergic to certain drugs) Lomotil, limit your diet for a day or two, and stop thinking in terms of amoebic dysentery. What you will probably have is a common variety of stomach upset, quickly gone and easily forgotten. In the meantime, study some Spanish, listen to the remarkable commercials and the bombastic piano concertos of which radio program directors are enamored.

RESTAURANTS

What you should know about eating in Mexico City is that it is Continental in some ways, American in others and of course, many kinds of Mexican. Restaurants deeply love the tourist and offer him many moods, cuisines, décors, and price levels. Also, new hopefuls alight, then fly away with the speed of hummingbirds, and although many restaurants are open Sundays, many are closed on Mondays.

Few restaurants will have lunch ready before one, and eight is fairly early for dinner. You might have your hotel phone the restaurant of your choice to make sure, or prepare a list of alternate choices. A lack of Spanish is no serious matter in the deluxe restaurants, since the menus and the waiters are bilingual, and not much more serious elsewhere in Mexico City, where much of the population is embarrassingly fluent in English. To feel safer in the more obscure places you might carry a phrase book. And keep in mind that like the rest of the world, these restaurants are becoming homogenized, that antipasto is rarely worth ordering and that lasagna can be an incredible mess in some venturesome restaurants.

As in the matter of hotels, check to find out whether they have survived earthquake damage.

Ambassadeurs   Reforma 12. Like a great aging tragedienne, aristocratic, a bit *triste,* and impressive. French cuisine. Expensive.

Hotel de Cortés   Avenida Hidalgo 85. Served in the appealing courtyard of the hotel, the food as appealing as the atmosphere.

Normandia   López 15, just off Juárez. The décor swings between French country inn and German *bierstube,* but the mood is distinctly Gallic down to the fine sauces and quality cheese (not always easy to find in Mexico) and the irascible tempers which electrify the air once in a while and lash down on an innocent customer. An ignorance of foreign languages comes in very handy then. Expensive.

Thirty years ago these were about the only elegant "international" restaurants the city could boast. There were a few gaudily *típico* places, some serious seafood houses, and near the market areas, a pocking of formidable holes-in-the-wall. Much of the rest of Mexico City's eating out was done near the omnipresent little taco stoves which dotted the streets. They were tin boxes with grill tops, fed by a few bits of carbon and carefully fanned by squatting, ragged women, often surrounded by children whose schools and bedrooms were these bits of sidewalk. The ladies and their children have now retired or been eased off the main streets by civic improvement, leaving the streets less tangy. The ladies rarely work the streets of the old city, and with their passing has passed a juicy piece of street mythology: when a person disappeared—a not uncommon occurrence among a restless people—it was often whispered that he wound up as taco stuffing, cheaper than beef or pork or chicken.

The burgeoning of good "international" restaurants has been attributed to the arrival of European refugees—loyalist Spaniards and big-city Jews—who were freely permitted entry by President Cárdenas in the late thirties. With their assorted knowledge and enterprise, they spurred the competition, and now the Niza-Londres area (the little New York–Milan of Mexico City) is crowded with restaurants of luminous décor and prayerful service at near U.S. prices.

Rivoli Hamburgo 123. Carefully wrought, soothing, and tactful, with very good European food. Expensive.

Focolare Hamburgo 87. This is a little outsize for real elegance, usually better contained, like chamber music, in a smaller vessel. One feeds well, though, at any one of the sea of tables. Expensive.

Delmonico's Londres 87. Histrionic, playful, overdecorated, and good. They do their florid best with excellent steaks, ladders of spareribs in a vigorous sauce, and practically anything on flaming swords whipped by Vesuvius-sized flames. Expensive. (A less vivid branch functions in the Gran Hotel.)

Quid Puebla 154. A little off the tourist belt, and very good, with fine grilled meats, excellent desserts (especially the mousse), and good music for dancing or listening to. Expensive.

Belinghausen Londres 95. Satisfactory in all categories, but particularly for its fish and the pleasant sounds of male voices and the clinking of glasses that seep into the street at lunchtime. High moderate.

Passy Ambéres 10. A serious place with a pleasant patio, dedicated to grilled meats; highly thought of by prosperous Mexican trenchermen. Expensive.

Several peaks of the current Olympus of dining are:

La Hacienda de los Morales A vast seventeenth-century keep at Vazquez de Mella 525 (reservations: 5-40-32-25). Past shops of choice objects, redone in Colonial style, and through a lordly courtyard, one comes to a ramble of exceedingly handsome rooms decorated with paintings, figures, carved woods, and grillwork to surround the equally handsome tables and chairs. Your drink, in an outdoor or indoor bar, will be served with a set of savory bits: a small taco, a little *tostada* pizza, a meatball. Then, in a dining room whose windows are adorned with lovely plaster-shell designs in the old manner, you might have the seafood cocktail or go right to the red snapper *en papillote,* or for that matter, anything on the menu. Save some appetite for the very good cakes or the strawberry mousse. The cuisine is French, Italian, Mexican, the service exquisite; for cuisine, service, and fine décor, prepare to pay.

Another peak is the **Restaurant del Lago,** in Chapultepec Park. (Even if you are a demon driver, go by cab; the roads at this upper end of the park are complex and the signs invisible at the dinner hour.) The place is a fantasy of luxurious, carpeted maze wandering through jungle extravagances of greenery. Somewhere in the maze, overhangs of vast triangles in several materials and textures, a pit for dancing, and—if you have a good table—a soaring wall of glass that reveals a multi-jetted fountain that purls, then jumps as plumes and as geysers. Somewhere near the center of this agglomeration of elements there is a tall, slender pyramidal thing that seems to act as a beautiful nail to hold them all together.

The service is attentive and the dishes "international" with a sprinkling of Mexican dishes treated with unusual care. Have the seviche, for instance, a common enough dish but with a difference here. The chicken in almond sauce is a remarkable dish and the duck à l'orange very French. Dining and dancing in this Mexican version of Angkor Wat will be expensive and worth it.

Les Moustaches Rio Sena 88. In a charming turn-of-the-century house adorned with stained-glass peacocks and French provincial prints, high cuisine of several countries is treated with great care. The vichyssoise is subtle and creamy, Mexican *huachinango* is served in a delicate anise sauce, the brochette of steak is zesty but done with restraint, the Spanish Casuela de Mariscos and the Sole Véronique are extraordinary versions of these classic dishes. The desserts—zabaglione, baked alaska, Grand Marnier soufflé—are of equally high quality.

For courtly service, attractive ambience, and the distinguished dishes, the cost will be high for Mexico but less than you might pay for a mediocre dinner at home.

NOTE: In this "Continental" category belong, too, the highly favored dining rooms of the luxury and first-class hotels. Expensive.

FRENCH RESTAURANTS

Although some of the above lean inevitably to the French, those below are more distinctly so, less showy, and, in most cases, less expensive.

El Bistro   (Still sometimes referred to as Chez Hélène) Lerma 9, near the Monument to Motherhood (disrespectful or amusing in shape, depending on how you feel about motherhood). The restaurant is dignified and spacious, with a quality of understatement that is mainly due to inadequate lighting. Try the omelets or the filet, and the desserts, light and fine-spun.

Chateau Boheme   Londres 142. A small, discreetly and charmingly designed restaurant that serves carefully authentic cuisine and choice grilled meats.

Napoleon   Huichapan 25, at Plaza Popocatépetl. Though its address is difficult to pronounce, and it is a bit out of the center, it is worth the hazards of blundering through speech and streets. Moderate to expensive.

Perigord   Yucatán 33. Uneven, but you can depend on the wide, generous spread of carefully prepared hors d'oeuvres which remain immutably good. Moderate to expensive.

La Madelon   Rio de la Plata. Consistently, reliably French. Moderate.

ITALIAN

La Pergola   Londres 115. A steady old-timer for the classics—pasta, veal, etc. The finest classic, the Italian salad, should not be ventured, here or anywhere.

Alfredo's   Londres 104, in the lovely shopping arcade. By a judicious use of color and arrangements of space, with a few engaging touches, the illusion is achieved of a small classic restaurant in Rome. As you might expect, the veal dishes are all done skillfully, but try—for its novelty and zip—the Sicilian steak, which has been marinated, had pepper and oregano passionately beaten into it, and then broiled. Moderate to expensive.

This *pasaje* has become a culinary annex of Rome. Dressed in various degrees of Imperial splendor you will find several treatments of Italian food.

La Gondola   At Génova 21. Serves generously and fairly late. Moderate.

Sorrento   Balderas 36. An old favorite, unremittingly trustworthy. Moderate, as is reliable **Cardini's** at Madrid 21.

SPANISH

Lar   Lerma 86, near Rhin. The clientele makes the doors bulge on Sunday afternoons and fills the air with the lisps and light gargles of *puro castellano.* Have the hare in wine, or the Argentine steak and/or crab soup. Because it is popular, and crowded, go before two for your lunch, before eight or after ten-thirty for dinner. As in most Spanish restaurants, eleven is a perfectly respectable hour for dinner. Some Mexican dishes. Moderate.

Centro Vasco   Aristoteles 239 (Polanco). The *comida* (the large mid-afternoon meal) is the *pièce* here. For very little you can ingest a stultifying amount of food until it becomes a pressing question—at an altitude of 7,340 feet—whether to breathe or go on eating. Although the food is decent Spanish home cooking, it is hardly superb (has anyone ever heard of really superb Spanish food?), but to the person who has just recovered from two days of pills, tea, and toast, it is a joy. Modest.

Centro Asturiano   Orizaba 24, near Hotel Luma. This follows the pattern of the Centro Vasco. Don't go unless you're prepared for a huge *comida* (somewhere between 1:30 and 3 P.M.) and a siesta afterward. Modest.

El Horreo   Dr. Mora 11, off west end of Alameda. Inconspicuously placed, almost secretive, and not an eating experience of importance. You should enjoy, though, the unreconstructed Spanishness: the restraint, the bullfight posters, and the dark-clad customers who manage to preserve their deep Spanish pallor in spite of the insistent Mexican sun. Modest to moderate.

Manolo's   López 1. Well spoken of by many Mexicans. Moderate.

NOTE: A number of additional Spanish restaurants appear under *Entertainments* because their emphases lie in that direction.

ARGENTINE-STYLE GRILLED MEATS

La Mansión   Insurgentes Sur 778 (and two other locations). Meats and chicken broiled on a large outdoor grill, and accompanied by a fine herb sauce, fresh salad, rolls, and beer, constitute the menu. The interior has a pleasant, arched whitewashed roominess, but the choice place is the outdoor patio. (Apt to be crowded; go early.) The location is attractive, the meats—in slabs or *en brochette*—quite good, but the strongest point is the heating grill put on your table, so that you may eat in a leisurely fashion without worrying about the lake of cold grease shaping up in your plate. Moderate.

NOTE: Insurgentes Sur is an endless stretch of refulgent grilled-meat places blossoming like May buds. Some have outdoor terraces. Try whichever you fancy on the way to or from the outskirts of town and give yourself plenty of time.

SEAFOOD

Lincoln Grill   Hotel Lincoln on Revillagigedo, a short distance off Juárez. Like its nice, stuffed leather seats, generous and sound. It doesn't have to show off, it knows its quality. The tablecloths always gleam, the waiters are quietly efficient, the rolls fresh, and the seafood famous. If it is available, order the Moro crab, which is treated like royalty, and justly. Moderate to expensive.

La Truca Vagabonda   Londres 104. A sort of sidewalk café hung with fishy sea things. Order crab bisque, crayfish, or the assorted cold seafood platter that looks like an old Neapolitan still life of nature's edible bounty. Expensive.

Prendes   16 de Septiembre 10, near San Juan de Letrán. Venerably reliable, with dignified elderly waiters who know their place—a paternally tactful notch above yours. The décor is strictly utilitarian, except for the gleaming refrigerator oases in the back (near the phone, whose use is free to customers). That, in contrast to the black-and-white of tablecloths and conservatively dark-clad customers, is dazzlingly bright with the yellow and red-gold of snappers, the pink of shrimps, and the creamy, veined shine of lambs' testes.

Pick any fish or seafood on the menu. There are meats here, of course, but why waste the opportunity to taste *pulpos* (cuttlefish) in their own vigorously flavored ink? Moderate to expensive.

El Danubio   Uruguay 3, just east of San Juan de Letrán. Even if your appetite is languid, this is a good, busy place in which to watch serious, middle-class eaters do full honor to their two or three hours of *comida* time. Slowly, steadily, they absorb a couple of tequilas with a plateful of solid hors d'oeuvres, a large bowlful of crab soup, a mound of crayfish, a red snapper, Veracruz style, and finish with a flourish of sundae stuck with tall flutelike biscuits, and as bright as the Mexican flag.

As in many seafood houses in Mexico (and elsewhere) numerous paper napkins are used and dropped on the floor. Consequently, El Danubio rarely looks calm or neat, but it is clean enough by most ordinary standards. Being crowded, it is inclined to be noisy, and made noisier by the large marimba which, since time long forgotten, has claimed the sidewalk and the helpless air.

Enjoy it all (without the napkined floor, the marimba tunes, the big eating, the soaring conversations, El Danubio wouldn't be its cherished self) and ask for *langostinos a la parrilla con mojo de ajo* if you want broiled crayfish, heaped and garlicked; *sopa de jaiba* for the crab soup; *huachinango a la Veracruzana* for red snapper in a zesty sauce of onions, olives, tomatoes, and spices; the paella, or *pescado en salsa verde,* which is fish in a piquant (in the Mexican sense, which means strong) green sauce, an old specialty of the house. Modest to moderate.

Boca del Río   Ribera San Cosme (which has been the streets of Guatemala, Tacuba, Hidalgo, and Puente de Alvarado, and will become others as it winds its erratic way), across the street from the Cine Roxy. The menu consists entirely of oyster, shrimp cocktails—small or large—cocktail of cuttlefish *(pulpo);* seviche of fish, crab, or oysters. (Seviche or *cebiche,* and variations thereof, probably corruptions of the more correct *escabeche,* is a marinade of seafood soaked in vinegar, onion, chiles, and spices—strong, but not brutal, and one of the very best items of Mexican cuisine.) Crowded night and day (it has been open twenty-four hours a day, but better not count on too odd an hour), the Boca del Río has the usual carpeting of napkins and cigarette stubs, but every three hours or so the place is emptied and swept. The shrimps are brought in fresh in daily carloads, and the sauces made in a clean, modern kitchen.

The streets, shops, people, vendors in this area are very unlike those you will find on the tourist beat. After a lunch of a tumblerful of shrimp cocktail, seviche of crab meat, and strawberries with cream (if it's the season and you dare) for little money, walk into some side streets, and if you're in the mood, visit the grave of Juárez, in the small dignified cemetery on the Plaza Guerrero, opening out of Hidalgo. Modest.

Nuevo Acapulco   López 9. Neither modern nor much accustomed to *Yanquis,* the old place goes on being hospitable and serves fine seafood. Expensive to moderate.

PURELY MEXICAN

Círculo Sureste   Lucerna 12, near Bucareli. As plain and neat as an old Childs, and there the resemblance ends. The restaurant is Yucatecan and serves some rare dishes; not formidable, just unfamiliar. They make little tacos stuffed with the best suckling pig *(cochinito)* outside of Spain; tortillas built around and incorporating *frijoles;* chicken in a Yucatecan marinade with onion *(pollo en escabeche);* dishes in Pilpil (or Pibil) style, which means that they have been cooked with garlic, butter, and the shells of chile—a bit sharp but not seriously. If all this is too challenging, order the shrimps in any style. They are large and beautifully flavored, and along with the Yucatecan Carta Clara beer—light, fruity, and not easy to find outside of Yucatán—make a happy lunch.

You might enjoy sitting toward the back of the lower level, near the counter where the tortillas might still be made by hand, to enjoy the rhythmic light slapping and patting, a sound which used to be a leitmotif of the country. And, for an introduction to Yucatán, stare at the white embroidered skirts and long, square-necked *ipiles* of the waitresses, the dress of the village Mayans. Modest to moderate.

Mesón del Caballo Bayo   Av. del Conscripto, via Avila Camacho. Open until 8, including Sundays, this is a good place to go on your way to or from the race track nearby. It is an old, rambling Colonial house with ivied walls and a large, shaded garden, obdurately rural, middle-class Mexican. The interior is an odd Swiss-Mexican combination of dark wood paneling and fancy *charro* (cowboy) saddles. *Comida* will start with country-style hors d'oeuvres: pork cracklings (the stuff sold all over in yellow-gold sheets), bits of lung fried with onion, pieces of pork with tortillas to wrap them in. To follow, there are the soups, rice, fish, meats—well and simply done. Don't expect much of the desserts; the atmosphere and particular style are what count. Moderate.

Hostería de Santo Domingo   Belisario Domínguez 72. Supposedly the oldest restaurant in Mexico City, but who knows? With the exception of a mural of the Zócalo done in the eighteenth-century Italian manner (the colors inconquerably Mexican) and a modest stretch of tile, the Hostería has the enormous appeal of no décor at all. The waiters, who rarely serve tourists, are delighted to demonstrate the pleasures of Mexican eating, and they will bring you a taste of this and a view of that. Try the *quesadillas* (tortillas made with cheese), or squash blossoms, or sausage and follow that with *carne asada,* usually surrounded by *frijoles,* tortillas cut up with raw onion, and *rajas* (strips of pepper, onions, chile). The desserts are usually cooked fruits and a variety of caramel custards (flan), the most ubiquitous of Spanish desserts. Moderate.

Fonda Santa Anita There are several branches, all big and showy, overdressed in the manner called "typical," but clean and friendly, aware and solicitous of North American eccentricities. Moderate.

Two antique favorites still sit on the crowded streets of the old city, not far from the great markets. You may not want to wander these streets at night without a Mexican friend, and taxis are not easy to find; better go during the day. They are close to each other and you may size each up before you decide:

El Taquito Carmen 69 A.

Las Cazuelas Columbia 69. Both moderate and frequently visited by *mariachis*. Authentically Mexican regional foods in authentically atmospheric streets.

Fonda el Refugio Liverpool 166. The prices are higher than strictly Mexican food merits, but the place is attractive and popular, and quite good, especially the *mole verde.* Moderate to expensive.

Los Comales Revillagigedo 28. A largish place with many small tables and a Veracruzan harpist from whom you could buy a song for three pesos. (He was a man of much imagination and little repertoire, usually variations of Schubert's "Ave Maria" in a long scale of moods, from hymnal to waltz.) A good place to go on a Saturday afternoon, to see the care and feeding of lower-middle-class and working-class Mexican children brought for a rare outing and a cheap, open-handed meal. Exotic note: Iced tea takes a long time to prepare—it is a strange, troublesome order—and is served, with straws, in a beer stein. Modest.

If you'd like to eat Mexican nontourist, middle-class style, try one of the restaurants on Serapio Rendon. Take a look, also, at the church of San Cosme and Damian, possessed of a soaring gilded altar manned by more than a dozen full-sized, full-colored saints. And, for contrast in neighborhoods, cross San Cosme into Santa María (page 39).

El Moro   East side of San Juan de Letrán (42, near Uruguay), if it hasn't been wiped out by a new highway. This one is for the boldest of adventurers, equipped with casual standards of orderliness, some Spanish, and Mexican friends. The time to go is at about 11 P.M. for *churros* (the thin, long Spanish cruller) and chocolate in varying degrees of intensity—"French" for thin, "Mexican" for medium, "Spanish" for thick and spiced. Not the roughest of places, but a good place not to look and act like the *Yanqui* Imperialist, and absolutely not for women alone, no matter what their number. The *churros* and the chocolate are delicious, and despite these warnings, and since it is a Mexican place, you may find enchanting, helpful people who will get you seats (even their own) and see that your order is quickly filled. Modest.

Truncated *comidas* called Lunch Comercial (15 to 25 pesos) are available and quite good in coffeehouses on López, Serapio Rendon, Bucareli; almost anywhere as a matter of fact, including Sanborn branches.

NOTE: For the more daring, there are numerous vigorous Mexican restaurants on San Juan de Letrán, on Gabriel Leyva, on Bolívar, on the main avenues of working-class *barrios* (districts), on the edges of tourist strongholds; there are a million *puestos* and *loncherias* on the streets and in the markets, selling chunks of pork and kid, or tacos, or magnificent *tortas* (*bolillos* running over with meat, tomatoes, onions, lettuce, and chile). Like the food on the stands near the bullfight arena, they all smell wonderful, but before you're carried away, try to remember that, often, the better the smell, the greater the danger. One of the first culinary lessons the world learned was that onions, garlic, chile, and mixed spices are effective disguises for doubtful meat.

SANBORN'S

For many years **Sanborn's,** on Madero, was home and mother to American travelers; it was "safe," it was "clean," it had an approximate understanding of the U.S. appetite and language, and its Anglo-

Saxon name cast a pink glow of comfort. With names like Woolworth's, Sears, Hilton now conspicuously part of Mexico's vocabulary, the complexities of the club sandwich conquered, and the presence of *animales* in dirt and stale food—even though one can't see them—acknowledged, Sanborn's is no longer exclusively home base, but still a stimulating place.

Is it still "safer" than other places? Not necessarily. The old-fashioned strawberry shortcake is a Taj Mahal of desserts, but whipped cream is as vulnerable here as anywhere else. Do all waitresses speak English? No. Or hardly. Or some. A waitress may be afraid of being drenched and left helpless by a deluge of English. Ergo, she will avoid the foreigner and rush for the order of a Mexican. These are minor hazards, and except for sleep and the more stratospheric ranks of culture (guidebooks, magazines, pocket dictionaries, and a mural by Orozco surrounding the ladies' room which supply *some* mind food), a fairly satisfactory tourist life can be lived in the downtown (Madero) Sanborn's.

The old courtyard was glassed over some time ago and the walls painted in late Victorian colors and images, but the size, pillars, and balcony are luxuriously viceregal. On a sunny day the glass ceiling translates the hot Mexican sun into a dark-gold dusk; on a rainy day, the light is a moody gray-blue. One can sit and watch the changes of clientele which make Sanborn's different places at different times of the day: the purposeful businessmen who meet for a *cafecito* and intense discussion between eleven in the morning and twelve-thirty; the Mexican matrons who stop for a shopping break at one; Americans who take over for lunch from one-thirty to three. Late in the afternoons, the amateur *políticos* and Mexican ladies return, giving way to American diners, and later, young Mexicans, who absorb mountains of cake and ice cream. On Sundays at noon, starched, white-gloved little girls are brought from local church services for a dish of decorated ice cream, as foamy as their dresses.

The more active tourist gulps quick snacks at the soda fountain, follows these with pills from the drugstore, taken with water from the fountain at the back of the restaurant, then to the drugstore for cosmetics or gloves or pocketbooks, munching on chocolates picked up opposite the cigarette counter. On to the magazine rack and the wheels of picture postcards and into the restaurant to write the cards beside a cup of coffee, then back to the stamp desk and the mail drop and, exhausted, back to the hotel for a siesta.

Mexicans like the Sanborn branches as well, especially the huge circular restaurant at Reforma and Fragua where they gather at about three o'clock in the afternoon for a lavish *comida.* An additional attraction are two Tamayo murals, a darkly glowing lunar painting above the perfume counter, and, in the dining room, his watermelons surrounded by a bounty of round pink-purple fruits.

MISCELLANEOUS

Pabellón Suizo   Plaza Miravalle 17. Off one of the many handsome, green plazas which adorn the city, terrible for drivers, a great pleasure to walkers. The restaurant has a number of Swiss characteristics: it is clean and sober, decorated in the expected combination of heavy, dark wood and cute cuckoo clocks. The dishes are French and German staples, wiener schnitzel under egg from one border and béarnaise sauce on steak from the other. The cakes are noble structures of sweet, rich things to which the waiter will add a glacier of whipped cream—a custom of the house and of the well-packed customers. Moderate.

Also German-Swiss is the consistently good **Chalet Suiza** at Niza 37.

Konditorei   Génova 61, opposite the Monte Cassino Hotel. Small and very crowded at lunch. The prime attractions are the open Danish sandwiches arranged around a small good salad (try the one lightly touched with curry). For the valiant or skinny there is a gorgeous child's dream of a pastry cart. Moderate.

Mexico houses a few "kosher-style" restaurants, which means that they are not kosher at all, but rather echoes and shadows of the substance of New York City's "deli-restaurants."

Carmel   Génova 70 (the "Lindy's of Mexico"). The pioneer blintzes and pastrami stronghold. Its highest point of interest was its proprietor, who brought his wit and sparse beard to the restaurant late at night, the time of intellectuals. He had a passion for writers and thinkers (the restaurant carried a respectable rack of paper books for sale) and had himself been writing a book—or a set of poems, or essays—always imminently to be published. In his absence, you might look for entertainment at an outside table, staring at other tourists who saunter through the attractive shopping plaza on which the restaurant opens, or study the Englished menu: cheese blintses, hembuerger, shrewded beef, sausagues, which may unfortunately have been corrected. Moderate.

Kinaret ("Vienna-Wilno meats from Chicago") at Hamburgo and Génova. It makes odd bedfellows of *carne asada* and pastrami, enchiladas and blintzes. If you are a connoisseur, you'll find the rye bread and the spiced meats not exactly what they are on Sunday nights in the Bronx; it has, however, pierced the mystery of the garlic pickle. The reputation for good sandwiches is such that your tablemates might be touring Nigerians or Japanese, living versions of the famous Levy's bread advertisement. Moderate.

Another in this category is the **Tel Aviv,** on the Reforma, at 105, whose menu ranges from Israeli falafel and hummus to Russian borscht and delicatessen sandwiches (more or less American) to Mexican staples. The prices are a bit higher than they might be, but you should pay something for an outdoor table in the deafening traffic, for the opportunity of listening to customers greet each other as *licenciado* (an honorific like the Italian *commendatore*), and for an interesting form of acculturation: the menu adorned with a menorah, the entrance edged with Mexican lava hardened to rocks and hairy, prickly cactus.

Incidentally, there was a truly kosher restaurant, **Shalom,** at Acapulco 70, and it may still exist. The more relaxed Jewishness of **Bondy,** Madero 408, may be more suitable to your taste.

Skandia On Homero in Polanco. And one thoroughly nonkosher restaurant (grilled ham with melted cheese) that yet features pastrami and tongue, lox and cream cheese in reasonably authentic style, except for the extraordinary pliability of the usually stubborn bagel. Hung with ropes of garlic and peppers, and serving good cappuccino, it also suggests an Italian trattoria—and an odd cafeteria since you must give your order at a desk and wait for it to be delivered to your table, when you find a table. Crowded, eccentric, and moderate.

El Paseo Reforma near the University Club. A delectable bourguignonne of beef filet and several other good dishes accompany the piano-playing and songs. High moderate.

For vegetarians: **Yug**, Varsovia 3; **Las Fuentes**, rio Tiber 38 B; another on Filomeno Mata, near Victor's (page 77).

Mauna Loa San Jeronimo 240. Shields, things of tapa cloth, lamp shades of turtle shells, various South Seas *objets* hang from the rafters and the walls, bathed in the dulcet *tristesse* of Hawaiian music. The stately menu lists a group of Oriental-like dishes—Chinese, Indian, and Island adaptations of these—served by handsome convoys of waiters. Expensive and a fair way out. Phone: 5-48-68-84.

Why anyone would want to eat American food in a foreign country eludes understanding, but it is an odd fact of travel life which explains the appearance in Rome, Paris, and Mexico City of cozy little nests of beef, pasty buns, and hot-and-cold running ketchup. If you must:

In addition to the various **Sanborn's**, who will give you ham and eggs or hamburger, several **Denny's** and **Vips**, dazzlingly decorated, will make you reasonable facsimiles of American favorites. You can find, too, a mushrooming of pizza places and a chain called **Shirley** that is thoroughly satisfactory for non-Lucullan dishes. The "cafeterias" (meaning "coffeehouses") of the big hotels offer good service and chic surroundings; not necessarily expensive. Very good broiled chicken revolves on numerous spits in the Gutenberg-Melchor Ocampo area, and the tacos in small places on Londres and Hamburgo are highly thought of.

For an afternoon or late snack most of the above will do. The **Café Suizo,** which has good cakes, is on Revillagigedo, immediately off Juárez; the **Flaminia** is a graceful, lyrical little *salón de té* on Reforma. The **Konditorei** serves afternoon coffee and cakes. The prima donna of the group is the **Duca d'Este,** Hamburgo 164 B, which proves its right to an Italian name by the quality of its cappuccino, the Italianate décor, the zuppa Inglese (sopa inglesa), all foam and meringue carried off in great quantities by elegant shoppers, and the almond cake threaded with chocolate that is a flake of Paradise. Also, keep in mind that the Reforma Hotel coffee shop once packed and may be packing inspired corned beef sandwiches.

Mexico City has the climate and temperament for outdoor dining. Unfortunately the downtown streets are too crowded and narrow for much expansive life, although strips of tables and chairs appear here and there: for instance, right off Juárez near the Museo de Artes Populares, and more numerously in the vicinity of the Hotel Reforma.

Roof of Hotel Majestic You are encouraged to have the Sunday lunch (1 to 4 P.M.) complete with souvenirs, *mariachis,* and all you can consume. But any day will do for this pleasant oasis and its view of the great old square, which was a heart of Mexican history long before it was recorded. Moderate.

Chalupas Reforma (through Chapultepec Park) at Monte Urales 537 (tell the taxi driver that it is near "Petroleos"). Lively and popular, especially for its Mexican dishes, the *quesadillas* and tacos, and for the resplendent ice-cream structures. The menu extends to much more than that, of course, but the important things are the shaded tables on a green lawn, the magnificent trees on the avenues, and the good-looking Mexican teenagers who drop in for club sandwiches or "hamburguesas." Moderate.

San Angelo's or **San Angel Inn** In the old suburb of that name. The dash of waiters, the clatter of dishes, the awesome Mexican Sunday *comidas* have been replaced by hushed elegance, courtly service, and a large menu of European-Mexican cuisine, a few items, like the seafood *en papillote* thoroughly *haute.* The cakes, a bit more ornate than the decor, are sinfully delicious. It is best on Sundays, even if you have to wait for a table in the lovely gardens, and good on Saturdays when the nearby Bazar Sábado brings a colorful international crowd to San Angel. Pleasant on slow, quiet weekdays, too, when the ancient stone buildings present themselves, regally undisturbed, to your eye. High.

Of several Chinese restaurants, the **Luaú,** at Niza 38, meets most nearly, as varied dinners for reasonable sums, the American conception of "Chinese" food.

THE EXPATRIATE; OR, THE WAY OF UPMANSHIP

Somewhere, via a telephone number or a letter of introduction or by accident, you will meet North Americans living in Mexico.

They will vary in texture, quality, riches, and cause of residency so far from home. Some are remittance men and women sent generous allowance checks by families in the States to stay away and do their drinking and drugging in Mexico. A younger group (with fewer members than a decade or two ago) leads the cheap, beat life of beards, rum, marijuana, and contemptuous dissociation from the rigid, conventional Stateside life with its jobs, taxes, television, and ties, supported by money orders from worried mothers. Here and there are inconspicuous groups who mind their work and their own business.

In small, mutual-protection clusters, one finds the colorful little spots of the frustrated artistic: the writer *manqué* who somehow could not write in the sterile, anti-intellectual canned culture of the States. He can't write in Mexico either because its color and impact have so overwhelmed him that he must give himself time—endless time—to absorb it. The painter who could not paint at home because art is in decay, the artist held worthless, life too materialistic, now can't paint in Mexico because of a paralyzing embarrassment of compositional riches which has him trapped in a long-lasting coma. The blank canvas grows gray with dust, the unused brushes in the jar scrape the indolent air.

Mexico shelters, also, a variety of U.S.-haters who feel that their native land didn't love them enough, and like sullen children, they hate back. They were unsuccessful socially or loathed their jobs or their wives or parents and blamed it on our distorted, exsanguinating society. They think they want the "simple life" of the Mexican peasant, whose life, actually, is a difficult, worrisome thing, an enmeshment of poverty, ignorance, and superstition which he would happily escape if he could. Mexico will not love these expatriates enough ultimately and in time they will try the promise of some other primitive paradise.

A good number, though, stay to live and drink cheaply and dully. Not gifted, devoid of the saving illusion of talent, not curious, and often too old, they neither understand nor try to understand the lives and the language around them. They spin out their lives in neat little cocoon-like colonies, speaking and living only with their mirror images, building a philosophy and a purpose on the high ideal of maids, gardeners, rum, and sunshine on $400 a month.

And, of course, around and beside these is a group of people who would love Mexico even if life were more expensive, whose temperaments and bodies are more comfortably nested there, who work and live without anger, defense, or exhibitionism.

In any of these groups, there is a subgroup which will make you miserable if you let them; these are the players of upmanship. Their Spanish is better than yours; they talk to waiters flowingly while you point to an item on the menu with a mute, hopeful, embarrassed look on your vulnerable face. They tell endless stories about contretemps with Mexican maids and traffic cops and how they outsmarted them. Debonair accounts of easy, inside-know bribery trip off their sophisticated tongues (they always speak of bribing, even in English, as the *mordida*). They will explain "the Mexican" to you (a favorite indoor sport among Mexican as well as American intellectuals) at great, psychologically complex length. They will be appalled at how much you pay for your hotel room, which you thought was quite a bargain—*they* know palaces which serve Escoffier food, charge $3 a day, with free beer and Spanish lessons thrown in. No matter what you've bought they know a little shop where it's infinitely cheaper and, besides, more indigenous, more authentic, more folkloric, and more made by hand. If you say you ate Mexican food, they'll tell you it wasn't—no *pozole*, no *atole*, no *panucho*, no *pibil* sauce, and other incomprehensible, ego-deflating terms; it was a bad imitation, drained of meaning and flavor and, as usual, you paid too much. At some point, with an indulgent smile and deadly intent, he says the dread word to you, he calls you a "tourist." You would, of course, rather be called a yokel or a pariah or a leper; nothing evokes an image of loutish gullibility more vividly than "tourist," and you wish you were home or dead.

Before your psyche collapses entirely, consider: Why must he make you feel bad? Why won't he let you enjoy your trusting innocence, the pleasure of being overcharged, the delusion of having "the authentic Mexican" experience. Because he is afraid of you. You are more successful and richer; you can afford to live in the United States and visit and waste your money in Mexico. Furthermore, he is also afraid of Mexicans. Listen to his charmed and charming stories about Mexicans—how childish, how irresponsible, how gay; such naïve little people. He is making them less strange and fearsome to himself by diminishing them, like the German hunter of crocodiles in the old story. (The German's technique was to go equipped with opera glasses, a pair of tweezers, and an empty matchbox. As he approached the river, he turned the glasses so that the crocodile he saw through them was extremely small, small enough to be picked up by the tweezers and put into the matchbox, which could comfortably be carried in a vest pocket.) That is what the expatriate does to the Mexican and to you out of apprehension. Remember the German and the crocodile the next time you are looked at pityingly or spoken to as the profligate fool of a corrupt society.

CRAFTS, QUASI-CRAFTS, BAUBLES, AND BURDENS

The happy old days of bargaining, of shopping as social occasion, of making a new friend or a temporary enemy, are passing in Mexico City, particularly in the golden streets to which most tourists cling. Greetings and thanks are sometimes courtlier than almost anywhere else, but big-city nerves and speed have set in. It can still be a pleasing experience, though, especially in the shops of the die-hard knights and connoisseurs who shut their doors against the rough winds of efficient commerce.

BASKETS

Anywhere your eye falls in a shop or market. Try the San Juan market, an enormous gathering of trinkets and baskets. Bargain and try the clasps before you buy.

CRAFTS

Authentic objects, like regional dress, have been slowly creeping farther and farther into the hinterland, hanging on stubbornly in some areas—Oaxaca, for instance—and more tenuously elsewhere. Craft villages have become company towns; the former makers of pots, baskets, and delightful, crude toys now prefer to earn in some other way the money for plastic bowls and plastic dolls. Or, country people have been taught by entrepreneurs to touch their simple objects with stylish flair, resulting in a bastard form which sometimes has great charm—a Miró painting as an Oaxacan *serape* is not bad but hardly authentic. The shops below will give you some idea of where to find the pure and the impure. And, keep in mind that a number of shops are closed on Mondays and on all days from, roughly, 1 to

3 P.M. And to repeat: a number of central shops were badly shaken by the 1986 earthquake. Consult with your hotel concierge about their condition.

Victor's Madero 10-305, second floor. Only a block or so from the Madero Sanborn's, Victor's has a fine collection of Mexican crafts. Here, too, you can find the paper cutouts used for witchcraft or fertility, the beribboned embroidered blouse worn by Mazatecas in the mushroom villages of the Oaxaca mountains, the straw hats blazing with ribbons worn by the young bucks of Chiapas. You will find large old, bold earrings like gypsy queens', authentic *quexquemetls* (the triangular overblouses hideously ubiquitous in cheap copies elsewhere), a few old toys. Once in a while Victor has an extraordinary Colonial painting, or a good copy of one; once in a while, an archaeological object. Nothing has been adapted or twisted out of its original shape and it might be a good idea to look around here to see what Mexican crafts were—rivers of skill and imagination running from practically every village—before the rivers began to dry or were diverted into more sophisticated channels.

Museo de Artes Populares Juárez 44. An old church, now a national treasure, has been converted by the government to a center which fosters, displays, and sells native crafts and current adaptations of those crafts. In the front, formal room you will find meticulously chosen silver crafted by the best silversmiths, a small, select group of handwoven textiles, and a few rare old-style oddities, like men's sashes hung with numerous small pockets (a good gift, by the way, for an adolescent girl with the courage to be different from her tribe).

The informal back room, open to the public, is the stockroom of cheaper, less polite items: shelves of brilliantly colored stupid chickens; rearing horses striped in carrousel colors; the crudely made, crudely decorated, and appealing pottery of Tzintzuntzan; a few well-made baskets; stiff-legged animal whistles; and on and on, endlessly.

In recent years, the government has, under the umbrella title of Fondo Nacional Para el Fomento de las Artesanias, taken on the job of fostering and subsidizing craftsmen and has leased shops on Avenida Juárez, not far from the older Artes Populares, that cover a wide crafts range of many areas.

At Juárez 18 is **Artesanias del Estado** (State) **de Mexico,** whose strengths are heavy sweaters, bright embroideries, and good pottery. At Juárez 70 are the almost overwhelming riches of Oaxaca in space arranged as enormous high vaults folding on each other, like the movement of slow waters. The several vaulted levels provide endless space for displaying a world of embroideries, weavings, dresses, pottery, enamels, basketry, ceramic figurines, *serapes,* jewelry, fat Oaxacan sirens, *rebozos,* belts, and straw *animalitos.* The prices are not market prices, but you will not find in markets many of the extraordinary beauties in this kaleidoscope of crafts.

Juárez 89, a stately old building, is used by the Fondo Nacional for a general compendium of sophisticated versions of Mexican crafts from several areas: the woodwork of Michoacan, huge devils wired for explosion during Easter Week from Guanajuato, painted gourds from around Uruapan, and ornate embroideries that are the work of Huichol Indians. Above the serene order of the miscellany, paintings of hands spinning, boring a minute hole in a piece of jewelry, painting a tiny deer, molding a bird—a pleasing homage to craftsmen everywhere.

Diagonally across the avenue, the Secretaria de Gobernación building usually gives rooms to an enormous general collection, reachable via Calle Iturbide. The ceiling is hung with magic cutout papers and the walls with Huichol weavings in shapes resembling voodoo symbols. There are Chiapas hats, strange animals, enameled boxes from Michoacan, but the emphasis seems to be on textiles: as bags, *serapes,* hangings, table linens, blouses, *huipiles* heavily and sparsely embroidered; a group of fine drawn work blouses and a dress embroidered with feathers. Again, these may not appear to be extraordinary bargains but they are, considering the cost and rarity of handwork elsewhere in the Western world.

If you're in the area, stop in at **Artesanias y Regalos Carmen,** 25 Revillagigedo.

PIÑATAS

These papier-mâché animals—frilled, curled, beribboned, and often remarkably expressive—are built around a clay vase which is filled with small gifts and candies, then suspended to be whacked at and broken by blindfolded children ready to scramble for the spilled treasures. Although they are usually used at Christmas in Mexico,

American tourists have been taking them home for birthday parties and showers and as decorations. The airport has a small zoo of them on hand, at prices which reflect that the seller knows that you know that this is your absolutely last chance to buy one. If you think of it in time, go to the Rodríguez market instead, where the stock is large and varied, especially at Christmas time. (See page 40.)

For good lacquer (some of what is called lacquer is crudely painted wood and hideous), stay with the shops that sell authentic crafts.

CRAFTS: TWENTIETH CENTURY

The odd wedding of Indian crafts and European styling (stimulated by an influx of Europeans in the thirties, and more recently, Americans) seems to be a fairly happy one, deplored by the purists, who find it difficult to recognize industrialization. Crafts anywhere are inevitably doomed, and without these mixtures there would be nothing or, worse still, bad copies in bad taste. These newer things have, also, the advantage of being attractive to tourists and of keeping a good number of people employed.

Tlachiualkalli   Copenhague 2, and **Artel,** at 30 on the same street, treat the old crafts well and use them skillfully in adaptations. The first has good small carpets and wall hangings, jewelry in the old style, and paper cutouts that have magical properties. Artel concentrates on rainbows of fingertip towels with deep fringe, crocheted drapes, bold metal jewelry, beguiling hand-painted boxes, pottery in delicate colors on a subtle gray glaze, and—echoing an ancient craft—angels and sirens with yellow tresses and pink cheeks, beige-bottomed Loreleis made of dough and preserved under shellac.

El Aguila Descalza   (The Barefoot Eagle) at 31F on the attractive little street of Copenhague shows sophisticated versions of Mexican crafts in boutique style. Its particular pride, an exclusive, are the distinguished—and not cheap—dresses named Josefa.

Los Castillos   The enterprising family which is usually one jump ahead of everyone else in the business (it was they who revived the ancient art of "wedding" metals) has two shops: one at Juárez 76 and the other, newer, at Amberes 41. The boldly arranged Juárez shop shows, among its showers of silver jewelry and gold rings, such novelties as modern silver crucifixes made by a group of Benedictine fathers and exquisite copies of small Byzantine panels executed by an order of nuns in Cuernavaca. Upstairs, they keep the larger objects: tables of marble embedded in fine wood, sometimes laced with inserts of metal and mosaic, of which their best example rests in the lobby of the Hilton. The crushed marble, lapis, obsidian, rose quartz dinnerware, simpler Tarascan pottery with old patterns drawn on modern shapes, serving forks, tea sets, trays in silver and in wedded metals are always interestingly designed, even if they're not for you.

The newer shop has set and spread itself in a rambling old house where you may wander freely. The street section is devoted to the Castillo classics in jewelry, chaste calm things of hammered gold holding crude stones, wonderfully assertive on a confident woman. Toward the back, one finds the applied crafts, which may consist of wooden screens parading incised, colored figures in a courtly procession, or imitations of the big-eyed, solemn-children paintings of Colonial days. Here and there, hanging on a wall or lying casually on a bench, may be a few Oaxacan figures, embroidered bags from the mountains, a clever piece of basketry.

Adapted crafts turn up at hotels, at various **Sanborn's;** in the innumerable shops on Juárez, Niza, Génova, Londres; and, in rather careless style, at the San Juan market. If you want to buy souvenirs that mean a friendly gesture rather than a cherished gift, San Juan is a good place in which to forage. Don't expect brilliance of design or execution, although some of the tinware is quite respectable, and bargain with all your strength and patience because the asking price hovers between preposterous and outrageous, and instead of competition among the stalls you may find understandable but annoying collusion.

Leaping sharply upward from the trinketry of the market, we reach the **Bazar Sábado,** open only Saturdays, from 10 A.M. to 7 P.M. It is out a bit, on the Plaza de San Jacinto, in the suburb of San Angel, near the large, busy Avenida Revolución (reachable by Insurgentes buses marked "San Miguel" or "Universidad"). It meanders tightly up, down, around, inside, and outside a Colonial house to show then-plus-now combinations, and the newly emerging styles of many artisans. It provides for craftsmen a place in which to show and sell, and for the tourist, an opportunity to see many kinds of objects under one roof in an engaging confusion of space.

The idea turned out to be as entertaining as it is worthy. There are few pleasanter places to spend a couple of hours than at the Bazar, which takes care to feed all your senses: the eye is fed by beautiful batiks, sculpture, dopey dolls, antiques, masks, paintings, children's clothing and women's, jewelry, glass (to mention only a sampling); the nose enjoys the smell of aromatic candles floating from the stall of a candlemaker; taste gets its satisfaction from the buffet lunch, attractively arranged and generous, in the courtyard; the ear by the *mariachis* who play from the sides of the fruit-decorated fountain; and for touch, there are myriad textures of things and the silky hair of one of the many children you will find at your elbow, quietly judging your purchase and you. Even if your schedule is very tight, try to go. Although it isn't the seriously indigenous folkloric thing some visitors insist on, it is a brilliant splash of taste and gaiety, recently expanded to an adjoining building that welcomes with out-door cafés and the nearby Pro-Arte shop, worth exploring. To make your shopping day complete, go to the Museo Colonial Carmen (a former church) and look through the reproductions they produce of Oaxaca jewelry, old silver pieces, records of folkloric music, color slides, and, possibly best of all, about two dozen pieces from the Museum of Anthropology, including a strange Olmec baby-jaguar-faced figure and a famous superb Mayan head.

So attractive and profitable an idea as the **Bazar Sábado** inevitably spurs on imitations. One now finds them in many parts of the city and in other cities. Coyoacán (page 132) for instance, has a vast *parian* (an ancient word for market) on its Av. Hidalgo near the crossing with Morelos. It is meant to be a total shopping center, shaping up in California-Mexican Colonial style. Surrounded by parked cars, it serves for shoe and clothing buying, house furnishings, barber ser-vice, baked goods, and beauty. A large craft section has areas deftly separated by various devices—a low adobe wall, a pierced terra-cotta screen, an enclosure of wooden beams, a large thatch umbrella.

Another enclave that promised to be a great beauty is the **Molina de Santo Domingo,** Observatorio 139 (Tacubaya), part of a rebuilt meander of fine houses. A long covered hall, cool and stately, with a handsome wooden ceiling (once a mill and stalls, it is said) has been divided into shops which have not quite decided what their areas of interest should be. Find out whether it has survived its growing pains before you venture forth. (There are so many crafts centers that some inevitably fall by the wayside.)

You may have wondered where the several million calendar-stone wallets are made, who sews the Mexican eagle on boys' blouses and plastic fringes on fake leather, who weaves the summer pocket-books—none of it the craft of Indian villagers or *avant* artisans. These are done in a survival of cottage industry ("crafts," silver, copies of Colonial furniture as well) in the *Colonia de las Fábricas,* around the **Calle de Tamagno** in Peralvillo, off Insurgentes Norte.

LEATHER

Aries At the entrance to the arcade of the Del Prado Hotel on Juárez, in the lobby of the hotel itself; next door to the gift shop in the Hilton; and part of the El Presidente Hotel.

Also on Florencia, just off Reforma, in a sort of noble's cottage—a bit French, somewhat Spanish—which enfolds shoes, ties, belts, leather accessories, some knits, some furs and clothing in suedes like silk for both sexes. There is a new branch just beyond the Petroleons statue, going into the Lomas.

Their carry-alls, glorified duffel bags, and small valises are noble objects and so are the suits and coats. The prices are hardly timid and neither are the salespeople—particularly in the Juárez shop—who seem to have been tutored in disdain by some of our Fifth Avenue experts. (The newer hotels all have shops something like these, but not quite.)

Ginatai Londres 91C. Covers the gamut from leather wine flasks to fringed jackets and floppy hats, with reasonably designed coats, wallets, etc. in between. Upstairs, the ubiquitous dolls, ceramics, glass in the local "every shop a bazaar" pattern.

Demian's Boutique Corner of Estocolmo and Hamburgo. Decorated leathers as skirts and bags, a few somewhat kitschy, most quite attractive.

Window-shop Juárez and the Zona Rosa for exclusively styled native leathers. They are indisputably high-class, with prices close to U.S. costs. For sliding much lower down the scale, try the old leather shops on Cinco de Mayo (it starts east of the Bellas Artes and goes to the Zócalo), which are large and darkly tall, smell of years of leather, and sport the magnificent saddles and other riding gear you will see on Sunday's *charros.* Or, still going downward, try Pino

Suárez in the old city, a bit east of the Zócalo, and a traditional street of leather shops, whose recent widening has diminished the leather goods. If you go, be prepared to bargain vigorously, or be taken. (The same injunction holds for the leather stalls in the markets.)

CAVEAT: A number of shops use imposing foreign names. Don't be carried away; there is often no authentic connection and the quality may be far from that which you might expect.

HUARACHES

You may stumble on them anywhere—in curio shops, in craft stores, in markets, and even in shoe emporia. Bargain, bargain, bargain. Should you be going to Cuernavaca, Taxco, Acapulco, or any other resort town, you'll find a boundless supply of well-made, well-styled sandals. For the fascinating crude ones with soles of discarded rubber tire, joints of metal, and straps of thick, indestructible leather which stinks forever, wait for the country markets you may pass, or Oaxaca or Chiapas.

GLASSWARE

One can buy Mexican glassware of several kinds in most of the craft and curio shops. For a number of reasons (the showroom, factory in its old house, the neighbors, the neighborhood), it is a good idea to go to the glass factory on Carretones (between Topacio and Roldan), at the risk of being crowded out by another set of tourists. The balcony of the ancient courtyard is ringed with pots of flowers whose colors are dimly echoed by the luster of the shelves of glass in the open storerooms below. The vases, lamps, pitchers, and dishes are mainly of customary Mexican design, but a number bear the imprint of Swedish and Italian influence. (No Mexican has yet acquired the skill to make a fine Murano handkerchief vase, but they're trying and the efforts have a wry charm.)

The actual factory is a composition of light and dark, suppressed flames, glowing knobs of molten glass, metal spears, and water wells. The boys darting in the gloom to the huge conical stove which holds the molten glass and back to the shaping plates, raising the glowing shafts high as they run, crowding against each other in the small space, look like spear carriers in Uccello's battle painting. In a dim corner, a wall shrine holding wax flowers looks down on glittering vats of broken glass.

As you leave the factory, look around. Several shops nearby sell the commonest tourist articles: cheap bags stamped in that calendar-stone design, gaudy "Mexican" skirts, "Indian" heads which look more like Sitting Bull than the noble, doomed Cuauhtémoc. (One of these shops was called "The Real McCoy," and still may be.)

On the step of one of the discouraged houses whose windows are hung with tired cloth sits an old drunk trying to read a torn page of yesterday's paper. Across the street four boys are reading one comic book. The two older boys take turns reading while the others peer over the reader's shoulders to look at the pictures. Diagonally across the corner is an *ostionería* (oyster bar) which occupies a narrow slit bulging with a large jukebox, a Coke freezer, and twelve slightly mashed customers. On another corner, a *pulquería* sends out its sour smell in waves synchronized with the swinging of its yellow door; on it a sign: "No minors, women or men in uniform admitted." Between oysters and pulque stand little cave shops, dimly lit by the thin slant of sunlight that touches the narrow street.

Through the quiet, gray half-light of the street run dizzying bands of noise and color, itinerant peddlers pursuing tourists relentlessly with plastic-fringed imitation-leather jackets, whips, bags, and very recent bits of archaeology. And the tourists, driven by the demands of time and guide, run, zigzagging frantically from shop to shop, brightening the lives of the old drunk, the literary boys, and the musing children.

SILVER

As iffy a subject as the bullfight and more fraught with responsibility for a guide; it costs more to make a mistake. Should you wait until you get to Taxco, the silver town? Is Taxco cheaper? Sometimes yes, sometimes no. Taxco is a funnel of silver and consequently offers many shops and much variety in a small, convenient area, but its best things may have just been shipped to Mexico City before you got there. If it's a question of small inexpensive things, buy what attracts you, wherever it happens to be. For larger objects of silver, do some comparison shopping in Mexico City, then check the Taxco possibilities if you're going there.

As you know, Mexico City runs rivulets of silver, too; shop after shop blinds you with its effulgent bargains. If you plan to buy a substantial item, find out something about its price at home so that you can evaluate its Mexican price (it should be considerably less), and remember that it is the weight of silver which largely determines price and the signature of the most gifted and reputable designer.

Sigfrido Pineda ("Sigi") designed and built himself a house-showcase at Hamburgo 171, an imaginative structure that blends the Colonial and the modern. His designs range from the ancient in silver through traditional—gold and ornate—to the simple sweeping lines of the modern. Despite the impressive house, one can spend as little as 300 pesos for rings with semiprecious stones and, of course, a great deal more for gold wrapped around gems. Whatever you buy—or don't—sitting in a circular pit around a lazy Susan and probably drinking coffee on the house, look around you to admire what can be done with brick arches, wood, good lighting, and discreet, varied display cases.

Platería Tane   Amberes 68, near Liverpool. (Branches elsewhere.) Displays of vermeil and heavy ornate silver in late Victorian and traditional European design. The trays are ponderous and the prices also, but you're paying for a large, unabashed mountain of silver and the impression it will make back home. The window displays are often amusing, in the style of Tiffany's in New York.

Sanborn's   This keeps cropping up in various capacities, now as purveyor of silver. All Sanborn shops carry some, but the Madero store, set off by itself, is the calmest and most extensive.

India Bonita   Juárez 14. A lively, enterprising shop which keeps itself informed about and stocked with the work of some of the best designers, selling it at just prices.

San Francisco   With a long-established shop on Madero and a newer branch at Niza 46. Carries a great range of designs and objects worth inspecting and considering.

J. Rosenberg   Londres 114. Serious, conventional, trustworthy.

Taxco   Londres, near the Génova Hotel. Small, bustling, and eclectic in its choice of designs. (It is possible to bargain here but don't press.)

Arte e Plata   Londres, near Insurgentes. Distinguished craftsmanship in an appropriately distinguished shop.

Flato, SA,   a highly respected designer, shows his wares at Amberes 21.

Moise   Juárez 58, Paseo de la Reforma, and Génova 98F. Attractive jewelry of several types and vermeil roses and baskets of fragile design.

Ponte Vecchio   Niza 22. Features Italian-style jewelry; in gold and lapis, for example.

The lobbies of the big hotels always lead to silver (and gold) at prices suitable to the lordly surroundings. For bits of silver—the kind of thing you may take back for a neighbor's little girl—look in the markets. The more unusual native jewelry is not easy to find. The **Museo de Artes Populares** may have some and the shops of authentic crafts may have a few pieces to show you. And see what is on display at the shops of the Fondo Nacional (pages 77–78).

FABRICS

The range swings very wide; from the insubstantial, loosely woven homespuns, which trail off market stalls, to prints of appealing chic.

Telas Típicas   Campeche 157, near Sears on Insurgentes. Displays miles of solid, durable Toluca cloth, available in juicy colors which won't wash out (Mexican dyes are much less volatile than they used to be). It is possible to "discuss" prices, although the asking sums are reasonable.

Like other crafts, weaving has become increasingly sophisticated, internationalized, borrowing a texture from Sweden, a color from Italy, a usage from the United States. The best places to view some of these developments are in the shopping streets of Londres, Génova, and Hamburgo.

Palenque   Londres 119. Native cottons in interesting prints, used also in a few simple dresses, some of them embroidered, and comparatively inexpensive. At Londres 106, Mexican cloth in a wide diversity of colors and designs; made up as dresses as well.

CLOTHING (see FABRICS, also)

Lila Bath   Niza 40. A handsome shop which designs and decorates imaginative resort wear, using native homespuns and skill.

Marisa Ruby   Niza 45. High-style originals just a shade off Paris prices.

L'Hirondelle   Niza near Reforma. A newer boutique in the same class as the above.

For adroit, worldly, and inventive styles of clothing and accessories that use native materials and handiwork, consider the possibilities of:

Girasol   Génova 39A. Admirable design here.

Taxco   Londres 184.

Acapulco Lindo   Hamburgo and Amberes.

Tomacelli   about Londres 85.

Georgette   Londres 81 or 83 (Mexican addresses insist on hiding).

Casa Lina   Londres 136.

Maya of Mexico   Copenhague 21.

And dozens of others, cheek by jowl.

NOTE: Small, semi-hidden streets like Copenhague and Oslo are opening attractive, unusual shops under their trees and pretty street lamps.

A man who feels expansive and fond of himself and thinks the mood warrants a nice present should examine the arcades of leading hotels for fine alligator shoes and sports coats, or adaptations of the *guayabera* (the white, tucked shirt of Yucatán and Veracruz). If you have to count your money to make sure of how much you may spend, feast on the window, go on to more moderate shops, and save your shirt-buying for Yucatán.

If you're a lucky girl who happens to be traveling with a rich, indulgent husband or a "sugar daddy" (what happened to that happy phrase?), guide him into the same arcades. The French blouses, suits, and other exquisite dainties are delectable and worth the prices, particularly since you're not worrying about them.

For bargains (with no regard for style, workmanship, or longevity, just basic cover), shop the streets around the markets, and on Tacuba, Venustiana Carranza, Uruguay, and the streets nearby.

FURNISHINGS AND ANTIQUES

You'll have to know how to judge quality, authenticity, and price, but you might look in at:

La Lagunilla   (page 43)

Monte de Piedad   (page 32)

At Copenhague 20 there are respectful copies of Colonial furniture and some stimulating objects of glass and metal.

Rosana   Florencia off Hamburgo. Shows beautiful frames which let the ornaments go in favor of balanced proportions and careful finish.

Galerías la Granja   Bolívar 16. Nowhere is the supply of Colonial furniture as rich as it was, but this is still one of the better places to look. While you're on Allende, look in on the secondhand shops along the street; also on Bolívar.

Mullers   Londres at Florencia. If you must have and can afford to buy and ship an enormous onyx tabletop (there *are* smaller objects), this is for you.

Artesanos de Mexico   Londres 117. Furniture in Colonial style and old-style ironwork.

Chiqui Londres 121. Art-nouveau lamps and fanciful decorative objects.

Lanai Hamburgo 151. An impressively arranged display of drapery and upholstery materials and a few unique decorative objects.

Bazar Mariscal Madero 37-3. A crowded miscellany of oldish objects and jewelry.

Here and there in the Zona Rosa, shops of impressive house decorations and accessories; combinations of stone and metal which make the most regal lamps and doorpulls.

BOOKSHOPS

The number of good bookshops in Mexico City puts us to shame, particularly in view of the fact that there is still a low literacy rate in Mexico in spite of vigorous and fruitful efforts to bring it up. One of the many endearing qualities of the Mexican is his reverence for the printed word—whether he can read it or not. Sometimes, when you are walking on Madero (examining its windows of church ornaments and vestments) or Cinco de Mayo, you may see a booth or small shop used temporarily to publicize the text and pictures of a new, ponderous work—a history of the Revolution, maybe. The most careful examiners will be people who can hardly afford to buy a secondhand comic sheet, let alone an expensive series. Take a look at the awed, eager faces bent over the books, drawing from them what magic of learning and understanding they can.

In the section on walks you will find mention of secondhand bookstores; and, in the description of **La Lagunilla,** the treasures you might or might not find there. Dignified old bookstores, European in style, solemnity, and learned dimness, spot Cinco de Mayo, Madero, Independencia, Argentina, Guatemala. Some bookshops, conveniently located, which may be variously useful or interesting to you are:

Librería de Cristal Once upon a time next door to the Palacio de Bellas Artes. Large and crammed with inexpensive books, the whole encased in vast boxes of glass which gave off longhair music. Branches, not quite so shiny or musical, in other parts of the city now.

Librería Bellas Artes   Juárez 18. Good technical books in English.

Librería Porrua Hnos.   ("Brothers" abbreviated.) Juárez, near the corner of López. A broad range of gift books—art books and fine bindings, and a fairly complete collection of English Penguins.

Central de Publicaciónes   Juárez, just off San Juan de Letrán. Carries dictionaries in many languages, *avant* paperbacks, Italian and French publications, records, and a gallery of contemporary Mexican art in its high, wide, and logical interior.

Arvil   Cerrada de Hamburgo 9, between Florencia and Estocolmo. An attractive showcase for chic art; alert, knowing managers who keep a sophisticated, varied stock of records and books in several languages, including your own.

Mercado de Paperbacks   Reforma at Neva. Should you run out of easily portable reading matter, here it is, in sizable quantities.

Librairie du Quartier Latin   Nazas and Sena, logically close to the French Institute. Although the city has a number of shops which specialize in French books, this one has the most style, and the liveliest collection of records.

British Book Center   Rio Ganges 64. All those wonderful British whodunits in paperback, plus all sorts of English books and publications.

Ritz Bookshop   Attached to the hotel on Madero.

MISCELLANEOUS

Dulcería de Celaya   Cinco de Mayo, east of Motolinia. Established in 1874, it is orderly and elaborate, miniature, like an expensive dollhouse, or a box of fancy candies. All the sweets are native— glazed fruits, stuffed fruit, *morelianas* (caramel disks) of Michoacán, coconut patties from the tropics—and the atmosphere is docile and retiring, refusing to recognize revolution, modern décor, changes in tastes, or the novelties of importation.

Every crafts, gifts, *curiosidades* shop sells paper flowers, but if you should like to concentrate on flowers only—in all colors and sizes, curled, furled, budded and open as full sunlight—see the paper gardens at Hamburgo 136, at Londres 164, and on Revillagigedo, a few paces from the Reforma.

On Tacuba (a continuation of Hidalgo as it runs eastward), at 14 and at 15, are two shops in which Mexican women buy their perfumes, ointments, elixirs, and extracts at bargain prices. From all reports, the products are stable and trustworthy. Be sure of what you want, or take someone who speaks Spanish. These are busy shops, English is rarely spoken, and there is no time—most uncharacteristically—to help you stammer through your phrases.

Cosas Hamburgo 231. For people who can't stay away from secondhand stores and their promise of glorious bargains, an amiable, rambling old house, flowing furniture, utensils, dishes, decorative pieces. You may find many things disappointingly priced (dishes, for instance, if at all usable, bring high prices in Mexico), or you may find a treasure cheaply wrested from a great household fallen on evil days.

In the course of an old-city walk do some window shopping—for example, at Carranza 155, which supplies dollmakers from shelves and windows full of a grotesquery of minuscule feet, hands, heads, and clothing. Then stop at **Tomás Guijarro,** Uruguay 83, a large place as neatly arranged as a pathologist's slides should be. The thousands of boxes are full of glass bits of every design and color twinkling out of neat rows. Dozens of boxes contain varisized pins for brooches, metal mounts for rings; for earrings, there is a universe of beads and miles of chain wrapped around large wheels. The street seems to be a center for supplying the makers of trinkets with several shops that show their window wares in pretty, shapely jars, the beads and bits of glass layered as in those big, showy antipasto jars one sees in Italian groceries.

Farther down on Uruguay, approaching the Merced market, there are, among other sights to relish, great sacks of dark chiles, yellow and brown grains, the reds and blacks and whites of beans, all pushing at the mouths of soft straw containers. (Watch out for the barrows underfoot and sacks of grain flying overhead.)

Having seen the markets, with their dozen pesos' worth of herbs and thin cotton *rebozos,* it is now time to see the movie-set market designed to lure heavier sums. It is the **Pasaje Jacaranda,** scooped out of the interior of a block (the easiest and most attractive entrance is at Londres 104) and designed lightly, almost playfully, with soft, Mediterranean charm. Pots of flowers and small, planted squares break the gray walks; outdoor cafés sit near flowing greenery; the decorative statuary is simple and peaceable, quite unlike the usual monumental heroism of Mexican sculpture. The shops are completely glass-fronted, revealing two levels arranged with enough variety to avoid horizontal monotony.

Have a cup of coffee first and stare at the young Mexicans at the next table; the osmotic effect of clothing and atmosphere makes them look like young Italian intellectuals, which a few of them may be. You will of course have taken your shoes off to air your protesting feet—perfectly acceptable and even expected of you. (Mexicans are impressed by the tourist's determined energy and sympathetic over the exhaustion which follows each wild foray. As for mild undress: this is still a country of public nursing, public urinating, and public delousing, so you needn't worry.) And having rested, put your nose to a couple of windows:

Jacarandas makes lots of white, lacy worldly things—resort wear and accessories of Mexican homespun cloths. The dramatic to startling color combinations suggest an interesting cycle: the strong colors of Indian folkloric objects were picked up and used in Greenwich Village, then seeped into Madison Avenue, and now are back in Mexico as high style. **Paulsen** is a highly selective jeweler, one of whose specialties is a set of finely worked plaques of silver on black in a semiabstract manner. **Peggy Page** shows well-designed metal objects, among them mirrors, and china in traditional designs. Diagonally across the walk there may still be a stall covered with chunky rings of dipped pewter around clusters of semiprecious stone. The work of an Israeli craftsman, they are dramatic, inexpensive, and shown in an increasing number of places. **Sevigné** offers beautiful candles—tall, short, dignified, plain, and frilly—which make the wall hangings and the curtains of this shop exceedingly attractive. Before you buy many, stop to think of how you can carry them home. It has been managed, but many visitors find themselves the proud possessors of a large lump of colored wax after a sojourn in the tropics. (In addition to the goods in the shops above, you will find crafts objects and souvenirs of some worth.)

Wherever a handful of Mexican Indians meet there grows a market, as true of the Zona Rosa as elsewhere in Mexico. There is one of baskets, clothing, hats, and souvenirs—nothing of any distinction—along Liverpool off Génova. Embedded between Amberes and Florencia on Londres there is a fuller public market of vegetables, fruits, frying tacos, and thousands of dresses—embroidered, ruffled, flounced; blouses gauzy, blouses opaque; onyx souvenirs, dolls, puppets, and even the immortal sleeping-Indian bookends. The prices are a bit higher than those in the old-city markets, but much lower than those in the area and particularly inexpensive for the extra piece of luggage you almost inevitably find you'll need.

The price will be higher, the styles more distinguished at **Jacinthe,** on Londres near Florencia. And while you're wandering the latter street, or pondering the price of Dior bags at **Le Sac et le Baggage** at Florencia 11, have a look at 41, one of several such art-nouveau-touch-of-Gaudí houses that once-upon-a-time lined the street, now given over to expensive trade: stately silver in several shops and exquisite candles—and only candles—at the corner with Hamburgo.

You will, as everywhere in the world, see displays of blue jeans, at a price. The Zona Rosa called one of its outlets "Bonnie and Clyde" to match in worldliness a nearby unisex barbershop that calls itself "Hair Lovers," complete with a pretty heart on the sign.

ART GALLERIES

As you probably know, art is duty-free (get documentation, sometimes requested by customs) and there's much of it, some dreadful, some superb, available in Mexico.

Central de Publicaciones   (see Books) Shows paintings.

Galería de Arte Misrachi   Génova 20. Shows the modern Mexican masters and other established painters, as well as an unusually large selection of art books.

Salón de la Plástica Mexicana   Havre, in from the Reforma. Uneven, interesting exhibitions; government-sponsored.

Galería Estela Shapiro   Varsovia 23.

Galerías Iturbide   Hamburgo 146A. Modern Mexican work and some old masters.

Kin   An enterprising gallery in San Angel, Amargura 12.

Mexican Art Gallery   Milan 18. Presents serious, good painters, though not necessarily always "names."

Galería Pecanins   Hamburgo 103. A sociable gallery, often full of the young painters whose works hang on the walls.

Galería Aristos   Insurgentes near California. Related to the university and capable of pleasant surprises although not always.

José Clemente Orozco Museum   Hamburgo 113. Stages shows.

A graphics atelier that produced impressive work may still be at Netzahualcoyotl 9; check address and existence.

The big hotels display art and so does **Siqueiros' Polyforum** (page 122) and they keep coming, mainly into the Zona Rosa. Check tourist information papers and booklets available at almost all hotels.

MEXICAN HOURS

11:45 A.M. *The café savants have diminished Reagan and Gorbachev, demolished Castro; the pope is now readied as target for Mexican scorn and wit.*

12:00 *An Indian farmer, in worn, rusty white and a broad, tattered straw hat, stands alone and motionless on a hillside, sculptured of the same bitter passivity as the cactus near him, as silent and isolated.*

12:30 *In Cuernavaca all the outdoor cafés are crowded. The broad stream of vendors flows between the rich in the shade and the poor in the profligate sunlight, as at the bullfight.*

12:40 *A collapsed bus disgorges its resigned passengers at Tierra Colorada. They saunter to the market to while away repair time and, attracted by a gay, laughing crowd, join it. In the middle is a young woman with a handsomely modeled face holding up for display a naked baby of about ten months, round, firm, and dark, with a vigorous thatch of coal-black pubic hair. The tourists turn away, uneasy. The villagers are delighted with the charming surprise in a changeless life.*

12:45 *A tired, hot tourist stops under the shade of the giant* ahuehuete *tree in Tule and wipes the perspiration pouring down her face. An old Indian lady nearby whisks a straw fan out of her shapeless reticule and fans the foreign woman. "La Francesa" (any fair female stranger is still a French-woman—shades of the Empress Carlotta—in rural areas) thanks her and offers a few coins. The old woman turns back the thanks and the coins: "It is for nothing." And with "May it go well with you" moves off in her torn skirt and great dignity. The American woman finds herself bowing her farewell, an obeisance to royalty.*

12:55 *On the outskirts of Mexico City a tall elderly Indian seats himself on a bit of grass in front of an upper-class residence and carefully, slowly, washes his feet in a rain puddle in the cracked sidewalk.*

1:10 *Outside the crypt of mummies in Guanajuato a little boy approaches one tourist for coins. Tourist: "Why pick especially on me?" Boy: "Because you're rich." "How do you know?" "Oh, because you're so nice and plump and your cheeks are so pink."*

1:20 *A passenger on the train reads aloud to his friend a sign attached to the wall: "This train was bought in Switzerland at great cost for your comfort: please help us maintain it." The listener picks up a banana peel from among the many that, by now, enliven the floor of this first-class car and stuffs it into his pocket.*

1:30 *The Mérida branch of the Banco Nacional is crisscrossed with lines of people. All work has stopped because a two-year-old girl in a dress like a wedding cake has been lifted over a counter and is being dandled and petted by guards, tellers, runners, and managers.*

1:45 *The train makes one of its frequent stops (this is an "express") and lets on a man festooned in plastic squares, for use as an impromptu raincoat, to wrap a baby in, to make a tablecloth or a curtain, or a carrying bag. He looks frantically for the not impossible her to whom he can make a sale in two or three minutes. His tense progress is impeded by two lean yellow dogs who boarded with him and who systematically search the long aisle and under the seats, row by row, looking for food. They are old desperate pros and pace themselves expertly for a thorough survey, and then back to the door, ready to leap as the train starts.*

ENTERTAINMENT

Nervous joy, music that tears at the ears and the drunken heart, the latest dance step stamped or jerked with stubborn gaiety, obsequious service with a subtle sneer, tables always too small, checks like the voice of doom—all are available in Mexico City as they are in Paris, New York City, Rome, and anywhere that money is. Practically all the big hotels have some form of entertainment, featuring North American or Mexican artists, and, once in a while, someone from Paris or Madrid. If you like dancing, this is the city and the country for you. Everyone dances, and beautifully, to a "name" group whose enthusiasm for volume sometimes drowns out tunefulness, to jukeboxes, to radios, to the voices and guitar of three boys who ordinarily work in the local supermarket, to the soundless music of an impulse.

Consult the hotel desk, the newspapers, or the numerous pamphlets which will find their way to you and check the times of floor shows. Below, you will find a few bright foolishnesses which may not be part of your ordinary *ambiente,* either live or via television.

Gitanerías   Oaxaca 15. *(Reservations: call 28-70-68.)* Not for the claustrophobic. A very low ceiling holds together a set of small cavern-rooms, further laced together by thousands of miles of paper streamers, supplied by the management and tossed by customers with the kind of vigor usually confined to little boys' birthday parties when the ice cream is finished and the restlessness explodes. The atmosphere is further enriched by two bands of musicians—guitarists, singers, clappers of hands and snappers of fingers in the Spanish style who, along with the customers, maintain a heady brew of sound.

The tiny Spanish olives served in bucketsful along with carrots and cucumbers, the chance to drink rough, red wine from the stream of a Spanish community bottle *(porrón)* held a couple of feet above you, and the entertainment may be worth the strain—especially heavy on Saturday nights. If you can possibly go on some other night (not Monday), do. You'll be able to concentrate on the floor show, which calls for full attention.

The flamenco singing is a flash of flames, the classical guitarist a fine artist with a remote aristocratic manner which suits impeccably his antique art. The *declamador* recites, with a reckless passion, Spanish poetry whose words may not be comprehensible but whose import will, particularly when he recites "Gachupín," a bitter poem which deals with the modern Spaniard's resentment of Mexican disdain and old anger toward him. "Your mother was the Mexican earth, but will you deny your father?" he shouts with a twist of sardonic sadness on his mobile face.

Then the flamenco dancer appears. His slight, tense body is wrapped in narcissistic concentration. He watches his own feet as they hammer out his impatient, exigent rhythms; his eyes are lowered, his face closed from his audience, responding only to a mysterious inner passion. He is frighteningly self-contained; his music is the snapping of his own fingers, the clapping of his own hands, the sound of his own heels. The narcissism, and total privacy of the tight body in the tight, revealing costume, absorb and disturb, as if one were watching a primitive rite of unimaginably ancient ur-sex. Expensive. (Check the check.)

Rincón de Goya Toledo 4. In several small, tight rooms (Spanish places apparently function best when they pull around them the closeness of the gypsy caves of Granada), and almost as violently gay as Gitanerías, though sober about its good Spanish food (paella, especially). The entertainment is the whole "Spanish" gamut plus Afro-Cuban. Moderate.

Los Infiernos Insurgentes and Tiajuana. Pounds out Veracruzana and Cuban music nonstop, or almost.

REMINDER: Check with bellhops and clerks for existence and addresses.

Fonda del Recuerdo Bahía de las Palmas 39A at Bahía de Santa Barbara. You may never get here because taxi drivers sometimes deny knowing where these streets are. It is a remote neighborhood and the city has grown beyond their knowledge. When and if you do, you'll find yourself laved in the insistent, fluid rhythms of the music of Veracruz, mostly the inexhaustible repertory of the dance called the *huapango,* whose phrases lap over each other like small waves. The musicians—a harpist or two or three, maybe a fiddler—wear the regional white, with red scarfs, and are often skilled virtuosi in the small harps of their *tierra*. Go at about nine and have the *empanados*, oily but delicious.

The Plaza Garibaldi is an old square in the lumpen section of the city, once a dim, sly square of *mariachis* and prostitutes. It is now better lit, its decayed saloons dressed up and gaudily painted, a market of eating stalls built to brighten it—a general cleanup to entice and calm the tourist. The *mariachis* still hang around in their *muy macho* tight pants and extravagant hats, and if you like, they will sell you a song while you sit in your car or on one of the benches in the plaza. Or you may hire them to play at your party or to serenade a friend's birthday, starting at three in the morning. As for the girls, they're not hard to find. They won't attack in the manner of Piccadilly Circus or Paris streets, but you'll know them if you're looking. The two strongholds are:

Guadalajara de Noche   It is wildly crowded on Saturday nights with a few tourists and groups of young Mexicans drinking and singing with red-faced vigor, and a few women, in groups of two and three, quietly waiting. Compounded of the voices of leather-lunged *mariachis,* the vociferous horns which call above their voices, the shriek of fiddles, the roaring customers, and the tightness of space, the noise is a thick, palpable weight pushing at the patient walls. Moderate. (Count your drinks and check their cost. Discuss any error with your waiter politely; don't dispute it. Let the valor go and settle for discretion.)

Tenampa   A long time ago when the plaza was still its own nighttown, the Tenampa was one of the favorite *mariachi cantinas* on the brooding square. It was an L-shaped room, the short end a bar just inside the entrance, the long arm a series of booths. The *mariachis* stood for hours at the bar, drinking tequila and mescal in swift short gulps, hardly interrupting their long, loud winding songs, hardly casting a glance at the parade of adolescents with old faces emerging from around the side, mouths, heads, shirts covered with blood, muttering and staggering in pain and drunkenness, lurching back toward more combat. They were coaxed, led, half carried by their women—girls of fifteen or sixteen, weeping, gentle, ragged, worn by their knowledge of knives and blood. The *mariachis* sang on, their eyes brightened by the loud effort and drink. They had no comment to make or help to offer.

The Tenampa has since been cleaned up and expanded, but something of the old flavor returns from time to time, a dour subterranean muttering under the incessant music; poison in the lacquered hair of the silent, watchful women; blind storms in the faces of the young men. The poor vendors ceaselessly, listlessly, offer things no one wants. Whether you'll want to go is a matter of your own responses. You may find it blithe and gay, through your own happy lenses, or be demolished by it. It isn't dull. Modest to moderate.

Los Turcos   Diagonal San Antonio 1107. After a journey through closed, anonymous streets you came to a small opening in a Persian arch. This led into a Stygian blackness in which you stood paralyzed until a voice attached to a minute flashlight led you through clouds of dim white veiling, a step here, a slope there, always downward. You were in one of London's most effortful fogs or a high school production of Orpheus' descent into Hades. A flash of the light upward showed spots of wall encrusted with the endlessly interlaced patterns of arabesque design, a scalloped arch, vaguely minaretish shapes. The idea, which you've already caught, was PRIVACY; you could drink and dance and hide in groups of twos, fours, and even sixes behind the gauzy curtains—full of holes, tears, and mends, if you cared to examine them by the light of a match. The dancing, in small clearings outside the tents, was as private as you liked to music supplied by a very good orchestra which sat in a miniature Saracen castle, back of the "Persian Room," a cluster of the darkest and smallest (cozy room for two only) warrens. It has probably changed; one hopes not.

Weird and wonderful, and quite innocent, like a child's view of grown-up vice. Open Sundays as well as other nights until quite late, unless the city's rectitude has caught up with it and attacked. (It has, sorry.)

Jacaranda   Génova 56. A huge, softly lit shell; something like sitting in a hangar draped in dark velvet or a heavy cloud whose only visible opening is a glass panel. The tables are set on shallow tiers and it takes a little negotiating to step down to the dance floor. As is the custom of the country, the music never stops and is about as good as you'll find for dancing anywhere, although you may find your best fancy footwork and long swoops imprisoned in the tight space that the rest of the crowd allots you. Just twist your torso and listen to the well-sung vocals in Spanish, French, English, Italian, Arabic, or whatever. Expensive.

El Colmenar   J. Teran 42. This one is of an older and less brilliant vintage than some of the other nightclubs, and its standards of entertainment a bit shaky: a remarkable French chanteuse one week, a tired belly dancer the next. Find out who's showing and decide for yourself. Moderate.

With a burgeoning middle class and a fantasy that the Olympic games and all its visitors will return tomorrow and stay and stay, Mexico City is opening, along with Taj Mahal hotels, many nightclubs and discotheques. Some last, some don't. A number of them are strung along Insurgentes, the longest and most passionately striving street in the city; a few inhabit hotels of the first-class and luxury variety. Again, the desk clerks will tell you about current favorites.

AT YOUR OWN RISK

None of the places below are guaranteed to be open, nor are they recommended unless you go with a Mexican, or you have a magnificent command of Spanish, including some sure slang, or you're a man alone looking for sociology-cum-adventure and/or trouble. If you're with a woman, incidentally, but importantly, *do not* let her dance with anyone but yourself—absolutely. Depending on the erratic games of police action and inaction (too complicated to go into here even if one understood them), any given place might be closed down when you get there. Hold the cab while you investigate.

Tio Sam, Delgado 1, threatened with closing, seems to have the skill to hang on. Big, big, big, with two bands, strippers of a sort, and available girls—only the dancing is guaranteed. In the area where San Juan de Letrán becomes Niño Perdido, you may find places with names like **Centro Típico, Siglo 20, Cha Cha Cha, Casablanca,** and plenty of dance partners. For a descending scale of size and shine, see what you can find (if you must) along Niño Perdido—**El Raton** possibly. And not too far from these a place or two in the neighborhood of Bolívar and Najera, where you can buy a dance for very little, remembering that you must order drinks (stay with tequila or beer) and that the sight of an American makes a whirlwind change in the economy. The décor is often intentionally nightmarish and funny: horns, excited swirls of thick paint, and snakes with women's heads, the eyes illuminated. If you want to investigate the décor in upstairs rooms you should know what you're doing and why.

Still moving a bit downward: at Libertad and Allende, a small dime-a-dance saloon, with a regular, closed clientele which may not like you. On and around the Plaza Netzahualcoyotl there may still exist some dives, terribly quiet and immobile—in spite of the music the customers are zombies. Look quickly, but don't stay, and have your taxi wait right at the entrance.

If you have an insatiable taste for this sort of thing, look behind some of the taco stands on Izazaga, which front tiny, crazy caves, and the *pulquerías* on Honduras or Comonfort, or wander Bolívar at about two in the morning. Girls in thin sweaters and papery shoes stand against the protecting walls while they haggle with thin, sharp young men. There is no playfulness in it, nor even much energy, just restlessness and several kinds of desperation and, if the night is cold and damp, the sight will depress you, which you may deserve or even perversely want, if you've come this far.

"NATIVE DANCING"

The native dance is rarer than you think, in spite of the ads and travel leaflets which portray a country on permanent vacation. (When it isn't water-skiing or lying in the sun it is stamping its heels, snapping its fingers, spreading its sequinned skirt in graceful turns, according to the posters.) Like our Ozark folk music, regional dances have been succored by the sophisticate and the paid entertainer, and readily relinquished by its original only begetters for something newer and zippier from the big city. Even country fiestas will have little dancing unless committee members round up a group and keep it corralled until performance time. With great good luck, you may stumble on a celebration in a village where there will be dancing or a small-town church-fund benefit which will feature dance and song competitions or a vaudeville show. Otherwise, you will have to do with carefully arranged and overarranged demonstrations, still not to be scorned.

There are stately dances and satirical dances, the complex toe-and-heeling and hot flirtatiousness of Veracruz, the regal, *triste* waltz of Tehuantepec, and a dozen others, including a monotonous stamping and turning which may be *muy auténtico* and dull.

Danzas Anahuac Alvaro Obregón 241. Performances (usually Monday, Friday, and Saturday at 8:15 P.M.) of regional dances, dressed in appropriate costumes and marimba music. Rewarding entertainment without an excess of "Olé's" and "Let's give the little girl a big hand." (Check times.)

Hotel Vasco de Quiroga Londres 15. Monday, Wednesday, Friday, and Saturday at 8:15 P.M. The dining room is given over to magnificent costumes and fairly capable dancers, chosen as much for their looks as their skill. Since this is one of the features of some city tours, it is likely to be crowded with prepaid diners and watchers, and the atmosphere charged with expansive Latin American bonhommie. But you can pay your entertainment fee and stay aloof if you choose to. (Check existence and times.)

Ballet Folklórico de Bellas Artes Palacio de Bellas Artes. Frequently on Sunday mornings and, depending on the season, some evenings as well.

The best of its kind that you're likely to see and a stunning show in any terms. Starting with the great hieratic dignity of ancient ritual and a solemn, hypnotic plume dance, it moves through times and regions skillfully and imaginatively, accompanied by varieties of appropriate music: a chorus which sings the songs of the Revolution, a combination of *chirimía* and drum which makes the thin, lonely sounds one still hears in remote churchyards, *mariachis* of good taste and musicianship, the nimble harp strings of Veracruz. The décor and costuming follow folkloric themes, bringing to life clay candelabra and primitive Spanish-Indian angels in bright crowns and wings, dancing around a stiff blue-and-gold Virgen de la Soledad. If there are now variations in programing, choose a performance of the Yaqui Deer Dance, a solo dance of a deer sensing the hunt—supple, rippling, quivering darts and hesitations—danced to maracas and ankle bells worn by the dancer and, offstage, the eerie, nervous shouts of voices and percussion. Well performed, it is unforgettable.

Companies of the Folklórico Ballet perform at Siqueiros' Polyforum (page 122) and other more impromptu groups in hotels, now and then.

One of the quieter, less costly pleasures is city-viewing at night, high up, drink in hand. There are several places, but one of the pleasantest is the **Muralto** at the top of the Latino Americana tower at San Juan de Letrán and Madero. The entrance is opposite Sanborn's and one takes an elevator to the thirty-seventh floor and then another to the observatory (small fee) or the bar-restaurant, where the viewing costs the price of a drink or dinner, rather high-style and expensive. The room is small and usually crowded, but with patience and a polite phrase you can make your way around tables, musicians, bars, and other viewers to look around and down through the long windows.

The city is large and diffuse, with as yet comparatively few tall buildings, and it spreads into its dark horizon on a field of Redon fantasy flowers. In the east, a line like smoke from a slow-moving steamer etches the outline of a settlement on a distant hill. Directly below, to the west, the cupcake of the Bellas Artes borders the Alameda, whose foggy glow is imprisoned by the dark-green mesh of its treetops. (The viewing is good on a clear day—the hours are from 10 A.M. to midnight—but make an effort to go late.) The view from the high bar-restaurant-clubs of major hotels is also excellent.

CHARROS

Ranchers disport themselves on Sunday mornings at the Rancho del Charro, on Ejército Nacional. The fancy riding and roping will remind you, vaguely, of our rodeos, but here they are performed by gentlemen riders on blooded horses. Skillful and handsome as the men are, and attractive as are the singers who appear for their turn at entertaining, the show is invariably stolen by the young girls: reckless; long-skirted, ruffled dresses whipping around the frail bodies; long, loosened hair pulled and spread by the windy speed—a flight of young Furies.

MUSIC AND THEATER

Mexico City's cultural life will ultimately catch up with its ballooning size, but it hasn't happened yet, so that your choices may not be many. As a general rule, the summer season is richer, offering Sunday morning symphony concerts as a regular thing and occasional guest appearances by fine artists. There is a short opera season which the Mexican public grabs with avidity, and often at great sacrifice. These performances take place in the auditorium of the **Palacio de Bellas Artes** while chamber groups and lesser soloists perform in the smaller halls of the Palacio.

Before the building of the National Auditorium, the popular-priced hall was the bull ring. One of our haughtier opera stars was invited to sing in it after an appearance at the Bellas Artes. She was appalled at the idea of wafting her silvery notes—she had outlived the golden—from a platform in an "abattoir." The concert committee, serious sons of democracy, tore up her contract, and the considerable Mexican sale of her records dropped sharply. Stravinsky had conducted to mink stoles and French jewels one night, to cotton *rebozos* and worn sandals in the National Auditorium the next. It was hard to know what the carefully washed and starched family from one of the poorer *barrios* made of "The Firebird," but it was a remarkable thing to watch their intense, closed faces concentrated on gathering, understanding, and never forgetting the whole strange experience.

The **Nezahualcoytl Hall** enhances its music with remarkable acoustics.

The Mexican rich find their theater in New York or London or Paris; the poor find it in their streets, in "futbol" and television. The middle class is just learning to need it; and the intellectual can't afford it. Therefore, not much theater, but try the **Xola Theater** (if it is still functioning) for classical drama, even if your Spanish can't stand it; the actors are usually of the first rank and the stagecraft inventive; and see what there is in the new **Social Security Theater** on Hidalgo. Little theater groups of varying degrees of talent and tenure perform in French, Spanish, Yiddish, and English, announcing the facts in *Excelsior* or *El Universal* or the *News*.

Manuel Fabregas, a versatile actor, has built a spacious, comfortable theater on Serapio Rendon. He often brings, and performs in, American plays translated for Mexican audiences. His Tevye in "Violinista sobre la Tejada" was a miraculously convincing performance.

In spite of television, movies are still the opium of this people, unbelievably cheap and in great supply. The prices are low at the showiest houses, even those with dancing fountains as added attractions. At these prices, it takes quite a while for large, important U.S. imports to cross the border, but you can practice your Spanish by reading the subtitles of an oldie you may have missed or avail yourself of the chance to see French, German, Russian, and Czech films which might not get to the States. The best bargains are double features of foreign gems for a small sum. (Newspapers run several pages of vivid, explicit ads.) The newspapers and tourist information leaflets available at every hotel desk will inform you of art films in "cine clubs."

FRONTÓN

You may know this as jai alai, a Basque game played by two men against two on a long court with three walls. The hard ball is caught in a *cesta* (a shallow basket) strapped to the forearms, and then whipped against one of the walls, to be caught and thrown, or missed, by an opponent. It takes rare skill and agility and the obedient body of a ballet dancer. To novices, the betting is entirely incomprehensible; hoarse men in red berets shout the odds with Castilian lisps in a constant high drone of urgent prayer, while the slit tennis balls which hold the bets fly back and forth overhead, from bettor to caller. If you're not betting, you won't stay as long as the enthusiasts; get the cheapest seat. (Every night except Mondays from about 6 P.M. on and on at **Frontón México,** off the Plaza de la República. And there was a girls' frontón team, not as skilled as the men's, but in its own caricatured way, as entertaining. Ask the desk clerk at your hotel if they are still performing and where.)

THE CORRIDA

Although "futbol" is replacing the bullfight, especially among the young, it still gives as much rise to passionate dispute among Americans as politics and the way to make a martini. Should you go, assuming you haven't and are doubtful? Most simply put, it depends on whether you are more a friend of bull or man. If you have been brought up in a pure A.S.P.C.A. spirit you will be horrified at the sight of an animal, red-ribboned barb in its neck, tearing out of a box, pained and infuriated, to be tricked, turned, speared, and killed; and, a padded, blinkered old nag repeatedly bumped and thrown by the crazed bull. (Don't believe the stories of horses' entrails pouring into the sand; unpadded horses are a thing of the past.) If, on the other hand, you have a great investment in the controlled insane courage of men, even the odd narcissistic ones who become *toreros,* it can be an immortal experience to see a slight man dressed like an expensive doll standing alone in the arena, legs together and poised, holding high two frilled sticks *(banderillas),* no sword, no cape, nothing but a pair of barbed wands to place together, and exactly, in the bull's hump as the man meets and eludes its rush; or to see the immobile shining man and the rushing black bulk embraced in a graceful cadence of red cape. At its thrilling best, a bullfight dispels the conflict; it is not man against bull as much as man with bull in a magnificent duet, stately and magical, the priests of an ancient rite performed against a ring of "Olé's" softly breathed by 50,000 voices in unison.

According to experts, the quality of men and bulls has declined in recent years, in Mexico as in Spain, and the season of great men is much shorter (roughly late November through March). At other times, you will see *novilleros* trying out their novice skills. Some are good, some are reckless fools, and the kill, a tricky job to do at once and cleanly even by the best, can become an unbearable, murderous hacking. On the other hand, a superb *torero* may, like a great diva out of voice, not give you the great experience you've heard and read about. To find again those moments when the bull, the man, and the spectators soar into impossible beauty and nobility is what keeps people going to bullfights. The superlative is rare, but worth hours of waiting through the ordinary when it finally happens.

Occasionally, the A.S.P.C.A. people win out—for Mexican rather than U.S. reasons. A bull will obviously be so tremendous an animal in shape and alertness that the audience, which sometimes calls the tunes, will shout to have him taken out for siring mighty progeny and he is trotted out like a docile calf between a pair of oxen. Such an event can't, of course, be promised you, nor can the rare performance and antique charm of a *rejoneador.* He is of an anachronistic breed which fights from horseback, in the old style. He is dressed in the black silks, velvets, and plumed cap of a Velázquez noble, and the mane of his blooded horse is as elaborately knotted and beribboned as the braid on his coat. He works with a short lance, turning the exquisitely responsive horse with his legs. At some point, he will break his lance in half and control horse and bull through the narrower, more exciting slit of space. It is an enthralling thing to see and feel, for its own intrinsic excitements and the power it has to pull you with it into the eighteenth century. If it should cross your path or even be inconvenient to get to, don't miss it.

NOTES: Like most literate people, you've probably read Hemingway, Tynan, and García Lorca; looked at Goya's "Toromaquia" etchings; and waded, at least, in the vast ocean of words about bullfighting: the acts of its drama, its ritual music, its roots in ancient Crete, what a *verónica* is, and how Belmonte and Manolete endowed it with art. If the subject has passed you by, however, pick up one of the pamphlets available in all bookshops and sometimes at the bull ring. In spite of the amorphous quality of Mexican time the *corrida* starts at four o'clock sharp. Give yourself plenty of time to find your seat, which is always at the other end of the huge arena. As for choice of seats, the *sol* (sunny) side is cheap and seats can be bought at the arena a short time before the bullfight. (This is the part of the house from which pillows, programs, and even pop bottles are hurled down in displeasure, and where, from time to time, men are frisked for knives and guns at the entrance. Leave your money and important papers in the hotel and keep a sharp eye out for flying objects.) The *sombra* (shade) seats are choice and most efficiently bought through the hotel, which will charge you a little extra—a great saving in time and trouble, however.

Getting out to one of the two bull rings is not too difficult. Getting back is another matter; either arrange for a car to meet you or leave early to avoid an exhausting, often futile search for a cab.

Cock fights are not permitted in the Federal District, which means you can find them right over the line. Guides know, desk clerks know, taxi drivers know where to find them—if you insist on the whirring, pecking monotony of the "sport." Leave your wallet and passport in the hotel safe.

The seeker of special pleasures might look into the public-baths situation, some of them with sybaritic suites for two or four and the use of steam rooms, shower rooms, rest rooms. Who and what you will encounter and in what combinations can't be prognosticated, but the possibilities are interesting. On the other hand: lectures and films at the Anglo-Mexican Institute, the French-Latin American Institute, or the Mexican-North American Institute. Or chess on Sunday mornings in Chapultepec Park. (Ask for *ajedrez*.)

Or, art openings offer you a peep at intellectual high life, particularly those of the chic, glossy galleries, whose devotees move silently, expressionlessly, from picture to picture, their slow, smooth progress a scene out of an *avant* film. The air isn't quite as chilly in less imposing galleries which parallel—cocktails, tidbits, smoke, and no room to view the pictures—our gallery openings.

The pyramids at Teotihuacán put on a show of *Son et Lumière* frequent evenings. Go with a tour group and carry a sweater. If you are driving and confident about getting back at night, go earlier so that you may stop at the convent of Acolmán (where there is a restaurant and entertainment, incidentally). It has a narrow, extremely high-vaulted church of the mid-sixteenth century and an adjoining monastery, both painted and carved by Indians on Spanish design and interesting for both the skill and essential naïveté.

POVERTY AND PROGRESS

American tourists are frequently appalled at the poverty they see in Mexico. It is appalling, as it is in Sicily, in Brazil, in India, in Africa. The small consolation is that it was much worse. Thirty years ago the doorways on Juárez and Madero were crammed at night with frozen bundles of homeless boys, plagued by hunger and cold that pierced their blankets of old newspaper. Now some of them have employed parents who can and do keep them, more of them are in school, and though we recoil from child labor, it is comforting to know that a number of them can work and keep themselves in bed and board, meager by our standards but infinitely better than begging, stealing, and trying to sleep on marble. Thirty years ago too much of the city's population had no shoes or sweaters. The only protection against the cold of prolonged summer rains or the icy crawl of winter nights was pulque for the men, thin cotton *rebozos* and prayer for the women. A barefoot person or one without some sort of sweater or jacket against the cold is now rare; the shoes may be of plastic or crude sandals and the sweaters thin and limp, but they exist. The doorways of San Juan de Letrán used to shadow girls of fourteen and fifteen, with despairing, listless faces bare of makeup, dressed in the undecorated grayed cottons of poverty. They hoped it would be understood that they could be bought; they had neither the courage nor the imagination to display the fact. Prostitution hasn't disappeared from Mexico but it is better fed and clothed, not quite so hungry or diffident, nor so young.

Soft-hearted, soft-living (and guilty?) tourists are pained by a slum populace that must buy one cheap cigarette at a time, rather than a full pack; which buys its spices in packages the size of stamps, and almost as flat, for a few pesos; whose sewing thread is bought in lengths of a few yards; and aspirins one by one. It might be comforting to know that some of these people picked cigarette butts off the sidewalks, stole pinches of herbs, and were too discouraged to sew some years ago. (Late note: With the drop in the peso, ensuing high prices and increased unemployment, and thousands from unproductive rural areas pouring into the big cities, the dreadful old situation may be returning.)

If any one single substance can be said to have changed the face of Mexico it is plastics. The baby once wrapped in an extra fold of *rebozo* to protect it from the rain is now better, if less indigenously, protected by a sheet of plastic. The round rush raincoat, like a thatched hut and strongly reminiscent of the reed coats in Japanese prints, has been replaced by lengths of plastic, often in a bright pink which leaps out of the gray of rain and sodden fields. Plastic flowers are more "high class" and last longer and have replaced the immense fresh bouquets and wreaths carried on pilgrimages. Plastic pants now cover the uncertain bottoms of little children—except in the tropics, where the babies are as bare as the piglets. Plastic covers the cakes and candy trays of vendors, replacing the old sheet of flies; it encases shimmery gelatins, potatoes, greens, soaps, and stockings in the *supermercado,* whose atmosphere is the shine and rustle of plastics.

All this is deeply deplored by the old Mexico hand (American, that is) who misses the aesthetics of beautifully arranged mounds of vegetables planted on dirty sidewalks and surrounded by small lakes of discards and mud. It was more "real," if plastic is "unreal," and more "human," if plastic is less "human," but considerably more hazardous; and fortunately, with considerable help from plastic, the old, fly-covered, stench-style market is becoming a thing of Mexico's primitive past.

MUSEUMS, MURALS, BUILDINGS

Pinacoteca Virreinal Across from the northwest corner of the Alameda. A plaque at the side says this was the place, precisely, of burnings sponsored by the Inquisition from 1596 to 1771. The place of ancient agonies now sits calmly among the newer agonies of construction shrills and shrieks, sometime to end, as the Inquisition finally did.

The former church and offices have been converted into beautifully lit and hung galleries to show not an important but an interesting corner of art history, the native work that filled Mexican churches in the sixteenth, seventeenth, and eighteenth centuries. It is, of course, a limited field, much of it copied from Spanish models, but while you move from saint to saint, admire the restoration of architectural details and the sections of late-sixteenth-century tiles that remain. As everywhere and always, there is something stimulating to find in a repetitious collection. A superpatriot painted a mural of the conversion of the Indians by Spanish friars filling the Indian faces with open, gentle candor while the friars tend to resemble Fagin, one of them complete with hooked, cajoling, and menacing finger. Or look for the very Mexican, yellow Christs and naïve Virgins surrounded by the floral ornaments still made and sold in tin and clay. In the organ loft, now an office, you will find several viceregal portraits, among them a plump, becurled, beruffled child whose Spanish cousin might have sat for Goya. The small price of admission and a half hour accompanied by good music from the guardian's radio are very well spent.

Academy of San Carlos From the Pinacoteca turn to and cross Av. Hidalgo, more easily said than done at this writing, an act that requires considerable courage and agility. However, once across, walk to Hidalgo 107, which was the old convent of San Hipolito and the first madhouse in Mexico. Now it shows—as what Colonial building does not?—a regal court, your basic reason for stopping here. Recross the avenue and a few blocks on turn into the street called M. Arizpe to a small park that fronts on the early-nineteenth-century house of a local Duke, now the academy which had been the principal art school in Mexico for almost two centuries and, for a long time, the only school of architecture. Since the time of the great mural painters, who led the way, there has been much defection from the rigidities inherent in such institutions; art students in Mexico City have moved to the freer air of other government-sponsored schools.

It is an interesting group of paintings—interesting not because they are particularly good or bad (there are a few at both extremes) but because they so heavily represent worn-out tastes and the kind of meager treasures sent to a subject country by a Crown which had gathered a world of art treasures. Whatever their intrinsic value, a good number of the paintings are large, dark, sentimentally religious, slavishly detailed, and for all their labor, piety, and gold frames, add up to little.

For their collective virtues and oddities there are a few paintings worth searching out: an El Greco, for instance; a small apocalyptic "Jesus in Limbo" by Bosch; a fine portrait by Mostaert; a few Flemish altar paintings. Look at a "Pietà" by Luis Morales, apparently modeled on the eyebrowless, green-yellow virgins of early Flemish triptychs plus the tortured look that makes her indisputably Spanish; a "Road to Damascus," decorous, elegant—it might easily be the Canterbury pilgrimage, without the Wife of Bath; and a portrait by Philip of Champagne: the long contemptuous nose, fine armor, lace tie, cynical expression, and air of profligacy are wonderfully pleasant after the moribund saints.

You will find a number of Zurbaráns, a couple of Tintorettos, a Caravaggio, a Gentile Bellini, a very good Rubens "St. Peter," a portrait by Lorenzo Lotto, one by Bronzino, and a Van Dyck. Other lustrous names appear carrying, unfortunately, the tag "attributed to."

Gone are the storm-tossed ceilings, many of the classic figures that enlivened the academy when it lived in the old city. One especially misses the hermaphroditic Apollos in chic hairdos, a sheaf of arrows held gracefully along a soft ripe thigh. They used to present an interesting puzzle: How could a punitive, Inquisition-whipped, sin-obsessed church permit the eyes of its young to be ravished by the paganism proclaimed from the old balcony of King Carlos III's art school? As consolation for the loss of the Apollo-Dianas, however, the public is offered a pretty coffee shop on a secluded little inside court.

Museo Nacional de Antropología Chapultepec Park. We might begin by saying that the museum (in spite of its name, it greatly concerns archaeology, as well) is the most imaginatively, generously, intelligently, and humanely designed collection in the world. It is a monumental masterpiece built to hold masterpieces. Like the cathedral of the Middle Ages, it was created by the efforts of numerous artists and artisans devoted to shaping a dedicated place, this place dedicated to the Mexican people, their imposing artistic achievements, and those of all peoples. The legend carved in large letters near the entrance says: "Valor and confidence to face the future is found by people in the grandeur of their past. Mexican, look at yourself in the mirror of this splendor; stranger, know also the unity of human destiny. Civilizations pass, but man has always within him the glory of those who struggled to bring them into being."

Led by the cricket that is the symbol of Chapultepec and his neighbor, the squat, massive rain god Tlaloc, one saunters through lordly space toward a large rectangle of glass and marble (notice the fine row of ancient symbols on the glass doors) surmounted by the eagle-serpent symbol of Mexico, the imposing entrance unit embedded in creamy brick walls, alive with tints and textures. You will notice the richness of tones and textures again and again: the enormous diversity of shades, shapes, and surfaces that make a varied and harmonious total of benches, mahogany screens, planters, ash receivers, panels, curves of steps, lettering carved in the marble, and especially, the arrangements and lighting of objects in the exhibition halls.

The logical place to begin—sometimes accompanied by kindergarten groups, solemn, silent, holding tightly to each other's hands—is the Sala de Orientación, a darkened amphitheater which shows hourly a dramatic presentation, accompanied by primitive music, of the development of pre-Hispanic Mexican civilizations from earliest times to the arrival of the Spaniards. Not only informative (there are earphones for translation) as a quick introduction to what you will find in the halls beyond, but also—with its uses of habitat groups, codices, pyramids, and gods that leap out of the darkened walls or rise from hidden platforms—a lesson in showmanship for education.

Then you pass into the inner court, which achieves the difficult goal of being both majestic and hospitable by means of a big umbrella fountain that spills lively rain, a long serene pool of water lilies and papyrus reeds, and, on the walls, the lean, noble poetry of ancient bards.

Although nothing should be missed, if only for the masterly arrangements, a traveler's is not the most leisured of possible worlds, so you might skip the "Introduction to Anthropology" hall and plunge directly into Mexico's past, beginning with "Origins," introduced with an ancient quotation: "There was no glory or grandeur in the world until there came into being the human creature, the full man." The displays, as you might guess, concern prehistoric animals and the primitive men who lived with them, one meeting represented by an artfully modeled scene of a dozen tiny men armed only with spears attacking a mastodon. You will notice that each hall has two main levels, one to give room for exhibits on an upper story and full height left for enormous gods, huge murals, and a maximum of natural light. A third level of sorts is the outdoor section, used frequently for appropriate scenic background, here a dry, inimical patch of desert, unfruitful to both man and beast. Then, back inside, the first awesome step forward, the cultivation of corn, shown in a case that traces it from a small weed to its large present types.

The Pre-classic and Teotihuacán hall confronts you with an imposing wooden panel suspended from the ceiling and grooved out to make space for extraordinary figures. Accompanying them in the vast hall, in subtly illumined cases, on plinths, on panels of terracotta and wood, the pottery and sculpture of this early time, several examples gathered together as they were found in an excavation site not far from Mexico City and, in the open area, a crude cave roughly scored with symbolic designs of ancient, lost significance. Outside the cave, and actually an annex of the upper halls, is a beguiling compound of Tarascan homes with ornately carved pillars (on the porch a rush raincoat used by local farmers), a neatly arranged kitchen, a carpentry shed, and a stall for the cow, a real cow wearing a restless bell.

The hall of Teotihuacán might be too much—so many incredible objects—each calling for close examination were it not (and it cannot be stressed too much) for the equally incredible arrangements using various heights and forms and materials as platforms and cases. It is a stunning hall, truly, as total entity and as the gathering of the artifacts of an awesome society—a strange vase like a fat chicken with the face of a vulture worked in bits of jadeite and pink shell; a baroquely painted wall, nervous with repetitions of running ornaments; a brilliant reproduction of a portion of the Temple of Quetzalcoatl with its jutting heads of plumed serpents, symbols of the sea, and terrible round eyes like the mouths of cannons; elsewhere (and what is placed where always seems the perfect choice) a fine polished green stone torso and groups of superb masks.

And on to the more naturalistic art of the Toltecs, which plucks out characteristic essences and expresses them in the sparest, essential means, as in a stone macaw and the plumed head of the god Quetzalcoatl. Then, if you've lasted, time for a rest in the long, calm court and continue on the other side, leaving the *sala* of local cultures, Tenochtitlan, for last. Oaxaca shows its ancient stelae engraved with the oldest recorded dates and calendar symbols, a section of the geometric designs of the walls in Mitla, the famous *"Danzantes"* panel in Monte Albán, and, against a diversity of backgrounds at differing levels, the fine, elaborate pottery of several periods of its long-lasting culture.

One can go on endlessly, pointing out, describing the wonders of each culture, the differences and the influences among them, through the extraordinary sculptures of the Olmecs, the naïve young gods of the Huastecs, the bent, slack-bellied old fire gods, the gleeful goddesses, the charming toys, and elegant pyramids of the ancient citizens of Veracruz; the aristocratic soaring genius of the Mayans; the less sophisticated achievements of northern peoples whose work is, reasonably, like that of our Southwest Indian tribes. But books have limited space and travelers have tired feet and distances to go. However, save time and energy for the climax, the central hall of local cultures, which uses, to show its terrifying splendors, strong porous dark-red stone contrasted with gray-brown dividers of several heights and terra-cotta platforms. The fearsome, fearful tone of the Aztec religion is set as you come, very soon, to the huge face of a nocturnal, jaguar god who guards an immense blood-sacrifice vessel whose base shows two figures of gods performing blood-letting on themselves. Back of him, dramatically centered and fixed in a disk of light, is the famous Calendar Stone, whose magnificence has not been, and cannot be, diminished by its billion reproductions on souvenir leather. Its immense bulk is masterfully incised with a multiplicity of Aztec symbols of time and the elements. The intrepid early church fathers must have found it threatening, since it was buried, rather than destroyed, shortly after the Conquest; rediscovered and reburied about a hundred years later and then, according to John L. Stephens:

> In the year 1790, two statues and a flat stone, with sculptured characters relative to the Mexican Calendar, were discovered and dug up from the remains of the great Teocalli in the plaza (Zócalo) of the city of Mexico. The statues excited great interest among the Mexican Indians and the priests, afraid of their relapsing into idolatry, and to destroy all memorials of their ancient rites, buried them in the court of the Franciscan convent. The calendar was fixed in a conspicuous place in the wall of the cathedral, where it now stands.

The widespread tight control exerted by the Aztec empire becomes vividly clear in tables of accounting: what tributes were received from which peoples as well as estimates of what might be expected, depending on the productivity and population of a province, careful bookkeeping that rivals that of the Romans. For such power to grow and endure, the gods had to be fed, and the hall shows how the human heart, the greatest of all sacrifices, which would keep the sun rising each day, was cut out of the bodies of living men, and the bowls and instruments that were used. But not all of the art served the gods; for his own delight and that of the beholder, the artist worked wondrously spare, quintessential, almost abstract figures of a large red grasshopper, a big green calabash, and a shining black monkey whose body swells to vase shape.

Then, back to fearsome matters in the shape of a group of skeletal women who died in childbirth and since disturb the night with their lamentations; nearby lie colossal stone serpents (larger-than-life was the usual scale of Aztec art) of a geometric, brutal beauty, and beyond simple brutality, a fearsome platform of skulls, and a headless earth-death goddess, Coatlicue, who wears a necklace of human hands and hearts and a skirt of woven snakes. For relief, again, look at the highly sophisticated pottery of the Aztecs: the masterful head of a warrior emerging from a serpent mask; a beautifully sculptured ring which narrates the deeds and powers of Huitzilopochtli, a war god; a large frog carved and etched with sure, knowing economy; and a huge lava-stone turtle of imponderable age.

Don't neglect the remarkable codex that tells, in a few significant, dynamically drawn symbols, of the wanderings of this people and, continuing on in an imitation of the codex style, panels that show the rapid conquest of much of the rest of Mexico by these same wanderers once they had found the place where their prophesied eagle held a snake in its mouth. The charts continue as codices to show the terrors of dreams and forecasts that weakened Moctezuma and, finally, the Spaniards with their horses. Nearby, a map of the city of Tenochtitlán before it was ravaged, a well-planned example of early urbanism, each street named and each part of a clearly designated section bordered by canals and roads and an artfully detailed model of the crowded Indian market. The climax of this section of the hall is a large-scale model of the sparkling, worldly city of gardens and palaces and temples, of great wealth and magnificent princes, so unbelievable that the well-traveled *conquistadores* could compare it only with the fantasy cities of high romance. Even Cortés, who could hardly be considered a sentimentalist or an aesthete, expressed regret at destroying "the most beautiful city in the world."

The upper floors, devoted to present rural descendants of the peoples represented below, is much lighter, appealing matter. Separated by handsome, easy, free-flowing dividers are habitat groups of the major living cultures, meticulously and colorfully arranged with life-sized figures working, hunting, taking care of children, dancing, participating in their particular ceremonies. Nets, crafts, costumes, the shapes and types of materials used for shelter, household objects, and musical instruments (and piped-in music they produce) are cleverly displayed in their dazzling variety and appeal.

The museum, which asks very little for the sight of its treasures, deserves a week's visiting, two slow hours each morning, to absorb some large part of what it offers in its unstinting magnificence. That, however, is much to ask of many a traveler; make it at least two sessions, selecting from a chart offered you near the entrance. Or, if you absolutely must, wait for a guide (free), who will give you a respectable, if confusing, once-over. Keep in mind that the museum is closed on Mondays, open from 10 A.M. to 6 P.M. (Friday to 8 P.M.) other days, that the Salade Orientación asks a small charge in addition to the entrance fee, and that there is a pleasant restaurant and a café-automat on the grounds. (You may be aware of or even controlled by an increased number of guards made necessary by a devastating recent theft.)

Chapultepec Castle   (Museo Nacional de la Historia.) As one hears again and again, the time for a visit to the castle is on Sunday, when the park is at its best. Spending Sunday in the park in Mexico City is an effective way to fall in love with all Mexicans, the girls in their hoop earrings and gauzy skirts, the boys with ascetic faces and strong black, black hair; the little girls shown off in the dresses of flamenco dancers—ornate combs in their hair, carefully lipsticked and powdered—the starched, dignified little boys, the baroque babies; the bundle-carrying mothers (lunch, a strip of cloth to sit on, changes for the baby), the fathers whose parental pride keeps them fussing over hair ribbons and collars askew. The park is vast and lovely, shaded by ancient trees which may have hung over the gardens and zoos of Moctezuma and laced by paths with romantic names: a path of the poets, a path of the philosophers. Inside the rich tropical greens the rowboats glide, the balloons float away, families engulf prodigious lunches. There is the man with the puppets, the man with the trained dogs, the man with the monkey act—all seriously attended to by wide, black eyes whose accompanying mouths are wrapped around soft-drink bottles or ice pops. In a modernized section of the park there is a perilous-looking loop-the-loop (shielded from the road by a big screen, so as not to distract drivers), a children's train, and a well-equipped and very pretty playground. Beyond, fountains and fountains and lakes centering on Rivera mosaics and one of the lushest restaurants in Mexico City or anywhere, for that matter.

The castle itself stands at the very peak of Chapultepec Park. Because Maximilian and Carlotta had extensive changes made and used the castle conspicuously in their conspicuous short-lived Mexican time, the castle is often considered to be of their founding. Actually, late-eighteenth-century viceroys built over what was very probably an Aztec fortress. Later the building was put to military uses, extensively rebuilt in a vaguely Tuscan style by Maximilian, and still later used as the presidential residence until the time of Cárdenas, whose egalitarian sentiments and principles could not sit comfortably in an imperial castle. No president has used it since and now it is the Museum of National History.

The museum has been for some time in the restoring and rearranging stage, but even as it now exists, it presents Mexican history, roughly from the period where the Anthropological Museum stops through the revolution of this century. Vestiges of the Conquest remain as early baptismal fonts, sections of armor and arms, early maps and books. One odd, crowded painting, sectioned and numbered, pulls together most of the events of the Conquest; inept, but it solidifies the reality. Another room hangs portraits of dour ecclesiastical worthies and, among portraits of Spanish royalty, the strange, narrow-eyed face of Juana la Loca (the Mad), who was the mother of Carlos V, the king of the Conquest.

Time and adroitly arranged space march on to the eighteenth century with a precise model of a ship which carried wealth to Spain and brought back products to sell, prelates, and governors. We soon reach the struggle for independence of the early nineteenth century. Its heroine, La Corregidora, is sculptured and colored to appear indomitably realistic, down to the holes in her ears. Father Hidalgo's chair, documents bearing his signature, his inkwell, bring him into the present, as do the mementos of Morelos, among them a colorful jacket returned to Mexico from Spain a century after it was carried off. Drums, small cannons, a Virgin of Guadalupe, carried by the insurgent forces in 1810, a large copy of the early "Bill of Rights" proposed by Morelos (whose tenets, as in all idealistic documents, have not yet come to full fruition) lead to a huge curve of wall painted by Juan O'Gorman, which gathers the salient conflicts and characters of the period of 1784 to 1814.

A long hall of furniture, exquisite glass, ornamental swords, fine vases, and portraits of the rulers of the first half of the nineteenth century. Then, the famous passionate mural by Orozco: an immense head of Juárez emerging from a red cloud of victory, leaving below a defeated church and army, monstrous politicos and monarchists, and the cadaver of Maximilian, a long rope of shrouded flesh supported by bloodless aides. A bronze of Maximilian, delicately featured with a luxuriant beard, divided and carefully curled, contrasts tellingly with the unadorned, craggy face of Juárez, to whom, naturally, much space is given. It is surprising, however, to find Imperial gestures in the homage done this egalitarian Oaxacan Indian—laurel circlets, a silver-leafed wreath, lavishly worked, and bejeweled medallions.

One mounts a lordly stairway to a good collection of photographs of the more recent revolution (notice how many Mexican women fought along with their men), this display followed by an interesting group of etchings, watercolors, and genre paintings that show certain aspects of life and dress in the nineteenth century. Juan O'Gorman appears again with a large, clumsy mural of the conquest of space which bears one interesting detail, the poet-king Nezahualcoyotl trying to fly with broad bat wings; he was apparently early Mexico's Leonardo. The revolution soon returns, roaring to its apogee in a theatrically angled mural by David Siqueiros, one of Mexico's prides and a bone in its now-temperate throat because he was an important functionary in the Communist Party. One branch of the government gave him a showcase for his talents in this museum while another put him into prison for disruptive acts inimical to the government. One hand blind to the acts of the other is a common habit—and possibly must be—of governments, but in Mexico the contradictions are starker. The mural, however: an endless row of bloody broken dead reaches into bleak hills under a violently hot sky and hundreds of figures, including Karl Marx carrying a red-bound copy of his *Kapital*—inevitably a reminder of Mao's little red book—rush forward into the struggle between the workers and the Díaz forces. Porfirio Díaz sits enthroned, his foot on the Constitution designed by Juárez, surrounded by top-hatted anguished cohorts and frantic can-can-shaped ladies.

Not too far away, several levels down from this crest of the hill, meanders the Gallery of the Struggle of the Mexican People for their Liberty. The rooms curve and coil, space is skillfully broken and adorned to avoid the monotony of a continuity of great events in Mexico's liberation—an illustrated history book that uses models, photos, music, and spoken commentaries to infuse interest and/or patriotism in the visitor. It all leads to a sort of Pantheon with a white marble floor that holds in its awesome space nothing but the Mexican flag, clutched by a cactus-design ornament, the Constitution of the United States of Mexico, and above it, an immense eagle holding, as always, his serpent.

(Small charge, less on Sunday. Closed Mondays.)

Still continuing downward (ask your way as you go), look in at the round museum of **Arte Moderno,** arranged in wedgelike sections to show its paintings, and the adjoining, more complex, building that shows sculpture and mounts exhibitions of Mexican and foreign art.

Anahuacalli   (The Diego Rivera Museum.) Calle del Museo, off the Calzada de Tlalpan, which carries a directional sign to the museum.

Rivera's extraordinary museum, built on a height flattened to resemble a Mayan ball court, was designed by the artist and furnished with his collection. It takes the architectural habits and details of the pyramids of several cultures and melds them into an imposing gray structure that carries the formidability of the pyramids of Teotihuacán and Tula. The same use of pre-Hispanic forms runs through the interior: Mayan arches used to enclose and set off gods and figures and pieces of pottery; slabs of onyx between strips of stone used as windows; ledges to hold objects suggesting stepped pyramids.

It is as fine a collection as one might expect from so ardent an antiquarian and patriot and brilliantly displayed under mosaic ceilings that repeat the ancient symbols. The objects range over several cultures in a long stretch of periods, and you may feel you have had enough with the Anthropology Museum. If you have the time, though, and enough interest, go—if only to see the arrangements made with a painter's eye to effects and the large collection of objects from Colima and Nayarit, for which he apparently had a great affection. Here we find the plump little dog-vases and birds, the affable, playful people busy at their various chores and diversions: a sleepy-eyed woman resting out her pregnancy, a woman rolling out tortilla dough with a young child clinging to her back (you might see her today in a remote village), a wary soldier, and the inevitable and always enchanting lines and rings of dancers. In a central section of this floor you will find a large photo of a plump, elderly, sad-eyed man at an easel, the artist himself. The photo is accompanied by sketches, studies for murals, and a startlingly precocious drawing of a train made when the artist was less than four years old.

Up and up one goes, past the fanged masks of Oaxaca, a photo mural of the pyramids of Tajin, highly sophisticated pottery, and a ceiling of rough, vivid mosaic depicting birds, men, plants, and animals, to the very top level. Surrounded by mosaics, figures, and an architectural ornament that resembles the Aztec Calendar Stone, one looks down to find the surrounding terrain still fairly rural and close by, neat rows of corn set in two high islands of earth surrounded by volcanic rock, so old and constant a Mexican sight that one feels it to be an essential part of the museum, a subtle summing up.

(Should you be there near the Day of the Dead, you will find an enormous display of objects that form Mexico's Monument to Death.)

MURALS

A good way to see the great three—Siqueiros, Rivera, and Orozco—together is on the upper floors of the Palacio de Bellas Artes, the **Museo Nacional de Artes Plásticas.** Some years ago, Tamayo was gathered back into the fold and given wall space, and although his subject matter is as nationalistic as the others', the differences in drawing and technique make clear why, in addition to biographical fact, Tamayo was not, for some years, considered to be of the "Mexican" school, although essentially unmistakably Mexican. And while you are in the Palacio have a look at the work of Goita, the masterly fierce engravings of José Guadalupe Posada, whose revolutionary anger and imagination strongly influenced the great muralists, the highly sophisticated "folk" art of Ferreira, and see which current painter, photographer, or craftsman is being shown.

El Palacio Nacional, on the east side of the Zócalo, is inhabited by a vast array of Rivera murals which march back to pre-Conquest days and forward into hopes for Mexico's future. If the strong, brilliant murals don't exhaust you, examine the building itself, believed to be on the site of Moctezuma's Palace; its wide Colonial body supposedly incorporates Aztec stone. It was Cortés' palace-fortress, continued in use as the seat of viceregal government, both before and after the destruction of the building by riot and burning late in the seventeenth century. It was later rebuilt to its present width, then heightened by a third story and remodeled and resurfaced in the late 1920s.

The **Ministry of Education,** on Argentina, near Venezuela, is a comparatively new building based on traditional form. The walls of the offices and special sections were painted by Goita (a very old man who leads the life of a slum recluse now—if he has not died—and who painted the powerfully moving scene of mourning women which hangs in the Bellas Artes), Mérida, Montenegro, Siqueiros. Whether one can see these paintings is a question of what rooms are in use or closed at any particular time. The stairways and walls of the patio are public, however, and almost entirely the domain of the luxuriantly prolific Rivera. Painted in the twenties, they provide a wonderfully rhythmic panorama of regional folk life, beautifully conceived and painted, and don't let the color blind you to the lovely grisailles.

El Palacio de Justicia, at the southeast corner of the Zócalo, is an Orozco showpiece, and there are smaller works (Mexican artists occasionally suspect their authenticity) in the **Orozco Museum,** at Hamburgo 113.

University City is a roll call, as you know, of established Mexican artists who, in the large dramatic Mexican gesture, sculptured, mosaicked, and painted vast areas of the fantasy school.

POLYFORUM CULTURAL SIQUEIROS

Rather far out on Insurgentes Sur, almost attached to the big, blatant, and for years unfinished Hotel de Mexico, resides David Siqueiros' monument to himself, which is not to be scorned or overlooked. As one approaches it from Insurgentes, an almost impenetrable wall of worked metal suggests waves, birds, and music, and beyond, a wall of abstract painted panels is followed by a section composed of many screws, locks, bits of metal pipe—the densely arranged (and quite attractive) detritus of a machine shop. On entering, one is greeted by a set of enormous polyforum murals in the darting, stabbing style of the Master, warm, strong busts of Orozco and Rivera, among other Mexican artists, and a close look at the deep-blue pools that will make part of the handsome surrounding area.

A modest amount buys admission to a show of modern ghostly shapes or beguiling Colonial paintings, for sale. Elevators like bullets take one below to yet another extraordinary large crafts shop, beautifully arranged and with choice pieces of the full gamut. (It's amazing how much of this exists and how engagingly it's shown.)

The heart of the matter here is the Foro Universal, which is shown fairly frequently as *Son et Lumière,* although even unlit and unsung it is an impressive Siqueiros work. It is an immense, almost circular room ringed with figures (some in relief) in a strong angry slant, reminiscent in portions of Orozco, that reenacts Mexican history. "Painted with violence" are the *conquistadores* and their monks; women fleeing with their babies; Mexican humanity wrapped in trees and fire; the great Mexican earth mother. A remarkable piece of punctuation halts this angular flood of figures and their flow into the ceiling as abstractions. These are, at either side of the room, two sets of outspread hands, one purportedly female to symbolize peace and love; the other masculine for science and knowledge. There are women who may not like the sharp distinction, but the hands are, nevertheless, a stunning conception.

Quite another sort of adventure is the passage through spiked, sculptural forms thrusting out of a fountain to the Hotel de Mexico for lunch (if that is still possible) in its sky restaurant. Unless work has progressed at a more promising rate, it will be an uncomfortable ride forty-two stories in an elevator that passes through open construction floors and is sometimes pelted with loosened stones. If the smog is not too heavy, the view of the endless city and its contrasts is fascinating; some prefer to view the sea of lights later on and dance to the music of the restaurant's nightclub combo. (Check before you go. Like a number of Mexican enterprises, this one can halt suddenly for lack of funds, dissension among owners, a strike.)

BUILDINGS

The first buildings after the Conquest were the dour Gothic fortress-church-monastery ghettos, still extant not too far from the city—at Tula, Tepoztlán, Cuernavaca, as well as other parts of the country. Once safely established, the Conquest gave way to more relaxed architectural amenities and began to import the very distinctly Spanish "plateresque" style—Gothic and Moorish overlaid with escutcheons, flowers, leaves, scrolls, etched in the precise, delicate manner of Renaissance silversmiths, from which the style derives its name, *plata* meaning silver. The reaction to the ease of the plateresque was a cold neo-classicism shaped after the Escorial in Spain and sometimes referred to as "Herreriano," after Herrera, who worked with Philip II on the stern monument of the King's self-immolation. The breakthrough came soon after, in the baroque of the seventeenth century, trailing wisps of the plateresque with its handsome, somewhat restrained ornamentation, then becoming thicker, more exuberant, more crazily convoluted, producing façades and altars which explode with excess. This style—or lack, as some critics would have it—is the dominant mode in Mexican Colonial architecture, the "Churrigueresque," a hyper-baroque named for José de Churriguera, a Spanish architect of the late seventeenth and early eighteenth centuries (and his numerous brothers and sons) who can hardly be reproached for *all* the jungles of decoration his followers devised. The wild laughter of the Churrigueresque was silenced, later in the eighteenth century, by a return to the rigidities of another bout of neo-classicism; and thereafter Mexican buildings followed—with some time lags—that which was fashionable in Paris and Madrid.

Armed with these notes of a very swift flight through Mexican architecture (pre-Cortés buildings are dealt with in other sections), you might like to look at some, all, or none of the following, remembering that many of them have only partially survived floods, earthquake, revolutions, changes of fashion, and civic improvement.

The patio of the **Convento de la Merced,** at Uruguay 170, in the Merced market area consists of a set of richly carved columns and arches surrounding a gracious, dignified courtyard, thoroughly worth searching out.

Banco Nacional de Mexico, at Venustiano Carranza and Isabel la Católica, built in the latter half of the eighteenth century, has a noble façade and generous stretch of gray arches and balconies, as appropriate to government wealth now as to private wealth then.

The **Church of La Profesa,** at Madero and Isabel la Católica, the remains of an important Jesuit enclave, is one of the best of seventeenth-century baroque buildings.

The **Iturbide Palace** was the residence of Augustín de Iturbide, the first Mexican emperor after Moctezuma. It was built by the same architect who designed the Palacio Nacional, in the eighteenth century, and is by some accident remarkably well preserved.

The three buildings above—as well as a good number of other Colonial buildings—can be combined with a visit to the **Monte de Piedad,** or breakfast at the downtown **Sanborn's** on Madero, architecturally distinguished in its own right. It was built in the late seventeenth century as a private mansion. The legend is that its construction was the answer of a worthless son to an exasperated father. Papa said son could not build a house of tiles. Goaded by what must have been in its time a stinging phrase, the son showed papa. The tile-covered surface (commonly known as "Puebla-style") brightens a corner of stolid bank and office buildings, and the interior affords easy lessons in Moresque tile work and Churrigueresque ornamentation.

Almost before the houses, bridges, records, and art works of Tenochtitlán had stopped burning, a church was built by the *conquistadores,* somewhere near a great Aztec temple in the Zócalo area, and of course incorporating its stones. Some twenty-five years later Philip II decided that Mexico needed a full-fledged cathedral, but it took another twenty years before the stentorian voice of royal command was heeded. Interferences of various kinds, by man and nature, delayed it further a hundred years, and the building of towers still another hundred. Finally completed at the end of the eighteenth century, it had grown in a variety of changing fashions, and although imposing, is neither pleasing nor aesthetically impressive. The cathedral bears fascinating details, inside and out, and its vastness and the life around it are worth some time, however.

The **Sagrario Metropolitano,** which appears to be a wing of the cathedral although it was originally a separate church, was built late in the eighteenth century and is a perfect bubbly Churrigueresque whole with an artfully worked façade and a collection of distinctive works of religious art.

Where the Calle Zapata meets Santísima, there is another Churrigueresque gem, **La Santísima,** a church of the latter half of the eighteenth century, with an exuberant façade and an interior stripped of interest.

On Vizcainas, just east of San Juan de Letrán, there is a superb baroque building (ask for the **Colegio de las Viscainas**) which bears not only the name of the street but the distinction of being one of the earliest schools in the city founded by Jesuit fathers. The caretaker, an amiable man (for a tip), will let you look inside if school is not in session. Beyond the proud Spanish entrance of gray stone in the dark-red bricks, a splendid courtyard centers on a great fountain. Take the time to walk around the building to find several little hidden streets of old houses and at the back of the school a row of low dark-red and gray early-eighteenth-century houses whose street floors are inhabited by small workshops. At Isabel la Católica and Uruguay stands the **Biblioteca Nacional,** which had been the Church of Saint Augustine in the sixteenth century, later destroyed and rebuilt. You probably won't get to see the documents, but it might be of interest to know that this is a treasury of Mexico's history, not all of it yet catalogued.

Before you sell yourself to the blandishment of markets, you might look around on Arcos de Belén, which is spotted with a few very early churches, and, quite near the market, a large and lovely Colonial fountain. (And, as was said before, and probably will be again, look sharply as you walk. Alexander von Humboldt, the nineteenth-century explorer and naturalist, called Mexico City a "City of Palaces." Many of them are desiccated old ruins, cut up into slum hovels, many have disappeared, but the searching eye still finds some.)

New buildings don't have to be located. They hit the eye with varying kinds of impact. Imaginative playgrounds and housing projects, diversely designed and decorated and—unlike some of ours—pleasantly mated to human living, are growing up all around the city; office buildings and hotels surprise, shock, and charm with their flights of architectural fancy. As for the middle-aged wonders of late Victorian accretions of turrets, gargoyles, stained glass, and conspicuous consumption, old neighborhoods still hold a few.

For those interested in inexpensive public housing, there is the large Alemán project in a working-class *colonia* east of Insurgentes Sur, along Cuevas; a pretty set of houses, decorated with mosaics and graceful stairways and balconies, near the city's immense new medical center on Avenida Cuauhtémoc; and the apartments near the Plaza of the Three Cultures (page 44). There are, of course, others just completed or in the building. Hotel employees usually know, or inquire of the bilingual policemen who patrol tourist areas. Find out, too, where there might be a new Félix Candela building or church, always worth searching out.

AND MORE MUSEUMS

The **Museum of Graphic Arts,** on Mar Arafura, number 8 (Tacuba), has a remarkable collection of seals, codices, books, printed matter, and matter for printing ranging from pre-Columbian to modern times.

The long-developing **Museum of the City of Mexico** is in working order, in the house of the Counts de Santiago de Calimaya, at Pino Suárez 30 (check hours).

The new **Centro Cultural,** near the Presidente Chapultepec Hotel, shows American, European, and Mexican art.

ON HEARING AND SPEAKING SPANISH

If the man is his words—which are an approximation of his thoughts, which motivate his conduct, which reveals his outer character—an examination of the eccentricities of his speech should give some clue to the "Mexican." The adroitness of Spanish verbs is a dance of letters and syllables slipping before or behind a root or noun to weave shades of meaning or neologisms. The verb *flitear* was invented to accommodate the advent of Flit, for instance. A change in one vowel in a verb may change flat, unemotional certainty to doubt, regret, sadness, happiness, hope—a gamut of subtle shades that plays like light on water and is often as evanescent.

One of the odd enchantments of the language is that it is heavily garlanded with diminutives. Most commonly, as elsewhere, they are endearments. Sometimes they serve as intensifications of meaning: *chico* means small; very small becomes *chiquito;* and further diminution brings us to *chiquititito.* Often, the more diminutives hung on to a word, the less its connection with verity. *Hay sol* means the sun is out, but if you are in an excursion boat under a cloudy sky and the boatman hopefully says there is *solecito,* beg to be taken ashore before the descent of a storm that maddens the quiet lake. The first lesson in Spanish that a tourist should have is that *ahora,* meaning now, when spoken with no embellishments usually means a sober intention of getting a thing done soon; the addition of one diminutive ending—*ahorita*—lengthens the chain between promise and deed; *ahoritita* propels possibility into improbability; *ahoritititita* becomes a joke.

Also there is the malleable, impersonal reflexive *se,* which not only changes meanings but makes possible a charming and bewildering climate of irresponsibility. One doesn't break a glass: *se me rompió,* which means that it broke itself for me, or against me, or at me. Bargaining elicits not the crude: "I can't sell it cheaper," but "one cannot"—*no se puede.* A woman doesn't lose her bag: *se me perdió*—it lost itself. To be late is explained away by *se me hizo tarde*—a mischievous unseen third-person "it" made itself and me late.

If *se* is not convenient or correct to use, it is thickened to the third-person plural: "they" did it; "they" told me, even when the agency is singular and easily identified. The aura of vagueness and shunning commitment clouds even simple purchases: three mangoes are bought as *como tres*—like or resembling three, avoiding the harsh statement of specifics.

Possibly, the use of the impersonal, uncontrollable powers—"it," "they"—and the carefully sustained vagueness may be both cause and effect of fatalism whose reverse side is a gay casualness. A Mexican will, with charm and the utmost sincerity, declare his affection, admiration, and profound need to see you again, very soon. The chilled Anglo-American temperament gathers this welcome around him happily, warmed by the charm and animation, the glow in the deep-brown eyes, the eagerly given gift of love, and settles into it as in a warm perfumed bath: he has arrived, he is being accepted by Mexico. Then, nothing happens and continues not to happen.

We begin to feel unloved, unwelcome, guilty about being awkward gringos with huge feet, each one of us responsible and defensive about the annexation of Texas, "Yankee imperialism," the mess in the Middle East, the threat to the world's monetary systems, and the Cuban economy. There is no solace in being hurt or angry with your new Mexican friend; it serves nothing and is unjust. *Se* intervened and manipulated his life in some untoward way and the untoward attracts the Mexican more than you do. Novelty and surprise are the salt and pepper of his life, which is why he is devoted to the capricious Mexican leprechaun-god *se*.

Also, death waits around the corner and time is an Indian giver's present, too erratic a thing to be caught and divided into boxes of hours and days. *Mañana* need not be precisely "tomorrow"; it may be a wave of tomorrows carrying unseen flotsam in the wash of time—a fiesta, a collapsed car, a change of mood, a new face—to be enjoyed as it swims by, if "God lends us the time."

Another fact to know about the language and the man is that the words "to expect," commonly used for "to hope," are the same as those for "to await." There are fine semantic games in this one: sitting in a rural station (or an urban station, for that matter), you have waited for a time beyond the most generous limits of expectancy; you continue to sit, having gradually entered the condition of hoping that there will be a train, any train, anytime. You made a date with a friend, expecting him at about four, since you had agreed on three o'clock. At eight o'clock you hope his car hasn't collapsed and he with it. The next morning you await a call of explanation, then you hope nothing has happened to him, etc. etc., and finish up with a combination—you expect and hope that he will be in touch with you one of these days and keep waiting for his call.

Overemotional and exaggerated phrases make a conversational baroque which the Anglo-Saxon ear rejects in disbelief. Ask someone his address, and having told you, he will add, "There you have your house" or "My house is your house." (Apparently, the only person in Mexican history who took the statement seriously was Cortés.

According to his chronicler, Bernal Díaz, Moctezuma said this to the *conquistador,* who took not only the house and later its treasures, but the complex of treacheries and fealties of the whole Aztec Empire.) Admire something—other than a child—and you will be told it is yours. A "thank you" may elicit "to serve you." An introduction is often acknowledged with "at your command." None of this is servile or self-seeking, or an indication of intense gratitude or devotion; they are simply leftovers of Spanish courtliness, the lace cuff on the plain New World suit.

In the realm of sentiment a wide gamut—from the lightest breath to the heaviest hand—is run. In *amor* anything goes: the limits are wide and gaudy, streaking the conversational sky with great criss-crosses of rainbow. Shelley's "I die, I faint, I fail" are bloodless mutterings compared with the locutions of a Mexican in the throes of romantic love. Elsewhere, the touch can be light and glancing: one doesn't slam a man down with "He is disagreeable." He is, instead, "little amiable." You are urged to be quick with the use of the sting-removing diminutive: *"Venga, por favor, temprancito."* To use *temprano* (early) might be construed as pressing. No one wants to press, you understand, but be sweet and come on time, gentled and seduced by little *ito,* the primary tool of Mexican persuasion.

The elusive, the uncommitted, the vague, the elaborate can make pretty knots of incomprehensibility, as in this sentence in a report concerning the denial of asylum to Dominicans in the Mexican Embassy at Ciudad Trujillo: "Asylum was denied [them] because it was distant from total doubt that one was not dealing with persecuted political persons."

There is no need to speak Spanish in the large centers. As a matter of fact, it is sometimes difficult to practice one's Spanish in Mexico City; everyone is dedicated to practicing English on visitors, shaming us with their fluid command while we totter through the simplest statements. No matter how Anglophile your tongue, learn some Spanish greetings and words of politesse which will open for you all sorts of doors. Mexicans are so charmed with a *norteamericano* who tries that they move with his mental processes in an extraordinary empathy (or, possibly, experience has taught them that all tourists have pretty much the same needs and troubles). They hand-feed you the essential words for which you are groping. A sympathetic Mexican can make you feel that you know Spanish; it's your tongue which is stupid.

Also, study the stances and attitudes of conversation. A Mexican conversation, tête-à-tête, is an animated, graceful act. People of the mountains have a great talent for silence, but the tropical and city Mexican likes sound—radios, jukeboxes, *mariachis,* and constant talk—and will fill any pause with conversation, as a piece of politeness, and because he has no doubt that anything he has to say is of considerable interest. He will repeat phrases and ideas several times, but rarely becomes dull because his straight man, the listener, is so intense a participant. His eyes glow, he smiles, he melts, he frowns, he is delighted, he is appalled; he is completely immersed in the flow of words and keeps it going with murmured encouragements: *"Claro, pues sí!"; "Qué bueno!"; "Qué linda!"; "Ai, lástima!"; "No me digas!"* Mexicans have a knowledge that we have lost or never achieved: it takes two to make a good talker—the confident actor and the responsive audience.

Other than its obvious usability, a knowledge of Spanish opens several arcane worlds. For instance, that of the truck and its driver who describe themselves in large hand lettering as "Old but Lovable," "The Undaunted," "Bloody but Unbowed." Or a country saloon which calls itself "What Are They Whispering?" Or, to translate back into Spanish from menu English, *"Douche en orange juice"* (they mean "duck") and *"Shrimps in Broobe He Venecia Styl."* (There are Americans who cherish the mystery of "Broobe" and go to some lengths not to find out what it is.) And there is the pleasure of picking up a newspaper to read about a few women who were sent to jail because they were *"pupilas de una casa de escándalos"* (pupils of a house of scandals), or an essay on Proust.

There is a particular reason for a woman to understand some Spanish. How else would she recognize the verbal flowers thrown in her path? And, if she isn't quite *that* young and lovely and the word *guapa* (handsome woman) is wafted to her, and she doesn't turn or smile (which she shouldn't) and is followed by an indignant "For God's sake! Can't you even say thanks?" she might enjoy knowing what has been going on.

Spanish will enable you to play the game of diminutives and discern the echoes of class attached to the courtly *"hágame el favor,"* to the middle class *"por favor,"* to the cajoling, peasant *"por favorcito."* And should you be attending to a day's attack of *turista* (in spite of the rumors, it is not inevitable), but are the intrepid type who doesn't take the first plane home, and you've finished your book, there's

Mexican radio. With Spanish one can inhabit the wonderful universe of Pepsi-Cola ads, for instance. An old, toothless female voice wheedles, "Buy me a taco." Old, toothless male voice: "Sure, they're delicious." Vigorous voice out of the wild blue: "Delicious? Pepsi-Cola is *more* delicious. Drink Pepsi!" Distraught female voice screaming: "I can't stand it any more! *You* pay the household bills. You don't give me enough money to cover them!" Sturdy, helpful voice, soothingly: "Calm yourself. Have a Pepsi." Siren's voice, dulcet, with a little rasp of passion: "Darling, please buy me another diamond." Salacious male voice: "What? So that you may be even more delicious?" Voice from the void: *"More* delicious? Pepsi-Cola is more delicious." With sequiturs quite non and a cheerful, mindless panacea spreading over a wide range of inappropriate situations, the possibilities are very diverting. Between the announcements you might hear a recital of Mexican poetry, a survey of cultural news around the world—what the Yugoslav Opera is doing and what paintings are being shown in Madrid—and a flat-footed, pedantic analysis of Mendelssohn's "Midsummer Night's Dream Overture." If you're for lighter stuff, there is plenty of "rok" in Spanish, complete with the taffy-pull syllables; the yearning and burning of love songs; the regional songs by turns poetic, cynical, sentimental, and bawdy. And, without Spanish, how could one be grateful for the sponsorship of *"Mox Foctorrr de Hawlywoot, naturalmente"*?

(A tip for sounding more "in" than you might be: Mexico City sounds the *s* in *"buenos días"* and *"buenas tardes,"* but chooses to say *"mucha' gracias"* and *"buena' noches."*)

Mexico City: The End

COYOACÁN, CHURUBUSCO

Among Mexico City's many endearing young and old charms is the fact that starting at some central point one can travel in almost any random direction and in an hour or two arrive at a point of high interest. Day after varied day one can meet with a country market, a crafts village, a hoary monastery, an archaeological site, deep woods and lakes, a spa, and often, a number of them together, ringed by mountains.

On your way to or from the inevitable trip to Xochimilco, leave some time for Churubusco and Coyoacán. The latter can be reached by southbound bus (check), marked "Coyoacán," on Insurgentes Sur; if you're traveling by car, follow Insurgentes Sur or Avenida Universidad.

On the historic square stands one of the oldest Dominican monasteries, in sad shape but still an impressive pile, and its accompanying church, San Juan Bautista, built in 1583, about fifty years after the completion of the monastery. Across the square is the local city hall, usually identifiable by the presence of a few non-militant soldiers. You will be told by locals that this was another palace of Cortés. That Coyoacán was one of the first seats of Conquest government is true, that Cortés was here is true, and that he tortured Cuauhtémoc here is probably true. The "palace," however, is baroque of the mid-eighteenth century, but—to assuage the romantic breast—it is quite likely that it was built on the site of Cortés' house and offices. Another such anachronism is a seventeenth-century house, a lovely old thing, attributed to Alvarado, Cortés' right-hand man, who must have been well dead when it was built. (Moral: Never altogether believe or altogether disbelieve anything you learn in Mexico.)

As you walk past the splendid gates and doors of the cobbled streets (Francisco Sosa, particularly) under the ancient trees, look for the simple sixteenth-century Casa Ordaz, and then go on to another old house, rather startlingly colored, at Londres 127. This was the home of Diego Rivera and his painter wife, Frieda Kahlo, who was born in it. It is now officially the Frieda Kahlo Museum. She had a strange and bitter history which displays itself over and over again in her paintings and in the objects she collected. A victim of paralytic polio at the age of five, she was later, at sixteen, in an automobile accident which broke her spine in several places. The crippling, the long imprisonment in casts, the pain, and the fact that she could have no children dominate her paintings. She pictures herself pierced with numerous large pins which hold her to a broken stone column, her own spine. In another horrifying painting she is on a hospital table holding a mesh of blood vessels connected to a flower, a machine, a cradle of pelvic bone, a fetus, and a puddle of blood. Still another depicts her own adult face—an unforgettable one—over a small body and baby legs, nursing at the breast of a huge woman whose face is a dark archaic mask, as if to say that she was revived and sustained by Mexico. Not all the paintings are so nakedly of pain and painful: she painted some vibrant portraits, and some of her early paintings— she was largely self-taught—have the innocent, literal appeal of *retablos* (votive pieces). But one always returns to death: two immense skeletons flank one doorway; everywhere, among the collections of toys and archaeological objects, there are Day of the Dead figures; in the studio, the wheelchair she lived in and, on her deathbed, the long cast she wore, brightly and defiantly painted.

Into the light and life again—the mellow gardens surround some good pre-Cortés sculpture and a miniature pyramid holding a thatched temple.

NOTE: Closed Mondays; open 10 A.M. to 2 P.M. on Sundays; 10 A.M. to 1 P.M. and 3 to 6 P.M. on other days (check). Small admission fee.

Go on directly eastward a short distance, to the neighboring suburb of Churubusco, for a stroll through its venerableness and its baroque Franciscan *convento*.

On the site, originally, there was a temple dedicated to the war god, Huitzilopochtli, whose image was found in a cave by early nomadic pre-Aztecs and whom they named the Hummingbird Wizard because he spoke with wisdom, and in whose honor they later tore a mountain of hearts out of captive bodies. Because of his potent influence—Huitzilopochtli was the Mars-Zeus of the Aztec pantheon—the church fathers demolished the temple and built a church on the site, using some of the early stones, the classic practice of the time. After the destruction of this first church a more ambitious structure was built to the glory of Saint Matthew, in the latter half of the seventeenth century. Like a number of monasteries it echoes the severe imperial mood in which Cortés pronounced, "We are the emissaries of a great king, a great God and a great Church and, as their spokesmen, we are right and have rights which cannot be denied us." The thick heavy walls, built to last forever, lead into an endless flow of rooms and in and out of subdued monastery gardens. One goes through long corridors and rows of ascetic cells, to a refectory containing a massive table, into a small ornate chapel, past religious paintings and portraits of Spanish worthies, and then to a door which opens on the well-kept church. In spite of its chapels and religious paintings, the building might have been a stronghold of medieval warriors; the only room which evokes the atmosphere of peace and contemplation one looks for in a monastery is the library with its row on row of large, handbound tomes.

One section of the monastery is now a museum which displays mementos and portraits and carriages which might appeal to the lover of minutiae or a close student of Mexican history, particularly of the Mexican-U.S. war. (One of the important battles took place here.) The edifice, however, is the thing: the ruthless might and confidence of the Conquest in one sturdy, stubborn structure.

Before you are lost in the lures of the Bazar Sábado or stunned by a monumental meal in one of the restaurants of San Angel (marked as "Villa Obregón" on many maps), walk around that suburb itself. The most imposing sight on the wide sky is the tiled domes of the secularized Carmelite church and monastery right off the Plaza del Carmen. The interior is a gathering of many periods, and some of it should not have happened. Much more interesting in its odd way is a crypt full—if they haven't been moved—of mummies, hideously well preserved (something in the air, altitude, and impenetrable walls) and distressingly stylish. Out of the still, cold air of the crypt, take the sun in the plaza and colorful streets (look for one called "Lágrimas" and its tangents) that surround it. San Angel is an artists' colony of sorts and some of the inhabitants of the suburb try to keep its flavor old and unusual even if that means Tudor-style beams.

A glance at the map will show that San Angel is neatly located for sharing a visit to Coyoacán and Churubusco, eastward, or University City and its accompanying piece of modern fantasy, the *colonia* of the Pedregal, southward, and further southward, the "pyramid" of Cuicuilco.

University City has to be seen to be believed—and then not quite. Carrying with it the students and faculty of one of the oldest scholastic centers on the continent, the university flew out of its Colonial buildings in the old city and soared right into the twenty-first century. And yet, by gathering dozens of its most notable architects and artists, and their large entourages of craftsmen and laborers, the city repeated an ancient Mexican ceremonial act, the building of a new, splendid learning and art center—as the Mayans had at Palenque, as the Zapotecs at Monte Albán, the Toltecs at Tula—displaying again the grandeur and the profligacy of decoration of the antique cities. Like them, it is a compendium of accumulated designs and skills. The low, thick walls along the paths echo the shape of pyramids, some of the stonework repeats the building practices of antiquity, enormous walls of the bold, big buildings are covered with murals and mosaics in wide overall gestures that stem from the temples. Stunningly contemporary it is, but the newer music is wonderfully blended with older sounds.

University City covers quite an expanse and you might be tempted to let the sports stadium go. One shouldn't: it is a remarkable structure which holds countless thousands of people and seems as light as a china saucer. (Also, you might look for the statue of the official founder of the City, ex-President Miguel Alemán. It was demolished during student riots in 1960 and later caged off for protection and repair. If he has been carefully restored, back to the original shape, he should bear a strong resemblance to Stalin.)

Just west of the university is the Jardines del Pedregal, a wild and wonderful dream of upper-class housing which floats over a sea of black larval rock. It shares the mood of its neighbor, an intensity of Mexican modern driven to excesses which are, in this place and in this country, thoroughly appropriate. Rocks and trees walk into the house, wood and glass walk out of it, brooklets run through it like household pets; shapes startle and colors dazzle out of the bitter, craggy black earth.

The lake of dried lava which covers this area is believed to be the result of an eruption of Mount Ajusco, toward the south. In its devastating flow it covered the "pyramid" of Cuicuilco (near the suburb of Tlalpan), a crude mound, built over earlier mounds—an almost universal practice in temple building—which suggests an ur-design of the grander structures to follow. There are no evidences of aesthetic drive or great skill, but you might want a look at the oldest building this side of the Atlantic.

TULA: CLOUDS OF ARCHAEOLOGY

An easy trip to Tula in the state of Hidalgo affords a shorthand account of a number of kinds of Mexico and a trip into a maze of Mexican archaeology. A bus or a train plus local taxi gets one there in a little over two hours, but it is better to hire a car or make a deal with a taxi driver.

The drive northward on the Querétaro Highway, direct and clearly indicated on maps, leads past the tall and strongly colored sentinel pylons which guard the busy Ciudad Satelité and through miles of industrial enclaves whose wastes spread a brown blanket on Mexico City and its wide environs. The road continues through agricultural country of green and yellow fields rimmed by white-capped mountains reaching into the low, wide sky and the restless clouds, and then into Tepeji del Río, an indication that Tula is a short distance away. (Watch out for the *topes* entering Tepeji, and other towns and avenues in Mexico City as well. These are mammiferous metal studs set into a road to remind you to slow down; that life is, in spite of all you hear, at least semiprecious in Mexico. A disregarded strip of *topes* retaliates with a nasty, sneering jar, disconcerting to the car and a driver's confidence.)

In Tula the road leads to the central plaza, typically Central American in its inviting thick greenness and forbidding stone benches sharply marked with the name of the donor. The band kiosk, absolutely essential whether it ever shelters one toot of a trumpet or not, is *echt*-classic in several questionable styles, a heavy roundness held by neo-classic pillars and surrounded by ponderous lattice supports that look like gun emplacements.

Off to one side of the square and dominating it is the Franciscan monastery and church built in the middle of the sixteenth century—a huge fortress and factory of new souls, built to awe, to last, and to protect itself from its recalcitrant savage neighbors. The church has suffered considerable improvement, particularly in the addition of the ubiquitous new white and gold on columns and on the graceful rhythms of the old vaulted ceiling.

The old-time religion which the monastery vanquished only partially was ensconced in the capital city of the Toltecs, a short distance outside the town. Now a wind-swept hilltop of ruins, self-destroyed by the poor materials of which it was built, beaten by weather, strangled by foliage, razed and stripped of its treasures by pre-Conquest conquerors, it was once the majestic city of the great Quetzalcoatl.

As in all sightseeing, there are two ways to approach the buildings: see them first and then read about them, or buy a leaflet full of measurements and other specific details, and as you go, check off fact after fact—like German tourists checking the catalogues of the Uffizi. For the casual visitor, it is probably best to approach the bare, half-hidden buildings and accept their assault without too much learning, at first.

Quite naturally, the lower sections of the structures and their carvings—some still in color—will be examined first. The height of the drama comes with the appearance, at the top of one pyramid, of a set of immense stone Quetzalcoatl-warrior monoliths wearing the intransigent expressions and wide headdresses of kachina dolls. Along with square, carved columns and round columns incised with beautiful serpent-feather motifs, these golems were apparently designed to hold the roof of the temple which once existed on the flat top of the pyramid. The atlantes, the experts say, represent Quetzalcoatl not only as a warrior, but Morning Star as well, a rather incomprehensible juxtaposition. Even for archaic Mexican art, which was often evocations of terror, they are forbidding; there is no run of curves anywhere along their height of fourteen feet and, in spite of their awesome height, they look crushed downward and inward, gasping for breath. The large butterflies which appear as heraldic symbols on the massive chests, the bows, weapons, sandals, and bracelets are all angular, squared-off, compressed by their rigid space. To place them in a more familiar context: imagine the issue of a Léger man and one of Piero della Francesca's impregnable Virgins, then press the monstrous child into the shape of a square column.

For most of us a favorite—because it is easy—conception of Indian cultures is that each was contained in a separate box: this was exclusively Mayan, that distinctly Zapotec, the other purely Toltec. Here, a conspicuous section of wall consists of horizontal bands of geometric meanders strongly reminiscent of the Mixtec patterns which cover the burial site at Mitla, in Oaxaca. One stumbles on a "Chacmool," with his raised knees and alert listening look, who belongs with the "Chacmools" in Chichén Itzá of Yucatán, Mayan country. He is not Mayan and may not even be "pure" Toltec. He appears in other cultures, but was probably taken to Yucatán by the Toltecs, who imposed their might and culture on the Mayans. Ergo, Chichén Itzá is no more "pure Mayan" than the Chacmool. A large, carefully marked area limits a ball court. The Mayans had ball courts, so did the Totonacs and so, it is believed, had the Olmecs, who are currently considered—by virtue of their antiquity, influence, great skills, and evidences of wide domain—the forebears of many of the later cultures. The collared jaguar of the Tula friezes appears in Chichén; the eagle-serpent-warrior here is also a constant of Aztec iconography; deified Quetzalcoatl became the famous "Feathered Serpent" of a number of peoples. Clearly no culture stayed for long self-contained, no more than it did in the Near East and Europe, nor could it resist the constant interflow of influences.

This mélange might sort itself out a bit with the help of Tula's still uncertain, tentative story. The story of the sacred city of Tollán (as it was referred to in Indian chronicles) starts, to our knowledge, in historic times—about A.D. 900—as recorded in Indian codices and, later, in Spanish records. From the northwest, a horde of nomads who spoke Náhuatl (the root language of Aztec tongues) descended into the central valley of Mexico led by Mixcoatl, whom Miguel Covarrubias describes as "sort of an Indian Genghis Khan." He became the first ruler of the kingdom of Tula, which comprised several groups of indigenous peoples in addition to his now domesticated nomads. His son, the resplendent Quetzalcoatl, was the next ruler, and it was in his reign that the Toltecs had their Periclean Age: the land superabundant, the people prosperous, the craftsmen richly productive, all their robust activity shone on by lordly palaces full of exquisite rarities.

A new invasion brought a wave of barbarians from the north and the Toltecs, under Quetzalcoatl, moved on to Cholula, where an immense pyramid—the largest in Mexico—was dedicated to the priest-king, who had begun to take on the blinding splendor and mystery of a god. In the repetition of invasions which were Mexico's history early and late, the Toltecs later migrated to Yucatán and pressed the Toltec stamp deeply and squarely into the refined flourishes of tropical Mayan art and architecture. Toltec art spread its long outstretched fingers southward and eastward, leaving its plumed serpents and guardian Chacmools scattered over a large part of the country, and the Aztecs who, like the Romans, had a good eye for the art of a subject nation, took over and built *their* crescent arts on older Toltec forms.

This schematic plan of the travels and influence of the Toltecs seemed to work more or less; and then a group of archaeologists found Toltec qualities in the art of the Huastecs of northern Veracruz, not quite the usual direction. At another time savants who had been sure that the Teotihuacán culture which produced the great Pyramids of the Sun and Moon outside of Mexico City was older than Tula, that Teotihuacán was "Tollán," reversed themselves and decided that Tula was older. They may change their minds again.

And to get back to the Huastecs; they are now believed to be an offshoot of Mayan peoples. Were they late migrants, already a mixture of both cultures? What was the course of *their* history?—all of which thickens complications.

These shifts and uncertainties in archaeology are indicated to comfort the nonexpert, to prove that confusion is not a flower of his own ignorance, to suggest that many problems of Mexican prehistory end either in a question mark or a swamp of collateral problems. To solve them fairly soon much of Mexico's population would have to be involved in digging up its 10,000 or more known sites and searching out those yet unknown; an army of guards would have to see to it that stelae and friezes were not carried off for farm fencing; a large labor corps would have to keep hacking away at voracious jungle; the government would need to train and pay a host of archaeologists. As it is, the not overrich Mexican government, with an assist from

North American foundations, is doing valiantly to clear the complex picture of pre-Cortés cultures, but until the distant day of sharp backgrounds and precise lines, one must accept some fact, much hypothesis, and a great deal of imaginative conjecture.

A short distance from Tula, at Actopán, is a church and monastery of the Augustinians, built in the middle of the sixteenth century. Unlike some of its compeers it has a certain chic, compounded of a rather jaunty tower, like those the Moors left in Palermo, and a stately fan of exterior decorations.

Or, if you're out for adventure, ask a boy to ride with you from Tula to the "Balneario" and he'll direct you over a minor road to a swimming place fed by thermal springs. Accommodations are fairly simple. Lunch can be bought, but it may be gone before you get to it on a weekend, or not there at all on a weekday. You will probably have packed a lunch, in any case.

MORE TRIPS NEAR THE CITY

Assuming that you want to spend some time in the hinterland, day trips around the city must be limited. However, for those with energy, curiosity, and time to indulge them, the following suggestions:

No one comes to Mexico City, or should, without seeing the great pyramids at San Juan Teotihuacán, about 32 miles from the city, northward. They can be reached by bus, first and second class, but the easiest way to do it is to hire a car or join a tour arranged by your hotel, making sure you will stop at Acolmán (page 108) as well.

By the time you get to the pyramids, you will probably have read and heard more than you can absorb or remember. If by some chance not, a tour guide, or a guide at the site, will dizzy you with measurements and statistics. Remember that they get carried away, as all good guides should, and that the Pyramid of the Sun is *not* larger than the Pyramid of Cheops, nor even the largest pyramid in Mexico. No matter how colorfully or fervently it is said, this was *not* an Aztec city; it was dead for centuries before the Aztecs came upon it. It was very likely *not* the great city of the Toltecs, Tollán. For lack of surer information, it is designated as the religious center of a very old people classed as the "Teotihuacán" culture. (In spite of the above, your guide may be conservatively well informed, clinging carefully to what he has been taught in the government training courses.)

Friday in Toluca (good bus service or by car on a smooth highway) holds as much as any day can hold. The market that day is enormous and the hawkers in best voice. What with the multiplicity of objects, the calling, and—once in a while—the being pulled into a stall in the manner of the old East Side in New York, exhaustion soon sets in. Stay long enough to see, among the thousands of things you won't want, many of the good crafts objects you will want. Try, also, the local fruit "wines"—more thin syrup than wine, but part of the whole experience—and look in at the Museo del Arte Popular. Then go on to Calixtlahuaca, a huge city, only partially exhumed, of a culture which indicates Aztec influences, earlier Toltec influences, and connections with cultures to the west, links which may prove very important in determining the chronology and spread of Mexican cultures.

Or, you might want to take a ride up Toluca's gleaming snow-capped mountain for some awesome views. (Check road conditions, and skip it if there have been heavy rains.) Or take a ride to the cool, remote beauty of Valle del Bravo, where you can lunch at one of its inns.

A few minutes south of Toluca, on the Ixtapan de la Sal highway, is Metepec, a crafts village which makes charming clay objects. Its market day is usually Monday, but any other day will do. These people want and need to sell and are happy to make the effort at any time. Or, you might instead turn off the road at La Venta (nearer the city) and take a stroll through the pine woods of "El Desierto de Los Leones," a former Carmelite retreat and now a national park. (Why this heavily wooded area is a "desert of lions" is a secret that died with the monastic fathers.)

More murals? An easy ride along the Mexico-Veracruz highway to Los Reyes, then left on the Texcoco road, takes one to Chapingo Agricultural College, once a hacienda, now a government school. It is a highly respected school and well equipped, but its high fame rests on an extraordinary set of murals by Rivera, considered by some critics the peak of his achievement. They deal, of course, with the Revolution, but here it relates to agriculture in a superabundance of colors and shapes.

Texcoco, the big market town nearby, had its days of glory when

Nezahualcoyotl, the poet-king, reigned. He was apparently a highly civilized man who tried to discourage human sacrifice, who established a center for arts and sciences, and was himself a prolific writer. Texcoco reflects little of that grandeur now, but it is the center of a *serape*-weaving area (bump your way through Chiconcoac, a *serape* village about three miles out), the market is lively—full of the coarse heavy wool sweaters you may or may not find more cheaply in Mexico City—there are a couple of Colonial houses and, all in all, Texcoco will present you with a picture of a typical town of the area.

More pyramids? More Churrigueresque? Take Insurgentes Norte and turn off northwestward toward the suburb of Tlalnepantla. Very close to it is the pyramid of Tenayuca, distinguished for the fact that it is supposed to be a purely Aztec edifice. At least its outer layers were Aztec (these were constructions superimposed on each other at intervals of fifty-two years, the Aztec "century"), built not very long before the arrival of the Spanish. Continue on from Tlalnepantla northward past Cuautitlán and on to Tepotzotlán, about 25 miles from the city. Very well preserved and lovingly cared for, Tepotzotlán is the apogee of Churrigueresque. Every inch is colored, carved, gilded; flowers, saints, urns, cherubs, squares, curlicues, trills, flourishes crowd each other in a wild splendor which the Counter-Reformation would not have dared in Europe. Very wearing for anyone with a taste for cool, spare modern but in its own insane way exceedingly attractive.

NOTES: As has been said before, one's own car—hired, with or without a driver—is best for these trips. But if that is difficult, a tourist agency will arrange matters for you, or include you in one of its frequent tours. And if you find yourself with a loose hour or two, head for any little village in the vicinity. You may hit a market day, or a local fiesta, or weaving or clay molding, or just dogs, chickens, children, and shy women around a dusty plaza around a foolish bandstand; some surprise or other always awaits.

Market days in the local villages are apt to be miniature repetitions of what you'll find in the city on any day, but the crafts villages are something else again. (No guarantee that they have not turned to other endeavors.) Several have already been mentioned but a few others, not always easy to get to, particularly when dirt roads turn to mud, are Lerma, on the Mexico-Toluca highway—for palm weaving, baskets, and furniture—and several villages southeast of Lerma:

Ocoyoacac, Tianguistengo (Tuesday market), and tiny villages nearby for more basketry, weaving, and embroideries. (You'll need some Spanish or a guide to discuss prices.)

MINOR SKIRMISHES

THE BATTLE OF THE MANGO

The mango, or sticky, season starts in May and ends in July, time enough to enrich the stay, glue the fingers, and stain the clothes of most summer visitors. There are several ways to eat a mango: one is to peel the skin down halfway from the thinner end, then nibble and chew around the flat, hirsute pit, then turn it and proceed on the other end; another method is to cut the mango in half and dig under the skin and around the pit with a spoon. The most refined method is to use a mango fork (one long center tine and two short tines flanking it) forced into the stem end of the fruit. Slices are cut off the sides and scooped out, the rest is peeled and nibbled at, runnily, like an ice-cream pop. No matter what the procedure, mangoes leave an aromatic, thick, moist sweetness somewhere.

Buy several mangoes (one is never enough if you like them at all) and take them to your hotel. Start running a bath, strip, and eat the mangoes while sitting on the edge of the tub. Then, slip into it to remove the rivulets of mango juice from hands, arms, chin, chest, and knees. (Advice given by Charles Flandrau over fifty years ago; it hasn't been improved on yet.)

THE BATTLE OF THE HAMMOCK

Since the essence of a hotel is beds (and many tropical Mexican hotels don't move far from the essentials), they have them in the inns of Veracruz, Campeche, Yucatán, and the Isthmus, but strictly for tourists, who steam in hot beds behind closed doors. An open door— availability to inspection by anyone who passes—is not conducive to rest; tourists are very private sleepers, particularly compared to country Mexicans, who don't consider it sinful either to be publicly asleep or to observe sleeping. Somehow—maybe childhood memories of hammocks on lawns—sleeping in a hammock seems less a violation of privacy, a hammock less shameful a place than a bed. Lightly dressed, one lies, or tries to, in one of the hammocks slung across a porch, or balcony, or the room itself.

A hammock can be, if not properly handled, a thing of light, playful malice. The single-bed size, considerably more capacious than our back-porch fixtures, gathers its fine cords into a silky elusive rope and mirthfully swings its slender length away from inept efforts. Once you've opened a core to lie in, the hammock may slip from under you and slide you onto the floor. If you manage to stay neatly plastered into its center, you may wake up with a stiff neck and mangled back. The secret is to lie across it on a diagonal.

The wide, hospitable *matrimonios*—double-bed size—are used head to feet by twosomes, on a slight diagonal. The physics of stress and strain create two long nests with a low mesh of wall between man and wife, a delightful situation for quiet, confidential talk, but what of other matters? One asks tactful questions; then, less tactful questions, with significant emphasis on the bountiful procreation of the tropics—practically no woman between fifteen and fifty-five without a baby in her arms or the visible proof of one soon to be carried. Love in a hammock still remains a mystery to the northerner. Here, as elsewhere, though, love obviously finds a way.

THE BATTLE OF THE TELEPHONE

The easiest call to make is over long distance to the States, via operators who speak fine English and have a wholesome respect for the probable importance of such a call. Long distance within Mexico is something else again. First of all "National" as opposed to the "International" is frequently out to lunch or getting her collective hair done, no matter what the time of day; the phone rings and rings in an empty world. Ultimately—while you've filed your nails and read a page or two of the current *Time*—there is an answer, to the effect that the lines to Guadalajara or Morelia are busy, do you wish to cancel or have her keep trying? While she does, you might go to the movies—double feature—or wander through the labyrinthine markets.

Local calls within the larger cities can be made, of course, from a hotel room, with a switchboard operator or desk clerk to pave the way. The more intrepid, ready for high adventure, call from outside. First, find the phone. To have a phone means owning one and owning one means buying stock in the phone company. Little shops and some larger ones can't make the investment, so going to the corner drugstore won't necessarily solve your problem. If you don't see a sign of a telephone in your immediate vicinity, go into a prosperous-looking tobacco shop and say, with a rising inflection, *"Teléfono?"*

Examine it carefully. It may be one in a familiar style: you wait for the gasping dial tone, drop your token in, dial, and wait for an answer. But it might be of the French style which, after you've dialed and received an answer, requires that you push a button when you hear a voice; otherwise, it won't hear you. After searching, after finding, after waiting, after wasting several tokens in being slow with the button, the phone may die, though its ghost keeps swallowing tokens.

For getting rid of the anger, though it requires some knowledge of Spanish, dial any number and roar, "Whom am I speaking with? What number is that?" It may be an echo of class war that the owner of a Mexican telephone is put on the defensive; it is *his* business to be the right number and not your error. Or have a tequila and give the whole thing up.

The big fat phone directory which looks as efficient as ours may not be much help in looking up a name and number. Apartments are valued for the presence of a phone but the lessee is not always listed for the reason that the landlord retains ownership of the stock and phone. Of greater help is the Anglo-American Directory, which you'll find in every hotel and which is kept rather carefully up-to-date. For other nationals, try the embassies, send a messenger with a note, or hop a cab.

THE BATTLE OF THE FAUCETS

If they are truly Mexican they will be marked *F* for *frío* (cold) and *C* for *caliente* (hot). However, the mechanic may have been illiterate—even to this degree—or a country boy who doesn't know what a shower is for, or just a funny fellow who will feed for a long time on the joke of having reversed them. If the spigots are American, the variations become more complex: *C,* cold to you, may actually *be* cold or indicate Mexican hot. On the other hand, *H* may mean nothing to the plumber's apprentice and he will place it according to his fancy. Between his mental set and yours lies a sea of hazards, including freezing or scalding, or a rapid alternation of both.

The high point of this indoor water sport is a shower of all hot or all cold, no matter what the faucets properly or improperly say, or a small hiss or Bronx cheer from the shower head and nothing more, no matter how frantically you turn. For this, there is no solution except the release of complaint, which will bring you stricken, courteous apologies and a bucket of water. Or move to another hotel or another town, and join the battle as before.

CUAUTLA

The true believer in the magic of hot springs can take himself to San José Purua, which sits in a beautiful gorge just off the Morelia-Mexico highway—about halfway—and serves up sun, mineral springs of varying degrees of temperature and salubrity, nightclub entertainment, colossal quantities of food, and a good number of refugees from Miami, when the weather turns unfriendly there. Or, he can go to Ixtapan de la Sal, a more recent explosion of enterprise. It used to be, a few decades ago, a sleepy village, with one large, neglected Colonial hotel, a square vat filled with thermal waters which smelled like hot ginger ale, and a small volcano one could climb to look into its boiling, steamy crater. Now it has a well-fed country-club air, complete with golf course, hotels, shops; the springs run through marble baths, which can be hired—and a bed to rest in after the salubrious wallowing—by the hour. They call them "Roman baths."

For a more indigenous and less expensive dip in curative waters, try Cuautla and the villages around it, a beautiful ride (the monotony with which this phrase is repeated is simply proof of the extraordinary beauty of all of central and southern Mexico) of less than two hours by bus from Mexico City. It goes on through fertile green fields guarded by the famous snow-covered volcanoes, Popocatépetl and Iztaccíhuatl, the "Smoking Mountain" and the "White Lady" (more often called the "Sleeping Lady"), which cast their majestic glow over much of the central valley. Both Chalco and Tlalmanalco are appealing towns, and both have sixteenth-century Franciscan monasteries, not in very good shape but worth a long look.

Amecameca asks for a little more time. First of all, it lies against the sides of the volcanoes, a staggering backdrop for any town, and it is the point of departure for climbing Popo (neither easy nor recommended, except for the expert). Secondly, Amecameca is a busy ceremonial center. A cobbled walk leads upward through old trees and Stations of the Cross to Sacromonte, a famous sanctuary dedicated to the memory and legend of one of the first Franciscan friars, Fray Martín de Valencia, one of the handful who endeared themselves to the Indians. Pilgrims, often on their knees, stopping at each Station of the Cross, make their labored way to the Holy Friar during Easter Week, often on All Souls' Day and the Day of the Dead. On the day of the Virgin of Guadalupe (December 12) they visit the chapel dedicated to her, not far from Sacromonte. For the less devout, there are the beautiful views and a voluble Sunday market.

The ride, by good road from Amecameca to Cuautla, takes one through Alpine scenery so convincing that its homes and hostels have names like "Little Switzerland," "Chalet Maierling," and "Wienerwald." (If it is time for lunch, resist the cuddly names and look instead for a restaurant once run by a Catalan family that made extraordinarily good sausages and pâté. Look for a sign, FABADA ASTURIANA, near the entrance to Popo Park.) The tropics take over before you reach Cuautla and the good-looking, traditional clay-and-thatch silo that stands near the road.

If Cuautla has any particular religious drive—other than the habitual Catholic observances—it is to take good care of its health. It strolls slowly through the lazy, tropical streets to air itself in the plaza and stops to buy a tonic in one of the innumerable drugstores. Sometimes it sits among the immense rubber trees in the plaza, trying to adjust to the ornate, silvered metal benches, gazing up at the tall, becolumned bandstand, or peers into the metalwork ateliers on the calle de la Union or Ayala. Or it searches the large section of medicinal herbs in the market for a more venerable elixir and then wanders on in the market to gaze at the new horseshoes, the carved baby chairs, at the unusually good huaraches and the red and gold velvet hearts of several sizes to pin on child-saint figures. To search, also, for juicy pineapples, neat, boxlike piles of thin, thin meat called *cecina,* and the pans of bugs—alive and crawling over each other—used for making tamale sauce. On its unrushed walk it looks into the very modern nursery school, decorated with ingenious paper work and bouquets of Mexico's enchanting young.

After an energetic day or two at the **Hotel Vasco**—walking to the pool (apt to be emptying or refilling in the middle of the week), maybe swimming, maybe sunning, ambling through its large gardens and maze of bungalows, and surrounding the long undistinguished meals in its dining room (or a cheaper meal, also large and quite good for the price at the Tlacuaut restaurant across the road)—one is ready for an outing. A few miles away, a short distance off the Yautepec road, is Oaxtepec, supposedly an area where Moctezuma did some of his gardening and, inevitably, possessed of an old monastery now brought up to date with thermal baths, a hotel, restaurants, and a sky-lift. Or, take the short ride to Agua Hedionda, where you can soak in a hot sulfur pool or sip the yellow water.

The time to be in Cuautla is the weekend, when half of middle-class Mexico City—especially its Middle-European citizens—pours itself, its bracelets, its water wings, its children, its maids, and its gaiety into the local pools. While you're in Cuautla you might want to nod at the monument which commemorates the victory of Morelos and a small number of men over the much larger Royalist forces which had held the town under siege for three months. And bow, too, to Zapata, who sits on his famous horse a bit out of the center of town. He was killed in this area, shortly after the more recent revolution, a hundred years after the early storms stirred by Morelos and Hidalgo.

NOTE: There is a road from Cuautla to Cuernavaca with a turnoff to Tepoztlán, or you can continue on to Oaxaca, via the road that meets 190.

OTHER POSSIBILITIES: The ride to Tlaxcala and back. Tlaxcala was the seat of government of a people who were furiously anti-Moctezuma and consequently pro-Cortés and died by the thousands during the siege of Tenochtitlán to prove it. The town has declined from greatness, but it still surrounds one of the oldest churches, San Francisco, and in its environs are the remarkable Tlaxcalan murals of Tizatlán and the dazzling white Sanctuary of Ocotlán, a foaming of Churrigueresque whipped cream surmounting nubby red tile. Nearby are the weaving villages that surround the towns of San Martín Texmelucan and Santa Anna, and the imposing monastery of Huejotzingo—romanesque, some plateresque, and the indomitability of the rest of its kind.

You might also look at the bulletin board of the Mexican-North American Institute at Hamburgo 115 in Mexico City. The Institute organizes frequent and inexpensive day trips (usually on Sundays) to interesting places near the city. Language will be no problem, since half the company will be Mexicans studying English, the other half Americans learning Spanish. If you'd rather cope with the French-Spanish combination, see what the French-Latin American Institute (Nazas 43) has to offer.

The Poster Route:
Taxco, Acapulco, Zihuatanejo

Once upon a time there was a couple in Idaho whose farm grew very prosperous during World War II. They bought a new, powerful car. She put in a supply of new, boxy housedresses and had her hair cut in a square bob. He bought several Hawaiian shirts and laced his chest with amulets of new camera. They got into the car with their new purchases and chased down to Las Casas, near the Guatemalan border, and back in ten days.

Silly? Not especially, if all one wants to do—as they did—is say he's been; and only a bit sillier than going to Mexico and avoiding it. It is possible—and even easy—to live the U.S. life in the luxury hotels of Mexico City, to shop in its Continental boutiques and eat its international dinners. Then, undisturbed by Spanish (a guide whose English grew in the public schools of Chicago, for instance) and Mexican smells and tastes, on to the enchanted forest of Cuernavaca, that Cuernavaca whose inns drip bougainvillaea and Southern drawls and from which sorties can be made to other Americans on the square and for lunch in other American-speaking *posadas.* (For other Cuernavacas, see pages 158–190.)

The next stop on the stereotype trail is Taxco, the well of silver and a national treasure whose shape and character may not be tampered with. It is a self-conscious charmer busied with hotels, expatriates, artists, crafts shops, firework bulls, hard-working tourist saloons, an extraordinary cathedral built with silver-mine money, old houses, new workshops, streets that tumble and bump into each other and spill each other's flowers. The town is small and tightly cupped in the hills and densely inhabited by shops and cars. To see the nonhotel, nonshop Taxco one has to go down to the market or outside the corkscrew town.

NOTE: Should you visit the cathedral—and you should—in inappropriate dress, you may be handed a large apron to wrap around your offending limbs.

Another "must" in Taxco is the workshop of Jana at Fundación 8 to watch craftsmen bend and polish silver, sometimes gilded, into exquisite naturalistic forms; a rose worthy of the Rosenkavalier, poppies with trembling stamens, long fine sheaves of wheat and thistles with delicate, spiny leaves. For use as well as gazing at in awe, there are pocketbooks of silver mesh or vermeil, napkin rings, cufflinks, and stately peppermills. The prices are necessarily high but less than they would be at Tiffany's, where Jana's work is often shown.

Next stop, Acapulco: everyone's dream—and nightmare—of beach tropics. In this never-never land of beaches overhung by stage-set cliffs and giant luxury hotels, the fish chase the hook and shrimp is eased into one's mouth by beautiful, satiny beachboys. Long brown muscles stretch, turn, and shine in the sun, and stride the water skis. Celebrities in Acapulco, straw hats heavy with cuteness, paddle in rivers of rum while amiable ladies guide them to *their* particular ports. The abundant sun shines and shines, melting the brain and caution. It is great fun, a gold-plated Disneyland for large tots, and there are people who take one look and turn quickly back to three-dimensional, earthy Mexico.

Quite apparently places that have been so successfully attractive as these of the picture-postcard route must have much to recommend them, and do. The unjustly sour-toned descriptions above, loaded with subjectivity, are exaggerations and meant to suggest that the reader who has come so far go on and deeper, not necessarily in distance but in flavor and meaning, and not "do" Mexico by skimming over everything but its gaudiest flowers.

HOTELS

Taxco *(All American plan):* The **Victoria** was and is a favorite, knowing and lively (moderate); the **Monte Taxco** hangs over the town prettily and sports a pool and gardens (moderate); the **Rancho Telva** is an old reliable (moderate). For nonhotel atmosphere, try the **Haci-**

enda del Solar, a bit out of the center, a Colonial estate, refurbished elegantly with fine accommodations and houses to rent on the lyrical grounds (expensive); **San Francisco Cuadra,** out of town, an antique hacienda with a modern pool and a country manner (moderate); **Los Arcos,** Mexican pensionish, oldish, nice-ish (modest to moderate); **Hotel Melendez,** an old house in the fervid center (modest); **Posada de la Mision,** pool, murals and not far from good shopping.

La Casa de Dona Clarita (its formal name was **La Cumbre Soñada**) was the Valhalla of a Dutch, multilingual lady painter. It sat high, high over and around gorges on a rough road and maybe still does. The houses are charming, the food reputable, but unless you enjoy tootling up and down the edges of canyons via taxi, hotel car, or your own, or are looking for the total escape offered by a flowery, hospitable eyrie, think twice. High moderate.

If you are not staying, but need lunch, try the spacious—indoors and out—**Cielito Lindo,** a few steps from the cathedral, or **Los Balcones,** a simpler place that gives you views on the side of the cathedral and down to the plaza.

Acapulco *(Rates go down one-third to one-quarter from April through November, for which times you may not need a reservation):* The supply of hotels is boundless and by the time this book is published a half-dozen new Versailles will be pushing the others off the cliffs. Consider the **Pierre Marqués,** about 12 miles out of town, super-deluxe, air-conditioned, exquisitely manicured and cuisined. **El Presidente** is big, imaginatively decorated, and run by the same enterprising people who direct the El Presidente in Mexico City. **Las Brisas** is a delight of gardens sliding off cliffs and individual pools in front of pleasant bungalows. The **Acapulco Hilton** and **Acapulco Princess** (out of town) are also sybaritic and expensive, and the large **Hyatt Regency** lures guests with free-form package arrangements. Or you might prefer the big, shining **Copacabana,** expensive, or the jazzy **Condesa del Mar,** expensive.

A notch or two below, not far down: the **Caleta, Prado Americas, Club de Pesca, Costera**—all agreeable. More modest and still good: the **Pozo del Rey,** the **Papagayo, Quinta María, Las Hamacas Boca Chica,** and the **Areca Club,** which requires a taxi or your own car for beaching—all moderate. In addition to these, there are innumerable small places (and cheap) which change quite rapidly; some of them slide downward fast while others flourish into splendor. If you plan to spend time and not much money inquire locally—there is a tourist office—and inspect.

SHOPPING

Although it has some good fabrics and lovely cotton blouses among other lures, remember to save silver shopping for Taxco.

Most of the good hotels and several shopping centers offer dashing to astonishing sportswear and souvenirs.

Many of the talented tribes of Mexico City have annexes here as do posh American and European stores—witness a Cartiers and a Gucci.

ZIHUATANEJO

By bus from Acapulco or plane from Mexico City, you can reach Zihuatanejo, an old photograph of Acapulco thirty years ago, trying to catch up but still fairly untroubled. They're now calling it Ixtapa-Zihuatanejo to emphasize the new colossi springing up about ten kilometers from one of the few easily reachable tropical paradises left in this country. At this writing Zihuatanejo is possibly at its best; a little order—a pedestrian shopping mall its main street, air-conditioned airlines offices, good peripheral auto roads, a self-respecting airport, and a spate of restaurants that afford variety in cuisine and price—and lovely jungle disorder. A five-minute walk from the beach that fronts the town (and watch out for the boys casting for small fish and not reluctant to catch a gull, too), toward the hill of the hotels, the road returns to its old uncovered earth edged by a dense patch of coconut palms, tangles of low bush and vine, hibiscus, and a lazy, muddy stream oozing by mud and thatch huts, dusky naked babies, and the smell of fish drying in the sun.

There's a lot to do in Zihuatanejo without much effort. You can record the ebbing of tension and I.Q. as the sun melts and the waters lull you. You can busy yourself with the choice of today's beach. Shall it be the long white sands of the Playa la Ropa and seviche (marinated fish) and *huachinango* (red snapper) under the thatch of Las Brisas? Will you saunter down to the town pier and join a boatload (cheaper that way) for the few-minute ride to the beach of Las Gatas of the pale-green, clear waters held in smooth check by a seawall whose legend says that it was built for an Indian princess to protect her from the undertow and inimical fish? And will *sopes* (small, fried tortillas filled with beans and a sprinkling of cheese) and a rich, coconut sweet flavored with tamarind do you for lunch? How about visiting the town beach for a chance to watch sunstruck tourists stagger out of the small beachfront hotels sheltered by a bower of palms? You could drive up to the Ixtapa compound and beyond about three or four kilometers to the Playa Quieta, endless and silken with a pleasant alluring view of Ixtapa.

Toward late afternoon, have a drink on the terrace of one of the Zihuatanejo hotels that climb their own hillside and look down on the broken circle of bay, and notice the even cadence of the hills that rise from it. On the far hillside, lights gleam from the few houses and the town lights have begun to glow. The shrimp boats have dropped their mesh wings and one last excursion launch skitters across the bay like a dark water bug. The western sky is smoky purple streaked with pink and orange rivers on which ride little flocks of gray cloud like distant ghost ships. As the bold colors turn to lavender, the ghost ships darken and meld as flotillas, the gold on the water pales to silver, and the black hills spread the silhouettes of their trees against the star-sparked sky. And soon to bed to ponder the problem of which jewel of beach to loll on tomorrow, or delay the problem and go to the open-air movie house in the village to see a double feature (changed every night) of films whose vintage goes back to the time when Kirk Douglas' chin-dimple was sharp in a taut young face.

First off, go to the tourist office in town for a booklet that contains many ads and maps of the village and the beaches. You will have made your hotel reservations beforehand, especially if you plan to go during the Christmas season. Consider the semidetached beach and garden bungalows of the **Calpulli** at the end of La Ropa, whose restaurant-bar is a huge concrete *palapa* (usually a round thatch shelter) and whose entrance greets you with a Siqueiros-style mural of a militant with intense eyes who pushes a gun toward you. It is a fifteen-minute walk from the village, pleasant but hilly, and you'll probably want a taxi one way, at least. A beach bungalow for two, at moderate cost, includes breakfast and one other meal; courtyard rooms are a bit lower and suites several hundred pesos higher.

The **Sotavento** has rooms that rise high on the hill with a stepped series of balconies; moderate to expensive. The adjoining **Catalina**, a ranging old hotel (once barracks) with a funicular to lift you from the beach to its several levels, asks moderate to high rates. The **Irma,** nearer town, is well run, speaks good English—as do most of the hotels—and, because of the lack of public rooms, is quite chummy. The best double, with a balcony on the bay and including breakfast and dinner, should run moderate to high. (All the above have pools and lower their prices by about 25 percent in the summer.)

For considerably less and the right to roam for your meals, consider two small hotels in town: **Tres Marías,** in what is still referred to as the "old fishing village," which you reach via a plank bridge, and right on the town beach, the **Casa la Playa.** For this one wear ear protectors; the waterfront sometimes leads late hours.

There are a surprising number of satisfying restaurants in the village. The **Captain's Table** is currently a favorite with its sophisticated dishes—try fish in "1,000 spice sauce." **La Tortuga y la Rana** serve pasta in several styles, along with the full repertoire of seafood at about the same prices. Their specialty is a mix of coffee, Kahlua, brandy, and sugar, made in a style that combines sorcery and ballet. Good to drink, fine to watch.

There are several simple places along the main street (go past the left ear on the heroic bronze head of Guerrero) that will feed you decently. One, two blocks from the waterfront is a cool open place bound in ironwork which serves excellent shrimp, a good-sized *huachinango a la Veracruzana* (olives, onions, tomatoes, pepper, and a touch of spice) for less than two dollars, and a complete lunch including fish or chicken and superb milkshakes (have the mixed fruits, including red papaya, melon, banana, strawberries) for much less than MacDonald's might charge.

Puntaremos, across the plank bridge, is an old and popular establishment; go fairly early and expect to pay about three or four dollars for a dinner of extremely generous portions of meat or fish. Almost any corner, particularly on the waterfront, serves seviche, freshly made and moving fast. This is marinated fish dressed up with onions, pepper, tomato and a bit of chile, and a glassful, usually accompanied by crackers, very cheap for food worthy of the gods.

IXTAPA

Ixtapa is on the mainland, though it takes its name from an island. A **Holiday Inn** and another hotel are in the building. They and the completed and functioning **Aristos** appear like three sudden shouts from the desolate landscape which takes on, as you approach, gardens, restaurants, beach. **El Presidente** has arranged its wood and concrete and thatch to move low and companionably along the contours of its beach and manages to be quite engaging to look at, while the tall **Aristos** settles for angled balconies that have endless views over bay, sea, and mysterious hills.

Several services of the ambitious resort have not yet firmly jelled. But the water sports are well organized, the boys who anchor your parachute after you've swung through the air with the greatest of ease are strong and reliable, and, because Mexican resorts representatives have been scurrying around Japan and Europe, your room neighbors may speak Dutch or Icelandic or French or Japanese.

Camino Real—as always handsome, unique.

Hotel Krystal Ixtapa—luxurious and lively.

Ixtapa is now served, direct, by Aeromexico.

SEVERAL WARNINGS: Prices change and invariably upward. The tropics, though substantially cheaper in the summer, are also hot. The undertow at some beaches is strong; unless you are a strong swimmer, save your fancy strokes for the pool which every middle- and upper-class hotel keeps.

MEXICAN HOURS

1:50 *The driver closes the door of his bus outside the Querétaro station just as an old woman, dressed in the rusty black cocoon of perpetual mourning, shuffles frantically toward it, waving her shopping basket to catch the driver's eye. He opens the door and through her thin gasps learns that she has just missed her bus to Guanajuato. He lifts her onto the bus, and with much style and pleasure tears down the road to overtake her bus, terrifying by his speed, bulk, and confidence every other vehicle on the road. He and the old lady make it.*

2:00 *Again, the train stops. This minute's arrival is a tamale woman who sells them both sweet and hot. She has differentiated one from the other by marking the husk around the sweet-corn mash with a dot of shocking pink (a Mexican color centuries older than fashion's invention); the strong chile-centered ones are marked with a poisonous green.*

2:15 *The sun pours into the bus returning from Pachuca, baking the American woman in the window seat. The shade doesn't work and there is no other seat. She sits in molten somnolence, not bothering to look out or ask why the bus had made another of its short, eccentric stops. Suddenly, the beaming driver's assistant thrusts before her face a cerise ice pop, begging her to take it. He had bought it for her, he says, because she looked so uncomfortable, because he felt bad that he couldn't fix the shade, because it was delicious, and for* amistad *(friendship). Pleased and awkward, she turns it down politely; if amoebic dysentery has a color, that of the ice is it. He is crestfallen and she, realizing it would be doubly tactless to give her reasons, is miserable.*

2:30 *A tourist buys the billionth wallet with the Aztec calendar stone coarsely bitten into its leather. Like all the purchasers before him, he is vaguely moved by the incomprehensible design. Now he feels closer to the indigenous, the authentic Mexico, more strongly linked to its ancient, blood-drenched mysteries.*

2:50 *The five-minute bus stop at Salina Cruz has expanded into an hour. The passengers have gone from one beer to three. Some have settled down to a meal, others to the joys of mounting indignation because the driver seems to have abandoned them altogether. He returns ultimately, looking fresh and breezy in the intense heat, his curly hair glistening wet. With no apology and a broad smile, he informs his flock that he has had a lovely swim in the Pacific two blocks away, and now,* "Vámonos, damas y caballeros, por favor." *("Let's go, ladies and gentlemen, please.")*

3:00 *A broad stream of sound bursts from the working-class district behind the Merced market in Mexico City. It is the public bathhouse whistle announcing that the water is hot and ready for use.*

Cuernavaca and Environs

One hears from far off that the rich of Mexico City spend their weekends in Cuernavaca, for a new infusion of oxygen ("getting off the altitude"), for the greenery, the flowers, the country quiet, and the swimming pools. The anticipated picture is that of a cross between a carefully landscaped rest home and exclusive country club. In actuality one comes out of the mountains into a nondescript scramble of streets, growing narrower as one goes down and down into the crowded center from which the centrifugal force of the town churns and sprays out. (Buses leave frequently from the Autobuses del Sud terminal in Mexico City.)

Two contiguous little parks and the sidewalk cafés that border them constitute the three-ring circus that is a Cuernavaca weekend. The townspeople and visiting Indians from nearby villages watch with flat, motionless eyes the frantic assault of tourists on Cortés' old palace (at the side of the smaller parklet) with its famous Rivera murals and crafts shops. Or they play with their scrubbed Sunday-in-the-park-clothed children or they just sit, staring into a private, timeless place, or quietly enduring the throbbing agonies of a hangover. The immense Mexican sky is embroidered with clusters of balloons in the shapes of benign devils and playful octopi. The supposedly fresh salubrious air is thick with the odor of sweets and the exhausts of innumerable cars which move in a slow, viscous stream around the plaza. Toward evening the veil of fleeting dusk is cut by the flight and chatter of thousands of starlings, darting into the dark old laurels of the parks—that is, those left after a recent laurel slaughter. Early on Sunday evenings, a vehement band concert takes place with frequent intermissions of pleading by the master of ceremonies: "Please keep off the grass! Please keep off the bandstand! We are not inclined to use force, but we will have to ask for the intervention of the police if order and the proper distance from the musicians is not kept. Please, amiable citizens, please!"

The *ricos*—Mexicans, Americans, and Middle-Europeans—sit in the narrow strip of sidewalk cafés inhaling gas fumes and coffee, trying to make conversation searching, inventive, revealing, as they imagine it to be in Paris and Rome (where it is ordinarily no more stimulating than it is in Cuernavaca). Their conversational efforts often decline into a palsied set of head shakes—no, no, no, no—to the plague of persistent vendors who hop from table to table like bees for the honey of pesos. Miles of lottery tickets are dangled between coffee cup and face, each worth 2,000,000 pesos, and you have to wait only until tomorrow to collect. Swarms of little boys cut into the conversations with thrusts of Chiclet boxes. A moving warehouse of bark paintings, bad copies of Chinese art, *rebozos,* puppets, lanterns, aprons from Oaxaca, interferes with the view of the trunks of parked cars, like the behinds of glistening rhinoceri. The beggars bring their blind, pockmarked faces and gnarled hands close in; a young boy carefully displays a hideously crippled brother whom he carries on his back—his burden, his treasure. (Curiously, the one café which bars these people is rarely full.) Another café attraction is the opportunity to be joyously venomous about the visitors who come in from Taxco or Acapulco in tight shorts and beet-red faces topped by Acapulco hats—straw confections hung with miniature straw bicycles, animals, fruits, embroidery, and ribbons. The view into the park is more appealing. It is a corral of artificial horses and ponies superintended by photographers of rider-children. Near each man and horse stands a case of photos to display the skill of their old hooded camera.

Outside the confused and glutted center, almost too colorful, away from the cafés and the central shopping street of straw baskets and silver trinkets as thin and bright as tinsel, there are large closed gardens sheltering quiet houses and *posadas,* deep *barrancas* (gorges) with narrow streams flowing through them, streets that wind and twist through Mexican color and slums, lovely churches, verdant green, clouds of purple and red bougainvillaea, and flamboyants. Cuernavaca then becomes something like its advertised image.

Although it takes more time to get there via the old road from Mexico City, that ride is infinitely lovelier; it climbs up over the valley into hills and forests, opening panoramic views of distant mountains and plains, then slides into the town. Having negotiated the hazards of the center, dropped your bags, oozed in and out of the pool, you might arrange to drive around the outer areas of the town. (There are few, if any, cars to hire in Cuernavaca. If you don't have one, arrange for a taxi through the hotel. Taxis are expensive, for Mexico, and since it is to be assumed that your genial host gets a cut, the cost may come as something of a shock, particularly after the generous *pesero* rides of Mexico City. But then, not very costly by U.S. standards.)

For views of the non-American or European life of the city, there are one or two short walks to take. One can begin with the inescapable visit to the building which was Cortés' "winter palace" as of 1530, and which now derives additional strength and importance from art (Diego Rivera murals) and patriotism (a huge statue of the hero Morelos almost overtowering the conqueror's palace). The murals were a gift to the city from Dwight Morrow, once U.S. Ambassador to Mexico and resident of Cuernavaca. Considering that many Mexicans have thought, and some still do, of the U.S. as the land of latter-day *conquistadores* (certainly Rivera thought so, to judge from his utterances and paintings), the combination of American capitalist and Communist painter collaborating on a set of murals depicting the brutalities of the earlier Imperialists and the triumphs of the Revolution is odd. But as has often been remarked, diplomacy, money, and art make strange bedfellows. Done in 1930, the wall paintings are full of the round, affectionate rhythms with which Rivera embraced even his most brutal objects. Zapata is, of course, heroically simple, an appealing innocent, and his famous white horse as winsome and gentle as a unicorn. But the most living strokes and rhythms flow around the bundles of sugar cane, the piles of graceful fish, and mounds of mangoes like polished gold.

Outside the battlements reflecting imperious Spain stands the glowering Morelos (all patriotic monuments glower in Mexico), and although fairly modern, the great cemented blocks of stone stacked to build his towers of legs, the smooth tight, stone cloth on his head, the blind, angry eyes recall the Tula monoliths.

From the lower end of the castle, cross the broad avenue of Benito Juárez and walk down the curve of Calle de las Casas, a modest street in immodest colors whose rooftops set off shifting views of church domes and towers. It slips into the Plaza of the Second of May of 1812, just big enough to hold a circle of flower market. Continuing up the hill, turn right on Comonfort, an *hidalgo* of a street, still and reserved, disclosing nothing but dignified façades.

Returning toward the center, there is an opportunity to observe modern Mexico's omniverous tastes in architecture. The **Banco de Londres** is rangy, dignified, and Spanish Empire. A short distance behind is the **Banco Comercio de Morelos,** of flat glass and marble in late-Mussolini style. And just beyond, the **Banco de Mexico,** very modernly jazzy and the busiest and noisiest of the banks. The absolute in class is the private **Banco del Sur,** which encloses orchid plants as well as finance.

Another walk which reveals much of small-town, tropical Mexico starts with a cab ride, unless you actually want to struggle uphill in Cuernavaca's insistent sun. Ask the driver to take you to the **Casino de la Selva,** itself an imposing resort hotel which you might want to walk through; it has everything and a great deal of it.

Across from this Grossinger's of Mexico, and dipping downward from the road, is a beguiling park, shady and gracious and a fine place for picnicking. At one side and above the park is the **Internacional,** which sits on the Calle Cuaglia. Walk down this street, among its walled adobe alleys whose doors open sporadically to allow views of messy, lively yards swarming with children, chickens, radios, and potted plants in old tin cans. Look upward as you go at the small and rusty balconies laden with miniature jungles of plants and vines jostling each other out of the sun. You will walk under the arches of an ancient aqueduct and over a deep gorge cut by a knife of river and clotted with banks of elephant ears and thick sprays of fern. (If it interests you, this is a good street on which to buy used Mexican comic books. The local boys set up business on the sidewalk and while away the time between customers rereading old, old numbers—unless they and their families have been moved out and replaced by bepooled villas; Cuernavaca is like that.)

If you're in the mood for Sunday in the park, Cuernavaca style, a small sum will buy you entrance through the toylike castle of the **Parque Recreativo** and its row of inconsequential shops, gardens on several levels, a moribund zoo, and a toy railroad jammed with Mexican children. For gathering your thoughts together, go to the contemplative, deeply shaded **Melchor Ocampo** park.

To see a superbly restored hacienda busying itself with varied cultural matters, ask your hotel-keeper for the new "centro cultural" on the outskirts of town.

It is a long walk, up and hot, but you can be driven to the community of San Anton on the edge of town to walk a path down to a strong waterfall surrounded by dreadful souvenirs, or to buy an inexpensive large garden pot and have a simple meal or beer in one of the shaded eating stalls. It may be slippery going in the rainy season, but you are rewarded with the sight of orchids flaring from the sides of the waterfall.

The much advertised Borda gardens of Maximilian and Carlotta are worth seeing for their own sad self and to belie the impression one often gets of the light, airy charm and French gaiety which hung about the singularly innocent, singularly foolish couple. The gardens are forgotten and disconsolate: few flowers bloom in the shade of the large, dark plants and heavy, drooping trees; things grow upward a bit and then fall with discouragement; some of the once pretty fountains are dry, others trickle anemically. The whole is a Doré illustration or a late-Romantic minor poem (except in those months when crafts classes are held here for American college groups) and a fine place to escape the sun.

One moves from this sad softness to stern hardness by crossing to the medieval city of the Cathedral of San Francisco. The cathedral, originally a Franciscan monastery begun in 1529, is of the fortress-church-castle type seen frequently in southern Europe, like the great dour warehouse in Albi or the smaller, indomitable stone boxes that sneer down from the high banks of the Garonne. From a distance, the dome and the tower lighten the town; closer by, the great lengths of wall—marked in curious waves of discoloration as if time and decay were moist and poisonous—seem to close out the world, forbid and frighten. On the inside, however, especially on a summer Sunday morning, the church-convent is a lively kermess.

A shell of pink and yellow plaster curves out of a building to suggest a stage shed for two itinerant "Aztec" dancers, in costumes only faintly suggesting the splendor and style of Aztec nobles: "Their cloaks and loincloths were richly embroidered, and their shining hair was gathered up as though tied to their heads, and each one was smelling the roses that he carried, and each had a crooked staff in his hands." (Díaz) One latter-day Aztec in a yellow rayon cape shakes a pair of maracas to mark the simple rhythm of the bare, repetitious tune. The leader, in a girdle of leopard-print cloth, trimmed with yellow fringe, bells of dried seed pods on his ankles, picks out the primitive tune on an armadillo-backed mandolin. Both men keep stamping, turning, playing, glistening in the hot sun while a small crowd of children and tourists sprinkle the earth around them with modest gifts of money.

Beyond these Aztecs, deeper into the yard, stand the inner walls of an old chapel, which suggests a proscenium arch, the buttresses' acoustical wings frequently used for concerts.

Farther inside the court, is the church, whose entrance is surmounted by a skull and crossbones topped by a cross, a building recently restored in cool modern handsome fashion, and its fascinating early murals, sixteenth to seventeenth century, brought out from its covering wall of plaster.

In the stirrings of dissidence from the established Catholic Church several groups and personalities of Cuernavaca have played complex roles, as American readers know. It is a fascinating story but not within the province of this book. However, three tangential effects of the controversy should interest all travelers to Mexico: a once-remarkable school, CIDOC, the EMAUS religious ornaments designed by ex-friars (available in crafts shops throughout Mexico), and the *mariachi* mass on Sunday. They start pouring in at about 10:30 A.M. or earlier—the respectable old ladies with fine lace triangles on their heads, the girls in brilliant sandals, brightly striped pants and sleeveless shirts, the Indians from the hills in clean threadbare shirts carrying babies, chic couples from Mexico City, the necklaced young of several countries, many children. The musicians in dark trousers and white shirts—no silver buttons, no elaborate braid—sing and play sections of the mass using unmistakable Indian rhythms, the lilt of old waltzes, the vivacity of regional dances. The tunes (not necessarily Mexican but clearly Latin American) are catchy and everyone sings along lustily, including the conservative ladies who might easily have attended a more conventional service. A sermon by the bishop neither warns, exhorts, nor thunders. Woven through the service, starting and stopping with "Let us think a bit about this. We will return to consider it," the sermon becomes a gentle questioning and invitation to question and in the process lends each boy, each poor farmer in the congregation the dignity life doesn't always offer him. At the end of the ceremony, bishop, priests, and acolytes descend to embrace members of the congregation who embrace each other as well and everyone saunters out humming the lilting "Hallelujah."

Under the shady trees, alongside the walk leading to the church entrance, sit the cripples on wheeled carts, surrounded by old lady beggars taking a few loquacious minutes off; babies are changed; families picnic decorously on stuffed chiles, tortillas, and chicken pulled out of market baskets; a solitary intellectual reads his comic book, comfortably stretched out under a tree, unaware of a man sketching him from under another tree. A couple has fallen asleep, undisturbed by the movement on the walk, the murmurs of the beggars, the cries of the ice-cream vendors in the street, the splutter of motorcycles, the peal of the bells, the soaring tones of the orchestra, the chatter of the dancer's ankle bells—a turbulence like the opening of the second act of *La Bohème*, Mexican version.

HOTELS

Habitual weekenders—those who don't have houses or lucky friends on whom to descend, all smiles, bikinis, and rye bread from Mexico City—are intense devotees of various *posadas* which resemble each other in many ways; they are small, have pools and gardens hung with profligate vines of red and purple bougainvillaea, are usually ruled over by American or European proprietors, and serve the best food in the town. Some serve only breakfast, others require that you live on the American plan; many sell meals to transients, if arrangements are made several hours ahead. Reserve in advance for a stay.

Jacarandas   The Villa d'Este of Cuernavaca—out of the hub-bub, extensive, beautifully landscaped grounds surrounding a dramatically placed pool and rather regal accommodations, including a small golf course and exclusivity. Expensive.

Casa de Piedra   Also a bit out of the center, with raffish gardens and small pools. If the cook and standards have not suffered through life's and Mexico's mutabilities, the food should be Continental good. Expensive.

Las Mañanitas   Small, very pretty, with lashings of flowers, strutting peacocks, charm, and curlicued furniture; extremely popular for its food. By Mexican standards it is fairly expensive but not more than the moderately well-heeled tourist—and which one, except for the itinerant youth, is not?—can easily pay. (Recently changed hands and there may or may not have been a change in decor and quality.)

Posada de San Angel Privada de la Selva 100. An engagingly redone hacienda with a pool, good manners, good food, and good cheer. As an extra, a slice of life immediately outside the entrance: a clinic conducted by nuns and the waiting girls with babies, the old men sitting on the benches or under the sheltering trees of an antique street. Moderate.

Arocena-Holiday Paseo del Conquistador. A large, somewhat formal modern hotel, its meals highly esteemed. High moderate.

Las Quintas Has the usual arrangement of rooms gathered around a pool and large gardens. The service, even for Mexico, is unusually eager.

Los Amates Los Actores at 112, about twenty minutes out of town. Spanish, and little English, if any, is audible. Quite reasonable.

Posada Arcadia Leyva 37. Lies a block below the Cortés Palace. It has a long, beautifully kept lawn which rolls down to a good-sized pool, complete with dressing room. The rooms are attractively arranged, the bathrooms distinctly "House and Garden," and the meals imaginative. Moderate.

Hacienda de Cortés Plaza Kennedy 90. Supposedly a rest house of the Conquistador now possessed of gardens, pool, and good cuisine. Expensive.

Internacional At the very top of Calle Cuaglia. Has the usual pool and lawn and modest, unassuming rooms. The clientele is largely European and Mexican families; consequently expect to be splashed by children and chase large rubber balls. Inexpensive to moderate.

For *the* Mexican experience, try (via information culled from waiters and policemen) to get into the house of a Señora who insists that she does not run a "Casa de Huéspedes"; it is her home, all the children have fled in marriage, and what is she to do with all those rooms? As in most Mexican houses, the rooms all come off a court and are dark. (There is enough sun outside, Mexicans feel, and that is where it should stay.) Meals served in the court are distinctly Mexican, as is the décor, jumbles of bright brocades in artificial silk. La Señora runs the house and the kitchen and her maids in a constant high-speed clatter of speech and slap of bedroom slippers. Her English is primitive, but she has nimble antennae for meanings and responses. If she has too much difficulty, her able assistant—a boy of fifteen or so—will help out with his sixth sense of what an American might want. Always modest.

The *very* Mexican experience may be La Señora's neighbor, who offers "apartments" and serves no meals. The entrance usually leads to a yard which is a knot of tiny stairways leading in a confusion of directions; the traditional courtyard is now stuffed with rooms. They have stoves and, most of them, bathrooms, and, of course, beds, all squeezed together into small breathless spaces, decorated loudly and casually in brilliant cheap cottons, like gypsy fortunetelling shops. The walls are stained with damp and the beds not luxuriously mattressed, but an apartment may be had for very little per day for two.

RESTAURANTS

As mentioned, various inns serve meals to transients. However, there are several restaurants you might want to try.

Don Pancho   At the corner of Morelos and Jalisco. Serves, plainly and artfully, zesty seviche; the shrimps in garlic sauce and treatment of red snapper are quite distinguished. Moderate.

Playa Bruja   Oaxaca and Galeano. Also deals in seafood, more festively, on a spread of brilliantly illuminated outdoor tables. They cook the white fish of Patzcuaro with delicacy and do well by Argentine-broiled meats. High moderate.

Los Canarios   Sets forth a large, inexpensive paella on Sunday afternoon, usually out-of-doors.

The Hotel Colon   Also feeds local food in Spanish style on Sundays at no great cost.

For a snack try the **Peñalba,** on Morelos, in an old fountained court adorned with flowers and twittering birds in myriad cages.

And at least once have the *Tacos al* carbon at Rayon 5. The specialty is pieces of pork, beef, or sausage on small, open tacos, cooked over charcoal. A few pesos for each bit of ambrosia, enhanced by roasted young, green onions.

SHOPPING

Shopping in Cuernavaca is inescapable; if you don't go to it, it comes to you, as explained. For choicer objects, not dangled by hawkers, try **Tianguis,** across the small park from the Cortés Palace. It holds a sizable collection of reproductions of Colonial portraits; not all of them are good or even passable as art, but they give out of their pinched frames an acid charm. Look also at the bed covers or large hangings done in heavy cross-stitch of stylized animals and exquisite boxes made locally. There are good copies of the fat, red clay Tarascan dog—a commemoration of the animal bred for eating by the pre-Cortés Indian, and judging from their girth and smiling expressions, they were a great deal happier than the lean hounds that drag their thin flanks and mangy pelts through the alleys of Mexico today.

Tikal   Across from the Borda Gardens. Has everything in the tourist gamut and also makes huaraches in many attractive styles.

Trini's   Very much like Tianguis, displaying variations on the same themes plus embroidered shirts adapted for U.S. wear and of course the ubiquitous tin—tin flat, tin fluted, tin tinted. By the time you get there or to Tianguis, there will be a still greater variety of objects, because the fertile minds of the proprietors keep inventing ingenious uses for Mexican materials and skills. Unfortunately, Trini's is disdainful of repairs and returns even when justified.

Bagatelle   A shop in which lovely embroidered robes and blouses in fresh and innocent floral patterns are embroidered and made to your order. This, however, takes some time.

Celia Harmes   Río Mayo 5. Creates silver and semiprecious stone jewelry in imposing designs.

Immediately on the outskirts, **Ceramica di Cuernavaca** makes white, often delicate ceramics: don't be put off by the Italianate displays in the window.

Artesanias y Decorados   Zapata 116. Offers the mesmerizing sight of potters at their wheels, rows and rows of objects waiting to be glazed and fired, and a large display of dishes, vases, and ornaments in old patterns and new. Look for the graceful vases usually placed on a high shelf near the entrance to the workshop.

Gundi   Domingo Diez 507. If the owner or manager is about, you may be conducted (and certainly you may wander on your own) through the atelier, from the vat of the first candle dipping, to the smoothing and polishing processes, then the application of decorations and final dippings. The candles emerge as sturdy towers, mushrooms of all shapes and colors, wax flowers that flicker in pools, charming Mexican children that no one would dare burn.

Las Campanas   Near the town center. A beguiling compound of shops, art gallery, and courtyards. Its wares are varied and choice, therefore fairly expensive.

Finally, don't neglect the big market, which carries a full repertoire of tourist goodies.

For golfers and riders: both are available short distances from town. For watchers of riding: Lienzo del Charro, five miles out on the old Mexico City road, a colorful show that may involve bull baiting. Saturdays and Sundays only: check times.

TEPOZTLÁN

Under 12 miles from the Cuernavaca of expensive taxis, manicured *posadas,* and "English-speaking here" sits Tepoztlán, privately, seclusively, a collection of things Mexican: dramatic landscape, a Náhuatl-speaking populace resistant to change, an Indian temple, a fortress-monastery built by the *conquistadores,* visible signs of the destruction and havoc of the 1910 Revolution. For these reasons, among others, it has been carefully scrutinized in recent years—its mores; its social, religious, and economic practices; what goes on in its pots and its beds—by anthropologists and sociologists, and has been stared at by the fierce Cyclopean eyes of Hollywood cameras. All this plus non-Mexican settlers and the worldly breezes wafted from Cuernavaca might have lured to unrest and change, but nothing seems to affect the town or its somber, laconic Indian life.

The trip from Cuernavaca takes less than a half hour over a flat, winding road which passes a graveyard like a toy shop of bird cages, miniature churches, and houses painted in naïve, clear pinks, blues, and whites. There are no strong colors or subtle ones; the innocence of babyhood returns to the dead. Around and beyond the cemetery spread grazing fields pressed by tall hills. One craggy upthrust dominates the landscape for a distance and then splits into a fantasy of massive, broken walls of rock with bristling beards of green shrub. The rocks become immense tablets waiting to be momentously inscribed, sections of castle cities, old green-wrinkled stone giants, monstrous stale wedding cakes.

Inside the ring of startling *Nibelungen* landscape lies the town, a shout of green—the dense green of crowded old trees; the light greens of vines lacing houses, fences, and trees; the obdurate steely green of cactus; the gray-haired green of dusty grass. The shaded plaza with its inevitable stone and iron benches (usable only by the totally exhausted or the Spartan flesh of the rural Mexican) leads into a large, dry square, the stage of dances and mock battles during fiestas. On both its sides are market stalls carrying fruits and vegetables of meager size and quantity; ribbons of sinewy strips of meat turned to the sun (and its friends, the flies) for drying to make the local jerked beef; coils of cotton lace (a few cents a yard) nesting lurid candies.

A short distance behind the market square stands the sixteenth-century Dominican monastery, one of Mexico's national treasures and a most forceful statement of the Conquest and its church. Its buttresses don't fly; they stand close and tight, like outer ribs, holding the building inward. The walls are large and heavy, cutting deeply into the earth. The interior is (or was, until restoration of murals was begun recently) almost as unrelenting as the outside—long stone halls cut by dim cells and decorated in a limited palette of black, white, and terra-cotta. The design, too, is meager, repeating endlessly the thorned bands and rosettes of the Dominicans, copied with sincere effort but little refinement by Indian craftsmen from Spanish design. The few figures visible in murals—where they were not whitewashed or scratched out during the Revolution, when Zapata used the building as headquarters—are curiously Asiatic, slant-eyed and high-cheekboned, much less Spanish than Indian. Whether it was simply easier, or a gesture of fierce resentment, it seems strange—and yet not—that the Indian painted himself in the conqueror's clothes.

A stairway leads to the heavily battlemented roof which adds its dour stretch of stone to the fantasy of the surrounding hills. Around the sepulcher of Spanish might, the alive and verdant spouts unquenchably. A mesh of trees and vines arches over the athletic hour of the local secondary school; the boys whirl painted wooden disks while the girls step and turn to the rhythms of a regional dance thumped out on an old piano. Down below, the church sits quietly in a newish dress of too much gold and white paint, but its beautiful door remains untouched as do the decorations above it, delicate carvings of Virgin and Child, plus moon, animals, angels, and bits of Indian fancy, in smooth naïvely symmetrical arrangement.

Behind the monastery sits the town's museum. Like a number of rural museums, it is a teaching institution that inspires, primarily, pride in Mexican art. "Europeans did not bring us culture. They brought their culture. Centuries before Europe produced culture, it flourished among us in splendor." "Never will we be completely Mexicans as long as we do not know, to love and admire, the marvelous art of our indigenous ancestors."

These signs set the mood for exploring the intelligently arranged displays created by Carlos Pellicer, who was also the donor and founder of the museums of Villahermosa (page 329). One begins with *the* basic myth in the form of a quetzal bird with green, shining plumage and a long tail, accompanied by a snake, which tells the story of the god Quetzalcoatl (page 175), who was born, they say, in Tepoztlán and brought up in nearby Xochicalco. One is then introduced to the chronology of Mexican art developments and examples of the major cultures. By way of prints, reproductions, photographs, and original pieces one becomes acquainted with the beamish or grotesque Totonac faces, the gray, indomitable naturalism of the Olmecs, grim Aztec figures, the small, serene figures of Jaina (one couple, more earthly than is usual for this aristocratic group, busy in sex play), a model of the orderly glyphs and famous figures of Palenque.

Assuming you have already seen the sublime collection in the museum of Mexico City, there will be no need—except for pleasure—to examine every case, but do look for a beautiful couple and their child isolated in a case in the Teotihuacán section, always the Jaina figurines, the small case of magical Teotihuacán heads, and the entertaining Colima warriors and their singing, dancing, maracas-wielding neighbors. Or do it chronologically. Begin with the very crude sculpture (some of it looks Cyclatic) that developed from hatchet shapes and follow through to the engaging Huastec sculptures made 1,000 years before the birth of Christ to the varieties of Tlatilco figures of 500 years later. Then watch modern crafts emerge disappointingly, as the boy who guards and dusts and collects your admission fee carefully carves the tiny wooden villages that appear on every souvenir stand. But then, working for kings and gods always produced better products than those turned out for hoi-polloi (here read "tourists").

NOTE: The museum is closed on Mondays. Open 10 A.M. to 2 P.M., 4 to 6 P.M., but don't rush; rarely does any door open precisely on time. Cuernavaca taxis will drive you to Tepoztlán (bargain a bit) and you can make it back in a local bus, with schoolchildren and ladies with bundles of tamales to sell in Cuernavaca, for under two pesos.

Above, 1,000 feet up, is the temple of the God of Pulque, Tepoztecatl. The local boys scale up to it on the steep side of one of the carved hills, scarcely touching the meager paths, swinging up the rope ladders in short, agile flights. The older and less indigenous will find it a harder climb. The footing is a bit uncertain, the improvised ladders cobwebby, but there is no real danger. The view from the top is large and majestic and there is, of course, the temple. It is a small structure, quite battered, whose stones bear symbols apparently related to the god, but he is gone, destroyed by the church fathers who had him thrown off the high cliff. A local legend favors the fact that the god reached the bottom intact—a proof of his great powers—and had to be hammered and smashed vigorously afterward. In spite of the efforts of the church, Tepoztecatl is still a vivid god-folk hero, given an affectionate, bibulous fiesta in September of each year. The church has its turn in January, when there is a fiesta and dance that celebrates the defeat of the Moors centuries ago.

NOTE: The **Posada del Tepozteco** is a rambling, terraced old hacienda overlooking the town and staring into the mammoth rocks. It has a pool, walls of roses, and monkeys and marmosets variously restrained. Being a self-contained unit, it provides bed, board, games, *artes típicos,* and quiet. One of the best of its attractions, which can be had for the price of a drink, is a sunset view of the hills when one crag burns copper red against the surrounding purple, deepens to blood red, and then melts into the dusty veiled blue of the evening. Moderate—American plan.

A modest inn run by a local family asks modest sums for room and meals; the address, Calzada Aguila 11. For a decent, inexpensive meal try the **Virreyes Restaurant.**

A new road through beautiful mountain country will take you from Tepoztlán (or Cuautla) to Amecameca and on to Xochimilco, on the border of Mexico City.

XOCHICALCO

There should be a bus that goes to Xochicalco; inquire. In your own car, go south on the Acapulco road as far as Alpuyeca, a distance of about 16 miles. From here, take the branch road to the right and begin looking for the Xochicalco sign.

A good time to get there is at about five in the afternoon, when the intense sun is beginning to loosen its grip, the late light turns the barren earth and scratchy shrub to dark gold, and the distant hills begin to fade into the low sky.

The work of excavation goes slowly and, consequently, most of the vast area, which was probably a religious-military center, is still uncovered. With the exception of a ball court and some underground passages, little is to be seen but the one extraordinary small building standing as a sentinel above the rest. Xochicalco was an abandoned city when the Spaniards came to it. It obviously stems from an older culture than that of the then incumbent Aztecs and has been attributed to the diffuse Toltec culture.

Whatever its lineage, Xochicalco is beautiful, much of it covered with remarkable carving (some restored) of involved, continuous

bands of plumes and serpents' heads surrounding noble aloof personages who sit cross-legged, with arms and hands extended in the
gesture of Hindu gods. The stylized plumes and serpents which flow
under and around the figures suggest that this, too, might have been
a temple dedicated to the god Quetzalcoatl, the "Plumed Serpent."
The shape of the building itself, rather than rising inexorably, like
other pyramids, with a rush of steep stairs, is of a more serene shape:
it pauses between the tightening pyramidal movements in a reflective
breath rare in these rigidly designed buildings.

For a view of the present with a tinge of the future, ride to Lomas
de Cuernavaca, an expensive housing development about five miles
out of the center of the town. Like the University and the houses in
the Pedregal area of Mexico City, it typifies what might be called
"Mexican Fantasy Modern"—bold mixtures of color, strong sculpture, stonework in unexpected shapes and combinations, modern in
techniques and concepts but anciently Mexican in that they are
elaborately carved and polychromed, rich and unabashed.

The streets are divided by undulating lines of figures in stone and
concrete, some suggesting prehistoric animals, others the ubiquitous
Aztec serpent, in blue or terra-cotta or ocher, colors frequently found
in ancient murals and sculpture. The serpentine and serpented streets
wind up and up to a newish church, the work of Mexico's leading
architect, Félix Candela. It is a white shell of concrete growing like
a great lily from the top of the hill, pure, uninvolved, and isolated
except for its one companion, a tall thin white pyramid of a cross
whose only decorations are the sticks set into it as pigeon roosts. The
shadow patterns the sticks weave as the light changes, and the restless short flights of the pigeons themselves, make a gently billowing
veil of movement around the cross.

Even if it means giving up an hour or two of swimming and
rum-and-sodaing, try to see it.

NOT IMPORTANT, BUT PLEASANT

About a half hour's driving time from Cuernavaca (less from
Cuautla) there sits a sybarite's Eden, the **Hotel Hacienda of Cocoyoc.**
In 1560 it was the vast sugar-growing and -processing estate of a
Doña Isabel Cortés Moctezuma (a name too good to be true). It has
recently been restored as the total luxurious retreat: regal rooms,

pools, old walls foaming with greenery, brooks, endless gardens plus diversions like riding, tennis, golf, bars, and a supervised children's playground as well as a nightclub. For romance, amenities, and cuisine you will pay a substantial price depending on the rooms or suites you choose.

Investigate the pleasures of the **Hacienda Vista Hermosa** about twenty miles out, once the home of Cortés, they say. It is Conquest in size and design, with a large pool and a restaurant in sixteenth-century cellars. You might ride in the small private bull ring, an exotic act which can assume romantic proportions in travel reports back home. Drive out to Palo Bolero, where one swims in and through small underground caves. Or, if you like wandering through forests of stalactites and stalagmites, go south to the grottoes of Cacahuamilpa (always go with a group) and see Xochicalco on the way back, or go on to Taxco. There is swimming in the river at Las Estacas, in the high lakes of dramatic Zempoala, and the resort area of Lake Tequesquitengo.

Once a suburb of Cuernavaca but now incorporated with the town and undergoing considerable restoration is Acapantzingo. It is becoming something of a cultural center with lectures in anthropology and sessions in the restoration of antiquities. The church is primitive, the garden across from it dominated by a cerise fall of bougainvillaea, but for you it might be interesting to know that besides being the site of a prison and once a busy red-light district, it was the place where Maximilian kept his local mistress.

A cheap way to look at village Mexico is to walk, in Cuernavaca, to the Monument of the Niños Héroes, and there board one of the second-class buses which bring country people to and from the town. Take any one—to Miacatlán, or Yautepec; any "pec" or "lán"—and make sure it is coming back. With luck you may bump into a country fair of pigs, rabbits, doves and chickens with fan-feathered feet. The decorations will be ingenious curtains made of strings of peanuts and paper straws and dolls devised by local children. The bodies are often soda bottles dressed in patches of velvet, the faces drawn on folded graph paper and surmounted by crowns and miters to hide the neck of the bottle. They are awkward to carry back as souvenirs, but they cost very little and are singularly good examples of the Mexican capacity to combine bits of this and that into clever, attractive objects.

MYTHS, HEROES, AND ANTI-HEROES

Mexico's history is as richly documented as that of any other country and a list of dates marking stellar events can easily be picked out of the dense mass. But such skimming is not necessarily instructive or interesting, a set of bleached bones which, lacking color and flesh, are something of a falsification. How can one pick up a few dry sticks and with them leap through the vast shadows of Mexico's prehistory (which might have been less shadowy if Indian codices had not been burned by the friars of the Conquest), through the incredible march of the Conquest, through the exploitation of the country by the Spanish Crown, through the elaboration of trade routes which brought silk from the Orient into Acapulco and silver out of Vera-cruz, through the emergence of a new indigene—the Indian-Spanish *mestizo*—through an exploration of Spanish society dancing uneasily on a floor of peonage, through the turbulence for independence and reform which began early in the nineteenth century, continuing on into the twentieth? How can one tear through the complexities which landed Maximilian and Carlotta in Mexico and Juárez in the United States, or the grotesqueries of Santa Anna's rule, or the refinement and corruption of Porfirio Díaz' dictatorship? Or the invasions, military and economic, and the political deals which changed the shape and wealth of the country?

For the interested traveler, there is printed matter—a good deal of it in English—on every breath Mexico ever drew. For the casual taster and viewer a glimpse of a few of the figures who dominate innumerable parks and plazas, whose names are the names of streets, cities, and states, whose existence is part of the national consciousness, part of the myth-history fabric which makes the personality of the country, might be enough.

The god Quetzalcoatl was the plumed serpent, the "beautiful bird" from the south; also, he came from the east. According to Indian record, he was actually a man born in 895 who died at the age of forty. On the other hand, he was supposed to have been a Viking explorer, a shipwrecked wanderer (either possibility would explain his famous white beard), a missionary who brought the cross to Mexico. Whatever his origins, he seems to have made the classic hero journey of mortal to priest-king to god, and by the time of the Conquest, had become magical. Numerous great temples in divers places had been dedicated to him; he was the Morning Star, the wind god, the god of fertility. He was the counterweight to the god of war and death who drank so much human blood. Between them they were the light and the dark, the Pluto and Ceres, God and the Devil, of late Indian religion. Because he was the god of light and good, Quetzalcoatl has been claimed as a precursor to monotheism—possibly a natural evolutionary development, possibly a Catholic invention.

The prophecy that the white-bearded Quetzalcoatl would come back from the sea to the east was persistent enough to half persuade Moctezuma that Cortés, a white man with a grizzled beard from across the sea and carrying crosses (a symbol the god had supposedly worn), was an enactment of that prophecy. Quetzalcoatl's imminent arrival was proclaimed in a widespread story that Moctezuma's dead sister had been resurrected and reported a vision of the coming of the white man preaching the True Cross. From Yucatán, from Cuba, from South America, and Hispaniola came news of just such bands of men, as the sky over Mexico flashed ominous portents—comets, unnatural lights, and eclipses of the sun. Wracked by prophecy, the terror of nature acting unnaturally, vague news of conquerors elsewhere on the continent, surrounded by a hostile empire, Moctezuma twisted and turned, evaded and yielded, and surrendered to the Conquest as something foreordained.

Moctezuma II was hardly a hero. He stands, rather, as symbol of Aztec power and wealth, of past magnificence and glory yearned toward now by a few supernationalists. It was his grandfather, Moctezuma I, who conquered much of the territory which became the Aztec Empire and it was the grandson's role to act as coordinator and emperor of the vast domain, as commander-in-chief of the large army needed to hold the conquered and to conquer the still unconquered. He was a high priest and a demigod. Remembering that extant reports of Moctezuma II were mainly Spanish, obliquely cast to please the Spanish Court and rationalize the Conquest, and that the fullest report (that of Bernal Díaz) was written many years after the events, one sees a picture of a cultivated man of paralyzing complexity, an experimenter in botany, a collector of rare animals (Chapultepec Park was the site of his zoo) and deformed people, a man who enjoyed art, music, jesters, perfume, the dance, and little boys—whether as food only is not quite clear. He was attended, it is said, by 3,000 servants in a hundred scented rooms hung with exquisite treasures. He bathed daily and changed his costume four times each day, never wearing again that which he had worn once. For his meals there were a hundred dishes from which to choose, and for his company he had princes and nobles of conquered civilizations, elegantly housed and clothed but still hostages. According to Díaz, the ornaments the Spaniards wrested from him (some of it drowned with the treasure-laden soldiers on their flight from Tenochtitlán—Mexico City—during the course of the battle for the city) required three days to take apart and amounted to 600,000 pesos—a colossal sum then—in gold, silver, and gems.

Vacillating, threatened, faced with rebellion in his own court and the victorious uprising against his rule elsewhere, beset by the furies of his priests, who saw churches going up on the sites of sacred temples, impotent in his double-dealings with Cortés—a master at that craft—he submitted to palace arrest, insisting that it was from his own choice and that of the gods who had finally broken their long, inimical silence. His tottering prestige collapsed when one of Cortés' captains caused the murder of a number of Aztecs. Moctezuma (now no longer the emperor; Cuitlahuac had been appointed in his stead) rose to the roof of his castle to announce that the Spaniards were leaving—who was lying to whom in this maze of duplicity is difficult to sort out—and please to hold off from killing them. Someone threw a stone which hit Moctezuma. His injury was apparently not great but being no fool and irreparably trapped between his own people and Cortés, he used the blow as his escape. He refused treatment and food, and as surely as he had handled nothing since the coming of the Spaniards, gave himself to death.

It was easier for Moctezuma's nephew, Cuauhtémoc, to be a hero; there was no more treating with the Spaniards and he had no choice but to pursue the clear, doomed task of trying to hold Tenochtitlán. He could not unite the rest of the country against Cortés, and in spite of his valor and the pride and will of the starving Aztecs, could not break the three-month siege on the city. Cuauhtémoc was taken prisoner, tortured to reveal remaining treasures, and conveyed—in the manner of conquering Rome—on the *conquistadores'* march southward. Somewhere along the way he became too troublesome and was hanged.

The Virgin of Guadalupe, to whose basilica in Mexico City thousands of pilgrims from all over the country walk and crawl at various times of the year, almost had to appear when she did. An Indian peasant boy, Juan Diego, saw her only a few years after the Conquest, at a time when Indians were submitting to conversion but scarcely in numbers large enough to constitute a mass movement toward Catholicism. The swarthy Virgin appeared to Juan at the place which reputedly held a temple to a local fertility goddess, and it was that spot on which a church was to be built. Juan was to tell the archbishop that she said so. The boy's report of the miracle and request was rejected several times; the friars wanted proof. Reporting back to the Virgin, he told her of his difficulties and she gave him miraculous proof: she caused masses of roses to bloom on the dry hill. He gathered them in his *serape* and dashed off to the monastery to show his miracle to the archbishop. On opening his cloak, they found, instead of a bouquet of roses, an image of the Virgin stamped on the coarse cloth. The story and miracle of the dark-skinned Virgin induced more conversions, her church was soon built, and by papal decree in the eighteenth century, she became the guardian of all New Spain. The devotion to the Virgin of Guadalupe grew so great in time that Father Hidalgo used her image as his banner in the 1810 War of Independence and his troops called her name as a battle cry. Since then, and before, she has been called on to help in other battles, in plagues, in drought—whenever Indian-Mexican misery and fear needed a mother protectress.

The record of Colonial rule is, from its very purpose, a litany of ruthlessness relieved by lighter notes of lassitude, chicanery, posturing, and simple stupidity. However, whether one admires the means or not, Spain did build a great empire with the help of some men who knew what they were about. Though their allegiance was unswervingly to the church and Spain, their methods were sometimes decently humane and their goals of achievement went beyond the immediate triumphs of forced conversions and mountains of silver.

Among the earliest wave of friars there were a few tormented Christians who could not separate Indians from humanity. One of them was Bartolomé de Las Casas, who spent most of his ninety years in a lonely, frustrating struggle for elementary Indian rights, relieved by work on a massive collection of information and praise of the Indian in an *Historia de las Indias.* Early in his career as a priest in Hispaniola, he began to agitate against the enslavement of the indigenous peoples and against the *encomienda* system—a practice which offered Spanish settlers both Indian labor and tributes. Fray Bartolomé made the long hazardous trip back to Spain to plead the Indians' cause, with no success but, being his own type of zealot, he continued his energetic shuttling among Peru, Guatemala, Mexico, and Spain to convert the Indian as a man, not as a slave, and to convince the throne that its role was to promote Christian justice as well as money. Ultimately his persistence won some paper measures which were thoroughly unenforceable. (What Spaniard would force another to relinquish the slave labor they were both enjoying?) However, the old man died with the wry satisfaction of knowing that although he could not change people much, he had forced a change in the law and had recorded for posterity an account of a people he pitied and loved.

Don Vasco de Quiroga, the first bishop of Michoacán, was a calmer man who did not set his sights quite so high. It was he who introduced new crafts to the Indians in his region and gave them further dignity by establishing schools for them.

Unlike many of his compeers, the Count Revilla Gigedo II (he of the unpronounceable street name in Mexico City), Viceroy in the last decade of the eighteenth century, was a just, imaginative man and extraordinarily industrious. He built roads and schools and subjected Mexico City to an expert job of city planning: streetlights, health measures, water systems, contained marketplaces. And, in the time left him from these activities, he stimulated the exploration and exploitation of Mexican territory, filling Spain's laden coffers.

Father Miguel Hidalgo y Costilla, the parish priest of the town of Dolores, in the state of Guanajuato, seems to have been a gentle, intelligent man with a taste for literature, discourse, liberalism, and music. In July of 1800 he was denounced by the still active Inquisition. Transgressions? He taught a few Indians music, well enough to organize a small orchestra; helped them improve their meager agriculture and encouraged them to establish small tile and brick factories; he learned the pagan Indian dialects; he had committed immoral acts with two women; and was a well-known heretic who kept himself informed about the French Revolution, in French. Obviously, he had a shaky reputation, but the charges were dismissed.

The situation in Mexico at this time (the opening years of the nineteenth century, which had witnessed Napoleon's meteoric rise and the collapse of Spain) was ripe for social revolution. The Indian-*mestizo* peon appeared sunk in his dark fatalism; it was the creole who was angry and restless. Creoles (of Spanish blood but born in Mexico) had little chance for advancement in the government or the church or lucrative businesses; their representation in Spanish councils was inadequate, and increasingly enormous taxes and loans were being forced from them by Spain. Since Charles II and his son, Ferdinand VII, were imprisoned in France, several Spanish groups named themselves the legitimate Spanish government, and to them went the fealty of Spaniards in Mexico. The creoles were still clamoring for representation, but since that did not seem immediately feasible, decided to take their chances with the deposed Ferdinand in the hope that his regime, when restored, would produce long-delayed reforms. Fair representation and more reasonable allotments of Mexican wealth and opportunities were the aims of the "Literary Society," which met in the house of La Corregidora in Querétaro, Father Hidalgo and Ignacio Allende among the members. Their timetable called for action early in October, but events were precipitated by betrayals and warnings, and in the course of a mass he was conducting in Dolores (on September 16, which has become Independence Day), Hidalgo called his famous *grito,* his shout for freedom. They came from the factories and the farms armed with scythes, machetes, sticks, stones; they took Dolores, the towns on the way to Celaya, and Celaya itself, gathering hordes as they went. Six days after the *grito,* the poorly equipped forces—women and children among them—already numbered 50,000. Spanish captives and treasures were taken; the mob, releasing generations of smoldering fury, sacked and looted to the point where Hidalgo had to threaten looters with death. Guanajuato was a hell scene of carnage, but still they joined, the Indians and the *mestizos,* equipped with little but the arms they captured and their monumental rage, outstripping the fairly reasonable aims of their leader (as in the French Revolution) and propelling Hidalgo to the unfamiliar grandeur of an "organized government" whose heads of state were his chief officers, whose treasury held 400,000 pesos, and whose *generalissimo,* in a splendid uniform, he now became.

The "rabble" army, soon abandoned by the frightened creoles, marched on Mexico City, where the Viceroy, uncertain of his troops and their strength against the victorious peasant army, was on the point of fleeing. His advantage, however, was Hidalgo's greater uncertainty: ammunition was low, his army undisciplined and unreliable, his officers envious and disgruntled. And quite possibly he was sick of the destructive furies of revolution. Against the urging of his officers, Hidalgo turned back and began his rapid descent, a very short while after the valiant *grito.* The troops were disappointed over not being allowed to take the principal city, they distrusted Hidalgo's judgment and valor (a Latin American leader must always be a death-defier whether it makes sense or not), and they deserted in large numbers. The Royalist forces, aided by accident and the willingness of the threatened creoles to treat with them, began to retake the towns Hidalgo had won. The priest gave over his command to Allende and himself remained a figurehead, a rallying banner for the dwindling faithful.

Hoping for aid from the United States, Hidalgo, Allende, and a few of their army started northward and were surrounded by the troops of one of their former officers, paying them back for refusing to promote him. They were turned over to the Spanish authorities in Chihuahua on March 26. Hidalgo was dismissed from his priesthood, always a meaningful thing to him, and, it is said, wrote a retraction, a confession of error. (Although the document exists, there is no certainty that he wrote and signed it.) On the night of July 29, 1811, Hidalgo, divested of his priestly garments, thanked his guards in verse, distributed candy to the firing squad, recited a prayer, and was shot.

On the face of it, the storm of blood and fire which Hidalgo sparked and his own incredibly swift passage from small-town priest to revolutionary leader to "Serene Highness" to dead hero came to nothing; the Royalists were again in control at the time of his death. He had, though, unleashed forces and concepts which could not be entirely reversed or suppressed.

Out of these abortive beginnings of independence came a towering organizer and thinker, a man who knew where he was going—toward total economic and political independence from Spain and democracy. José María Morelos y Pavón was a *mestizo* who worked as a farm hand until he was twenty-five, then studied for the priesthood in Valladolid (now named Morelia for him) and took on a poorly paying curacy in an obscure town. In 1810 he offered his services to Hidalgo, who made him an aide without troops or arms, for which he was to forage as best he could. He marched out of his parish village of Carácuaro dressed in the large cloak and pirate's headcloth of his many monuments, accompanied by an army of twenty-five. They soon grew to thousands, whom he kept orderly and disciplined and for whom he appointed leaders astutely chosen for their valor, their devotion, and their military capacities, particularly in guerrilla warfare. In spite of bouts of malaria and the pain of injuries and denunciations by the church ("Instead of leading souls to heaven, you are sending thousands to hell"), he directed armies which took town after town and stretched across the mountains to Mexico City. Later, with troops starved out and decimated at Cuautla, plagued by the news of Royalist victories in towns he had taken earlier, Morelos reorganized his army and moved on to recapture Oaxaca.

Early in 1813 the insurgents held western Mexico from north of Oaxaca down to Guatemala, large sections of the center of the country, and part of Veracruz, but the Royalist forces, under the forceful command of General Calleja, were hard on their heels, maintained their control of Acapulco, and took again the key towns of Puebla and Querétaro. At this point Morelos thought it important to pause for clarification of purpose, and the Congress of Chilpancingo was organized. It declared Morelos its chief executive, issued an Act of Independence from Spain, and began to draft a constitution which is considered mainly the work of Morelos and contains the basic tenets of the long struggle for reform: equitable agrarian reforms, abolition of the privileges of the church, including the confiscation of church lands and the abolition of tithes, and the guarantees of democratic processes within a democratic governmental structure.

The Spanish armies prevented Morelos from seeing his reform in action. Steadily, surely, the insurgents were driven back, losing town after town, losing men and leaders and prestige. And his Congress, the ruling body of the new republic (which was to have as citizens no "Indians, mulattoes, or castes, but generally Americans"), removed him from leadership and handed it over to a committee of whom none had his capacities or integrity. The Congress and its war leaders dissolved into the common Latin American swamp of caciquism. Except for a few men, Morelos was abandoned (the parallels with Hidalgo become strong at the end of his career), hunted, and ultimately captured by one of his former officers. Except for a couple of guerrilla leaders, none of his dedicated officers was left.

Morelos was taken to the prison of the Inquisition in Mexico City and there stripped of priestly dignities after a long accusation which called him a heretic, a seducer, perverse, seditious, guilty of *lèse-majesté,* a traitor, lascivious—among other charges—and was shot just before Christmas of 1815, a few years before Mexico's independence was established. Like Hidalgo's, his public career was a flash of lightning, and his immediate achievement seemed failure, but he had designed specific goals for shaping the revolutionary passion which sank, flickered, and burned, sank, flickered, and burned, but could not be extinguished and ultimately achieved independence from Spain.

Benito Juárez, a Zapotec shepherd from the hills above Oaxaca and later governor of that state, became the welding force of liberalism and anti-clericalism in Mexico. He is, in the simplifications of popular history and myth (and overlooking a few expedient retreats from his staunch position), The Reform. He was a taciturn anti-uniform, anti-display man who declared his purpose early in his political career; it was that "of working constantly to destroy the doleful power of the privileged classes." His Mexico was a seething caldron of conflicts and power pulls: growing liberalism strengthened the unity of the opposing conservative landowners and clergy; Mexico had given an immense part of itself to the United States (1848) after a war which had depleted the monies not already lifted by corruption.

The seesaw of Mexican politics thrust the conservatives high, in 1853, under the erratic leadership of the opportunistic General Santa Anna, and pushed Juárez and his cohorts into exile in Havana, and later, New Orleans. Santa Anna's regime collapsed (1854) and it was again the time of the liberals. Juárez returned to become the Minister of Justice and Ecclesiastical Affairs ("Anti" would have been a just prefix to the latter title). One of his first acts was to abolish clerical *fueros,* the right of ecclesiastics to be tried only in ecclesiastical courts, outside of civil law. He also proposed the dissolution of the army, a suggestion which—among other points of dissension—cost him his job; and he went back to Oaxaca as governor, still anti-clerical, still anti-militarist. The liberal central government lasted for a while, trying to establish a usable constitution which included the abolition of *fueros,* prohibited the corporate ownership of lands, called for a federation of states, and guaranteed a long list of measures to ensure individual rights.

That government fell, and again Juárez went into exile, pausing at Querétaro to be appointed the president of the liberal government and then on to the Pacific coast and the long water route to Veracruz. Rebellions kept exploding; tension between liberal and cleric, land-owner and Indian, region against region, became increasingly tense and "that great but feeble and distracted country," as Stephens called it, continued to run blood. In his tropical seat of government, the stubborn Juárez continued to map out his Reform: a total separation of church and state and the ultimate erasure of all church power. No convents, nunneries, or new churches were to be built, church fees for all ceremonies were to be suspended, civil marriages were to be made legal, the church was to accumulate no property and give up all its holdings except those specifically and currently in use. (These seem to be almost vengeful rulings, steps for total annihilation, but it should be remembered that the church had vast estates and monies and often lent its tremendous political and financial power to corrupt regimes, provided they were pro–status quo.)

The political tide washed the liberals back into favor and, by the winter of 1861, Mexico City was ready to receive its somber, civilian president Juárez. Now there was peace of a sort in a ruined, depleted country harassed by debts to foreign powers which could not be paid. England and Spain took the sensible course of resignation and de-cided to wait. The French had more complex motives for continuing to press, mainly Napoleon III's yearning for an empire of his own. Stimulated by the wishful fantasies of Mexican conservatives in exile, he conferred the honor and title of "Emperor of Mexico" on the Archduke Maximilian of the House of Hapsburg. French forces en-tered Veracruz and started on their way to Mexico City. Rebuffed by Puebla, they retreated to the coast, only to return the next year to take that city and then move on to Mexico City. Clearly, with practi-cally no army the city could not be defended, and once again Juárez and his government fled northward to Texas, while the French troops spread and conquered.

Maximilian was "elected" Emperor by what he sincerely believed was "popular demand"; his naïve liberalism and his ego could have it no other way. Maximilian was not a villain; his heart was in the right place but his head was not. He was an innocent—gallant, ideal-istic, touched, like many young Europeans with romanticism, and a tragic dupe. He and his Empress, Carlotta, genuinely loved Mexico and Mexicans and were certain that they could create a New World Utopia for these enchanting, gifted peasants who would live colorfully and contentedly in a beautiful world whose center was their glittering court in Chapultepec. Between the realities of Mexico (the people's devotion to Juárez, among them) and the duplicity of France, Maximilian's lustrous bubble burst; the clergy soon deprived him of support, and France of money, and he was trapped.

In 1865, the quiescent forces of Juárez—with armed aid from the United States, helped by U.S. pressures on France and general disgust with the whole venture in France itself, to which Napoleon responded by withdrawing the French armies from Mexico—began to return. Maximilian could hardly believe that his enlightened reign could come to an end so soon. Nor could Carlotta, who went back to Paris, and getting no help there, went on to Rome to plead for the pope's good offices. (She never returned because it became obvious in Rome that she was quite mad, and so she remained until her death in 1927, an insane relic of a half-forgotten dream.)

Although there was considerable pressure for releasing Maximilian, who would soon be facing a firing squad, the implacable Juárez refused to permit it. "To this foreigner we owe neither blessings nor evils," he said. "History has told us that the representatives of his ancestor, Charles V, buried my progenitor Cuauhtémoc, considering his patriotism a crime." (Like many Indians, Juárez had a long, stubborn memory.) Maximilian was shot in Querétaro in the spring of 1867, a few months before the Juárez government was reestablished once again. Slowly, slowly the treasury recovered and the country began to resemble a coherent whole, while President Juárez found himself in the ironic position of being too conservative and cautious for younger liberals. When he died in 1872, he left a field for dissension and rebellion to sport on and a body of law which was for a long time neglected but still a blueprint for Mexico's future.

Zapata and Villa remain symbolically the emotions of the Revolution of 1910—and on. Zapata had a principle: agrarian reform, the distribution of the lands of vast haciendas to the Indians who had been tied to these lands by peonage. Villa had a fleeting idea or two for social and economic reform, but his principle was the thunderous might of rebellion, directionless and anarchic. Each—and briefly, both together—represented the myth hero, the great warrior and savior of his people, the sword for the oppressed, the Moses and the Robin Hood.

The fall of Porfirio Díaz, who had maneuvered countless reelections for himself through a dictatorship that lasted about thirty years, and had handed out much of Mexican resources and property to foreign interests (to do him some justice, it had been going on for a considerable time before), was the signal for the usual struggles for power among an ambitious band of politicos who had been waiting to pounce, one eye on the presidency, the other on U.S. policy and favor. Outside these palace battles, the Mexican peasant was spurred on by much simpler motives. Through Hidalgo, Morelos, and the flights and returns of Juárez, Mexico had been threading its tortuous, bloody way to economic and social justice, toward some semblance of education, toward diminishing the strong hold of the church, toward a vision of democratic architecture. Now, with the collapse of the Díaz dictatorship, was the time to solidify those often nebulous gains and to wrest the long-envisioned land reforms. The popular uprisings for "Land and Liberty," as the revolutionary banners read, found their leaders.

Emiliano Zapata of the noble white steed, the white peasant suit, and broad-brimmed peasant hat indelibly stamped on the Mexican eye by Rivera and Orozco, was an illiterate peasant born in 1879 in the state of Morelos. At the beginning of the Revolution he led a local uprising of Indians and *mestizos* in a scourge of burnings and killings—and being killed—of the big haciendas and *hacendados*, distributing the land among themselves, and when the exigencies of battle permitted, working the land. As under Hidalgo and Morelos, the peasant army burgeoned, always under the one slogan and purpose. There was the senseless destruction of nihilistic fury and, of course, wild looting, but Zapata never took a peso; he was a man wearing blinkers, his vision fixed in one direction, that of redistribution of lands. With popular passion behind him and the support of adroit guerrilla fighters equipped with U.S. guns (the result of one of the convolutions of Mexican-U.S. dealings), he entered and left Mexico City three times, one of those times to rendezvous with the forces of Pancho Villa, arriving from the north.

Francisco Villa (Doroteo Arango) was one of the great unleashers of the Furies of revolution—the excesses, the brutalities, the plunder, the chaos—and himself a Fury. He has been so wrapped in hatred and adulation, in blame and the glories of myth and ballad, that the man cannot be extracted from the matrix of exaggeration and emotion. Like Zapata, he was a peasant boy, but unlike Zapata discovered early that tilling someone else's soil was for other peasants, and he turned to cattle rustling and banditry. Early in the Revolution he too had U.S. support and arms, and with his violent, lawless appeal, gathered fellow bandits, peasants, and camp followers to him. Fairly soon he controlled a good portion of the north of Mexico and started southward to meet Zapata.

The month of Zapata-Villa occupation of Mexico City was a storm of anarchy which ebbed when the tides of fortune and politics defeated the peasant leaders. Villa went back north, where, in a fury of disappointment and anger with the United States because it now supported his opponent, Carranza (once an uneasy partner of Villa), he took part in—or directed or condoned—the murder of Americans in northern Mexico and New Mexico. In 1916 General Pershing was sent out with U.S. troops to get Villa dead or alive. They never did, and after a fruitless year, went back to the United States. Villa was still around, and in 1920 established some sort of accord with the government then in power in Mexico City. No one quite trusted his word or his explosive temperament or his talent for peace and, in 1923, it was seen to it that he was assassinated.

By this time Zapata had been dead for four years, also assassinated. He also had retreated to his native territory and would make no truce with the existing government. Suspicious (and justly) peasant that he was, he trusted none of the powers to foster his dream of immediate agrarian reform. His *Zapateros* continued raiding and managed, at least in the state of Morelos, to capture and hold sizable tracts of land.

Villa, as the giant *macho* of flamboyant courage and defiance, and Zapata, equally courageous but channeling his energies into a revolutionary principle, are both living legends of whom many stories are told and songs sung. *Zapatismo* is a common word in Mexican political discussion, and *Villismo* is praised or deplored as a symbol of undirected human ferocity. The more telling contribution of the Revolution's heroes is that they brought the peasant to a knowledge of his potential power and stature. He is still watching the *Revolución* as it has become a dynamic of Mexican government, as it promises him and the growing urban working class progress and greater prosperity. (All Mexican politicians must be for the Revolution, as U.S. politicians must be against Communism.) The meaning of the word often becomes misty, but it stays in the national vocabulary as reminder and ideal and as a spur, urging the Mexican toward his own progress: it is for the Revolution to teach your father to read, to go to night classes, to have your children inoculated, to keep the parks clean, and almost above all, not to spit on the floor of the bus. (Unfortunately, the school system is so frail and lax that not too many rural citizens can read these exhortations to improvement.)

In the state of Michoacán a peasant tells the story of a city man coming to his field to talk to him about the drought and the high cost of animals. The city man asked the peasant what he most needed. "A bull," the farmer answered. Within a few weeks a bull (white and large, as a bull in a legend should be) was delivered to the farm—free. "San Lázaro" had sent it. In Morelia, a physician whose family were once and no longer are large landholders insists that Lázaro Cárdenas is evil, corrupt, in the pay of Russia, a prime mover for Fidel Castro, and the dictator behind the P.R.I. (the Partido Revolucionario Institucional, the majority party and the only one with any power). Nothing, he says, down to an increase in the cost of matches, could be effected without a nod from Cárdenas.

The saint-devil, Lázaro Cárdenas y del Río, of Tarascan-Spanish blood, was born in the state of Michoacán in 1895. His early career—little formal education and soldiering in the Revolution—was in the common mold of his contemporaries except that he was more intelligent and more capable than most and was rapidly advanced until he became a general and head of the military forces of his state. At some point he was chief of militia in the oil center of northern Veracruz, where he learned something about the foreign-held oil interests and earned an awesome reputation for incorruptibility; against all custom, he turned down generous bribes to overlook this and turn his eyes away from that. In 1929 he performed the extraordinary act of "campaigning" for the governorship of Michoacán, although there was no doubt that he would win. It was a long journey of clarification and self-education; he talked with townspeople, farmers, schoolteachers, laborers. He questioned and saw and learned firsthand, and made himself known and responsible.

Moving into the national picture, later, he found himself being groomed to succeed President Calles (1924–28). Early in his career, after the fighting stopped, Calles had been one of the Revolution's most energetic catalysts; the school system was enormously expanded, church power carefully contained, land distribution and public works vigorously promoted. However, he began to suffer the usual affliction of aging revolutionary generals. A life of power and comfort (he had been an underpaid schoolteacher) felt good and he did not want it disturbed by the young radicals pressing for more rapid progress as he slowed down. The solution was to promote a quiet, steady candidate with no convivial vices who would give him no trouble and still please the younger men. The man was Cárdenas, who, however, had to wait through his governorship and a period which witnessed four presidents in a six-year (1928–34) period.

Again, Cárdenas campaigned, although he did not need to. Again he traveled thousands of miles, listening, talking, learning, crystallizing his policies and the thoughts of his supporters. What he hoped to achieve in his six-year term (1934–40) was roughly a strong, united labor movement, improved standards of living, vastly greater educational facilities, more and faster land distribution, and the return of the national wealth to Mexico. To Calles' surprise and opposition, Cárdenas and a fairly united Mexican people made great strides toward these achievements. Cárdenas had the vision and organizational ability to see the whole as well as the parts: industrialization had to be fostered, wages had to be raised, the land had to be more profitably used, and the national wealth had to work for nationals rather than foreigners.

The first move of expropriation came in the north, where an extensive tract of land held by American and British interests was nationalized and redistributed. In 1937 the foreign-held railroads were expropriated, nationalized, and turned over to the railroad workers. Mexican oil, controlled by a web of British and American companies, was reclaimed and handed over to the Mexican government and the oil workers. In each case, the change proved wasteful and inefficient for a few years: there were few adequately trained native technicians for the skilled tasks, disputes over claim settlements were long, loud, and acrimonious; but after a while things settled down. More land was distributed, more roads were built, more children went to school, more peasants ate more corn.

There was, as indicated, much apocrypha surrounding Cárdenas. He was not a dramatic man and rarely made a public show. He may or may not have been the motivating agent for the nationalization of light and power (also formerly held by foreign companies) in 1960. He may or may not have coached presidents. He may or may not have made the next presidential candidate. Several facts are more certain: He organized a rational economy, fostered a strong labor movement, restored to Mexico some of its wealth, made a functioning unit of people and principles, and established Mexico in the twentieth century.

Queretaro to Patzcuaro
via San Miguel, Guanajuato,
and Morelia

One can take a bus to booming Querétaro, maybe soon a train, or zip along the toll highway (some of it deep in industrial smog), a ride of three hours or so. Or make it a day, with a stop at Tula, at San Juan del Río to buy baskets and toys and cheeses at Walter's, then lunch and swim at Tequisquiapan. On your way, by a short deviation from the highway, look for an industrial zone still in the developing outside Querétaro. (There are thickening rumors that it is being developed as a capital annex to relieve Mexico City of some of its overpopulation and smog-making industry.) It centers on a major electrical plant, complete with laid-out streets and American ranch-style houses popping up here and there on a treeless plain. The climax of this new village is the enormous, as yet almost unused, luxury hotel in Colonial style, called **Jurica.** Or try the converted hacienda, **La Mansion Galindo.**

Querétaro, as everyone will tell you, had two famous citizens, one rather temporary. It was the home of Doña Josefa Ortiz, La Corregidora, who, as the wife of an important provincial official, lived in the municipal palace on the main plaza. Later, the palace was her prison for the role she played in warning Hidalgo and Allende that Spanish officials were aware of their revolutionary plans. Still later, in June of 1867, Maximilian, who was not very good at coping or surviving, although he tried valiantly, was shot just outside the town on a site now dominated by a stone colossus that represents Juárez.

Other facts you'll soon find out are that Mexico's Constitution was fought out and signed here, and that in spite of the Lotusland motels brought to it by the highway and busy shopping streets, Querétaro still has some lovely old houses, a monastery, several interesting churches, dignified old trees, and a local museum on the main plaza dedicated to the town's dense history.

Ordinarily the logical places for a pleasant meal would be the **Casa Blanca** motel, the **Baron,** the **Azteca,** or the **Flamingo,** but at Christmas register at the old careless hotel in the square, the **Gran.** On Christmas Eve, huge floats of biblical subjects, often crude and very moving, make their shaky way through the town, circling and circling the square. Before this solemnity, *fantoches* (huge papier-mâché caricatures) gambol along the streets, with music and firecrackers, Carnival crowding Christmas.

The Palacio Municipal, now the local museum in the center of town, was built about 1750 and decorated with strong, coarse, baroque design, more effective than elegant. The high points of Querétaro's architecture, however, are the two churches restored by Tresguerras, Santa Rosa, strangely buttressed and towered and deeply rich in its interior ornamentation, and Santa Clara, all polychrome and gold. Sit for a while in the squares that surround them and then on to the Calle del Biombo, past a few stupendous ancient doors and archways into a view of the tiled domes of San Francisco. Continuing on from San Francisco, along the side of a square where La Corregidora, dressed in her long earrings, holds the torch of liberty, you will find a vestige of very old market, a set of low cavern-shops that sell only modest things made of straw and rope—hats, sacks, coils of cord and leather.

The urban planning that surrounds La Corregidora will be completed as you read this. This end of 16th of September will have become a shopping mall and Cinco de Mayo, also free of traffic, a lovely walk as it leads into the engaging Plaza de la Independencia, its handsome surrounding buildings, its walks and benches centered on a peculiar statue of the nobleman—and his hungry-looking hunting dogs hanging from the corners of the monument—who ordered the aqueduct that brought water to the city. One of the most highly ornamented buildings you are ever likely to see is the Plaza's Association of Culture, hung with convolutions of ironwork that include two crowned eagles and, as if there weren't enough ornaments, a spread of stone drapery that frames nothing.

The plaza narrows into Venustiana Carranza, a street of turn-of-the-century houses adorned with more ironwork, etched glass, and, invariably, densities of lace curtain. At the top of this photogenic street resides the Convent of Santa Cruz, a stronghold of the Franciscans who were reputedly the first missionaries to wander on their own through the Mexican wilderness. It is now an almost empty complex of halls and cloistered gardens, one of them with an interesting myth. A monk unknown to the locals stopped in to rest in this cloister and on leaving forgot his stick. The stick took root and from it grew, and continues to grow, a hairy, rough cactus whose thorns are in the shape of a cross.

The other significant place in the convent is an upper room equipped with a cot, a chair, a desk, and a chest. Here Maximilian was held prisoner before he was taken out to be shot on the hill outside of the city where there now stands the huge monument to Juárez.

Continuing on toward the view of the imposing old aqueduct, one comes on a dignified open area of cypresses and dark purple bougainvillaea that surrounds the well-proportioned red stone sarcophagus where La Corregidora and her Corregidor were buried. Beyond the aqueduct, new housing.

Tresguerras, one of Mexico's "Renaissance" men, was born into the lap of a rich landowning family in the middle of the eighteenth century. With the talent and enthusiasm to use his fortunate birth well, he studied painting and later broadened his horizons to wood carving, engraving, poetry, music, and—rather informally—to architecture. Tresguerras was responsible for the design of the imposing bridge over the Laja River, some of the altars, and a painting in the church of San Francisco, where he was buried, and a monument or two, but the church of Nuestra Señora del Carmen, on the main square, is considered his great work. Its beautiful dome lightens the serene, large building—a judicious work of intelligence, imagination, and taste. The interior echoes the mood and, in addition, displays some of the sculpture and paintings of Tresguerras, not necessarily comfortable to modern tastes, but interesting in that they present still another facet of an extraordinarily gifted man.

Bursting with enterprise, Querétaro has recently become fairly busy with tourist life, and spotted her environs with new roadside hotels.

La Mansion, a large Colonial-style motel that has space for golf and tennis, etc., had a reputation for careful cooking, but slips when it is overwhelmed by busloads of tourists.

Galindos, in from the opposite side of the highway, is becoming a strong, elegant contender.

The Motel Azteca, on the road to San Miguel, is not too ambitious in size and décor and does well for sleeping and eating.

As for restaurants in town: Ask to be directed to the pleasant **Fonda del Refugio** (near the ropes and straw) or **La Flor de Querétaro** or the **Fonda San Antonio** or, for seafood, **Tampico.** If you can stand it, order goat *(cabrito)*, very well prepared in this part of the country. To enjoy the "ambiente" of a Colonial palace, seek out the **Hosteria Marquesa** on Madero.

Opals, for which the region is noted? Try **El Rubi** on Madero or see what the men on the big square are offering out of their bits of cloth and little jars.

SAN MIGUEL DE ALLENDE

San Miguel de Allende is reachable by fast highway, via Querétaro, on frequent buses from Mexico City. It is a number of towns. The bottom layer is the village of the Indian who works in the local fields, when there is work; when there isn't, his woman keeps the children in food and him in mescal by any sort of labor she can find. Another layer is the small restless village of scraggly beards, colossal rum consumption, and strong whispers of marijuana and sexual oddities. The more obstreperous are occasionally deported, in vigorous municipal house cleanings, to be supplanted by others whose names only are different.

Much quieter is the foreign population, which has settled in to write, paint, or, retired, to make their gardens grow. A few have adapted the native crafts to clever, exportable things and have given training and employment to local girls. Others provide medical care, books, and food for children who might otherwise have stayed primitive little beasts of burden, hardly as valuable as a burro. Then, there is the Colonial town whose splendor was the spill-over from Guanajuato's rivers of silver, still evidenced in baronial doors, in fountains and niches and the wrought-iron lanterns which cleave to the old walls.

San Miguel is a town which calls for slow strolling, although its cobbled hills are not especially kind to breath or feet. (There is a tourist office near the main square which will give you a map.)

Having donned thick-soled shoes, walk out at about two o'clock, for instance. Few people are out—most are either hiding from the sun or preparing for the midday *comida*. Nothing sounds but the scrape of one's shoes and, always, the bark of a dog in the far distance, muffled by layers of heat and sun which pierce the narrow streets, leaving sharp, hard shadows on the houses. Or, take a walk at about 6:30 P.M. to see the long shadows in the cool light which falls on the town at the end of day and to watch, from any side street, the flow and ebb of sunset colors.

In walking, you may come across a library or a school housed in refurbished old rooms around serene old patios or a bouncing Churrigueresque façade, like that of the Church of San Francisco. One of the many Colonial buildings, formerly an eighteenth-century convent, is the government school of ballet, music, arts, and crafts. (Ask for Bellas Artes.) It was meticulously restored, the floors laid in the patterns of centuries ago, the small bricks of the beautiful ceiling arranged to repeat the ancient lozenge-pillow shape, the pink brick curving into graceful white and gray arches. Some of the rooms show murals (including an unfinished set by Siqueiros), others contain paintings and displays of crafts; they all surround one of the stateliest patios in Mexico. Look into the recently restored Bonamax building for a view of its unusually tall, Italianate courtyard of high arches, sienna-red walls, and austerity; and stroll through the deep-shadowed "French" park. In an area of old market giving place to new, a recently cleared and cleaned square held a green, excited equestrian statue of Allende, now moved up to the Querétaro road. At one side of the square is a pleasing old house and nearby, the church of Nostra Señora de la Salud, whose Christ and Mary wear rich brocades and velvets.

The cathedral was an eighteenth-century church like a thousand of its compeers until it caught the ambitious eyes of Ceferino Gutiérrez, an untutored builder who took it upon himself to give the church a "Gothic" façade and tower via European engravings and the brashness of the innocent. Although it bears a wispy resemblance to the lace of Milan and Chartres, its lightly crazy style is none at all and adds an appropriate touch, some say, to a town which has its other loony aspects.

About seven miles out of San Miguel is a hamlet of adobe, silence, few stores, and the usual depressed dog. This is Atotonilco, which has a famous monastery, founded in the eighteenth century, that later served as sanctuary for Hidalgo and his followers, and now houses a nuns' school and a shrine for pilgrims. Groups of *penitentes* travel long distances to it through rain and heat, and after prayers and obeisances, leave their crowns of thorns (real thorns) in careless heaps in a patio yard for tourists to pick up and cherish. (Shrewder pilgrims sell them, as well as scourges.) The large church, some of its rooms recently restored, demonstrates every kind of drama and decoration a church can: a realistic life-size tableau of the Crucifixion and Christ figures everywhere—with bleeding backs, with bleeding hands, some wearing shorts of white satin with gold fringe and crowns of sugary angels. Around them stand velvet-robed saints, walls encrusted with paintings and endless reiterations of leaves and flowers; one section is completely covered, ceiling and all, with lively Breughelesque murals. A forceful rough-hewn saint's figure which might be primitive or archaic hides in an obscure corner, away from the clashing fanfares of color; he deserves a search.

For the pleasures of the unrepentant, take the ten-minute ride out to Taboada. It has a hotel and restaurant, a warmish pool, a quite hot pool (both supplied by mineral springs), lockers, benches to sit on, drinks and sandwiches, Mexican families for you to stare at, and an American blonde or two for Mexicans to stare at. (Make no energetic plans for post-Taboada hours; it relaxes to the point of enervation.) Unless you want the big smorgasbord lunch, don't go on Sundays. **Cortijo,** along the same road, is quieter and cheaper, with one pool, no lunch, and an eccentric proprietor.

Nearby is **La Gruta,** also a popular spa.

NOTE: For a long stay and schooling, investigate, along with the Art Institute, the promising possibilities of the Academia Hispano Americana, in town, which offers small classes in Spanish, history, and literature, and the writing classes, workshops, and lectures of the Centro Internacional, Pila Seca 1.

HOTELS

Because of the wobbly peso, you may be asked to pay your bill in dollars or traveler's checks; credit cards are not accepted in some places. You may have to pay a deposit for a couple or three nights and add a 15% tax to your bill.

The newest hotel here is the **Hacienda de los Flores,** at the top of the street called Hospicio. Small, attractive, and chic with views into the hills and sunsets, and a pool. High moderate to expensive.

The **Hotel Aristos** at the Instituto continues to be favored by long-term winter residents.

Villa Jacaranda, Aldama 53, is small, engaging, and exceedingly well kept, not always true in the best of Mexican hotels. High moderate. The most convenient and popular is the **Posada de San Francisco** on the Plaza Principal. Colonialish patio and rooms and generous meals. Moderate.

El Atascadero, above the town, provides attractive small suites, a pool, and walks to watch the changing lights and shadows of the town. (A steep walk from town, but you can arrange to have a hotel car transport you.) High moderate.

Casa de Sierra Nevada, at Hospicio 7, is an elegant old house of lovely spaces and remote times. The rooms are large and light, the food usually good. Not cheap but hardly expensive for what one gets.

Hotel San Miguel has gone through a number of changes of ownership and mind. However, it *is* an antique mansion, the costs are low, the company youthful, and the town gossip horrendous. Look before you buy. Or go on to the **Posada de las Monjas,** basic, or the **Casa Sauto** (both modest), and the nicely located **Mansion del Bosque.** As well: the pension **Casa Carmen** at Recreo and Correo; the **Posada Carmina** (moderate) on Cuna de Allende 7 in the company of cathedral bells; the **Quinta Loreto** and the **Meson de San Antonio,** both modest to moderate.

SHOPPING

El Colibiri, on the plaza, is a good place for books, art materials, and English conversation.

Casa Maxwell Calle de Canal. A ramble of shops sells a variety of pleasing things from all crafts areas and in every shape and texture;

one section concentrates on furniture in adapted traditional designs, cushions, spreads, and rugs in extraordinary colors and textures.

The **Pegasus** gift shop across from the post office has a popular coffee shop as well as good objects.

New shops keep springing up. See what's new on Correo, on Hernandez Macias and adjoining streets.

Carmen Beckmann   Hernandez Macias. An atelier, and a small shop nearby, can sell you jewelry for $5 or $2,500, in silver or gold, with or without stones, to your design or hers, or repair an antique piece of jewelry. Both workmanship and prices are trustworthy.

Tequis,   on the square. One section contains many things of finely woven straw and pins—butterflies, birds, brooches—of woven strands of vermeil. The other section shows woolens as carpets and subtle hangings, and, from swatches of wool, you may pick the color you want for a round cape with two slits which can be worn in a variety of ways. (Allow several weeks.)

At Zacateros 53 there may still be a craftsman who will mend jewelry for you, or design it or, if you and he have the time, teach you how to make it.

Casa Canal,   Canal 3, for a few respectable antiques and colorful, seductive dresses.

Casa Cohen   on Calle Reloj is a hardware store which shows good-looking metal fixtures and ornaments, and buckles and tic-tac-toe in metals that make good gifts. One of the distinctions of the house is its façade, studded with stars of David, gargoyle animals, and lines of smaller animals headed for Noah's ark at the top.

Anguiano's   Carries a large and inexpensive assortment of hand-loomed textiles and artifacts.

Shops proliferate here as they do in all tourist centers. Local tin-ware and art fill the central streets. See what's happening on tangents of the central square: the streets of Sollano, the meeting of Zacateras and Pila Seca, Hernandez Macias and Ancho de San Antonio. The

Plaza Colonial is a new shopping complex of art supplies, gifts, interesting odds and ends, such as the antiques at **El Atico**.

RESTAURANTS

The best eating is in the hotels and inns: the **Jacarandas,** the **Sierra Nevada,** the reliable spreads of the **San Francisco Hotel,** the simpler *comidas* of the **Carmina.** Then, the restaurants: **La Bodega, El Patio** (try Sunday afternoon buffet), **Mama Mia** (for pizza with noise), and fine enchiladas Suizas at **La Terrazza.** There is good food and bright decor at **El Circo,** at **Sr. Platas** and the appealing restaurant called **La Bugambilia.** Try, also, in the attractive court of the Plaza Colonial complex, the dishes of **La Casona** and those of a coffee shop, **La Dolce Vita.**

For entertainment, the skittering lights and thumping beats of the **Labarantino** discotheque, the **Ring,** and more undoubtedly to come. **Mama Mia** has a tiny nightclub, the **Fragua** is a seasoned and tough entertainer, and, except for Mondays, you get mariachas at **El Patio.** For more passive entertainment, see what's going on at the **Bellas Artes,** the **Centro Internacional,** and the **Angela Peralta Theater,** which offers a variety of attractions, including ballet and chamber music. The newly opened museum, in the old Allende house, often has interesting displays.

TO REMEMBER: Sunday tours (except in December) offer house interiors about which you may have been curious.

San Miguel has a bull ring and occasionally capable *toreros* come out of Mexico City to perform. If you don't understand the legend painted on the outer bull-ring wall, just beyond the entrance, this is what it says: "The citizens of San Miguel are noted for their good breeding and culture. Please do not throw bottles or rocks into the bull ring." For surer safety take the daily video shows in both Jacarandas and Sierra Nevada.

And also to remember: The rudest postal clerks, infinitely ruder than even French clerks, command the package shipping section of the post office. Avoid them; they will sour your day, your week.

Should you be staying for a while in San Miguel, using it as center for exploring Querétaro and Guanajuato, consider also taking a picnic lunch among the vast number of abandoned silver and copper mines of Posos, forty-five minutes away by car. Take the Querétaro road past the Pemex station and on until you see a road sign to the village called Dr. Moro. Follow that road, crossing Route 57, until you come to a generating station where you take a road to the left which leads directly into Posos. With no car and plenty of time, take the bus to San Luis de la Paz and a taxi or bus from that town.

Although dreaming an ambitious dream of mines again pouring copper and silver, probably mercury and possibly gold, and a hearty increase in population, all as the result of a French-Mexican trade pact, the town is a ghost in a ghostly area. Since there is little water, the land is not arable and the gaunt hills are a dry yellow-gray accented with the dusty black of slag hills. A map of 1895 shows Posos as a spot centered among boxes on boxes that indicated mines over a great expanse. There were over 300 mines then and enough mine workers to fill the town with a population of 60,000. Local history does not make it clear whether the Revolution destroyed the town and the mine works or whether the mines became unprofitable at about that time; possibly, a combination of both. Now Posos is streets and streets of abandoned houses, of large, unused schools, of the shell of a substantial church that was never finished, of a population that barely reaches 2,000. There is no restaurant, no decently supplied shop; for even basic shopping one must take the bus to San Luis de la Paz 8 or 10 kilometers away.

As you walk along the desolation of mines at the lower end of town, watch out for square, open wells where the ore was washed, and the immense holes, 800 to 1,000 feet deep, where soundings were probably made, the depth at which the miners worked. (Throw a rock into one of these holes and listen for the length of time it takes to land.) The area is not the cheeriest place for a picnic yet extraordinarily evocative: the bitter hills, a minute chapel at the top of a steep climb, a retaining wall to hold back a mountain, the old castle of a mine owner tucked into folds of hill.

A good portion of depleted Posos lives on the handicrafts—embroidery, beadwork, trapunto, painting on cloth, hooked rugs—taught by a remarkable woman, Juana Molinero de Molinero, the Mayor of Posos. She sees to the schools, to the poor, to the cleanliness of the town, to the health of her citizens, paints, gardens, makes cheeses, sausages, and preserves, is a keen photographer and archivist of her town, always has several pieces of handicrafts going, travels, keeps in constant touch with her five daughters and twenty (perhaps more by now) grandchildren. She is a handsome old woman who, the locals say, "carries Posos on her shoulders" and they should know since it was they, in fierce opposition to the provincial government, who appointed her mayor for three years and three again and will not let her resign. Should you pass her striding through the town in her old-fashioned high boots and swinging woolen skirt, give her a deep bow.

GUANAJUATO

Over the hills from San Miguel, via Dolores Hidalgo, is the historic-tour approach to the city of Guanajuato. Dolores Hidalgo, the birth-place of Hidalgo and the site of the famous *Grito* of Independence (still called out on the night of September 16 each year), is a listless place of no great interest. Avoid it and shorten the route by a broad newer highway.

Beyond it the road runs through plains at first, but soon the hills begin to flow together like billows of green and blue silk brushed with golden light. Near Guanajuato one or two small mining villages tucked into the folds of the hills appear. The great wealth of silver mining of former centuries is now played out and the small quanti-ties, wrested out of these tired workings along with baser metals, provide the most meager of livelihoods. These villages give way to a pure, undisturbed vista of great, lonely mountains cupped around Guanajuato, far below, minute and densely packed on itself, like a coiled cat.

Guanajuato was a magnificent old cat of a city, tired, battered by too much history, and like a cat, didn't try to be lovable. Moody, evocative, held by mountains and clouded by higher mountains, it made no effort to be other than a beautiful ruin of what it once was, untainted by greed for tourists although it was poor, cultivated with-out self-consciousness, strikingly dramatic without postures. With the recent opening of broad avenues, of an arched-over roadway which was once a discouraged riverbed, the city has taken on a welcoming charm and the breathing rhythm of Italian towns: a calm piazza leading to tight alleys that lead, again, to a serene piazza. Travelers say it looks like Toledo, in Spain; Mexicans say it is more beautiful, and it is.

Coming down from the austere mountains into the city, one is confronted immediately by the most telling symbol of Guanajuato's past and its declined present: the immense ruins of one of the local mining empires currently worked as a cooperative that shows no great yield as yet. Sections of thick buttressed wall stand crested with high stone triangles arranged in an immense ring, ostensibly to imitate and flatter the Spanish Crown should the immense quantities of silver extracted from the mines and sent back to Spain not be pleasing enough.

The Spaniards who made their way over the wild, arrogant mountains may have heard of the great silver deposits from the Aztecs (themselves no mean hunters of silver and gold) or stumbled on them by accident. Whatever the means of discovery, within forty years of the Conquest, the earth gushed forth precious metals—quantities of gold and copper accompanied the silver—in a dazzling river, whose largest branch flowed eastward to Spain. Great fortunes were made; baronial houses were built, and richly elaborate churches, whose legend insists that their mortar was mixed with silver and the best Spanish wine, grew from the silvered earth in great flourishes of Mexican baroque, thanksgiving gestures, and propitiation. Guanajuato was the richest mining city in the world, the site of the most highly productive single mine, and its aristocracy, made royal in exchange for large gifts to the Crown, scattered millions of pesos as if the fountain of silver would never dry.

It did, though. Some of the mines began to give out at the same time as the patience and docility of the semienslaved indigenes who worked the mines were wearing dangerously thin. In addition, intellectuals were sensing the breezes of revolution and change in Europe which neither an ocean nor the Inquisition could keep out of Mexico. The combined ideals and furies overwhelmed the city in September of 1810 and kept it bathed in flame and blood for some time. Some months after the insurgents, led by Father Hidalgo, conquered the city the Royalist forces took over, and the accomplished promise of the viceregal general that he would take "this city by blood and fire and razing it to the ground" further poisoned and corroded the once stately city. And, as it suffered one of the first, Guanajuato suffered one of the last monstrous acts of the early, abortive struggle for independence: in 1811 the four insurgent leaders, Father Hidalgo among them, were shot in northern Mexico. At the insistence of the head of the Royalist forces, their heads were sent to Guanajuato, put into iron cages, and nailed to the four corners of the large old granary (Alhóndiga) in the center of town. There they remained ten years.

As if this were not enough, early in this century a great flood drowned works, churches, houses, and people, leaving the lower town a desolate de Chirico landscape—a curve of heavy meaningless arch, a scarred, half-drowned church, a stretch of aqueduct topped by headless saints dominating dry shrub and cracked earth.

But this area, Marfil, experienced a brilliant renaissance, brought about by an Italian-born sculptor, George Belloli, who saw in the old stones—an act of imagination amounting to genius—the possibilities of making an extraordinary luxury housing development. Working with the hilly terrain and the meandering of the subdued river, he changed the ancient vats into pools and the blind arches into high, noble doorways. The houses are beautifully proportioned and the decorative elements perfect and often rare. In order to avoid desecration of his houses by the ferocities of bad taste, the many-gifted artist decorated and furnished a number of them himself: a stone musician-angel made by an Indian craftsman to hang over a fireplace; a crudely carved, lively baptismal font to make a birdbath; the gilded carved side of an old chest became the headboard of a bed; and a bald, black Christ dominates a tall white wall.

The upper, unreconstructed town has its own mellow charms and splendors. Pushed in by the mountains, the town coils, curves, leaps up, and drops in unexpected patterns. The streets and alleys spray out of large-fountained small plazas like the petals of a flower, or creep through and around each other like a tangle of vines. Some streets are narrow sunless slots, whose balconies almost touch; some seem to hang from stone arches; others stare down at scallops of stone or up at a series of long, flat stairs. Fountains of Roman size and boldness crowd modest, haphazard corners. The scratched, shell-torn wall of an alley will suddenly reveal an old door, its lintel defaced, its ancient wood still belligerently studded. Above, below, are immense stone buttresses and lantern-hung walls washed in the infinite tones of aged white.

Having wandered the streets and alleys and tasted their antique flavor, you might ask your way to several specific points of interest. The basilica, originally the Church of San Francisco on the Plaza de la Paz, is of a number of periods of reconstruction and addition. Its major interest lies in its "miraculous" Virgin, not in herself a notable miracle maker, but miraculously preserved in a cave in Granada for about 800 years, having been hidden there by the devout when the Moors invaded early in the eighth century. Subsequently she was sent by Philip II of Spain as a gift to rich and generous Guanajuato. The legend is a pleasing one and the Virgin highly venerated, but the style of carving might belie the excess of centuries attributed to her. The Church of San Diego, facing the Jardín de la Unión, has a strong, uninhibited Churrigueresque façade, in contrast to the somewhat calmer La Compañía, nearby. You will notice as you pass this church and others a sign, TENGA LA BONDAD DE NO ORINARSE EN ESTE ATRIO ("Please have the kindness not to urinate in this atrium"); the signs are attached to already deeply stained corners.

Next door stands the formal Colonial-style entrance of the university at the top of an infinity of stairs, giving a suggestion of a house of learning as Olympus. Education at this breath-eating altitude might be sobering for the young, but what about elderly professors and lowland visitors?

A short drop to Juárez and you are on the street of the main market, one of the most brilliant in Mexico. Built with immense pride—and speeches and photographs of dignitaries—early in the century, it retains its Victorian-railroad-station style of ironwork and vaulting glass and a balcony from which one can view the globe baskets of eggs, the great abstractions of fruit and vegetable arrangements, of breads and shining soda bottles. A newer adjoining building, tiers of shallow arcades, is the site of attractive eating stalls, neat, warm, and inviting—if you dare, and you might.

Another marketplace shapes on the days before the Day of the Dead, in Plazuela de San Fernando. Exquisitely, meticulously made flowers, coffins, skulls, miniature television sets, minute churches, lambs, birds, and a dozen etceteras, all candy, are sold here by the women who make them.

The orderly and interesting museum shows the expected Mexican talent at dramatic presentation in a cryptlike area that holds huge bronze heads of heroes, among them Morelos, Hidalgo, and Allende. In adjoining rooms, the crafts of the area; groups of old photographs, some entertaining, many moving; a history of mining from pre-Columbian times, through the Conquest and into 1910 when the Revolution broke out. One amusing room holds early donations: locks, maps, stirrups, church sculptures, and silver organs in a curious miscellany.

By way of the expected heroic murals one goes up to a rewarding surprise, the limpid, dignified, and remarkably expressive portraits by Hermangildo Busto. These are largely portraits of neighbors who lived in his native small town in the late nineteenth century (he died in 1907) and a magical collection, made more evocative by the fact that Busto had practically no formal training and is consequently referred to as a "primitive"—actually as primitive as the great English portraitists.

The Alhóndiga (now the museum) was built in the late eighteenth century to store grain against the possible recurrence of a famine such as the city had once suffered. Since then it had several public uses, but its fame rests on the stellar role it played in the War of Independence and as the stage of the heroism of El Pípila, whose much larger-than-life statue now stands on a hill overlooking the city. He was a peasant boy who, carrying a stone slab as shield and a torch, crawled through the Royalist bullets to set fire to the door of the Alhóndiga and thus opened it to the insurgents.

Another native citizen-artist was Diego Rivera, born on a street called Pozitos, at 47. It is a rambling alley that managed to keep its tall old lights and the Rivera house, now a museum, shows vestiges of stateliness as pieces of neo-classic plasterwork and attractive balconies.

One of the town's much advertised attractions is the cemetery (Panteón), at the top of one of the hills. It affords wide views of the countryside and entry to a crypt of well-dressed mummies. The viewing of town worthies who should long have disappeared from view is a perverse delight and an active local sport. It can easily be skipped. See, instead, the opera house, the Teatro Juárez, ringed by columns and topped with neo-classic figures, as ornate as Juárez was plain. For a small admission charge one can enter its world of courageously excessive decoration, culminating in a beguiling foyer of faded brocade settees, chandeliers, and the required classical heads of composers.

Below the steps of the theater, decorated by students swigging bottles of Coke, is a big iron planter that once served as garbage recipient and is still marked *"basura,"* the Spanish word for garbage. A few paces below that is the stop for the bus that takes one through the tunnels, some green-hung, some like medieval dungeons, that now cover the city's river and ease traffic most picturesquely. Buses make frequent stops, a few specifically cover central tourist attractions, so you won't be taken too far off your intended route.

In this massively churched town, most of the churches built with mining money, the two most interesting are at opposite ends of the economic and social scale. Halfway up a funnel of alleys, sitting on a brightly refurbished square that might be a set for *The Barber of Seville,* is the Iglesia de los Mineros—the Church of the Miners—its more formal name Mineral de Cata, for the silver-mining bonanza that exploded out of this area early in the eighteenth century. It is not large or rich, its facade not particularly meaningful as art or display, but its walls are astonishingly and solidly hung (except where there has been a theft or two) with *retablos* and mementos of thanksgiving for miraculous recoveries from illness and, particularly, accidents. The *retablos*—small, votive paintings on tin or wood—are painstakingly literal, done in the meticulous, repetitious detail of most primitives and the rigid color schemes of children's paintings: blue is for sky, brown is for earth, pink is for flesh. Row on row, they speak eloquently of mining accidents, of limbs crushed by fallen rock, of noxious gases pouring into vaults of rock, of inundations, and all held back by the miraculous intervention of the miners' Virgin. Whether by talent, or accident, or intense emotion, a few of the *retablos* approach strong naturalistic art; one, for instance, shows a group of trapped men waiting to be rescued, obviously with little hope, from waters seeping into their cave. The air is heavy and dark, the rocks of an ominous color, the only light rests on the huddled figures, whose heads, legs, and arms hang in utter despair. The mementos—babies' shoes, braids of hair, the silk cord used to enlace a couple during the marriage ceremony, a vial holding a preserved appendix—are not only gifts for aid received, but offerings for future protection, an amassing of potential help for the next disaster, which might come tomorrow. (Take your opera glasses; because of many thefts of *retablos,* the best and most valuable have been moved to upper reaches.)

At the top of the city, at the top of the money heap, sits the Church of San Cayetano, the Valenciana. It was built by the owner of the richest mine in the area in the latter half of the eighteenth century, an act of gratitude and piety and certainly a piece of conspicuous consumption—one of the few, after the amassing of servants, carriages, concubines, and palaces, available to a *conde* in those days. Although he reputedly squandered unbelievable sums of money, he did not bear the cost of the opulent church—more strictly, his private chapel—alone; a vast number of miners helped in its construction (no overtime) and, in addition, were required to contribute a large lump of silver weekly to defray costs. What the *conde*'s contribution was, other than issuing the orders, is not surely known. At any rate, he built well: it is one of the most beautiful churches in Mexico and one of the most dramatically placed, high above the town, cresting a slope of rough hills and staring across the vast, angry ruins of the old mine. Its façade is of a delicate, light style, neater and more restrained than similar Churrigueresque fronts. Its interior is joyous music: three fantastic altars spread and soar to the ceiling, exuberant and laden like an orchard in season, a dance of gilded cherubs, angels, saints, flourishes, curvings inward, bellyings outward—scarcely Christian or dour Spanish. It might all be very foolish if it weren't so exquisitely worked and, within the variety, wonderfully balanced, the figures and details of ornamentation differing infinitely but placed in similar rhythmic patterns. In a small chapel in back, there are a few saints' figures one can examine more closely and in the calm of simpler surroundings. Though these are not in flight, they are of the same lovely, finished quality as the swinging, bouncing saints in the church proper.

Opposite the church is the former house of the *conde* himself, much of it now redone by an architect who retained the essential structure and proportions of the old rooms as well as the sturdy old beams. It may not be open to the public, but if access is at all possible, the old portion of the house is very much worth seeing. There may still exist the beautifully sized rooms slipping from the classic inner court and closed from it by heavy wooden doors with thick, broad metal studs, like the breasts of Iron Maidens. The graceful shell carving which melts into the thickness of the wall above the windows and doors may still be there, and the light coil of stair which leads to the nursery, the covered trunks whose leather has survived the centuries, the many-sectioned, intricately carved chests and, above all, the magnificent view from the back of the house, an appropriate sight for the owner of all he surveyed.

Guanajuato has one of the best orchestras in Mexico, and since it doesn't perform too often, a concert is quite a gala affair. If your visit includes a Sunday evening, spend some of it watching the *paseo* in the Jardín de la Unión, at the bottom of town.

Two or three times a week during the spring, the university per-forms classic Spanish plays in the appealing old squares, one of which resembles, and may have been a conscious imitation of, the beautiful Plaza de los Faroles of Córdoba. The performances, authentic to the point of requiring that local householders wear the dress of the period, are called *Entremeses Cervantinos,* since it is mainly the short plays of Cervantes (*entremeses* means side dishes) which are performed. In addition, Guanajuato (and to a degree, San Miguel) attracts at that time international theater and dance companies of high accomplishments.

HOTELS

The **Castillo de Santa Cecilia** (moderate) is the classic hotel, a thing of battlements and rose gardens. Even if you don't stay and your visit includes a Sunday, have the *comida,* the full spread, including paella, in the wide and deep dining room. The cost will be truly modest, the food unremarkable, but the old-fashioned atmosphere, the old-fashioned service, and the old-fashioned middle-class stolidity of the clients make a stimulating experience.

The newer **Hotel Real de Minas,** the **Hotel Carruaje,** and the **Parador San Xavier** follow the popular hacienda-modern style, which works well and attractively. (All the above high moderate.)

For more modest and convenient accommodations there are the **Posada de Santa Fe** on the small central Jardín de la Unión and nearby, on Juárez, the **Hotel San Diego.** A short distance out of the center is the **Posada de la Presa,** small and full of personality. (The above are modest to moderate in price and, like almost all Guanajuato hotels, offer meals. You might as well; the city seems indifferent to cuisine, although the food at the **Motel Guanajuato** frequently rises above the general standard.)

Several motels have cropped up on the highways near the city. Look in at the **Motel Guanajuato,** on the road from Dolores Hidalgo, or the nearby **Hotel Valenciana,** both moderate.

SHOPPING

Above the **Posada de la Presa** you should come to the **Plazuela de Calle Hidalgo** and above that to an airy, colorful place of local *artesanias.*

The shops in the **Real de Minas** may reveal something you want. As may its neighbor, the **Bazar de Carreton,** a flea market's flea market that crawls up a hill dragging brass beds, stone doorways, papier-mâché figures, books, *mariachi* sombreros, horseshoes, locks and unrelated keys, old banners, buns, wheels, dolls' legs—junk at its purest and rustiest.

A contrast is provided by the **Alfareria Tradicional,** Pastita 45, not easy to find but worth the effort. A meander of Colonial houses, workshops, yards, and kilns produce, or rather reproduce, singularly lovely pottery on traditional designs.

On and around the Plaza de la Paz you will find a few shops of interest: a few worldly adaptations of Mexican crafts, antiques like the bald, black, starved Christ common in this area—possibly because he looks like a middle-aged exhausted miner. Here too you may find the old silver coins which make good, small gifts, if you want to pay the price for authenticity. The shops may have bits of old glass, some furniture, a few *santos*—not much of any one object, but interesting conglomerations. If the shop of the Posada de la Presa is still functioning, you might find some attractive things there.

For inexpensive souvenirs, your best bets are the market and the local prison. The latter's most famous products are walnut shells, opened carefully in two unbroken halves, hinged and hooked to open and close, and peopled with numerous microscopic figures: a wedding scene for instance—the bride veiled in white, the groom in black, and a varicolored set of relatives—or a bullfight complete with agitated spectators. They are unbelievable and make fine souvenirs, and your friends are hardly likely to be oversupplied with them.

Guanajuato, and the area around it, is noted for its semiprecious stones, about which there is no sound advice to be given. Just remember that they aren't to cost too much. The same holds true of the copper, and the leather goods in the market.

Should you be traveling northwestward from Guanajuato, stop for a while in Aguascalientes, a lively agricultural center and the home of an enterprising populace, which restored an imposing Colonial building and turned it into a Casa de la Cultura, which instructs almost one thousand students in various arts and crafts. In April the city holds a fiesta in honor of San Marcos, and for his delectation stages plays and concerts, arranges art exhibitions, and—on the lighter side—gambling on just about everything from cock fights to roulette, and there are bullfights and folk dances of several regions. After a long rest, there is a Feria de la Uva (grape) in August, which coincides with the Feast of the Assumption, and there is a modified repeat of the April pleasures.

With enough time, give Zacatecas a couple of hours; it is a pleasing town not far from Aguascalientes.

HACIENDA

The Mexican Revolution of 1910, the culmination of the struggle which began a hundred years earlier, has had its bloody face painted in miles of murals, its raw screams sung in Mexican music, its tortured complexities explored in oceans of words; and in all of them figures the fat, feudal life of the hacienda, whose glories and excesses were like those of our great Southern plantations and, like them, suffered destruction and decay. Many haciendas were burned and pillaged during the Revolution, others were taken over and used as public buildings, some are now country hotels, some have been left to rot, and a few are still going through shadow-play functions.

The Hacienda San Francisco, in the state of Hidalgo, probably still produces pulque, as it has for centuries; now it may run in rivulets compared to the gushing rivers of former days. Pulque is the whitish ferment, in taste something of a cross between beer and buttermilk, derived from the sweet water *(aguamiel)* produced and stored by the maguey plant. The maguey makes much of the strong scenery of the Mexican highlands, marching through the landscape in forbidding rows, more like carvings of gray-green stone than growing, organic matter. The one plant provided the Aztecs with many of life's necessities. The fiber was made into cloth and sewn with a needle and thread which were the point of a maguey leaf blade and its attached length of fiber-thread. A drinking vessel was made of its inner membranes, easily shaped and impermeable; the same layers of leaf provided the paper for Aztec codices. The snails and worms that settled in the thick, sturdy blades were eaten—and still are. Most importantly, of course, it provided pulque, so satisfying a drink that a number of deities were created in its honor. Pulque is cheap, lightly alcoholic, reputedly full of vitamins, and an ancient habit of the mountain country. With the improving economy of Mexico, however, some pulque drinkers can now afford beer, and village children who once lived their short lives behind veils of pulque stupor now drink *refrescos,* soft drinks of jewel-tone colors and the sweetness of melted lollipops. Maguey fields have been turned for corn or uprooted for factories, but enough of the sour comfort gushes in *pulquerías* to support a number of plantations and families.

The Hacienda San Francisco is in part very old, having been expanded and refurbished in the 1880s. The complex of buildings stands utterly alone, rising from an endless stretch of stolid maguey and ringed by crusts of brown hills. The generous semicircle which fronts the main house was designed to hold fifty carriages at one time. The walls surround innumerable gateways of convoluted grillwork and long flourishes of floral-patterned tile on arbor arches and fountains. Once the family had its choice of two swimming pools and could amuse itself in its own bull ring or spend its time supervising the fifty gardeners imported from Japan to plan and maintain the landscaping.

To get around the estate conveniently, tracks were laid and a small trolley (Toonerville-style and possibly still standing as a rueful witness of passing splendors) was installed. Its terminus was the large building in which the pulque had been processed, a building still enlivened by robust primitive murals painted by the pulque workers themselves, depicting the processing of pulque, its pleasures and mythology. In the center of the plant there stands a large boxlike cage carved in the heavy rhythms of German-Gothic-Victorian-Díaz style; it was here that the pulque was weighed and payment doled out, supervised by a saint painted high on a nearby wall.

In an alley beyond the plant are the huge stables which recently housed one carriage, still used when a car breaks down, and an assortment of pigs, goats, sheep, an old horse, and bloody sheepskins hanging from a beam overhead.

Back of the house, the plant, and the stables is the small feudal city of narrow streets in which there still live pulque workers, carpenters, blacksmiths, repairmen, and their families. Their church is the private chapel of the *hacendado*'s family, a well-preserved baroque church with much fresh gold and white laced around lugubrious, overripe Italianate paintings. It is in good shape because it is so rarely used, coming to life only when an itinerant priest finds his way there.

The house itself is of many rooms, ranged in the classic Arab-Spanish style around a flowered courtyard, eighteenth century except for a pioneer crank-up phone on one of its walls. Two bathrooms are fairly recent innovations, innately efficient but made impotent by the scarcity of water during the dry season; then they smell like medieval Dijon in July. Other old discomforts have been partially erased by electricity, a modern phone, and a television set which, in this remoteness, must function mainly as a sign of prosperity and progress.

The spacious salon is a repository of late-eighteenth-century extravagances: ornately delicate tables, brocades held by heavy gold sashes, deeply tufted velvet couches, and silk chairs—overstuffed and spilling a little, like greedy cheeks; everything placed in military four-square stiffness. The furniture was imported from France, via ship to Veracruz, and then carried on carts, burros, and human backs into the mountains and across the wide plain.

The huge dining room holds a table of baronial size, surrounded by precisely placed sentinels of high-backed chairs. Their formality is oddly set off by the bare feet and black braids of the numerous shy servants who offer pulque and tequila and, later, immense platters of broad beans and fresh-picked corn sprinkled with grated homemade cheese, lime, and salt. Nothing is served in a small dish or in a moderate quantity; like the rooms of the house, like the hospitality, every gesture is wide and lavish, bespeaking a time when dishes were ordered by the barrelsful from France (service for fifty was an ordinary measure), when fifteen members of a family, accompanied by a retinue of servants, made their leisured royal progress on the Grand Tour of Europe's capitals during Mexico's dry springs or rainy summers.

The great old enclave, the aging furniture, the home-grown food on royal salvers, the barefoot shadowy servants are vivid and real when one sits among them, but they fade into a misty limbo as one leaves through the maguey fields, which are like the dark woods of myth. No flowers blossom in the maguey, no bee explores, the spare trees have few leaves and many thorns, no birds fly or sing, only silent creatures, worms and snails, move secretly through gray-green blades.

MORELIA

As you approach it from the Bahío (San Miguel, Guanajuato, Salamanca, etc.), riding over strange lakes among lovely hills, past the old convents of Yuriria and Cuitzeo, Morelia presents no astonishing presence. It is a restrained town, from its beginnings a town of intellectual endeavor and elevated tastes. Among its numerous Colonial treasures are the university, which stems through a long line of scholastic antecedents from one of the earliest colleges on the continent, and the church and convent of Las Rosas—now a music conservatory—a development of the music classes introduced in the nuns' school of Las Rosas two hundred years ago. Morelia has a sense of continuity—not jelled in its antiquity like San Miguel or passing it by, like Mexico City; rather, moving in a stately pace with its heritage. Originally, the city was probably a Tarascan settlement ruled from Tzintzuntzan. In the middle of the sixteenth century, it was granted the status of "city" by the Spanish Crown and named Valladolid, after the birthplace of the Viceroy Mendoza; and in the nineteenth century, named Morelia, in honor of the hero Morelos. (The Morelos house is now a small museum devoted to the hero's life and work.)

As elsewhere, the best thing to do about Morelia is walk in it. Get to the central square bordered by wide arcades—one side all cafés with bright tablecloths and busy vendors of mats, lottery tickets, and shoe shines; another is bordered by a handsome pedestrian mall, on Corregidora, holding a very, very old pharmacy—for a look at the cathedral, considered by the cognoscenti to be the most beautiful in Mexico. It took a hundred years to build, from the middle of the seventeenth to the middle of the eighteenth century, but the confusion of styles one might expect did not happen here, nor did the joyful jungle of decorations hung on so many Mexican churches. Its plateresque exterior sounds the keynote of the town: reserved, well-balanced, subtly aristocratic.

Walk back on the main boulevard (Madero) past the cathedral and the parks which flank it and, if you haven't done so already, ask for a map of the town at the desk of the **Hotel Virrey de Mendoza,** or the **Hotel de la Soledad.** Continuing on Madero, one passes the Colegio de San Nicolás, once a Jesuit church and monastery and the oldest college in Mexico. It knew Father Hidalgo as a student and professor and is now part of a complex of colleges, one section frescoed by Marian Greenwood, an American artist. A great part of its current charms is the gaggles of students lolling in the small gardens. Still walking in the same direction and then right on Gomez Farias, one comes on broad new arches that hang over a raised side of the street. This is the new sweets market, one colorful, crowded cave after another crammed with jars of *cajeta* (caramel sauce), *ates* (fruit candies rather like Turkish delight without the powder), and *morelianas* (flat disks of burnt milk and sugar, somewhat like caramels but only in the way that a da Vinci Madonna is related to a chromo). (If you know someone in Mexico City who deserves a small gift, bring *morelianas,* a great favorite not easy to find in the big city.) *Caveat:* the disks are wrapped, which makes it all right to feel the package before you buy. If it is stiff and brittle put it down and try for one that gives and bends a bit, meaning the *morelianas* are fresher.

Down the hill, on either Guillermo Prieto or Nigromante, with careful attention to their noble palaces, one enters the eighteenth century of Las Rosas. The church of Las Rosas has an impressive façade of stout old doors, gargoyles, and lovely plateresque carving, and an interior brought to life by a gay baroque altar with cherubs' heads, like candy dolls, embedded in the elaborations of gilt. The convent, though it houses a serious and highly reputable music conservatory whose boys' choir is widely famous and whose practice rooms give off hard-working sounds, is a hushed place of high, stern walls studded with gargoyle waterspouts, of the horizontal calm of an arcaded upper walk, of size and sobriety.

Before you go back to the busier world of the main streets, examining doors, street lamps, and lettering as you go, look in at the School of Fine Arts, on Guillermo Prieto, which is, in general design, like the music school and also felicitously appropriate for the cultivation of the arts. (This liveliness of arts, education, the many young running among regal old buildings, is strongly reminiscent of English university towns.)

Back on Madero, and having crossed, walk away from the cathedral to León Guzmán, and just inside the block you will come across one of the most fantastic façades in all of Mexico. Massive columns of broad, heavy ornaments of Oriental complexity weighing down the charming little baroque church of La Merced; pressed into tight space, without the air of an atrium, her steps worn, a downthrust design pushing at her heavy door, she seems ready to topple from exhaustion. For calmer air, follow Guzmán to the Plazuela de Rayón, sit down on one of its benches, and look around the little formal square of the empty fountain at the somber cypresses and three palms surrounded by low houses of faint ocher, diffident blues, and palest yellows, their walls hung with old grillwork lanterns on graceful stems.

Allende leads back into the plaza and passes three majestic Colonial structures: the Municipal Palace, whose murals by Salze manage to be both sturdy and lyrical, the Palace of Justice, and near them the Museum of the State of Michoacán, whose halls display a variety of Tarascan objects, period furniture and costumes, old books, some stunning pieces of religious art, a fascinating collection of engravings showing Valladolid-Morelia at different periods of its life. Once upon a time the museum showed flagellants' chains hanging on a wall, crucifixes hung on barbed chains, and a Christ made of an untouched tree and limbs, only the face and crown of thorns carved, the face gashed, and the forehead covered with blood. Now they have been replaced by nineteenth-century watercolors, and numerous birds in cages singing to the flowers in a pretty courtyard.

Although Morelia's climate is pleasant, she still shares the vivid Mexican sun, and this might be the time to take a shaded drive to the outskirts of town, to the Church of Guadalupe and the aqueduct. As the long parade of high stone arches comes into view, notice the way a mass of houses melts into the arches; then both disappear, like a channeled stream, into the formal shape of the city below. If you can, take a short walk through Cuauhtémoc Park, whose entrance is at the meeting of fountain and aqueduct, and then go on, past the arches, to the Sanctuary of Guadalupe. It sits at the side of a small park (as you may have gathered by now, Morelia tastefully surrounds its antiquities with bountiful quantities of living green, except when she decides, in the cement fever which has attacked all of Mexico, that blank blazing space does better and is more fashionable) in a rather isolated, subdued area. The architecture is not memorable, but the interior is: not one inch of space is allowed to breathe easy. Huge flowers of white, blue, and pink surrounded by loops, scallops, and filigree so thickly encrust the walls that the large paintings recede into a flatness beyond that lent them by mediocrity. The *retablos* in the chapel at the side are quite another matter. Carefully, painstakingly worked, they are acts of devotion to the Virgin of Guadalupe and San Antonio of Padua, thanking them for curing a husband's addiction to drink, for the recovery of a child from illness, for the miraculous healing of a deep bullet wound. Those who cannot afford to hire a *retablo* painter and feel their own painting skills inadequate write their messages (the near-illiteracy is betrayed by the common spelling of *Virgen* as *Birgen* and *vida* as *bida*) and, so that the Virgin or Saint Anthony might know who is writing, attach photographs to their letters.

The old market which stood behind the cathedral in traditional partnership has been replaced by a new one, on the Calle Lazaro Cárdenas. Stroll through to peer into the bowls offered by the eating stalls: fish stews, iguana eggs, steaming lungs, heads and innards. As always, the fruits and vegetables make delightful compositions and the baskets of beans and grains still lifes in earth colors.

HOTELS

The calm, the climate (occasionally tricky in wintertime), and the intrinsic charms of Morelia make it a good town in which to catch one's breath for a few days before going back to Mexico City or continuing westward. Also, Morelia is the proud possessor of one of the most engaging of inns, the **Villa Montaña** in the hills of Santa María, a few minutes' ride from the town. Each little house—one room or two—is quite different from the other, and all imaginatively furnished. The bathrooms are gaily tiled and pour *hot* water; the pool is warmed; the meals are handsomely served. High moderate.

For a short stay in the center of town there is the **Hotel Virrey de Mendoza,** popular with tourists and tourist agencies for its "Colonial atmosphere." (Keep in mind that the phrase sometimes means too much dark wood and weak light bulbs.) The **Alameda,** across the street, is its modern annex. (European plan, modest to moderate.) Smaller, lighter, and very attractive is the **Hotel de la Soledad,** a block from the main square (at Zaragoza and Ocampo). The building is a genuine old coaching inn, recently restored and decorated in a nice blend of traditional crafts and modern comfort. (European plan, moderate.)

Suites Normandie, also downtown, and its restaurant are highly respected, or you might prefer the newness of the **Hotel Presidente.** The hill of Santa María, in the vicinity of the Villa Montaña, is sprouting a considerable number of inns: the **Hostal Las Camalinas,** the **Posada Bella Vista,** the former increasingly popular for its meals. For more basic accommodations examine the possibilities of the **Hotel Michoacán** behind the bus station, the **Casa de Huespedes Perla** on Madero, and, even more basic, the student hotels on the main square.

Although eating out is not a habit of small-city Mexicans, one is not limited to hotels' dining rooms. There is good food available at **Las Comensales,** at **La Cabaña de Vic, La Posta del Gallo,** and in the coffee shop of the **Alameda Hotel** if you don't want a large meal. Sandwiches, eggs, tacos, chicken soups can be found in the cafés along Madero.

Or try the small restaurants near the big spread of cement flanked by streets named for two great churchmen, Quiroga and Las Casas, or follow the portals past the **Virrey de Mendoza** and turn into what remains of the ornate old marketplace for modest eating places, some quite appealing, all very Mexican and never ready before six in the evening.

SHOPPING

The **Virrey de Mendoza** and the **Villa Montaña** have gift shops, and there is the general market to browse in and the stalls attached to the sweets market. **Vicki** has interesting shops in the **Hotel Mendoza** and on the hill of Santa María, which specialize in hand-embroidered blouses, casual wear, and table linens, also unusually fine cutlery, some clay objects, some of metal, and an old gun or two. **Cerda,** on Zaragoza, divides itself into exquisite lacquer work and equally exquisite embroidery, each the domain of a Cerda sister. One doesn't buy this remarkable craftsmanship for centavos, but you will not be overcharged. Up beyond the hills of Santa María, **Señal** produces extraordinary woodwork, some of it carryable—like a salad bowl—and some of it large, but shippable—like benches and tables. The respect for grains, patina, workmanship, and design produces beautiful things. (Some of the smaller objects may be on view at the Villa Montaña.) Back down in Santa María: **Bizet,** who does careful work in iron and handmade cutlery; **Jacques** and **Maja,** whose smart things are based on local crafts. In the dusty or muddy, depending on the season, village of Capula, a few miles away, there is a family called Espinosa which shapes ceramics on one or two of the patterns you may have seen in the museum of Pátzcuaro.

REMINDER: It is not worth elaborate rearrangement of travel plans, but if you can be in Morelia on Sunday, so much the better. The music and art schools will be closed, but the market is busy, there is a band concert—replete with Juan Strauss—in the square and some *barrio* or other (this takes a little wandering off the main streets) has set some benches up in the street, collected a band and a strong-voiced *ran-chera* singer, and entertains itself, at small price, for the rebuilding of the local church. There might also be something—a concert, a film—at the museum or the Mexican-North American Institute.

MEXICAN HOURS

3:10 P.M. *A boy of nine grasps the hand of a passing American whom he has never seen before. The child murmurs "amigo" and, hand in hand, they walk down the main street of Morelia.*

3:30 *The gateman of a large hotel in Cuernavaca, having admitted some visitors, helps them stare at a new poured-concrete structure, an immense moth with half-folded wings. Asked what use it will be put to, the gateman answers, "I'm pretty sure it's a soda fountain. . . ."* (Long pause.) *"Or, very likely a church. . . ."* (Pause.) *"Who knows? Pretty, though, isn't it?"*

3:50 *Just off the road near Champotón, a* zopilote *(buzzard) swoops blackly down on a dead iguana, followed immediately by a cloud of his confreres who crowd him, push, peck, and torment him to get the prize away. Like a fat old lady on hot sand, he hobbles and waddles awkwardly to escape them; they follow in the same erratic, painful gait. He flies straight upward. They come after, beating him down again. He tries frantically to swallow his catch whole, before they can tear a piece from him. He can't and must disgorge some of it. The friends pounce, but he is too fast for them. He regains the morsel and flies away with it, still pursued by the flock, now in strong, efficient flight and screaming like sick babies.*

4:00 *Two blond young men wearing long-sleeved white shirts and black ties order club sandwiches and* malteadas *in a café in Mérida. They order in painstaking Spanish and continue their conversation in English over a detailed map of the city. They are apprentice Mormon missionaries, systematically covering house after house and street after street. Mexico has special importance for them because it is here, some believe, that sacred tablets of the Mormons are buried. One of the ironies of the quest is that although it has not yet unearthed the tablets or inspired much conversion, it has scratched up impressive pieces of Mexican paganism.*

4:15 *A woman in a second-class carriage of the train prepares to nurse her month-old infant. As she unwraps it from the folds of her rebozo, the tiny hands shoot forth to display ten minuscule dots of blood-red nail polish.*

4:30 *A peasant from Miacatlán welcomes a friend from Coatlán just boarding the rural bus. They ride silently through drought-wearied fields whose horses are long rib cages on skeletal legs. The cows are too starved to stand up. One man turns to the other: "Two days ago we put the Virgin out to feel the sun bake, to feel the thirst of the earth. But the whore didn't come through. Tomorrow we put out Tata Chuchu [diminutive and endearment for Jesus Christ] and he'll give us rain."*

From a window of a chic café in the modern, classy, and expensive Zona Rosa, an observer notices a man leading an unbelievably large, black shambling dog, both followed at a distance by a straggle of youngsters. A closer look proves the dog to be a bear. The man taps him; he rises to his hind legs and "dances" a few tired turns to the man's drumming and tuneless song. The short, desultory performance goes on several times in the shadow of a sleek hotel and collects a respectable amount of pesos from tourists to whom this is as legendary as Aztec gods.

4:45 *The majestic Tehuanas are now in Oaxaca's museum. Having spotted an American couple, they move toward them. Displacing the man with their bulk and might, they greet the woman and proceed to examine her. They feel the cloth of her dress, touch her hair, and discuss among them whether its color is natural or dyed; differ about the seemliness of so much lipstick, and as if she were a doll, turn her for a better look at the cut of the dress and hair style. After a leisured survey, suspecting that she might possibly be human and sentient, the eldest and largest asks her where she is from. She answers, "New York." Unimpressed, the Tehuana answers, "We're from Juchitán. We'll be in the market on Sunday. Come. Don't forget. Good-by." They move off like ships in full sail.*

5:00 *On a fairly crowded street in Mexico City, a beggar approaches the one impossible touch, a man who has a stack of records under one arm, a valise under the other, and in his hands two heavy baskets. It cannot be stupidity; it must be a private Mexican joke, to beg of this one burdened man when there are so many others around, and curiosity as to what the beggee might possibly do or say.*

PÁTZCUARO

Pátzcuaro is a heaped-up, scrambled town whose streets live between incomplete collapse and incomplete repair; its "perfect" climate includes frequent rains; compared to Morelia's neatness it is as free-form as a stain, and the famous butterfly nets are not as commonly visible as advertised. Yet Pátzcuaro is the dream town of many travelers. This may be due to the combination of vivid Indian life and decent accommodations and, of course, its lake, studded with steep, green islands.

Pátzcuaro might make a two-day trip out of Morelia by car or bus. You might stop at Quiroga, a village which has dwindled into a market for the local wood crafts, and at Tzintzuntzan, whose onomatopoeic name ("Place of the Hummingbirds") and fabled splendor as the capital of the Tarascan kingdom (proof, the Tombs of Kings is now being disinterred on the outskirts of the village) hardly prepare one for a village of little character except for a plateresque church exterior and the good-looking local people at their many stands of crude though distinctive pottery. However, the pottery, like the wood of Quiroga, can be bought in Pátzcuaro on Friday, the big market day, and Morelia at almost any time.

If one of your days is Friday, dash to the lake in the morning to watch the Indian dugouts streaming in with their loads of produce and sturdy, handsome people. Then follow them to the market just off the larger of the town's two squares. It is a big Indian market like many others, but there is something about the looks and manner of the Tarascans—or maybe it is the sound of the language—which makes it seem more efficient and sharper than others; no one dozes in the sun hoping not to be disturbed. The Tarascan is serious and enterprising and wastes little time. (Sometimes, winding among the distant hills, one passes a group of women walking briskly, gossiping, keeping the children to the side of the road, and spinning busily, all at the same time.) Not nearly as chatty, nor gleaming with shrewd good will like the Zapotec, the local people attract by their quiet independence, a stalwart *amour-propre* which permits no one to say "the cute little Indian" or "the poor little Indian." The mountain Mixes break one's heart, the Tehuanas terrify, the Totonacs appeal shyly, the Zapotecs charm the sense out of one's head, one respects the Tarascan. Not nearly as haughty as Tehuanas—only Edith Sitwell was—the women are quite regal in their long-sleeved, high-necked blouses (Gibson girl with a rural flavor) tucked into long dark skirts of heavy homespun wool, worn smooth in front, falling in folds at the back, and held by a bright band which circles the waist a number of times, one of the regional costumes that has not yet altogether disappeared. Above this there are the native endowments of dark-golden skin, black, black eyes, and lustrous black braids pulled back to show ornate earrings.

After walking up and down the cobbled streets (like San Miguel, Pátzcuaro requires heavy-soled shoes), looking down at its tiled roofs and old courtyards, and up to slender carved pillars of the houses above, go to the arts and crafts museum (anyone will direct you to the *museo*, a short distance from the plazas), which is one of the most engaging of regional museums anywhere. It is housed in the original Colegio de San Nicolás, which was later moved to Morelia, and a thoroughly appropriate place it is, since it was the local Bishop Quiroga who organized the school and was responsible for educating the Indian and reviving in him an interest in his own and imported crafts. The courtyard gardens are ancient, careless, and bountiful, and the various rooms—an enchanting Colonial kitchen, a room of religious art, myriad objects beautifully arranged—should be seen, even at the cost of missing a few interesting but not indispensable churches. However, there is a Carmelite monastery dug out from under the houses which covered it that is worth a long look. It is called the "House of the 11 Patios," revealing elegant columns, alabaster windows, and lovely decorative detail. The ensemble has in recent years been arranged as a crafts center: weaving here, carving there, jewelry making, embroidering, etc. The prices are not at market level, but then, neither is the craftsmanship.

One of the regional crafts specialties was, and still is to a diminished degree, the making of figures in corn dough. There is such a figure, a miraculous Virgin, in the Colegiata church and several saints in the modernized Church of San Francisco. Not far from the double market square—one section large, the other small, and both almost denuded of trees and grass—there is an old house (Casa del Gigante) that keeps in its patio a monumental figure. On another side of the market plaza, a movie theater embedded in what was an Augustinian monastery, and in the middle of the small square a literal monument to a local heroine in the act of being tortured for information, and resisting.

Leaving the heroine's plaza by way of the street of Zaragoza, one soon reaches the large dignified square dedicated to Don Vasco de Quiroga. Here much of the serious business of the town is done and that of surrounding villages. Here country people find a veterinarian to consult, numerous pharmacies, a notary, baskets for carrying grain, coarse sacks, and ropes, and, if they can afford it and haven't made their own, the charmingly carved furniture and boxes that are uniquely of the area. Along with rural supplies, the square offers worldly crafts objects, the clever things based on old crafts that might appear in the Zona Rosa of Mexico City. The combinations of basic and luxurious, of old houses and new shops, enhanced by the presence of elderly country couples resting in the shade of Quiroga's statue, make the plaza a rewarding place to linger and learn the role of Pátzcuaro as county center for numerous villages.

The lake trip should be made early in the morning, while the fishermen are still dipping their nets for shimmering whitefish and the small white herons have not yet flown from their marshy nests. Ideally, other villages in the lake and on the shore should be explored, but this takes time and arranging, so that most visitors content themselves with a trip to Janitzio, the most picturesque and self-conscious of the villages.

Once one could take pictures of tiled roofs, spilling nets, and flowered vines, and with permission, an old fisherman mending his net or a group of children leaping up the cobbled streets. It cost nothing but a polite request and thanks, until the value of being photogenic became a peso, then two or three or more. The area near the dock announces its devotion to tourists with a couple of restaurants and the crudest of souvenirs. Beyond that first stretch of too eager welcome, though, the island becomes more thoroughly itself, allowing one calm for looking at the steep red roofs, the graceful swing of the skirts passing by; and, as one climbs, the expanding views of the lake, the other islands, and the curves of the shoreline. The first, and minor, monument one comes to near the summit is the odd church, modestly tucked away, and containing some interesting Indian carving on European models. Behind it is the graveyard, which looks like any poor graveyard except on the night of the Day of the Dead. Standing on the top of the island is a colossal statue of Morelos, a colossal aesthetic affront to a great man. To house masons, to transport material, to prepare ground, to work in sun and rain in so inconvenient a place was an act of great devotion, and one wishes it were more successful, or successful at all.

Much more easygoing are the pleasant islands of Jaracuaro, Yunuen, and Tecuen, and the shore towns of Erongarícuaro (where fine textiles are woven) and Chupicuaro, which has a sort of beach. Or take a bus trip to Rosales or Tacámbaro. (Make sure there is a return bus; the countryside is magnificent, the villages and villagers delightful, but you won't want to stay even if you could.) For pottery, take a trip to Santa Fe (near Quiroga), and for hand-hammered copper to Santa Clara del Cobre, a village of family enclaves like those of gypsy tinkers.

HOTELS

The famous one is the **Posada de Don Vasco,** on the road that leads from the lake to town. Besides bed and board, it offers advice, guides, entertainment, and a bowling alley. Its companion motel, the **Toliman,** across the road, is newer and much more like home. On the square fronting the main church, a short walk up the hill from the plazas, is the **Posada de la Basílica,** a favorite whose rates are moderate. There was a hotel on the large plaza, an erratic and casual inn, with enormous rooms, beautiful potted plants and bird cages on the balcony, and practically no service. Also, it was extraordinarily cheap, even for a place in which one bathroom served four couples. The rumor is that it has been brought to near efficiency, and become the **Posada de San Rafael.** Have a look before you commit yourself. They may not meet your standards but if your pockets are almost empty: **Pito Perez, Gran Hotel Concordia, Posada de la Rosa,** and others off the squares. A safer bet is the **Chalamu Motel,** on the road at the edge of town, or the **Motel San Carlo,** near the lake.

WARNING: Check the number of blankets on your bed and ask for more. Pátzcuaro nights can be very cold.

RESTAURANTS

If you want to try the local specialty, the small whitefish dipped up by the butterfly nets, ask for **El Gordo** (Fatty's). Or go to **El Patio** or **El Meson.** Whitefish is also available in the small restaurants near the market, the hotels, several attractive restaurants on the road up to the town, and the restaurant in the loggia above the monastery-movie house.

SHOPPING

Attractive crafts and adapted-crafts shops as well as furniture ateliers almost line the road up to town from the **Posada de Don Vasco.** There is a **Vicki's** branch and a couple of shops in town, but there isn't much you haven't seen or won't see elsewhere except the local jewelry, which, like many crafts objects, is becoming scarce. These are the silver pins and necklaces of fish and dugout designs, sometimes combined with red beads or bits of coral. The **Casa Cerda** (Dr. Coss 15) is old and large and has a few rare specialties of local pottery, delicate lace tablecloths, and furniture. One shop on the big square has a huge variety of sombreros, huaraches, and knives; another makes fine carved furniture, particularly open credenzas in the local style you have seen in the museum. The serapes and mats of **Salina's Artes de Mexico** are well worked and may interest you. A travesty of local crafts peers through the stalls of a small market near the Biblioteca Pública; amusing and the right place to buy small horrors. At the other end of the scale, the beguiling things, not cheap, at **La Galleria** on Quiroga's square.

Here we have one of the frequent pauses for decisions which no one can make for a traveler; they are made by urgencies of time, money, and temperament. If time and tolerance for crisp morning air permit, check into the possibilities of a three-hour Sunday boat trip, past a number of islands, to Erongaricuaro. Arrange the trip at your hotel a day or two before and be prepared to leave at about 8 A.M. to reach the market where fish are still bartered for wood and vegetables. It is possible to go back to Quiroga and take the highway northwestward to Zacapú, whose neighboring village of Cheran produces distinctive, ornate pottery. Farther west, halfway to Zamora, a southbound road leads into Carapan and on to Paracho, a village whose craft is mainly making guitars, although it does other wood work as well. Stop awhile for a walk through rows of guitar backs— dozens of them—drying in the sun. Then continue on to Uruapan, an agreeable, pretty town which produces a good deal of the lacquer-ware found in this region and which has an enchanted forest of tropical gardens where waters play and paths are mossy and every vista is a Rousseau painting. Outside of Uruapan, as everyone knows, is the now extinct volcano of Paricutín, which suddenly burst through the quiet cornfields in the early 1940s and covered the town—leaving only a bit of church spire visible—with black ash and rock. When the volcano was still spitting, it was fascinating to take a car at night (better not to see the narrow wooden planks which straddled deep wide gashes in the earth) and ride horseback up toward the roaring red mouth. Now it is worth seeing as a hellish view of utter desolation quickly coming back to life.

As the map shows, it is possible to go back to Highway 15 and continue west and north to Guadalajara. But Guadalajara leads to other places, and those to others. It might be time, then, to return to Morelia and circle back to Mexico City, leaving Guadalajara for a plane trip, or an overnight train ride, if only to see the murals of Orozco.

PORTRAITS

Sunday in Chapultepec Park in Mexico City is the Coney Island, the backyard, and the parade ground of the Mexican working-class family, a time and place in which the father is most appealing. He is shiningly proud of his little boys in their freshly pressed shirts and the bright ribbons in his little girls' elaborately braided hair. He indulges them in large bottles of pop, candies, and rides on the horses and small trains and holds them for long periods on his hard-worked shoulders so that they may see performing monkeys or dogs over the heads of the transfixed adults. On trains and buses, fathers are enchanting to all children, their own and others—patient, amusing, yielding, gentle, generous, incredibly model.

To the less fashionable streets of Mexico City, to the plazas of small towns, to the poorer markets, come young Indian women—young girls by our standards—each carrying a baby wrapped in a thin, torn *rebozo,* a child of two or three trailing listlessly along at her side. They are shoeless and taciturn; neither child cries or demands anything; the three are a trinity of inherited Indian fatalism, of ancient outrage and stillborn hopes. The once model father has left them—for another woman, for another atmosphere, for more liquor, for no particular reason he can give.

There must be a number of historic and sociological reasons for this, and the problem has been given much study and conjecture. The Indian family structure was polygamous in many areas and still is in some, a matter of convenience. In the mountains, for instance, a man will have a wife in the village and one far up in the hills, a day's walk away, where he cultivates his field.

Custom, convenience, economic freedom—as among Yucatán's *cordeleros* (ropemakers) when henequen was very profitable—dictate the pattern even in the cities, where multiple families are made and visited in various degrees of casualness among the poor, the middle class, and the rich. In the cities, one family is usually church-based; poor country families are more hit-and-miss about it. An itinerant priest may not be coming to the village for too long a time to wait, the cost of the simplest wedding dress and feast may be prohibitive to a family whose earnings are solely the ears of corn pulled from a small, rocky field. Needed papers have to be dug out of town halls and often they can't be found because parentage is vague and births not always reported. So, a *licenciado* (lawyer) must advise on further procedure, and *he* must be paid. With the proper papers a civil marriage can be performed; there are fees to be paid for that, and then, the church wedding and its costs. Consequently, between economic stringencies and weakness of the marrying habit, not too many marriages per population are performed. Once in a while, the government will arrange a mass civil marriage of several thousand soldiers with children in their arms and ripe bellies on their young women and, occasionally, the church makes the same gesture, bringing respectability to some percentage of the rural population. This does not greatly decrease the number of unchurched babies "given light" (in the lovely Spanish phrase for childbirth); they swarm through the mountainous landscapes, conceived, born, loved, and given up to death in stolid resignation.

The male drifting from place to place and family to family reflects also a facet of economic uncertainty: a drought burns the land, the corn crop fails, there are no jobs on the local *ranchos*. A man leaves his family to try elsewhere, and elsewhere again, and continues wandering, leaving a child or two here and there, his original family growing dimmer as image, responsibility, time, and places fade away.

Consider, too, Mexican history: years of conquest and submission and the consequent irresponsibility that stems from being kept enslaved too long, of not being in control of one's life; the generations born hungry and dying hungry; the unleashing of freedoms and furies during the revolutions; the omnipresence of death—all made planning, a tenacious hold of the long view, foolish and futile.

By a dreadful paradox, the adoration of and dependence on the mother, expressed as intense Mariolatry in the church, leaves the role of total responsibility to the mother. The man knows that she will take care of the children somehow, as his mother did of him. She will beg or sell newspapers, sitting late on the sidewalk, the children hanging from her like sad fruit; she may set up a stand of twelve small, wrinkled avocados and a hundred peanuts. If she is lucky enough to have only one child she may go into domestic service or, as women in Harlem do, leave the children in the village with her mother or aunt and try her luck, unhampered, in the big city. The children may die (the child mortality rate, in spite of sporadic public health measures and education, is still fearsomely high) or survive to work as darting Figaros in provincial hotels, as waitresses in village eating places, as vendors or shoeshine boys, as anything which requires no literacy or training, only the habits of touching politeness, patience, and searching, knowing, appraising eyes.

When the children are gone—dead, working, married—the mother is left with what? Her need of men has long worn itself out; if she were to verbalize her attitude it would be one of mild contempt. The church, to which she had earlier been devoted, has shown her less devotion. She treats it more lightly, more and more careless of the steady round of observances, but she never forgets the Virgin, her sister, for whom she keeps a flower-trimmed altar in a corner of her shack. She sets herself up in a market, buying and selling toughly and shrewdly. She likes a bit of sharp bargaining, but not too much; she will no longer be victimized by anyone—dealer or tourist—and refuses to be excessively polite about it. Her world is the marketplace, but in dealing with small wholesalers and with sanitation officials, paying license fees, looking and watching, her world expands. She wants to understand, to partake, and to know her rights. She borrows or buys a primer and stubbornly, laboriously learns to read and write (and, should you make a purchase from her while she is studying, make it quick; she's impatient of such interruptions). She takes to herself the old woman's right to be eccentric and smokes publicly—still somewhat an oddity in Mexico.

And there she sits—dragging on her cheap, throat-ripping cigarettes, plucking out the mysteries of the printed word, monumental,

skeptical, unafraid, beyond disappointment or fear or loneliness because she's known them all well—possibly the freest woman in the
world.

ASK THE LITTLE BOY

Some of the best-informed, most capable, faithful, knowing, cynical,
polite, energetic, interesting guides are the little boys aged eight to
fourteen who haunt the railroad and bus stations of small towns and
the highway entrances. Sometimes they are dreadful birds of prey,
pushing, mauling, pulling at you for the pleasure and profit of carrying your bags. Mostly, they gather around more gently, trying to
outcharm each other. Whomever you choose—the one with the sad-
dest, most opaque black eyes, or the whitest smile, or the showiest
collection of English words, or the hungriest look—he will teach you,
if you want to learn, something of the children of Mexico. He may
make witty, skeptical comments but never complain. He will wait
and wait for you and never feel the need to be patient; he just is. He
has many fine antennae which search out your mood with fine delicacy: if you want silence he will be quiet, if your mood is loquacious
he will babble away. You need never tell him that you're displeased
with him; he'll know by the tone of your voice and the set of your
face, no matter how well you think you're dissembling. No matter
how hurt he is—and he is, like all Mexicans, extraordinarily vulnerable—he will not cry or display injury; his is a built-in stoicism,
painted over by a winning smile and fine manners. He will never ask
you for anything to drink or eat, although he may be quite hungry.
If you offer him food or drink he will accept it gravely, eat it slowly,
in small, delicate bites, as if he weren't hungry and it didn't matter
whether he was fed or not. (During the siege of Tenochtitlán, just
before Cortés finally took the city, the Aztecs were reduced to eating
roots and the bark of trees, women and children dying in the streets
of hunger. But, reports Bernal Díaz: "Two of the chieftains who were
talking to Cortés drew out from a bag which they carried some
tortillas and the leg of a fowl and cherries, and seated themselves in
a very leisurely manner and began to eat so that Cortés might observe
it and believe that they are not hungry.") He will not fight the other
boys (that happens when they grow older, more stupid, and less
confident), nor bully the younger ones, with whom he is very solicitous, as he is with his own family.

The favorite Mexican toy is a baby. They are constantly handled, hugged, caressed, and admired by men, women, and children. The infant emerges from the inner womb to the outer womb of the *rebozo*, wrapped and tied against its mother's body, and carried that way practically all the time, which, it is generally said, explains the tranquillity, amiability, and confidence of the Mexican child. (It might also explain the tranquillity of the rural Mexican mother, who while protecting is protected.) The baby is breast-fed at fairly frequent intervals, not "on demand" but before a demand can be heard, and this effortless, peaceful life goes on until the next baby takes its place. The older infant is then handed over to the next older child, boy or girl, and both of them are watched, washed, fed, and petted by one older still, and so forth. It is not unusual to see a five-year-old boy taking total, attentive care of a three-year-old sister, lifting her over puddles, devising little stick toys for her, smoothing her hair, carrying her around because he's proud of her and loves her. (If there is sibling rivalry in working-class or peasant families, it is, to the usual forms of evaluation, imperceptible.) A little girl of two, with no baby to handle, will carry an improvised rag doll in an improvised *rebozo*, imitating the nursing gestures of her mother. And even in sophisticated areas, crowds of little girls gather around the street to beam at someone's freshly starched baby sister, as if she were a prodigious novelty or something good to eat. Worldly teenage girls of the big city will croon over a baby, partially to impress the boys, knowing that baby-loving is considered a moving and important characteristic in a girl; still, it is sincerely meant, an honest and natural expression of temperament and custom.

A young child is rarely punished, and unless all available arms are already occupied, he has the right to be carried when he's tired. If he can't be carried he trots along, as docile and patient as a little burro and as uncomplaining. At home, in his village, very few demands are made on him until he is of school or working age—often the same— at six or seven. He wanders around at will, rarely far, coming back at intervals to touch the warm stove of mother, grandmother, or aunt, and out again into complete familiarity and uniformity, where every house is like his own and every door open to him.

The result is a singularly aristocratic, serene child, polite and poised, who is not afraid to ask—never demand—a favor, a present, or a coin. He may be disappointed when told "no," but he is not afraid to hear it, nor does it discourage him sufficiently to keep from trying elsewhere. Very rarely does a child cry in Mexico, never is a child rude, and temper tantrums belong only to the adolescent princelings of middle- and upper-class families. The child has great, intelligent curiosity, but will never pry. Give him more than one candy or cookie and he will put most of them into his pocket to share with his friends or family. Give him a job to do and he will tear his young heart out doing it well and quickly.

All this might suggest excessive sobriety and responsibility. Responsible he is—much more than his father, often—because poverty makes him so at a very early age, but once you know him and between you has grown the bridge of his little English and your little Spanish, he is gay, playful, mercurial, inventive, and deeply, warmly affectionate.

Often the most competent member of the staff of a country hotel is the young general factotum who sleeps on a *petate* (mat), guarding the entrance. He does the gardening, runs errands, sweeps and washes floors, and waits on table, always on call to do the odd bidding of guests and *dueños* (proprietors) with no time off. His biography often follows a common pattern. Abandoned by his father at an early age, abandoned again by his mother's death, abandoned a third time by his uncles, who could not keep him, he walked and trotted the sixty miles to the nearest big town, begging food or a coin as he went, picking up the overripe bananas thrown from a market stall. In the city he hung around a garage—skinny, large-eyed, alert, and silent—until the attendants noticed him, gave him an occasional coin and tortillas from their lunch. As he became more confident of being accepted, he began to help: he carried water, ran errands, wiped windshields, learned to make change, and at seven or eight was already a well-ensconced employee—not formally paid, but fairly well cared for, the care including a *petate* on the floor of the garage. An innkeeper, one of the regular customers of the garage, had watched and spoken with the child and was impressed with his eagerness and capacity to learn, his affable manner, and his quick tongue. For the equivalent of $25, he bought the boy from the garage owner and made him his own helper.

By the tenets of our psychology this should make a bitter, sullen, rude, knife-wielding adolescent. Instead, it produces the appealing, bright, resourceful boy who will pick flowers or pimp for you, with perfect, unruffled, worldly grace. (What happens when these delightful, beautiful children—girls as well as boys—grow up? Grown Mexicans can and do have many charms, but not the glowing perfection of the young. What happens to the quick intelligence, the loyalty, the enterprise, the accepting and giving disposition? The answers are many: poverty, racial mixtures uncertainly melded, profound inferiorities, and other possibilities which Mexican thinkers ponder and ponder, almost obsessively.)

Oaxaca and Environs

Oaxaca de Juárez is several states of mind, succeeding each other in the unfolding of days. The first is relief. If one has come by air from Mexico City, it might have meant making a plane at about eight in the morning (there is a later one, but that means losing half a day). The ride in the cold early morning with sand-grated eyes and cracked bones is tormented by the certainty that something of value was left in the bathroom or closet. Were the proper boys tipped and was it too little? Did the desk clerk actually make the Oaxaca reservation as he said he would? Where can one get a cup of coffee? Coffee is available at the airport but there may be no time for it—or too much, depending on weather conditions and the obscure decisions of the airlines mind. However, you're on the plane, *finalmente,* strapped in, motors and fears in motion. The plane leaves the valley of Mexico and then flutters, for most of two hours, like a heedless butterfly between rows of mountains, stroking the snowy sides of Iztaccíhuatl and plunging almost into the mouth of Popocatépetl, very exciting if you're a sanguine flyer.

Or, you've come by querulous, nervous night train or by bus, with a night stopover at Puebla, or by car with a very early start from Mexico City. After Puebla and its multichurched neighbor, Cholula, the landscape turns to patches of field wrested out of eroded hills which are hospitable mainly to rigid organ cactus that darts like prickly arrows from the rock, or spreads as metallic modern candelabra. Here and there, a minute settlement, its white church isolated on a craggy hill, and decorating the primitive houses, round adobe silos with jaunty thatched cone covers. Notice the use of cactus trees as storage places for hay and the ingenuity of goats who will make anything do as food when the riverbeds are dry and the soil arid. You may come on a village with an unusable hotel, a gas station, and, should you decide to rest on the shady piazza, a goggle-eyed young man sucking on a little rag of cigarette will sidle up to you and ask, "You wanna pot?" Another town may offer you a neat little shop and restaurant and a church that flourishes a minute Byzantine cupola.

The most impressive man-made structure along the way is the mighty Dominican church and abbey of Yanhuitlán, whose size bespeaks an early large population that must have fled disease or exploitation, or both, many years ago. The tall church, recently restored, has high complex vaulting over layers of ornate gold and mediocre paintings. Behind the altar, on a gold wall that lists, there are skillfully carved figures in colored robes that imitate brocade. At the sides of the altar, equally vivid figures climb up, up toward the vault on an elaborate interweaving of designs. As you go toward one of the chapels and halls, which should shape a museum, notice the broad, serene arches and the beautiful wooden coffering between them.

The collection has been changing. One would regret the loss of a Virgin in a smart nineteenth-century cloak and hat and a Christ in a wind-tossed wig on a burro; a pensive Christ; a Christ rather surprised to find himself in a crown of thorns, and a bald doll whose large body is swathed in gold-fringed blue and red velvet, the legs in blue and red embroidered boots. Some say he is Gabriel, some say Michael; whatever his name, he is, in several ways, peculiar. Whatever saint is in or out at your time of visiting, try not to neglect the grand carved doors, the floral decorations, and the remains of a mural which shows a huge Christopher-*conquistador* carrying a small Christ, in the act of blessing, on his shoulder.

(You might choose, however, to ride a shorter, less interesting route: via Cuautla, Izucar de Matamoros, Acatlán, Huajuapan.)

The second Oaxacan state of mind, which descends after a rest, a meal, a walk around the plaza, a beer under the *portales,* and an assault by the colorful army of confident vendors, is ease—a mellow ease, not the loosening of the tropics, but a sense of the blood running in a peaceable rhythm and one's skin fitting well. In spite, somehow, of the dense traffic that tears at the central plaza.

Like many other Mexican towns, Oaxaca has its colony of expatriates, North American and European; some drink, some paint or write, some drink-write or drink-paint. The town has also acquired many European visitors and a conspicuous number of well-heeled idle American young. Toward evening they gather at the tables under the *portales* of the **Marqués del Valle Hotel,** or some bar on the square, to make an exotic contrast with the general populace. The town abounds in native intellectuals, too, and the people of cultivation really are, with surprisingly urbane tastes; the troubled university is small but a couple of its faculties are nationally renowned for their excellence; the city maintains a mobile library and the weaving village of Teotitlán has its own; the bandstand in the plaza shows off one of the best marimba bands in the country several nights a week, alternating with a polished band which often plays music exalted beyond its brassy capacities.

Possibly the mellow, homecoming feeling of Oaxaca emanates from its people, compounded of singular good looks, grace, calm, and un-Indian worldliness. Unlike many other Indians, the Oaxacan is neither shy nor suspicious and is delightedly interested in new people and new ways and quite aware of a large world that is wider than he can see or stand in. Much has been written about the Zapotec who is one of the indigenous strains of modern Oaxaca. It has, at times, been sentimental, exaggerated, making of him the folk hero of Mexico, the invincible warrior, the noble nonbloodletting primitive, the fount of archaic cultures. He cannot encompass all this virtue even though both his past and his present are imposing. Nor is it likely that the present Zapotec is the "pure" man who built Monte Albán; he is now a mixture of all that centuries can bring of invasions, conquests, and migrations, and their subsequent human impurities. Whatever he was, he is now—and she—a skillful craftsman; a quick trader with a healthy respect for a good bargainer and a sharp eye for the vulnerable or unsure; a gentle, patient persuader, dignified and capable of yielding; hospitable, witty, and an appreciator of wit. His good-looking wife wears her *rebozo* in the most attractive manner of all Mexican *rebozo*-wrapping: she pulls its long ends forward around her head, twists a knot high in front, and then lets the fringed ends fall, one back over one shoulder and one in front. If the sun is very hot or a bundle has to be steadied for head-carrying, the ends are laid on top of the knot. Flowing or bunched, it makes a turban of considerable dash.

One of the pleasures and pains of sitting on the plaza or in the *portales* is the occasional locust-plague of these handsome women laden with the *rebozos* of Mitla, dangling gilt-filigree earrings and bracelets, flowers made of bright nylon thread stretched over fine wire, lace antimacassars, aprons of hand-loomed cottons. The only way to avoid them is to leave Oaxaca or hole up with a good book. One might as well brave them. Given a high degree of stamina and not so much sales resistance as charm resistance, it is possible. They use everything: the big old women stand like huge, accusing monuments, commanding, with their silent numerous presence, that you buy. The less dignified younger women flutter, flatter, cajole, and murmur attractive prices. The youngest sell their shyness and youth with the diffidence of a whispered, "Won't you buy something from me, too?" If none of this works, the battalion retreats, only to descend again and again—en masse or singly. One noble crone, with the profile and angry golden eyes of an eagle, who plied between the plazas in Oaxaca and Mitla, missed no trick; she played all roles from the avenging goddess to wheedling adolescent, and had still another gambit for women tourists who spoke Spanish. These she would engage in conspiratorial tête-à-têtes: "Make your friends buy; they look plenty rich, with those real leather pocketbooks. If you make them buy I'll give you a good discount on a fine *rebozo,* the best I have. If you make them buy a lot I'll give you one as a gift. Tell them to buy from your friend. I'm your friend. Remember me. Remember me." Her repeated injunction became as momentous and haunting as Hamlet's father's.

A younger woman, one of the numerous Rosas, has the makings of a big-city businesswoman. She loves the bargaining and horse trading, breaking down sales resistance, scurrying off to some mysterious hiding place to extract yet another color or quality of *rebozo,* smiling radiantly, or heartbreakingly crushed as the negotiations go up and down, and beyond the others, she has a good idea of what will appeal to most tourists. Not being able to clinch a sale in the city, she will invite a customer to her house in Mitla, where she has the most absolutely perfect, cheapest, finest *rebozo.* Getting into an Indian house is not difficult around Oaxaca, but most tourists don't have the opportunity and are timid about making it. The invitation is a plum which tourists can't resist; Rosa has her customer hooked.

The men who sell the *serapes* made in Teotitlán del Valle keep their distance—about three feet—standing with arms outspread displaying the total design of one *serape* while the others lie in a neatly folded bundle nearby. If you don't want a *serape,* don't venture even a side glance. The subtlest indication of interest is seized on, you become "*Amigo,* my fren' "; all the *serapes* are unwrapped and displayed; prices are quoted in "little dollars"; you must feel the fineness of the wool and admire the beautiful patterns. "Look, see beurrriful, chip *serape*. Look more, nice pitchur, more big. For you, my fren', chip, berry chip." The good-natured persistence is inexhaustible. Your few words of Spanish have, as usual when needed, vanished; just shaking one's head or bleating, "No, no, no" seems dry and weak; to turn a back seems very rude. But, unless you are eager to buy a large *serape* of heavy wool, say no firmly and go back to your meal or conversation or plaza-staring. The Zapotecs have a long history and their experience has encompassed sharper rebuffs than yours. To suffer about their hurt feelings is to reduce them to children whom you can dominate. You can't, except economically—and that only to a degree. The proof of that lies in the fact that the same vendors will be back in a short while with the same stretch of *serapes,* the same smile, the same English vocabulary, the same patience.

LATE NOTE: The invasion of numerous visitors, the proliferation of cafés, and the traffic are diminishing the open-air salesmanship, a thing soon to be, one suspects, one of the snows of yesteryear.

Although gentle combat with enterprising Marías and Miguels can absorb much time, there are other things to do and see in Oaxaca: the town itself, for instance; its drawings of grillwork; the plaza, and the youngsters making the circular rite of the *paseo.* And, of course, the churches—to be tasted, at least, by even those who have no real taste for them.

The baroque tour of Oaxaca could reasonably start with the cathedral, just off one of the corners of the plaza. It was begun about thirty years after the Conquest, and in the nature of cathedrals, took about two centuries to build. It has a façade rich with fine stone carving but as a result of periods of anti-religious fervor when many churches were gutted, and the not too adept restorations which followed, the cathedral's interior is rather impoverished. Quite in contrast is the immense glowing church and monastery of Santo Domingo, a few blocks away. It was begun about fifty years later than the cathedral and took almost as much time to complete. The façade of large saints in columned niches, flanked by two wide, firm towers which end in tiled domes, is imposing, but gives no hint of the ebullience inside. Imagine a tree with a thousand branches, all of thick gold, and among the golden leaves, polychrome figures and ornaments, the whole overwhelming tangle backed by dazzling white to make the most baroque of churches, and one of the most beautiful. In still another mood is the Church of the Virgen de la Soledad, of dark stone importantly set back and high over a stepped yard, which occupies most of a city block. Here again, the façade is a variant of the baroque combination of classic pillars and niched saints skillfully carved. The hardly distinguished interior houses one of the world's numerous population of "miracle" Virgins, this one especially adopted as the protectress of the city. A fiesta is held for her about two weeks before Christmas, a lusty one, possibly a little chummy for so formal and rich a Virgin. Some of the small buildings flanking the church have turned to more secular matters, except one, which is a workshop of church art, where on weekdays you may find a group of apprentices—anywhere from ten years old into the teens—carefully carving saints and wooden leaves.

An infinitely more antique and refined art is displayed in the showcases of the city's museum. This is the lapidary art of the Mixtecs, of which the spectacular early specimens (true of other Mexican arts, also) found their way, via the court of Spain, into various European museums and a few private collections. The great fairly recent find was made in the famous Tomb of Monte Albán, a Zapotec city which was, late in its history, taken over by its neighbors and enemies, the Mixtecs. They apparently used the city as burial ground for their priests and nobles, surrounding them, as so many civilizations did, with the splendor of their earthly goods. The Monte Albán jewelry is almost impossible, and even foolish, to describe: the gossamer fineness of its gold arranged in exquisitely designed necklaces, the transparency of its crystal and alabaster bowls; the incredibly precise small carvings in jade—all have to be seen. And although the jewels are naturally Oaxaca's pride, the museum shows a stimulating collection of local crafts, regional costume, and artifacts from the surrounding historic sites. It is an impressive place, part of the vast monastery of Santo Domingo, itself a museum piece of Colonial church might.

The Museo de Arte Prehistorico on Morelos—practically every corner bears arrows pointing to it—is the gift of Rufino Tamayo. Off a lovely old courtyard banked with camellias and bougainvillaea, his pieces of several cultures sit in attractively designed boxes suffused with soft, mysterious light. You have seen similar and many more examples of pre-Hispanic art and artifact in the grand museum in Mexico City, but the comfortable, human scale, the judicious placement and other-world quiet of this small museum are thoroughly appealing and the knowing selection informative and pleasing.

As anyone who can say "Oaxaca" knows, it has a famous market which sits contentedly in and out of the sun every day but mushrooms into a large Indian village on Saturday. Long before the days of the Conquest, Oaxaca was the market and trading center for many of the villagers in the distant hills, and the routes they now ride and walk were well trodden long before the Spaniards marched through the valley. If you can, get to the market on Friday night to watch the hill people unload their burros and their wives, bed the animals down, and arrange the family in a protective ring around the core of burro, grasses, and onions. Years ago the place for this was a set of *mesones*, now gone, but the same arrangement will be devised impromptu under a market overhang, or at the entrance of a shop. (It is difficult to take something permanently away from a Mexican, he simply devises another means of getting the same thing.) It will be dark, however, and to see the faces and costumes you will have to go to the market on Saturday morning—fairly early, since it begins to sag about noon.

The local Zapotec ladies are there, of course, but now is the time to keep an eye open for the turbaned hill girls in white girdled by magnificent belts of red; for the tiny Yalalag women in long white loose shifts with immense knots of colored thread at the chest and back, their loose hair falling straight and heavy. Somewhere you may come across a Yalalag mother sitting on a curb or a doorstep surrounded by her young, feeding them bits of meat and vegetable on tortillas, her hands moving as lightly and delicately as a hummingbird's dart for honey. Shyly off by himself is a Mixe from the far mountains, dressed in patches and wearing a conical felt hat, his face alert and full of apprehension, like a frightened young animal. He has walked innumerable miles to come to the big city, and in his furtive way is enjoying it hugely, but he brings with him the solitariness of his mountains. A sunnier delight is the jazzy market mode which calls for a large bunch of small green onions or garlic to be pressed down on the head, making a pearly cap with jaunty green ribbons sprouting out of its top. Only the prettier young market women sport this style, of course, and some of them, by the slant of the cap or a twist of the green onion ends, achieve great chic.

The appeal of the famous market derives from a composite of

many appeals: the worldly people who are still Indian; the conversation and laughter that go on as gay background music while no one misses a trick or a sale; the masses of brilliant flowers with faces among them like dark roses; the emerald cucumbers, the amber gourds, the ruby chiles; in the side stalls the specialties of Oaxaca—*serapes, rebozos,* the varied, individualistic pottery; the long mesh bags which start with the shape of an emptied banana peel and grow, when stuffed, to watermelon size; the thick-soled, pointed sandals with many straps and an air of antiquity—the blending of bright color, vigorous humanity, and light stench. It is an earthy market, but who could think of it as garbage when a magnificent heap of golden pineapple husks, bristling with gray-green spikes, and cups and coils of orange peel shine back at the full sun?

HOTELS

The **El Presidente** chain has placed a stunning hotel, with large pool and baronial meeting halls, in a section of the ex-convent of Santa Catalina. They have had the good sense to leave the haughty arches and vestiges of Indian colors in Conquest designs on the walls as well as old paintings, patios, and little inner gardens. It serves bountiful buffets in the morning and a grand one on Sunday afternoons. High moderate to expensive.

The Marqués del Valle (named for Cortés, who was given a land grant of the Valley of Oaxaca by Charles V) is the busiest and most popular hotel, not so much for its intrinsic merits as the fact that it accommodates many organized tour groups, and consequently, maintains a busy, efficient tour schedule run by English-speaking guides. High moderate.

The Hotel Señorial, on the square, is low-slung and modern; restaurant and pool. High moderate.

The **Victoria,** 545 Carretera Panamericana, a few miles outside town, has a handsomely planned main building, separate bungalows, gardens, a good-sized pool, evening entertainment, and a view. As in most of the local hostelries, you may live on the American plan, which could be a convenience if you don't want to trot back and forth into town. High moderate to expensive.

Calesa Real 306 Garcia Vigil, a short distance from the Zócalo. Modern, convenient, unassuming, with a decent restaurant and a small, beguiling pool. Moderate.

Hotel Mision de los Angeles, a short distance out of town. Moderate.

Casa Colonial is run by Americans in a picturesque house. Moderate.

The **Plaza,** off the square in another direction, has no dining room, which gives you the freedom of eating around town. The manager, Señor Raul Rodriguez, speaks English and is a repository of charm and information, both of which he gives of generously. He is preparing to give more by way of bulletins, books, maps, and tour suggestions to anyone who comes in. And for his guests, a Saturday night cocktail party to dispel the isolation he sees and pities on so many faces. One hopes that he is still there and thriving. Modest.

For a longer, rural stay, investigate the possibilities of the **Rancho San Felipe,** an antique hacienda which, from time to time, accommodates a few guests. Really cheap (and no other guarantees offered) are two hotels on J. P. Garcia in the market area, their walls sometimes hosts to mounds of pottery and garlic: **Hotel Palmar** and **Hotel Palestina.**

The most satisfactory place for an authentically large tasty *comida,* served family style (one to three are safe hours), is the house of **Doña Elpida** at 413 Miguel Cabrerra, a few minutes' walk from the center. There is no sign; one enters the gate into a well-kept garden hung with bird cages supervised by one big tropical toucan let loose to wander and scold. The dining room has one big and four small tables to serve the locals or visitors from surrounding towns. There is a short menu of choices but you would do better to have the dinner, efficiently, smoothly, and politely served by members of the family. One usually starts with crisp *chicherone* and bits of chop, then on to soup, good fish, and a nicely seasoned meat dish served with mounds of rice. With a custard dessert (flan) and coffee the satisfying meal comes to \$4 to \$5 for two.

The market, which is becoming more and more its own city, devotes one section entirely to food counters usually named for the women who run them. Currently, **Abuelita** (grandmother) is the favorite for rich soups and *chiles rellenos.*

The **Hotel Victoria** feeds you views as well as satisfactory comestibles.

Several hotels serve decent meals, but if you'd like something simpler while staring into the endlessly fascinating square, have sandwiches *(tortas)* or tacos at the **Bar Jardin** or **El Tule.** The **Bum Bum,** across the square, a hangout of local university students and their hippy friends, serves fruit juices, sodas, and coffee.

El Patio, on Hidalgo off the square, can be erratic, but try the shrimp diablo or hamburgers (not as inexpensive as you might expect them to be).

El Asador Vasco and Mi Casita serve you generously and allow you to stare down at what goes on in the zócalos.

SHOPPING

The four crafts specialties of Oaxaca are the long basket-bag, the local *serape,* the Mitla *rebozo,* and pottery. The rope bag, usually striped longitudinally, comes in several sizes and degrees of fineness. It makes an inexpensive, packable gift, and used as a potato-onion-paper bag catchall can lift the dreariest kitchen; besides, it makes an attractive and commodious shopping bag. Oaxacan *serapes* are highly valued, mainly for their solid workmanship.

The Mitla *rebozo* has gone through stages of refinement and trauma in recent years. Some travelers deplore the improvements, yearning for the old *auténtico* days when no *rebozo* was all of one shade, the many tonalities of one color melting into the other as they do in nature. The wool was thick with burrs and thorns, and pulling them out of the rough wool made occupation and entertainment through a long bus ride. Recently the colors have become more subtle and sounder, the weave finer, and the prickly plant life carded out beforehand. The authentic *rebozos* have been glamorized by quasi-bohemian high fashion, but the dignified, unadorned length remains loveliest and most useful, though no local woman wears it and very few Mexican women, except for fiesta dress-up.

Of the black Coyotepec pottery, there are several popular designs—the girl whose long skirt conceals a bell, a group of four bells, and the fat, flower-covered woman who is repeated in size from holdable to unmanageable in clay of dull luster or high shine. In any size or shine her insipid face and dumpiness are irresistible; in the size of a manatee (which she sometimes resembles) she makes a staggering garden ornament; small-fish-sized, she makes a talented corner brightener. Much rarer, worth patient search and inquiry in the market, are the green animal musicians from Atzompa: flute-playing deer, drummer pigs, goats stroking violins, and a hippogriff or two on cornets, small, appallingly sincere and hard-working, wonderfully droll.

The regional sandal is fascinating and, besides, wears and smells forever (carry a heavy plastic bag to wrap them in); the gaily colored cotton goods are attractive in small doses, the knives of Oaxaca are sharp and well sheathed and bear heroic legends—"I die for love!"; "Death for insult!"; and other such bits of *machismo.* Samplings of all the above—and much more—can be found in the market and the plaza, along with such seasonal delights as radish figures on Christmas and palm ornaments at Easter time. Finer examples of the important crafts can be seen in some of the shops tangential to the square, and immediately north. The choicest adaptations of many crafts in ceramics (an enormous gathering), baskets, tin, wood, woven cottons, some silver, chic embroidered dresses, attractively displayed, can be seen at **Yalalag,** M. Alcalá 104. They make a serious and usually successful effort to pack and ship securely and accept credit cards. Through one of the many market streets, by way of miles of redolent dried cod and green mangoes manned by Tehuanas and palisades of oranges, find your way to **Casa Aragon,** J. P. García 503. It is a house that specializes in knives, very fine ones, and ornamented machetes etched with little sayings like "There are bedbugs one doesn't feel but they draw blood nevertheless." The specialist for hammocks is **Francesco Cruz,** Diaz Ordaz 21.

Victor   P. Diaz 111, near Morelos. Related to the shop of the same name in Mexico City and, like that one, dedicated to authentic crafts of several areas—some disappearing—and a few rarities, oddities, and antiquities. Minute animal musicians and enchanting animals of painted tin may soon be rare; pick them up at a few pesos apiece here—and don't neglect the masks. Also ask to see the collection of regional costumes in the back. The owner has, incidentally, taken over a weaving establishment next door and it should be worth exploring.

It isn't necessary to go anywhere in particular for copies of the Monte Albán jewelry; it glitters out of every jeweler's window, on and off the main square, making comparison shopping quite easy. **Ortiz,** Independencia 36, is noted for his silver. And look in at **Galván,** Díaz Ordaz 309. For pretty, inexpensive jewelry—especially earrings of seed pearl and filigree—try the government pawnshop **(Monte de Piedad),** very near the center of town, and myriad jewelers. To measure the degree to which prosperous international tourism has invaded Oaxaca, visit the highly polished Champs Elysées-type jeweler on Alcala and look at the noncrafts, sophisticated wares. Or you might hit the **Presidente Hotel** when its desk is wading in a sea of good Austrian luggage, the property of a tour group from Vienna.

Inevitably, you will be handed a card to visit a textile and/or pottery workshop. Don't scorn it; the pressures to buy are minimal (usually), watching the looms has a hypnotic, soothing effect, the stock is widely varied, prices are not wild—and you can order in colors and sizes you prefer. (If you've been left out of the card distribution, try **Brena** at Pino Suárez 58 and **Casa Acevedo.**) Among the many textile, dresses, blouses, and general "artesania" places: **Ramona,** Hidalgo 807, and more opening constantly.

One of the least roomy and most interesting shops in Oaxaca (Mexico?) is **El Arte Oaxaqueño,** on the market corner of Mina and J. P. García. Only the slender may enter, to be sure not to knock something off the maze of shelves. A very quick and pleasant man and his not so quick but equally pleasant father are *dueños* of bags, mats, toys, tin boxes, wooden dolls, clay trees of life, birds and harps made of dry flowers; the sort of primitive toys that are becoming rare; tin fruits and fish, clay animals, and seductive rocking elephants and lions in tin; bags, gourds, and baskets of several areas hanging from the rafters; the difficult-to-find Azompa clay musicians and old crosses of Yalala in silver—all naïve and untouched by worldly designers. And, in a breathless space toward the back, extraordinary regional dresses, hand-woven, embroidered, and beribboned which, in their pristine state, make the most stylish of house or beach coats.

The **Artesianas** in the Casa Mexicana on G. Vigil, next to the Calesa Real, seems to be shaping up into an interesting shop. Wander in and, possibly, take a chance on the tacos and beer in its pretty courtyard. (Look at the myriad ceramic angel bells hanging from the ceiling of something called the "Ladies Bar.")

Very near **El Presidente**, on the Plazoleta Labastida—anciently called "The Blood of Christ"—one comes on banners and flags of brilliant color hung on ropes from tree to tree. Below, pretty, smiling, barefoot, and dirty little women sit and weave these gaudy lengths to use as shawls, *serapes*, and wall hangings. They are their own looms, the threads wrapped around their waists and attached to a bench or a tree. They speak little Spanish but rely for negotiations on one tough old crone and a young Spanish-speaking man. Bargain and bargain; they expect you to and it is part of the amusing reward for having trotted for miles from distant hills.

Taly, Vigil 116, carries a respectable collection of blouses, silver, tablecloths, mats, and craft objects. Also explore the stalls of the street of the 20th of November, part of the market, for small craft objects.

REMINDERS: Oaxaca is especially addicted to fiestas, both of folk and local-pride origin. It is a good idea to reserve hotel space ahead for December and the Lunes del Cerro dance festivals (two Mondays, late July or early August) and especially to inquire about local festivals. Quite unexpectedly, some neighborhood may be honoring its patron saint with dancers, huge papier-mâché *fantoches* (puppets), and giant *castillos* (fireworks), bigger, better, and noisier in Oaxaca than anywhere else.

If you prefer to avoid the drive through Puebla, the trip to Oaxaca can be made via Cuautla, where there is a road which leads into the Pan American Highway. Recommended only for the adventurous and leisured is the flight between Acapulco and Oaxaca, in a series of short hops to places like Jamiltepec and Cacahuatepec (the Hill of the Peanuts) and Tututepec, to drop a teacher and carry off a pig. For these meetings with the indigenous Mexican earth, inquire locally.

If you are planning to drive to Yucatán, consider following the rough but usable road that goes across the mountains, past Ixtlán de Juárez and Tuxtepec down to the dense, fruity green of the Papaloapan area, then meet 180 to travel south and eastward; or north to the city of Veracruz and beyond.

Check road conditions, particularly during the rainy season, even though roads are improving rapidly.

Puerto Escondido, something like Zihuatanejo and San Blas in their unspoiled primitive years, is now reachable by plane. Get there before everyone else does (200 miles south of Oaxaca).

MONTE ALBÁN, MITLA

The Zapotec Olympus sits on one of the mountains surrounding the modern town, a few, steep miles away. The vast majestic site, which offers a superb view of the city, is on a terraced plateau (countless years of labor for people who had no horses, mules, oxen, or the wheel) only partially uncovered, as yet, to reveal several platformed pyramids, an immense stairway superimposed on earlier stairs, wall slabs carved with strange, stunning, human dancing figures (the famous *Danzantes*), and mute hieroglyphs. Near this central area are the tombs which have yielded much of the Monte Albán funerary art (especially urns) one finds in many museums, wall paintings, and the unbelievable jewelry. Beyond the plaza and revealed tombs there is the rise and fall of innumerable mounds, a sea of buried buildings, tantalizing and promising, which disappear into the surrounding mountains.

The intrinsic importance of Monte Albán, to the nonexpert, is its own hushed immensity and its complex antiquity. As mentioned, it is referred to as a Zapotec city invaded by the Mixtecs, simplifications which brush lightly over the crust of a cultural center of numerous layers and mixtures. To arrive at some schematic order out of a confusing mesh of unknowns, scholars have designated the local cultures as Monte Albán, in periods of "1" to "5," with "3" divided into two periods of its own, cautiously suggesting blendings with other cultures. Allowing the leniency of a couple of centuries in either direction, the first period begins at about 500 B.C., bearing strong resemblances to the Olmec (itself a blanket designation for a culture complex whose dimensions are vague), particularly in the astonishing *Danzantes* (interpreted by some as figures of the diseased and abnormal) and characteristics of the innermost, earliest buildings and tombs. Quite apparently these founding fathers were a highly developed group who had a calendar, a writing system, and fairly sophisticated pottery. At about 300 B.C. new influences—possibly through a conquest, as a few glyphs suggest—appear, mainly in the large, vigorous funerary urns and figures, the strangely shaped "Mound J" building, believed to be an observatory, and changes in ceramic style, all possibly attributable to Mayan and Teotihuacán influences. Still carrying its accumulated characteristics, "Period 3a," which seems to have lasted into the early centuries of the Christian era, shows intense stylization and elaboration of earlier forms, mainly concentrated in a frenzied production of funerary arts and architecture.

"Period 3b," which hovers around the time of the fall of Rome, is a time of excess and decadence in art forms and the ultimate decline. The Zapotecs of this later time seem to have made way, for a time, to the ascendancy of the Mixtecs (periods "4" and "5") whose achievements were the decoration of the temples of Mitla (basically Zapotec buildings) and their beautiful jewelry. The story of Oaxacan cultures ends as a number of such stories do: then came the Aztecs and, soon after, the Spaniards. (Incidentally, recent excavations not far from Mitla may reveal reasons to change the chronology of these periods but nothing sufficiently substantial yet.)

Equipped with a government booklet in English, available in book and gift shops, this is an easy visit to make on your own, particularly since there is usually a guide-caretaker on the premises. Local taxi drivers are often well informed and helpful, and always *compadres* of the caretakers; there is a regular city bus schedule to the ruins, or you might take one of the frequent, satisfactory tours. For a tight schedule, this trip might best be made Saturday afternoon, wedged between the market in the morning and the relaxed plaza life of Saturday night. Also, the late afternoon light is more gentle and evocative as it sifts down on the ruins through the surrounding hills. Take time, however, for the small museum, the well-designed coffee shop and bookstore.

Unlike the trip to Monte Albán, which is for and of itself, with nothing but a curve or two in the mountain road to detract from its imposing presence, the journey to Mitla and back is a tour of varied and pleasing distractions. Almost immediately after turning south on the Pan American Highway (190), one meets the village of Tule, a somnolent little place with no distinctions other than its harvest festival and its incredibly large and aged (several thousand years) *ahuehuete* tree screening its small church. Walk around the great green ghost, examine the elementary charms of the church, and spend a few minutes negotiating the purchase of a few oranges or souvenirs from the little ragged girls who hang around the churchyard, practicing their indigenous, engaging blend of delicacy and forthrightness, and stay for a few minutes with the *serapes* across the road.

On the other side of the highway, a short distance off the road, is Tlacochahuaya, an old village whose town hall is a low, unimpressive building surprisingly surmounted by carved animals vaguely like Chinese lions. Right next to it is a lovely, gay Indian church, a dazzle of native color and decoration over Spanish symbol and design.

The village of Tlacolula dozes in the dust (or mud, depending on the season) during the week and comes to high bloom on Sundays. Except for some very simple pottery, there are no crafts here, but the market is a composition of sure old women, some in high-necked, long-sleeved blouses, skirts down to their bare feet, and cotton *rebozos* draped on their heads in a regal twist and flow; a few sociable farmers; shy, quiet little girls; the indispensable snorting, shaking bus, unloading livestock and tangles of herbs; pigs, burros, turkeys, and kids, all protesting; the smells of dried fish and ripe fruits; the colors of pink blouses, green herbs, and copper skins meeting and parting. (Try to see its fancy gold-touched and gilded church, said to be the earliest in the valley of Oaxaca, and if you can, find the rosaries sold here, of seeds strung on shocking-pink or bright-blue woolen thread, ending in a bit of metal—with no identifiable image, merely a suggestion—and short strands of the wool. A few of these twisted together make a unique necklace, an unusual gift at practically no cost.)

Teotitlán del Valle lies at the end of a short spur off the road and is a maze of paths and cactus fences surrounding the huts of *serape* weavers. Not everyone enjoys this visit; although the people are, as always, courtly, the pressures to buy—spoken and tacit—can be burdensome. Mitla, on the other hand, helps by its insistence; the dogged importuning of the whole town that you buy *rebozos* and beads and *ídolos* automatically stiffens sales resistance and you have no difficulty making your way to the ruins shaking your stubborn head.

There is some evidence that the tombs of Mitla were begun as early as the first Monte Albán period, but in the main, this Zapotec city of the dead was built during the decline of the earlier ceremonial center. Although Mitla might have been one of the temples dedicated to the ubiquitous Quetzalcoatl, the general opinion is that it was the burial place of Zapotec kings. The site was never, as far as is known, very large and was reduced by the church, which used much of Mitla's stone to build its own edifice. (One of the first visible sections of Mitla is a stretch of pagan wall which helps support the church buildings.) The scheme is a calm horizontal series of patios with low tombs built around them, some rectangular, others cruciform. Other than a row of six columns spaced along a large hall or passageway, and another tall column in a tomb (here a guide will ask you to put your arms around the column; the open space between your finger-tips determines how long you have to live and rational objections will get you nowhere), there is little of marked architectural interest. The decoration, attributed to the Mixtecs and clearly related to their lapidary skills, is the attraction: practically every wall is covered with fine, precise geometric patterns which change from panel to panel—over twenty different designs in all. At first glance it appears as if the patterns were carved in relief out of the stone slabs; actually they are mosaics of stone so carefully cut and tightly fitted that it is often difficult to see lines of jointure. How was it done by a people who had few if any metal instruments? Where did the immense stones of the carved lintels come from, and how many men did it take—since there were no wheeled platforms or animals for the job—to bring them from distant quarries? No one knows.

The town of Mitla itself can be nerve-racking, as indicated, or entertaining, or both. *Rebozo* selling is vigorous to violent, and the *rebozos* which hang like jousting pennants from the crossbars of selling sheds grow more experimental in color and combination each year. Unless you spot one you very much like, go to the ateliers of a couple of weavers, apt to be hospitable sheds of babies, pigs, ancient crones, and a large crude loom worked by a man. Look in at **Rufino Reyes Díaz,** Av. Internacional 24, whose wools are more carefully combed and dyed than those one finds in the plaza and whose workshops have expanded to hundreds of *rebozos,* quexquemetls, embroidered dresses and blouses, and many etceteras at good prices. And while you are in Mitla, see what pleases you among the hand-woven fabrics of **Felix Olivera,** Morelos 38, and at **Albert's, Artes Regionales,** and their neighbors on the road from Díaz's to Olivera's.

For a rest from ruins, *rebozos,* and fresh-baked *ídolos* you might retire to the sizable ceramic collection—one of the most extensive in the area—of Mr. Frissel, and his gift shop, which has a small, tasteful group of objects you may not find elsewhere. Here you can get precise directions and information about the condition of the short, rough road to Yagul, an archaeological site nearby, but if the rains have come and the road is still unimproved it can be more adventure than you might want. Like other ceremonial centers in the area, Yagul shows symptoms of both Zapotec and Mixtec occupancy, and like many fortress cities of the New and Old Worlds, sits on a terraced hill, sloped at the side facing the road and dropping off at the north in protective cliffs. The site is apparently quite large and work of this sort goes slowly, but by this time a few buildings should have been exhumed and another crack of light beamed onto the messy confusion peoples make when they migrate, conquer, and mingle. For a good American-Mexican lunch try the **Posada la Sorpresa,** near the ruins.

With the impossible boon of enough time, one can make trips by bus, car, or even local train—if it hasn't melted permanently into a state of *descompostura*—to surrounding pottery villages. (Not on Saturday, when the villages empty into the city market.) Directly to the south, on Highway 175, is Coyotepec, of the shiny, black pottery, its shaping sometimes demonstrated by an old master, Doña Rosa. Beyond that, Ocotlán, which has a bright, hearty Friday market that encompasses the pottery and toys it makes and also a section for the selling of poultry, little pigs, and, a short distance away, horses and burros. Stay a while and watch the careful, almost medical, examination of tongues and teeth. Nearby, a bit off the main road, is Santo Tomás, which weaves. North of Monte Albán is Etla, which, among other things, weaves flat bands of mild cheese into complex rounds (one loosens a strip and tears it off at the desired length). Each village has its market day, easily ascertained at hotel desks or the tourist center inside the government palace near the square.

Should your route take you toward Puebla, stop for a quarter hour, or more, at Atlixco, an enterprising town with a restful, shady plaza, masterly plasterwork at the side of its church, and a bandstand bubbling with various charms. Acatepec, nearby, brings one (ask for directions locally) to the presence of Santa María Tonantzintla. The façade of the church, with its crude, pagan saints and strange flowers, gives only a measure of what is inside: an unbelievable and utterly beguiling ebullience of carved and painted giant mangoes, chiles, leaves, flowers in faithful color and enlaced with gold. From this Fauvist Garden of Eden peer very pale faces, probably an Indian's conception of the white man's suffering saints, and hardly noticeable as the apples and the putti and tomatoes scramble up and down and everywhere, colors and shapes glittering and laughing as they encircle Saint Michael at the top of the altar. Certainly not the most devout but probably the happiest church in Christendom.

If you have the time and the will, you might try Oaxaca's beaches: Puerto Angel, a long, rough drive away, and Puerto Escondido, reachable by plane from Oaxaca. Both hope to be great resorts, but present accommodations are rudimentary to simple.

Tehuantepec and Environs

Several turns around the mountains, through crags of lavender, ocher, and sulfur-yellow rock opening to patches of cultivation and glimpses of a lake, and a long descent into the tropics (about 170 miles altogether and few attractive eating places) bring one to the fabled land of the Tehuanas, the proud Amazons who run the markets, the meager commerce, and even the local politics. They have been photographed, painted, studied, and described fully and enthusiastically: their matriarchal society, their statuesque bearing, their sweeping costumes of square *huipiles* over long graceful skirts edged in broad ruffles, the stiff ruffled headdress with dangling ends like rudimentary sleeves (probably the residual effect of a Colonial baptismal gown an imaginative Tehuana arranged on her head centuries ago), *huipil* and skirt thickly embroidered in fat roses, the whole imposing structure emblazoned with necklaces and earrings of old American gold pieces.

Unfortunately, except at weddings and fiestas (frequent, though, and impressive) the empresses wear no such clothes and one discovers that the best of Tehuantepec is in Covarrubias' *Mexico South,* and outside of the area—in the city of Oaxaca, in Mexico City—where the Tehuanas may be attending a meeting or a fiesta or just getting around, full-panoplied. Quite unlike most Indian women, who stay at home unless they are sent or taken somewhere by the men of the family, these Zapotecas leave their men at home—in the distant fields or bent over sewing machines, busily stitching away at the *huipiles* the wives will later sell in the market. They travel in groups of splendid, arrogant threes and fours. At home, on a dull, common day, they are less remarkable. The skirt made of many gores falling to a wide swish is still graceful but the color is drab, and the everyday *huipil* is usually two ordinary squares of cotton sewn up the sides to painfully tight armholes. The women are frequently barefoot, and although the local style is to arrange braids in a shallow crown with a wool cord or ribbons woven through the braids, many of them let their hair fly loose. In other words, on home grounds a good number of Tehuanas look as if they had just leaped out of their hammocks and hadn't bothered to dress properly, since there is no one around to impress and tourists don't count, coming from a lesser world than Tehuantepec. The legend has it that all Tehuanas are tall. Some *are* tall for Indian women and the older women run to imposing girth, but their height in general is not extraordinary; they walk tall, as befits matriarchs, their long skirts and hairknots lend height, and their gypsy look of suppressed vitality and bad temper adds dimension. One large Tehuana with a basket on her head striding toward a shrewd deal is all by herself a full parade. A cluster of young women and girls in their ribboned crowns, laughing, babbling in Zapotec, dark eyes and earrings glittering as they pass in a two-wheeled cart or hang around the ill-kempt square, make a vivid bouquet of tropical flowers.

A male tourist is often uncomfortable in Tehuantepec. Trousers are rarely visible except on Syrian or Lebanese merchants (whom even a tribe of Tehuanas can't frighten away) and on a row of men sleeping away the powerless days and nights under the overhang of the post office. If he tries to take a picture of a Tarascan woman, the male tourist will be asked for money; if he tries to photograph a Mixe, she will turn her head away or draw her *rebozo* over her face; a market Tehuana will try to smack him with the biggest fish she can grab. A lady from the city of Oaxaca will deal sweetly and flirtatiously with the husband of a foreign woman, knowing he has the money; a Tehuana is just as smart, but she doesn't like him and slights him as if he were blank space, concentrating her charms and light caressing touches on the woman. Men need not altogether despair, however, particularly if they travel alone and if one of the immortal stories about Tehuanas, sworn to as true, is true. A Scandinavian traveler—tall, slender, blazingly, exotically blond—was strolling the streets of Juchitán, carefully observed by the women selling bundles of iguanas outside the market. Two of them, after a short exchange, assigned the care of their merchandise to a friend and proceeded to follow the man, soon flanked him, stopped him, and after careful examination, spoke: "Would you do us the favor . . . ?"

There is no public end to the story. He may or may not have done them the favor, he may have jumped on the nearest bus.

To get back to present concerns, the trip from Oaxaca, either by car or bus, will have taken the better part of a day, so that one must stay here. (The ride to Tuxtla Gutiérrez, which has the next nearest hotel, is again as long a ride, if not a bit longer.) If you haven't already done so, buy some strong insect repellent and prepare to bathe in it, and if you see one, buy a fan. The **Hotel Tehuantepec** tries to keep out insects and to circulate the tropical air, but nothing can shut the tropics out altogether. For related reasons choose fish likely to be freshly caught, rather than meat, soup rather than salad, and bread without butter. This should hold, also, for the **Hotel Calli,** somewhat younger.

Except for a few well-made sandals and the elaborately machine-stitched *huipiles,* there is little local craft, but you may want to take a bus or drive to Ixtepec, or Juchitán, once a bit more self-respecting than its sister towns, with a more colorful Sunday market, but now grimmer, and still bra-less and sullen, in spite of new paint, ghastly new gray-white statues, and the promise inherent in a new electrical installation at the edge of town. On any day, the general dry-goods stores of these towns are something to see: baskets piled on each other in tight corners, heaps of *huipiles* on shelves to the low ceiling, bolts on bolts of cloth for skirts and on the counters, large jars of multicolored buttons.

Tehuantepec likes iguana stew and iguana eggs, both savory, if you can get past black skin and rubbery egg shells. Or try some cooked armadillo, or settle for the large, sweetened tortillas, *totopes,* which will rush at you in high mounds on any square.

LA VENTOSA

Like the Tehuana, La Ventosa has a highly romanticized reputation, which does not always hold up. From October to May it is sun and sea, and shade under a wide, thatched lean-to which shelters crude tables and benches, a few hammocks, the family chickens, pigs, a burro, and the ghostly dogs which gather wherever there are human voices and the promise of food. Lying in a hammock, one listens to the rustle of the breeze in the palm trees on the beach and the soft lapping of the ocean. The blue sky hangs over two hills and a light-house (supposedly built by Cortés, the Busy), then flows into the green sea. After a swim, there is the luxury of a shower in a private locker. The house provides fresh, inexpensive fish, tortillas, beer, hammocks for the night, and fish again for breakfast at very little cost. The little pigs oink and grunt through the night, a neurotic rooster keeps announcing dawn at all hours, the water sometimes smells a little fishy, but in spite of these—or because of them—La Ventosa can be a great comfort after a long drive and the hot dust or hot damp of Tehuantepec.

During the May-to-September rains, Eden becomes tainted. The water is thick, angry mud (the locals blame this on the crazy river in Tehuantepec, usually low and sluggish, but wild when it dashes into the sea swollen with rains) and everyone will offer to take you to a better beach nearby, a beach of clear water near nests of beautiful white herons. Don't go. It is likely to be a Calvary over smooth rocks for spills, sharp rocks for cuts, impossibly hot sand, more rocks, marsh, and cowdung, and no clear patch of water anywhere in sight.

NOTE: For a long time the only completely reliable hotel in the area was the **Magda** in Salina Cruz whose restaurant, though simple, was equally reliable. It is almost always full, so if you plan a slow trip through the area, using Salina Cruz as headquarters, reserve well ahead. The **Hotel Guasti,** whose lower section, around a yard of ghostly pillars, was a collection of cobwebs and rust, promises to improve itself. Maybe; have a look if the **Magda** won't have you. For a small meal and a rest from driving, stop at the **Café Colon** on the highway north of Ixtepec.

TUXTLA

The journey from Tehuantepec to Tuxtla Gutiérrez will absorb most of a day and should be started early for full views of the country and to avoid being caught in the wilderness at night. (If you are driving, take extra gas, water, and food along.) No one can accuse gaudy Tuxtla of quiet good taste, yet it is, once the eye recovers, a very pleasant town in which to stay awhile.

The plaza is inviting in its tropical Mexican fashion, with a pool whose shallow depths pay impartial homage to the two main branches of local heritage—a Mayan god and a Spanish crest in sparkling mosaics, travelers' palms which fan their unreal fronds into the light breeze, and all around the *puestos* of fruit drinks. (Try liquefied *pitahaya* or *guanábana,* and for peace of mind and body, an intestinal assault pill right afterward.) Tuxtla had a regional museum which was being systematically sacked (but may have been replenished) and a delightful small zoo of local animals, among them beautiful, fierce little wildcats and a pair of harpy eagles with nervous crests and baleful, haunting golden eyes.

As in most tropical towns, the plaza really comes to life in the evening, full of walkers and sitters, eaters of ice cream, drinkers of coffee, and watchers of girls. Dinner at a restaurant overlooking the plaza is a pleasant possibility. Later you might wander through the streets of the town for glimpses of life behind the long grilled windows or the sounds of marimbas and horns playing for a private dance. Or see if the Chinese restaurant just off the Zócalo is still there. It claimed an "internationally known cuisine for the most refined palates" and listed an Oriental rarity called Chau Min.

For a night's sleep, the **Hotel Esperanza,** in town and inexpensive, will do satisfactorily. The **Hotel Bonampak,** on the highway near the entrance to town, is a place for resting and expanding. At moderate sums, the Bonampak offers country-club living: a largish pool surrounded by tables and seats for poolside drinking and eating; a children's pool and play area; jai alai courts; gardens; airy rooms with porches; and the best food for miles around. Moderate.

About equidistant from Tuxtla and Chiapa de Corzo, eastward, and reachable in a half hour's ride (inquire about road conditions) is the Cañón Sumidero, a dramatic gorge at whose bottom slides the Río Grijalva, supposedly carrying in its long meanders the ghosts of Indians who leaped into it rather than submit to Spanish rule.

LAS CASAS

As the crow flies, San Cristóbal de las Casas is less than 55 miles from Chiapa de Corzo. As a human drives it should take more time than normally allotted for such a distance. It is a rise from an altitude of 1,500 feet to 7,000, an absorbingly beautiful and demanding spin through the mountains, with an occasional village to halt the rise and turn of green. As the road begins to slope into the town, watch for the hamlet of Navenchauc at the right of the road. It is a gem, a perfectly designed Japanese-print village which sends out on the road to greet you, for a few pesos, clusters of children and flowers.

There is nothing in Mexico—or possibly in the world—quite like Las Casas, a seclusive town which lives with its eyes downcast and a small voice. Its square, streets, and churches (interesting to see for the uncomprehending work of Indian apprentices of the sixteenth and seventeenth centuries) are not especially impressive. It is the local Mayan men—the Chamulas, Zinacantecos, Huixtecos—striding through the town with the somber dignity of ancient warriors who give Las Casas its unique character and style. They carry themselves with a classical nobility which derives from the immaculate whiteness of their handsome costumes, from the Greekness of their beautifully sculptured brown legs in the high-backed sandals of Hellenic art, from their stately gravity, and sure stride. The women, on the other hand, are shy, unkempt arrangements of dark, shapeless folds of wool, hung with babies and bundles, dim backgrounds for the brilliant men, a covey of dusty little peahens trotting behind the lustrous peacocks.

There is fortunately little to "do" in the town. The great Mayan cities are many miles away; closer ruins are enmeshed in jungle and take planning and fortitude to see. You might look at the façades of the churches, which, except for the chaste Caridad, look as if they had been decorated with giant cookie cutters. You might go out to the regional section of I.N.I. (Instituto Nacional Indigenista), a government bureau which—if it still exists—operates in backward areas. Its function is an interesting combination of the educational, sociological, anthropological, and medical, bringing primitive peoples into the twentieth century as gently as possible. You might play the game of strolling the cobbled streets to pick out which foreigner is tourist and which anthropologist. (The state of Chiapas is the anthropologist's Happy Hunting Grounds.)

In the late afternoon one goes for coffee and cake, for a small charge, to the **Casa Na Balom,** the Colonial manor house of Dr. and Mrs. Franz Blom, the defunct King and present Queen of Chiapas. He was a Danish anthropologist for many years connected with American universities and one of the begetters of Chiapas anthropological study. His widow is the baker of the very good Middle-European cake you will eat, a talented photographer who has documented much of the region, and a wonderful sight to see as she strides through her realm in riding boots, surrounded by dogs, with the same grand confidence as do the Chamula dignitaries. The whole state is her fief: the villages in lost hollows, the obscure jungle paths, the town itself, where every child knows the house.

The paying guests—if they'll talk to tourists at all—can be stimulating people, usually groups of anthropologists or students. Most stimulating and nonpaying may be the jungle Indian sometimes brought to the big city. Some years ago it was a Lacandón (a rapidly disappearing Mayan tribe from the tropical forests around Bonampak) named Bors, whose wife had died, leaving him with two little boys and no one to care for them or his house while he was off hunting. With his long straight hair and long white gown, flanked by the little boys dressed and uncombed exactly like papa, booming deep jungle sounds of greeting guests, he was a startling sight. And he was no less remarkable in the marketplace, where he spent hours dangling strings of beads at the local women to entice one into living with him and taking care of his children.

Las Casas at night has an unsettling quality. It is quiet and dark, closed on itself, but beneath the calm, restless. Santo Domingo Church glows into the crisp, dark night, a luminous curtain for the silhouetted soldiers who guard its stairs. From behind a black window come the strong sounds of a Beethoven piano sonata being hammered out in practice. One dimly lit *cantina* throws a startling shaft of light over the dim sidewalk; from its back pool parlor float the muffled sounds of a radio or a quarrel. None of these are phenomenal, but in nighttime Las Casas one's own footsteps sound disturbing, anyone else's ominous, and the brush of a dog is shocking.

The heart of Las Casas is the market, the streets near it, and the street of Guadalupe, just off the square, where many of the village people do their buying, selling, and bartering. The market doesn't sell much except foods, rolls of salt wrapped in banana leaves; dark-brown sugar pressed into the shape of an upended tumbler; tiny boxes of Tide, always shaken before a purchase, to determine quantity.

Guadalupe is the street for tourist wandering and shopping, for wide loose shirts of unbleached cotton (cut, sewn, and machine-embroidered to your order within a few hours), sturdy huaraches, woven sashes, bags of string or leather, and brilliant cottons which show unmistakable Guatemalan influence. The outstanding shop was **La Segoviana,** whose *dueño,* Señor Joaquin Hernandez Umbrias, came out of Spain (apparently from Segovia, to judge from the name of the shop and his shade of Castilian lisp) many years ago and found his way to this distant town. He learned enough of the local dialects, of the thinking and the customs of the Indians to trade with them in an atmosphere of mutual respect and affection. Consequently it is in **La Segoviana** that one found the unusual handloomed scarf, the old piece of embroidery, and, once in a while, silver pieces of eight which Don Joaquin, being the principled man he was, would tell you were modern copies, if they were. One hopes Señor Umbrias and his honest shop are still there and thriving.

HOTELS

The most rewarding place to stay is **Casa Na Balom,** if there is room, and you've written ahead. At the **Español,** a moderate sum buys three meals, a room off the courtyard, and intense sociability in the minute *sala.* The **Posada de San Cristóbal,** right off the square, has had its ups and downs and outs (for a while it was run beguilingly and peculiarly by two children), but take a look at it and, before you settle in, find out if the toilets have yet resumed flushing—or if the hotel has sustained life at all. Or examine the **Hotel Jardín,** on the square. None of these (except **Na Balom**) has the faintest trace of "gracious living."

To arrange a trip to Bonampak or Palenque or some other point in the Chiapas jungles, consult the intelligent tourist office *jefe* (who commutes between here and Tuxtla Gutiérrez), or try to latch on to a Blom group if possible or, if you have the money and time, Mrs. Blom may arrange a trip into the jungle for you.

REMINDERS: These are people who live in elaborate systems of witchcraft, to whom a strange-looking foreigner suddenly seen on one of their village roads may appear to be a dread *espanto* (an evil spirit which appears, interestingly enough, as a man to women, as a woman to men). For his odd appearance and the fact that he is taking photographs, thus robbing the streams or fields or children of their life essence, a stranger may be stoned to death. With a little elementary trickery, like holding the camera sidewise, or getting another tourist to make conspicuous photographic poses while you slant your camera subtly away from him, you can get good market photographs. Some of the young gods in bright-ribboned hats are often glad to pose for a couple of pesos, although their elders—much handsomer, in wrapped headcloths like pirates—rarely stoop to such ignoble trade. The town doesn't offer too many problems, but the villages require tact, especially during fiesta time.

Finally: It is cool in Las Casas. Bring sweaters, a raincoat, and socks to wear in bed.

WHERE TO NOW?

The fastest way to get to Palenque and Yucatán is by plane from Tuxtla Gutiérrez to Villahermosa and on (if the line is still in service). You might go back by bus from Las Casas to Ixtepec and pick up the railroad that connects with Coatzacoalcos and Mayan points beyond (if *that* is working).

The auto road which meets the Pan American Highway just east of Juchitán (185), traveling directly northward to a meeting with 180 at Acayucán, is a more civilized way to make the journey, through changing landscapes and hamlets (pleasant or to be dashed through). From the low cultivated plain, one rises to hills covered with wild shrub that lead to Matias Romero, a town for a gas stop, a look at longtime "temporary housing" as old railroad cars, to notice the frames of gold around the front teeth of many women and the density of dust and flies.

Alternations of crag and green fields, of up and down, continue to Jesus Carranza, which deserves a stop. At first look it is a tropical village inhabited by winter dust or summer mud, and tin-roofed cottages and stalls. The village is dominated by old railroad cars and a rarely used track which acts as tall esplanade for a view of a lovely bend of river that embraces a gentle island, thatched cottages, and long strips of golden beach—the perfect hideaway for a week's lazing in sun and water at a cost of practically nothing. You will notice that some of the houses near the river are built on stilts, since the river floods once in a while. Others, equally close, don't bother with stilts; it is so easy and cheap to put a few new beams and some new thatch together.

The terrain widens to broad ranches of grazing and corn and large birds that float, turning slowly, like white petals, to lacy trees. Soon there is Acayucán, whose charming plaza still holds on to its old trees and surrounds itself with many open, amiable cafés. The market is busy and vivid and you might do worse than stay at the air-conditioned **Hotel Plaza** (inexpensive, large, and no beauty) at the side of the market, before you attack the Yucatán peninsula.

Sea, Sand, and Sun: Guadalajara and the Pacific Coast

Like the east coast (see Veracruz and on), the Pacific coast is a string of beaches and eager fish. Most of the beaches are trying for splendor in the "international" style; a few don't yet give a damn, happily settled in their tropical torpor, letting the fish do the running and jumping.

The western sea-pleasure route is achieved by entering Mexico at Nogales, following Highway 15 down to Hermosillo, where a west-bound drive of an hour and a half or two hours (check road conditions) leads into Bahía de Kino, which has aspirations toward resort-hood but hasn't yet made it. Eighty-five miles south the highway reaches Guaymas of the fishing tournaments, flowered houses, deep hills, and resort hotels. From Navojoa a westward road (twenty miles) takes one to Huatabampo, considerably less showy, lovely, and teeming with fish. The watering place for Los Mochis, farther south, is Topolobampo, another fine place to spend the day swimming, fishing, eating seafood, bird watching, and admiring the view.

Or, if you choose spectacular scenery, take the train that does the Los Mochis–Chihuahua City run, past gorges, over bridges, to a meeting of several canyons called **Barranca del Cobre,** claimed to be wider and deeper than the Grand Canyon. Down in the canyons the Tahumara Indians cultivate their fields in the equable, sheltered temperature and bring their crafts up to Creel souvenir shops to sell to freezing tourists. (This is high and cold country; be prepared.) You might stay at the **Hotel Divisidero** or return—the trip is worth making twice—or go to Chihuahua on the newly refurbished, well-equipped train that runs quite frequently.

Much of Mazatlán is a shrimp-catching, -packing, and -shipping port, but there are, not too far out of the busy center, long, peaceable stretches of beach and not-too-wily fish to catch, and, of course, new beach hotels. By consenting to live across the road from the beach, you can buy decent accommodations plus meals moderately priced at the **Jacarandas Hotel.** The nonfisherman can watch the slippery, vivid life of the fishing pier in the morning, or swim, or lie in a thatched beach hut drinking rum, or walk along the *malecón* (sea wall) to watch the sun settle into the ocean, or gorge on seafood at **Mamucas** or **Copa de Leche.** Although the port is growing rapidly as a pleasure spot, there isn't much hoopla yet, but it will come. (Should your next goal be Baja California, here is where you'll find comfortable overnight ferry service to La Paz.)

About half an hour south of Tuxpan a good local road (Nayarit 46) winds its way through deep jungle to San Blás. If it has not been wrested out of its lethargy, San Blás should still be a typically over-ripe tropical village which—particularly in the summertime—moves at a slow ooze, melting under the forceful sun. Bananas and fish are abundant. Why strain? Accommodations are hardly deluxe and in the summer evenings the mosquitoes zoom down in massed billions, but its careless charms are good for the driven North American soul. It provides swimming and fishing off endless miles of white empty beach near the town or, via a short car ride to Matanchén, a gem of a bay whose hotel may be usable (or completely impossible) by this time. A short distance from town, at the side of the road, one can board a boat for a slow, dreamlike ride through an estuary of the sea closed in by orchid-bearing jungle brilliantly painted with unreal birds, and in the shallow waters, hand-painted fish who loll and laze and turn without hurry to show their masks and shoulder stripes of gleaming color. The ride ends in a hamlet of naked brown children threading the air and the water like flying fish, against a background of thatched huts and banana palms.

The map shows a road from Tepic (a singularly characterless town) to Puerto Vallarta, temptingly close yet much better reached by plane out of Guadalajara. Between Tepic and Guadalajara, the road becomes "Mexican" scenic, more varied, running through hills and wide plains, past rough gorges and into the moteled strip which introduces most cities. Guadalajara has, in recent years, progressed itself out of much of its Colonial flavor. In spite of the zealous but, up to this point, sage city planning, it has kept many lovely stretches of green and a regal spread of old plaza bordered by some of its most interesting buildings: the government palace, with a baroque façade both gay and dignified, a majestic courtyard, and rose gardens; the state museum in a proud old palace; the confused cathedral; the grand, grand-opera becolumned Degollado Theater. In spite of its occasional look of Pittsburgh, Guadalajara is still the *mariachi* city, a cultivated city whose boulevards are lined with jacaranda trees, and most important, the city of Orozco murals. The painter was born in the state of Jalisco, and its capital city has used, displayed, and commemorated his genius in the university, in its public buildings, and in the Orozco Museum workshop. The most awesome set are those in the Hospicio Cabañas, a vast Colonial building, now an orphanage and shelter. The tremendous, symbolic figures of the elements—air, fire, water, and earth—and the thunderous heroes of Mexican history gashing and roaring through the walls and ceilings are, in their own idiom, not too distant from the awe and emotion of the Sistine Chapel.

If Orozco leaves you the time, see the richly exuberant façade of the Santa Monica Church, the fine theater and library near the railroad station, the intelligently planned and large, attractive market, and, for a look at comfortable modern design dressed with imagination, see the airport and the enormous shopping center.

D. H. Lawrence has indelibly linked Guadalajara with Lake Chapala, 35 miles south of the city. It is no longer the place he described and loved-hated; a number of verdant towns have been taken over by craft enterprises usually run and organized by Americans. The **Chapala Country Club** offers golf and "social activities." Unconquerable Mexico pushes its way through, though, and makes a journey through the lake villages—Ajijic, Jocotepec, Tizapán—a pleasant way to spend a day.

As mentioned, one can fly from Guadalajara (frequent service) to mosquitoless Puerto Vallarta, a green-ringed Lorelei, with appropriate rocks in the sea, luring increasing numbers of people to its sybaritic hotels. It has become popular enough to have grown its own escape land, Yelapa, reachable via a couple of hours at sea, and equipped with cottages for tourists. Southward and seaward, one reaches Manzanillo, an easy, not-too-ambitious port town from which flowed endless miles of empty beach, a few huts here, a small hotel there, nothing much but peace and sun and a little swimming and fruitful fishing. Now the town is larger, busier, though still entertaining in the casual manner of the tropics, and the communications point for travel inland and northward through the spate of beach hotels and fantasy resorts that have settled into the lovely Pacific bays to Puerto Vallarta and beyond.

Should you be driving, the closest large town will be Colima, whose westward road will lead you into a fascinating amalgam of mountains whose soft folds, like old drapes, enfold new enterprise— hydraulic stations, cement plants, and miles of pipes waiting to be placed—as well as the classics of corn and cane and immense cactuses. The slide off the hills introduces orchards of bananas and mangoes, coconut palms, and, sheltering among them, thatched huts on carpets of lush grass and scatterings of waterfowl in still marshes.

In Manzanillo, a possible lunch stop is **Ray Coliman**, built over a pier surrounded by fishing boats. It is a pleasing introduction to this sort of open, inexpensive seafood restaurant available through much of the area. Having had your fill of shrimp and/or lobster, stroll through the town to catch a glimpse off one main street, Carillo Puerto perhaps, of streets that are bright, gay tangles of stairs, trees, houses flying up the close, surrounding hills.

Manzanillo's bay and beach, the Playa de Santiago, holds on to its old, cool family houses but has begun surrounding them tightly with condominiums, some rather tacky, others quite luxurious, and almost all of them willing to rent rooms or suites for several days. The esteemed and fairly simple **La Posada**, on the beach near town, provides bungalows and some single rooms at moderate rates. Among the more lavish: **Las Gaviotes**, whose rates for beach suites are higher, and the **Roca del Mar**, meticulously maintained and handsomely decorated suites complete with bar, kitchenettes, laundry room, and a beach restaurant. Since accommodations are proliferating faster than they can be reported, you might, if you plan to spend some time in Manzanillo, settle into the dignified **Colonial Hotel** in town for a day or two, eat some of its fine seafood, and then explore beach-living possibilities.

As mentioned, you can eat well in town and equally well along the beach. **El Dorado** is quite elegant and well mannered with outdoor tables swept in a breeze of coconut palms and a fine way with red snapper *(huachinango)* in several styles, crayfish *(langostinos)* with or without garlic *(mojo de ajo),* and shrimp, high for the area, but not very. Its opposite number is **La Estancia**, the most modest of shelters, which houses a few tables and a family of talented cooks who ask modest to moderate prices for their generous helpings. (Their schedule is erratic; if they're closed one night, they might be open the next, or the next, depending on the supply of fish and seafood or a marriage or confirmation in their expanded family.)

From Santiago Beach, looking northward toward a graceful curve of coast topped by green hills, is a white mirage town, a distant vision of fairyland, named appropriately for such a land, **Las Hadas.** Closer by, from the road that climbs to a peak of the protective hills, two magnificent views down on curious white architectural shapes, a small yacht harbor, lagoons, palm trees, and limitless sea.

The architecture and planning—which include a little swinging bridge, baby waterfalls, flower-bedecked pools, and thatched open *palapas*—seem to derive from several sources: the long horizontal balconied buildings that are modern resort style, a strong tendency to repeat the mosques and towers of Moorish Spain, and, from Catalan Spain, the sculptured forms of Gaudí. With such interesting introductions, the interiors are disappointingly conventional: big spaces, highly ornamented but essentially Colonial Mexican. There is a golf course, not the full eighteen holes (only fifteen) but spectacularly laid out and a challenge to play; there are attractive shops in an oddly appealing plaza and outdoor eating in sea breezes that sometimes cool the hot tacos pretty fast. There are suites that contain their own pools and simpler rooms on a scale that runs from high moderate to expensive ($50 and up, modified American plan). The best deal is an American-plan package tour of a few days that your agent can arrange.

Whether you plan to stay or not, spend a few hours if you can at Las Hadas, a dream that was meant to be peopled by the rich and beautiful but, disillusioned as such places often are, settled for the less erratic, plump middle class. If you decide to stay awhile, take a look at the steep Italian village, **Puerto las Hadas** (rented through the **Las Hadas Hotel**), and the apartments of various sizes of the **Villas del Palmar,** equipped with a reputedly remarkable golf course. Moderate to high.

The coastal road, still going northward, returns entirely to the tropics, the only buildings huts, the only industry cultivating bananas and papayas, and the beaches pristine except for a few naked local boys splashing in the shallow waters. A spotting of villages with large, white churches; and nothing more until one reaches Barra de Navidad. Barra, like San Blás (page 262) has been the secret paradise of a small number of Mexicans and resident Americans for a long time and, like San Blás, resists mass adulation. There are a couple of casual hotels—the **Delfin** is long-established—and houses and shops, but what is most engaging, very little ambition. And very likely the best lobsters on the coast. Go to **Rancho's,** a big thatched area on the beach, and have an enormous fresh lobster at a quarter of the price you would pay at home. Then paddle around the sandbar in a narrow cove at the end of the beach in the company of the local golden-brown young and a few of their American sun-worshipping friends.

The landscape out of Barra pulls its plantations up the mountains, each curve in the road revealing yet another composition of creamy scallops of beach enclosing white-frosted sea. Hills, sea, beach, jungle green, are all that happen for miles and one wishes it will stay that way, until one reaches Chamela, which threatens development. Soon one sees a sign for the **Hotel Carreyes**, which sits prettily on the slope that rises from its very own cove.

Almost immediately around the bend (you won't see a sign; the arrangement is that you be picked up at the airport in Manzanillo) is the Playa Blanca branch of the **Club Méditerranée.** As you know, plans for a stay have to be made well ahead of time, and these are carefully protected places with all fees, except for drinks, paid in one advance sum. As you have heard, the clubs abound in singles of several sexes and sociability among them is fervidly encouraged.

What you may not know is that Playa Blanca's accommodations scramble up its hills like the houses of Italian Riviera towns, looking down on a beautiful assemblage of tiny bays and dramatic spurs of rock. You may not know, also, that the planning is extremely intelligent—something for everyone at any time of the day from tennis and horseback lessons to yoga to Greek dancing. Or you can do nothing but lie on the beaches, both shaded and open, and watch the gorgeously decorated and draped hosts and organizers organizing tactfully and charmingly. Lunch is miles of platters of a great variety of foods set into small gardens of flowers and plants, self-service and all you can eat, plus the wines and beer set out on the tables. The big surprise is the increasing number of middle-aged and older people and families with young children who find the fun and games and food and the "singles" entertainingly satisfying and not, for what they get, expensive. (See your travel agent about the week package.)

A short distance to the north (actually thirty miles from Barra de Navidad) is the town that growed like Topsy, Puerto Vallarta. If you can tear yourself away from the sybaritic and expensive hotels with their alluring décor and shops, their ornamental clientele and lavish dining, wander through the lively town and especially its market, full of peculiar shell jewelry and objects and attractive sandals. Have a meal at the **Río Quale,** which lists a good international menu with a little emphasis on the Italian. The attached **Hotel Río Quale,** by the way, is satisfactory though modest, and at least one room has a small balcony with table and chairs that makes a fine viewing place for watching families stroll home from the beach, a man hammering out the dents in big gas cans, and a wandering old, white horse who impedes traffic and seems to be no one's concern. Another modest hotel, quite near the water, is the **Molina de Agua,** which asks no more than $15 a day for a double, no meals. The antiques of pre-Burton-and-Taylor days, the **Oceana** and the **Rosita,** have undergone some face lifting but still ask moderate rates.

SHOPPING

Several very good shops are found at the side of the **Colonial Hotel** in Manzanillo; **Las Hadas** shops; the large hotels and shopping streets in Puerto Vallarta, with especial attention to the distinguished jewelry at **Ric's.**

If you plan to return to Guadalajara from Puerto Vallarta by car, assume that it will take the better part of a day and that the drive will be dramatic and, for most of the stretch, sharply curved mountain driving in competition with trucks and buses. The early phase is smooth and tropical with a promise of distant hills that come closer and grow higher. Miles of the pale, gentle green of sugar cane stop for spills of rough, larval rock, as black and menacing as if they had just cooled. The mountains then heap up as bare sandy yellow, one base holding a round ruin which might have been a pre-Columbian observatory and is the promise of more buildings to be excavated. The mountain curves now come dizzyingly one on another, opening occasionally to spreads of enchanting valley like green patchwork quilts and smooth little hills stippled with green like adolescent beards.

Then, the big city signs of Guadalajara.

NOTE: All coastal areas are hot and wet in the summertime; save them for a winter trip or, if summer is your travel time, stay in the highlands, unless you like heat.

WITH TIME TO SPARE: Roads and accommodations keep improving throughout Mexico, yet not fast enough to obliterate "adventure" travel: to Shark Island (Tiburón), one of the last strongholds of the Seri Indians, or the remote, timeless fish and beach hamlets of Boca del Río, Agua Dulce, Playa Novillero, Los Corchos. And remember that roads and tiny planes go, or soon will, everywhere—or almost—and that, should you be approaching or returning from Mazatlán by way of the San Luis Potosí area, the ride between Durango and Mazatlán is quite spectacular.

GUAYMAS

Hotel Playa de Cortés,   bountiful and pleasurable, fairly expensive and worth it.

Guaymas Inn Motel,   satisfactory, companionable (modest to moderate).

ALAMOS *(east of Navojoa)*

Casa de los Tesoros,   considered one of the best inns in Mexico; usually closed late spring through September, but check (moderate to expensive).

If you prefer to stay in Navojoa or Los Mochis, both will provide decent food and shelter, and the highway keeps sprouting new neon and chrome wonders.

MAZATLÁN

Newish is the imposing, expensive **Camino Real.** Oldish, balconied hotels at one end and a line of new motels at the other, a few middle-aged beach hotels in the middle. It is simply a matter of driving slowly to see which appeals to you, especially off-season. For the safety of reservation, get in touch with the **Cantamar Motel** (moderate to high), **Playa del Rey,** in the same category, **Hacienda Mazatlán** (moderate), the **Sands** (moderate); or the nice big old hotels, much more indigenous: **La Siesta** (modest to moderate), or the **Freeman Apartments,** moderate, or the rangy **Las Gaviotas,** moderate. The rangy **El Cid** is a large, almost self-contained village. Expensive. The **Holiday Inn Mazatlán** is more modest in size and price.

SAN BLÁS

The **Hotel Bucanero** in town is undistinguished but *there* (modest). On the beach, a fresh, well-furnished inn, the **Posada Morales** (moderate). Look in at the **Los Flamingos,** an antique mansion modernized with a good dining room and modest.

GUADALAJARA

Since Guadalajara is the second city in Mexico, there is an infinity of shelter available. Your agent might have some information about a new wonder that suits your pocket. Or consider: The **Gran** and the **Fenix,** both popular and central (moderate); **Del Parque,** pleasant and backed by greenery as the name implies (modest to moderate).

El Tapatio   winds up and up on its own hill to hacienda-style units with balconies that afford twinkling night views of the city (not so good in harsh daylight) and refrigerators which are filled daily with snacks and drinks and sweets for which you pay as contents are checked and replenished. The complete life such hotels try for includes tennis, stables, and a close-by golf club. Maintenance and service are not always what you might like them to be, but that is, as mentioned, a general Mexican condition. (High for Mexico.) Also high is the **Excelaris Hyatt Regency** built in the dazzling vertical Hyatt style.

At similar rates, with more reliable service and less "palatial" décor—tasteful in its own modern mode—is the **Camino Real**. There are also in this category the **Guadalajara Sheraton** and the **Holiday Inn Guadalajara**.

Back in the "moderate" area, the **Hotel de Mendoza,** with a small, heated swimming pool in an inner court and an exit that leads into old Guadalajara. It is back of the theater and next to an ancient royal tobacco factory and a restored sixteenth-century building. One of its neighbors is a happy church that sings all day.

Besides its numerous hotels the city offers many motels, most of them with swimming pools: the **Posada del Sol, La Estancia de Guadalajara,** the **Motel Chapalita, Del Bosque,** the **Giralda,** the **Campo Bello,** the **California** (all modest to moderate). For housekeeping suites: **Del Campo, Monte Bello, Lila, Andrea,** and **Margarita** (moderate to high moderate).

PUERTO VALLARTA

Puerto Vallarta's almost monstrous growth has produced a **Camino Real Hotel** a short distance out of town that is twelve stories tall and described as "indescribable." **Fiesta Americana,** also new, reaches only seven stories but is quite splendid and expensive, as is the **Buganvilla Sheraton** which is one of a group of "Golden Six Hotels" whose facilities you may use while staying at one of the group (several airlines go from major U.S. cities to Puerto Vallarta). The **Garza Blanca,** a few miles from town, provides each of its suites with a pool and all sorts of luxuries. **El Mirador** and **Las Campanas** concentrate on bungalow apartments and decent monthly rates. The **Rosita,** the **Rio,** the **Tropicana,** the **Oceano,** and the **Paraiso** (you may remember it in its ancient, careless guise in *Night of the Iguana,* which inspired the Puerto Vallarta boom) if they still exist all ask reasonable sums. There are cheaper places still—the **Pedregal,** for one—and those that soar, like the **Plaza Vallarta.** As you might expect, there are many restaurants, including Chinese, and clubs. Look around or ask old hands (visitors who came to Vallarta two days before you).

CHAPALA

Hotel Real de Chapala; entertainment, pool, sports. Moderate. **Villa Montecarlo,** a thoroughly luxurious motel with an enterprising restaurant. For less splendor, but still a satisfying restaurant, look in at

La Terrazza. Ajijic's **Posada,** ranged around a court in the old style, is famously hospitable. **Hotel Nido**, central and handsomely ornamented. Modest to moderate.

RESTAURANTS

Guadalajara: The venerable **Copa de Leche** has clothed itself in chic new décor and added music to its respectable meals and solicitous waiters. More Mexican in menu, décor, and brouhaha is **El Farol. Recco** tends to the Italian, the **La Vianda** more to the international, **La Fuente** at least partially Mexican. Fast-food places appear, as elsewhere, in larger numbers, among them **Denny's,** which stays open twenty-four, or nearly, hours a day.

Coastal restaurants have already been mentioned in sections dealing with their areas. Motels and hotels, of course, serve meals, quite lavish but not immutably best at luxury hotels.

SHOPPING

Local markets may yield a meager crafts find now and then—not much; the best place to search is the Guadalajara market. For adapted crafts, textiles, and sportswear, look in at some of the shops on Juárez and Hidalgo: the immense, variegated, government-sponsored **Casa de las Artesanias** (Parque Agua Azul), **Arte Real** (Lafayette 27), **Taller del Museo** (Constitución 104). The ride to famous Tlaquepaque to see glassware and pottery is pleasant, but be sure of what you want, don't be swayed or charmed, and select carefully; a few of the many places are good, others are tourist traps, museums of ineptitude and dynamic bad taste. Chapala has some good crafts and clothing, and Puerto Vallarta is planning and bursting with new shops, as is Manzanillo.

MEXICAN HOURS

5:15 *A boy strolls through the* colonia *Condesa selling clay pots and dishes. He has arranged them in a web of strings which crosses his back and chest, runs across his forehead and along his shoulder, ending in bracelets of toy pots on his wrists. He is beamingly proud of his ingenuity, less interested in selling than in showing the clever, attractive ornament he has made of* *himself. The visitor remarks that the rural* mestizo, *through ancient usage and present necessity and because it is company, seems always to be laden with something, and recalls Stephens' description: One Indian set off with a cowhide trunk supported on his back by a bark string as the groundwork of his load, while on each side a fowl wrapped in plantain leaves hung by a bark string, with only the head and tail visible. Another had on each side of his load strings of eggs, each egg being wrapped carefully in a husk of corn, and all fastened like onions on a bark string. Cooking utensils and water jars were mounted on the backs of other Indians, and they contained rice, beans, sugar, chocolate, etc. while strings of pork and bunches of plantains were pendent.*

5:30 *A local radical is making a fierce speech to an assemblage of ten in a plaza in Mexico City. Following the straight line of the devout he damns all imperialist capitalist countries and finishes with: "With the help of the Holy Mother and Jesus Christ we will yet win."*

6:00 *Twilight settles its light, purple dust over the village of Tlacochahuaya. In the dry, bare atrium of the church two musicians play to the dusk. The small, monotonous drumbeat strengthens the thin, plaintive thread of sound from the flutelike* chirimía, *repeating and repeating an ancient tune of loss and longing unremembered.*

6:30 *In the hills of the state of Guerrero a city man returns a horse he had hired for the day. The house of the farmer is a shack made of bits and pieces over an earthen floor, the bottom of poverty. The rider asks, tactfully, where the owner bought such a fine horse. "Oh, our son won it in a lottery and gave it to us to sell. We haven't enough land to use it here." The city man asks how much for the day's hire. "Nothing. It was a pleasure to have you enjoy my horse." "May I offer you a drink then?" "No, thank you. When I am a guest in your* tierra *then you may buy me a drink. Here you are my guest and for that reason I cannot accept a drink from you. I should like to have drink and food to offer you, but all I have is the horse. Should you come back this way and the horse still be here, please know that he is yours to ride."*

7:00 *A group of boys are sitting in the square of Papantla, plucking at their guitars, singing quietly. One strikes up a lively tune and sings to it: "If I must be killed, O God, let it not be by a cow. Make it a Cadillac."*

7:30 *The train arrives at its station and all the relatives of arrivals are on hand for emotional meetings with those who had been away only for a short while. The women kiss, the men thump each other in hearty* abrazos, *the children are examined and hugged and laved with endearments. The elaborate, warm greetings over, they pick up their shapeless bundles and trudge off, everyone talking at once of the day's great adventures.*

8:15 *The bus from Veracruz accosts the bus coming from Jalapa. They slide toward each other in the middle of the well-traveled road, and then stand head to head like whispering lovers. The drivers exchange salutations, chitchat, arrangements for meeting at the movies tomorrow, and a few playful insults, while other drivers tolerantly wait out the tryst of the hippopotami.*

8:30 *A farmer totters through the swinging doors of a* pulqueria *with the democratic name of* El Sol Sale para Todos *(the sun shines for all).*

Veracruz:
Hot, Sweet, and Strong

A good way to see the city is to mount a trolley. (Pray that they have not been replaced by buses.) It may have bursting leather seats or be an old-style summer trolley mountable anywhere and completely open. The latter offers the advantage of being airier and avoiding the cling of sweaty skin to gray seat stuffing. (Veracruz is warm always, hot in the summer, and miserable during *nortes*—monsoons.) The trolley clatters past the narrow shopping street named, inevitably, Independencia, having passed one side of the busy *zócalo*—also, inevitably, named the Plaza de la Constitución, but that name is spoken only in the silent voices of street signs. The noisy little tram will, with the best speed it can muster and with a sailor's roll—this is a mariner's town—take you past a few newish apartment houses, all balconies and glass, a few varicolored mansions more interested in variety of decoration than "good taste." One flashes by a green park which houses a large outdoor, shaded refreshment place and a bright, imaginatively designed playground; skirts a vast set of market alleys, and skims by a beautiful abstraction of house-front colors— pink, yellow, blue, red, ocher-toned, fused by the bleaching of the sun and scraped by the violent winds and rains of the "northers." (A bus will cover the distances but not half so picturesquely.)

A walk brings more leisured and closer views of the area and the people. Much of the populace will look considerably darker than other Mexicans, quite like Cubans or Puerto Ricans but, as a rule, more fully packed; Veracruz eats and drinks well. The darkness of skin color is accounted for by the darkness of the indigenous peoples, the universe of lavish sun, large infiltrations of island Negroes and ships' crews from all over the world. The music, as well, echoes Afro-Cuban rhythms.

The speech, too, shows island influences and laziness—slurred, *s* lost in the rattle, syllables incoherently swallowed, like that of Portorriqueños and Cubanos.

Preserving its Latin dignity (and in a much less windy manner), the state of Veracruz is to Mexico what Texas is to the United States. It doesn't exactly boast (bad manners are left to Tejanos) but is richly verbal about its firsts and mosts and largests, its variety, virtues, speed in progress; and lets no visitor forget an item of its excellence. A good deal of the satisfaction, if repetitious, is justified: Veracruz produces a major portion of Mexico's petroleum, all the sulfur, all the vanilla, much of the sugar, some of the best cattle. Its coastal areas and lowlands grow a large variety of tropical fruits—coconuts, bananas, pineapple, mangoes, mamey, *zapote,* oranges, among others; its waters yield enormous quantities of seafood; from its highlands come sizable crops of cereals, vegetables, corn, and temperate-zone fruits. Veracruzan coffee is choice, its orchids flourish in hundreds of strange and beautiful varieties, among them the frail, petulant vanilla plant, which has to be cosseted and pampered. Its educational program is one of the most active. (It even affects the upper echelons: one lieutenant governor was the translator of Norse sagas into Spanish.)

Veracruz has managed to harness its rivers into a vast TVA operation; it has one of the most beautiful regional museums in the country, supervised by the energetic anthropologists and archaeologists of its university; its infant mortality rate has dropped conspicuously in recent years.

As every schoolboy knows, it was from the coast of Veracruz that Cortés launched his conquest of Mexico. Fewer schoolboys know that for many years the city of Veracruz was the port which sent to Europe tons of Mexican silver and goods from the Orient (via Acapulco), and consequently was often prey to pirates and buccaneers, among them Sir Francis Drake. Because of its geographic position as place of entry and exit, the port which Cortés called "The Rich Town of the True Cross" (Villa Rica de la Vera Cruz) has seen some other momentous comings and goings. It was here that the optimistic and doomed Maximilian, caught in a web of transoceanic politics, disembarked to a welcome of silent, closed doors. Benito Juárez, the Abraham Lincoln of Mexican history, fled through the port to exile in Cuba and later the United States. In 1847 the U.S. Marines invaded to take over the "Halls of Montezuma," and again in 1917, and some Mexicans can't forget it.

None of these comings and goings seems to have ruffled the port's temper or frayed its nerves in any apparent way. The beer and coffee flow; the shrimps, crabs, and gleaming red snapper leap from the sea; the *huapango* hammers out its staccato heel taps, the small harp exhales its retiring, dulcet sound in rolling, circular rhythm; the hips roll, and the merchant mariners roll from one outdoor saloon to another while the sun shines full, wide, and strong. Veracruz is a pleasantly fleshly city, not witless but certainly casual about things of the intellect, leaving that domain to the state capital, Jalapa, the "Athens" of the state of Veracruz.

The crowded alleys of the market, the odors, the mounds of tropical fruits, the dark-gold energetic vendors and customers deserve at least a half hour of Veracruz time. At one end of the market is the fish area, which begins with a clean, inviting stall of seafood cocktails—fresh shrimps, crab meat in an ice-cream-soda glass and sold for only a couple of pesos each triple helping. To have some or not? This much be assured of: Veracruz fishes much, consumes a respectable amount of its catch, and has a keen nose for the freshness and delectability of seafood. Having eaten or not, move on to the rows of fish stalls, which are a little smelly and wet underfoot, particularly when it has rained; but what fresh fish shop isn't at least a bit smelly? The yellow and gold and pink red snappers are neatly arranged in rows of graduated size or layered head to tail making a lovely running rhythm of shapes; the little ones are placed in circles, mouths inward, like a water ballet. Mounds of enormous cooked and raw shrimp clouded by millions of threads of pink shrimp whisker lie with green bundles of crabs—sixes and eights, neatly tied together with palm thongs. Beyond them hang jaws and unrecognizable sections of what must be latter-day leviathans and smooth, white, decadent little dogfish.

Out of the market streets, from the park, walk up Independencia, the narrow main shopping street once laden with flower-covered and girl-hung balconies, some of them held up by dusty caryatids with fancy-free art-nouveau hairdos. Now the buildings are prosperous glass cases filled with sporting goods, expensive watches, Chanel soaps; fancy bake shops; big pharmacies; and the newish, twentieth-century Mexican sound: hammering, drilling, and chiseling out new buildings.

At the end of Independencia as it enters the main square, across the street from the cathedral, is the **Café Parroquia** which serves—most of Mexico says—the best coffee in the country. It has to keep its standards high because many of its customers are coffee merchants and this is their exchange, where deals are discussed and argued with great vigor and no visible speed. (Trading in Mexico, except among States-trained or States-efficiency-enamored businessmen in Mexico City, follows a long, slow, convoluted line: first the elaborate greetings, including a clinched, back-slapping *abrazo,* then a few minutes of teasing and counter-teasing, exchange of information about mutual acquaintances, a lavish description of someone's fiesta, coffee and more coffee, discussion of some length and asperity on world and local politics and, finally, a slow slide into economic conditions, which may bring them to the price of coffee, or sugar, or a piece of real estate.)

After coffee at the Parroquia—as hot, sweet, and strong as love, Veracruzanos say—cross to the church and follow the tall *portales,* past a few pleasant, small restaurants, to Zaragoza Street. Turn right, where you will find a row of souvenir shops crammed with the ubiquitous baskets and shell work and, a bit beyond, a pretty handkerchief of a park where you might sit awhile under the oleanders and imagine what it might be like to live in the sullen little hotels nearby or to drink at their bars when a crowd of seamen hit the town and the bottle.

Having looked in at the crafts (too often stuffed turtles and dead baby alligators) on the Calles Zamora and Zaragoza and their arcades, continue on right, past the park and toward the sea, at whose edge you will find a junk heap of little shops and stalls crammed against each other, full of incredible objects made of clam shells, tortoise shells, and plastics that imitate both, anything over a half-inch in size stamped with "Souvenir of Veracruz." The sheer multiplicity and sameness are fascinating, and occasionally a breathtaking peak of bad taste is reached; for instance, a ceiling hung with dozens of bread baskets made of small shells surrounding a picture center—a view of a drunken lighthouse, curdled sea, and clouds like stale bread.

The statelier shops across from the sea wall, near the hotels **Ruiz Milan** and the **Victoria,** carry crafts of other regions and copies of small pre-Columbian figurines. The best of local crafts, of which there is not much, are the white baskets of flat, wide palm weave, well proportioned and worldly though not as strong as some of the cruder baskets of other regions. They come in several sizes, at a small sum each, which helps pay the fines of the prisoners who make them, and are available practically nowhere else.

Take some time to walk along the waterfront and look at the freighters. The *Brandenburg* is in from Germany, the *Trolleholm* from Norway, the *Covadonga* from Spain, the *Texas Star* in from Galveston. Farther out to sea, the fishing boats are returning homeward with the yellow gold, the pink gold, the red gold of *huachinango* (red snapper). Little boys are sitting on the sea wall hooking up garbage. A round woman in a blazing blue dress which shouts back at the sun is having her photo taken by an itinerant cameraman with a 1920 camera. A robust old lady in an improvised bathing suit steps out of a launch with a dangle of crabs she has just bought. The yellow "Hot-dog, Hamburguesa, Coca-Cola" stand positions itself for the customers who will take their *paseo* in the cool of the late afternoon. The huge Bank of Mexico, hard modern and glassy with flat, hard pillars and "strong" sculpture, stares across the water at the old fort of San Juan de Ulúa, whose flattened, crumbled battlements look like a seasoned cheese. At a distance the fortress is soft and small, belying its vigorous history as a prison and as the last bastion of Spanish Royalism after the War of Independence of 1810.

Back toward the main square again—follow the crowd and the energy that flows from it—past the deep murky sailors' bars and the dim hotels, to the large vista of seats and tables in the plaza cafés, bordered by men speaking all languages, wearing varying tones of sunburn, all kinds of weather-wrinkled and beaten skins, all types of caps, and in a large gamut of moods from the young, bewildered, tropic-struck, to the old, uncurious, and belligerent. Among them weave the shrimp vendors and the sturdy men with large voices who carry trays of crab, little wooden spoons to eat them with, and an array of strong sauces in old-fashioned hair-tonic bottles to be splashed on the *jaiba*, translated as "Estofe crob" for the foreigner.

Just before the corner of **Prendes,** that venerable institution serving *huachinango veracruzano* and vats of varied fish soups, look for a serious shop of antiques and the rarer popular arts: a few very good *serapes*, some choice ceramics, unusual regional costumes, and a few *santos*. The square you will emerge on, again, was once a comfortable, jungly, careless place. Later its buildings were covered with a pasty white glaze and peculiar lighting that made poison plants of its flowers and trees. The sun and rain, and tropical laissez-faire, are happily softening the harshness.

For other confrontations with Veracruz modernity—announced earlier by the industrial plants on the outskirts of town—take a look at the hard cubist benches and planters (no plants; maybe they are garbage deposits) on the waterfront. A few blocks away, a once playful area for fairs, carnival performances, etc., was turned into a large sententious rectangle whose dark stairs lead to bronze eagles with serpents in their mouths and, in a circle of marble stelae (each commemorating a constitutional advance), an enormous black Juárez holding a scroll marked "Reforma" in one hand, the other in his vest, Napoleon-style. Around the corner (Morelos and Juárez) from the tall white lighthouse building on one side of the rectangle, you may find a city museum which appeared to be the destiny of a building that held only a few heroic statues a few years ago.

Admittedly, any tropical city needs face-lifting from time to time, but the heroic-monument style is least suitable in a city like Veracruz, if it is suitable to any modern city at all.

The local beaches, a short trolley ride from the center of town, are lively and tuneful. On Sunday afternoons the young of the town, and a good number of their parents, turn out to swim, eat, and dance under big sheds right off the water. The music is usually good, and the stiff-shouldered, swivel-hipped, flat-faced, understated dancing—restrained but blatantly sexual—a rare and mesmerizing sight—when, of course, it isn't the spastic movements of "rok." Evenings (especially Saturdays) spent on the *malecón* watching Veracruz stroll by strumming guitars and witnessing the universal battle of wits and bargaining between vendors and sailors are low in cost and highly entertaining. (Ask for Playa Hornas, Costa Azul, Villa del Mar, all near the center.)

Launches hug the sea wall eager to take groups around the harbor or the more distant Isla de los Sacrificios, on which there isn't much to see or do unless you have the luck to pick up a bit of artifact (not impossible to do anywhere in Mexico), but the ride is pleasant and the cost nominal.

Deep-sea fishing can be arranged with the desk of your hotel. Within a half hour's drive or less are fishing villages where you might catch your own dinner and have it cooked for you at one of the local eating stalls. If you lack the energy or interest for sightseeing or fishing or dancing, it is still comforting to know that the greatest pleasure of Veracruz is its own gay, musical, sensuous, carefree company.

VERACRUZ CARNIVAL

FOUR DAYS BEFORE LENT

A huge, exultant jukebox which plays a hundred fragments of song simultaneously; a party of thousands of children, wrinkled and unwrinkled, basking in confetti; colored paper singing in the air; a gorging on shrimp and colored ice; a little salacious, a touch morbid, a bit perverse, innocent, and marvelously funny is the Carnival of Veracruz.

Veracruz provides a much less dangerous set of release days than the other famous carnivals. Río reports 47 dead, 6,000 hurt, and 10,000 arrested during its Saturnalia; the comment on New Orleans invariably contains some variant of "My God, you get mauled!" There are, of course, thieves (Veracruzanos swear they all come from Mexico City) and there are knives and guns in a number of pockets, but the owners forget to use them. The fleeting, intense affection which is one of the prime Mexican charms—and faults—blooms and grows like a great flower, shedding pink pollen of happy dust.

An old man, three tequilas and two beers in his skinny stomach, picks up two sleepy babies wearing caps of confetti on their newly washed coal-black hair, dances a few steps with them, and returns them with a kiss for each, and one for mama and one for papa. Two middle-aged gentlemen toast an American lady, assuring her that it is being done with "all respect," and repeat beamingly the one English word all Mexicans know, "Byurrifooool." Then, somehow, streams of amity and beer lead to Mexican-United States friendship, toasts are drunk to the memory of Kennedys and to the kindly brother to the north (no longer the threatening, octopus-armed Colossus). A young buck pressing his way through a crowd, politely and gently, stops to present an old lady with a flower. She beams up at him and inspired, revived, pulls her *viejo* (old one) up for a few steps of dancing on the seething sidewalks.

It isn't necessary to stay the four days: the last two are best. By the third day, everyone who intends to has come to Veracruz; people in costumes now move freely in their new skins; the atmosphere has become soft and perfumed with light fleshliness, playful, casually amorous, and beerily sentimental. Most of the floats and public, organized festivities that take place on days one and two are repeated, with limited variations, on days three and four. The most elaborate are outfitted by competing beer companies; historical floats of the great pre-Spanish days—the white man-bird who might have been Quetzalcoatl, warriors in tiger skins carrying great plumed fans, a jaguar-masked man and a few musicians in antique Indian dress playing native instruments.

Later in historic progression, Father Hidalgo and the lady on the disappearing five-centavo piece, La Corregidora, surrounded by revolutionary cohorts, move into view, in carefully arranged period costume, faces set in inhumanly high purpose.

The small improvised floats—usually on an open truck—of the various neighborhoods are less austere and much livelier. Bands of pirates play, sing, and gyrate (the Veracruzano prides himself on being related to early pirates; one of the local songs says, "I have the soul of a pirate"); girls in the lovely, lacy traditional costume and boys in white dance the local dances, involving some swift and intricate footwork. Truckloads of children, like huge baskets of fruit, trundle by.

However, a float is a float is a float. The best of the carnival pours by on foot. Sometime before noon (and maybe it would be safer to go earlier), find a seat in the *portales* of the main plaza. Any café will do, although the **Diligencias** café has an overload of Americans whose eager participation is too frantic. As at home, these North Americans work very hard at gaiety. Afraid they won't relax soon enough, that the merriment will run out before they can run with it, they drink too much rum too fast. They sit and shout, reluctant and yearning to dance their stiff-waisted Arthur Murray steps in this mass of whipping torsos. Then they pass out.

The cavernous bars of the **Colonial** and **Imperial** attract the most marimbas and *mariachis,* almost one to a table, the musicians outside outyelling each other and the four or five bands indoors. All this sounds deafening, and in another atmosphere, it would be, but during Carnival it becomes one of the natural elements, like the sunlight and sudden breezes of confetti. Where the most music is, there are the most released spirits—the dancers on the tables, the heapers of monumental piles of shrimp shells surrounded by battalions of beer bottles, the lustiest *ranchera* singers, the most dynamically affectionate types.

You've found, miraculously, a seat and before you is a paperful of large cooked shrimp just bought from a vendor. The waiter is trying to bring your beer but is blocked by an old weather-beaten man who is offering you a beautiful little kitten with a lovely spotted coat—an infant jaguar. The waiter slips your beer adroitly on your table, between the arm of the jaguar salesman and a new armful—this one trailing strips of lottery tickets. The extended arms come in a steady stream—tickets, candies, wallets and bags of hide and alligator skin, a cigar three feet long, Chiclets.

Still another group of *mariachis* saunters up. In their tight short jackets and trousers covered with buttons and braid, in aggressively large hats and flowing ties, they look anachronistic, like their prototypes of a hundred years ago—the *"mariage"* (hence *mariachi*) musicians introduced by the French of Maximilian's time. As the hours wear on, they push out with their massive formality and shouting style the more timid Veracruzan harps and marimbas, who nevertheless keep trying. A woman hails the *mariachis* and asks for one of the old songs of rural heartbreak. They oblige and she sings with them, head back, throat full and tight—in appropriate, rough snarls and high whoops.

A band of little boys in white trousers and red, ruffled rumba shirts are strutting and shuffling along the *portales.* Their moist, excited faces are heavily rouged and gold dust plasters their hair. They look like depraved cherubim, particularly the solemn little fatty whose tympani are two inverted frying pans loosely set in a wooden frame and banged on in a complicated Afro-Cuban rhythm. Their queen and soloist is a skinny twig of a girl in a bright satin G-string and bra. Her thin little face is heavily made up and dully immobile except for the jaw, which keeps discreetly chewing on a wad of gum. From outside the *portales,* a frantic, sweaty woman screams at her to stop and dance before a group of *turistas.* The exhausted child gyrates in a burlesque of burlesque, tossing her straight little side into what might be a lascivious curve if there were hip to curve; thrusts out and weaves her meager belly muscles, and now and then, in a mindless, automatic gesture, strokes her nonexistent breasts. Mama screams directions and inspiration.

A plump man dressed in beribboned baby panties, loose, sleeveless top, and an attractive straw bonnet, calls for music, and all alone, begins to dance, fetchingly, gracefully, coquettishly. Later he will continue to dance down the street, in the square, near the waterfront, always alone and smiling sweetly. There are several such happy solitaries, completely, joyously in love with themselves. One lithe little man with a boneless torso, which he thrusts and twists as if he wanted to be rid of it, appears one day in trousers and shirt and the next—still wearing his mustache and savage smile—in a ripply, ruffled dress, slashed up the front to show his hairy, frantic legs.

The night brings more music, more entertainment, more spectacle: a show of popular singers, and an American group that plays country music and local varieties of "rok." After midnight a dance band takes over.

In the meantime, in the central plaza, a group is performing local dances. The girls' costumes are all foam and lace and ornament; the boys are in white *guayaberas* and white trousers. These are hardly the Indian dances one sees elsewhere—based on simple steps with unimpressive variations and monotonously long. The Veracruzana dance is short, lively, flirtatious, and tapped out in the brisk rapid toe-and-heel work of the Spanish *zapateado.*

In the *portales,* the professional ladies have taken their places at tables or in laps; some of them are the crestfallen, local products who ply the freighter trade; others, with high-style hair arrangements and extremely *pegado* (clinging) dresses, cut far down and far in, with skeptical, brilliant eyes, bring their swinging beads and hips from the big city. They don't try too hard. If trade isn't very good, it's still Carnival. (Whatever twists of the human psyche produce it is anyone's parlor analysis, but it is a curious thing that the whores are most eagerly sought after as dance partners—and what dancing!—by the most exquisitely dressed transvestites.)

Which brings us to the rarest of Carnival entertainments. About five or six blocks from the center of town, in a large area adjoining the firehouse (ask for *bomberos*), two long rows of eating stalls, tables and chairs (try *pozole,* an indigenous porridge of corn, pork, onions, garlic, and chile), and a large inner space for dancing are arranged for the evenings of Carnival. The cooks and waitresses wear evening clothes, some girlishly graduation-dance style, floating in ruffles and bows; others slick, smooth, and compact as knives. Their manners are sweetly feminine, without caricature, and only their voices betray the fact that they are, by a great biological mistake, men. Some have a little difficulty trotting around on evening sandals with very high heels, a false breast slips now and then, but there is so rarely a sense of travesty or insult that one begins to speak of one's hostess as "she." In the center of town are the murderous caricatures of women, while here the imitation is kindly and, in a curious way, natural. Here are the men who don't want to kill women, but simply to *be* women, to cook, to serve and lead biddable lives. One young man in an exquisite hat and beautifully made dress keeps circulating among American women asking for a household job which would include cooking, cleaning, dress- and hatmaking, preening in his own skillful products as advertisement.

Just how this institution of public drag grew no one seems to know or want to say; certainly it is internationally known and watched for by *aficionados*. It is innocent and salacious, the weight of either quality depending on the moat in any particular eye. The Mexican youths who go to the *bomberos* to eat *pozole* and drink beer mark the fact of he-shes with the tolerance of a people who have lived with conquerors and outlived them, a people whose Janus head is empathy and violence, who live with flowers and blood, love and abandonment, to whom the human condition is all its varieties, not a plastic-wrapped selection.

The hinterland American doesn't note and let it go. He is staringly mired, fascinated, and confused. He feels he should deplore where he is charmed, should be appalled where he is attracted. Only after a while—after counting the monumental sins of the world—can he concede that he is witnessing a humane thing; in its special context, a healthy institution, an opportunity to be openly what one kind of human being wants to be, for a few days, at least, and in the world's eye.

Like a throbbing mesh of arteries feeding the transvestites of grace, of elegant cruelty, of happy narcissism; the confetti-coated children, beaming old ladies, and metallic prostitutes; toothless old tramps sifting the confetti for a dropped coin or piece of jewelry, the rhythmic music keeps pulsing. The babies bounce up and down, the little children move their feet expertly to it, waiters strum on trays and clack beer bottles to the rhythm; strollers dance their promenade, a band of sugar workers in sugar sacks clank coins in chamber pots—asking for more—in rhythm. The erratic darting of adolescents dressed in black dominoes and hoods submits to the rhythm. Everyone dances because he must, carried on the irresistible tide of music.

HOTELS

For Carnival, reserve hotel space early and expect to pay more than usual.

The **Emporio,** on the waterfront, has a pool and balconied rooms (moderate to high). Also away from the square and on the waterfront is the **Hotel Porto Bello,** quite good-looking and air-conditioned. A block or two below the Emporio are two smaller hotels, the **Victoria** and the **Ruiz Milan,** whose amenities, like their prices, are more modest. The **Diligencias** (moderate) is an old favorite. The **Hotel Imperial,** on the square, asks more modest sums. The **Hotel Colonial,** on the square, is the most modern and most expensive if you are alone, but since the rooms have several beds and couches, the prices drop considerably for family groups. Incidentally, if you decide to live on the square, carry ear plugs; life jangles early and late. The **Hotel Mexico,** whose rooms ring an inner court, may be more quiet.

There are cheaper hotels on the square, and cheaper ones still on the waterfront and the streets off Independencia, but not recommended unless you absolutely have to save money. A huge Italian villa of a seaside hotel, about five miles from town, is the **Mocambo,** colorful and livable although it suffers from occasional lapses in housekeeping (high moderate). The **Villa del Mar,** once a place of popular seaside jollity, has had its gaudy face lifted and is now quite refined (moderate). These have, of course, the virtue of being right on the sea, and the concomitant fault of not being near or on the effervescent plaza. Back in town, the **Hotel Prendes;** small, in colonial style and moderate in price.

In recent years Mocambo Beach (with easy access to the city) has added to its one elderly and appealing **Hotel Mocambo** a good number of others, among them the **Hotel Playa Paraiso,** equipped with a pool and air-conditioning, as is the **Hotel Torremar** (both comparatively high).

RESTAURANTS

Always eat seafood if you can: it's fresh, plentiful, expertly cooked, even in modest places. **Prendes** is the Rock of Gibraltar for seafood, as in Mexico City. It is not as cheap as other restaurants, but the service is courtly and smooth. Have the red snapper with onions, pepper, olives, capers (called *huachinango a la Veracruzana*, although it is Spanish), shrimps or crab-meat cocktails or the *langostinos a la parrilla* (broiled crayfish) without or with garlic *(con mojo de ajo)*. For less expensive and elaborate menus, try one of the clean, pleasant places directly across the square which also serve seafood. The cafés on Independencia—which is one side of the square—such as the **Diligencias** and the **Parroquia** (good coffee), serve sandwiches, chicken dishes, and eggs, should you be easily bored with seafood. Or, if a vendor looks pleasing, buy his shrimp or crabs and eat them in the park or at one of the cafés where the price of hospitality is a bottle of beer. You will find several restaurants, one in pastel New Orleans style, on or near the waterfront, and for a light refresher, one of the conesful of fruit dispensed from carts all over the city.

HUNTING

Hunting is reputedly very good in this area. Best make *absolutely sure* of gun regulations and inquire of the Mexican Consulate about local hunting regulations. Or you might inquire at the hotel, but don't hope for much.

VERACRUZ ENVIRONS

Follow the sea wall southward and then the continuing road, past the Mocambo and a few Mexican Newport-style beachhouses (here, as elsewhere in Mexico, the largest and gaudiest is always attributed to a wife of a former president; it might almost always be true), a few eating places, and, by our standards, little slatterns of hotels and a statue of George Washington.

In about fifteen or twenty minutes by car there will be a bustling swell of the road, hardly a town at all, a little sleazy and full of oilclothed tables and elementary benches, exactly like a thousand tropical eating places in Mexico, including the cases of soft drinks, the chipped crockery, the two-year-old calendar with the pretty picture of Brittany, a chromo of the Virgin of Guadalupe, and a pair of well-packed proprietors, teeth gleaming goldly. This is Boca del Río, where a confluence of rivers pours into the sea and sprays out a large, generous variety of seafood, caught, cooked, and eaten in less time than it takes a New Yorker to make his way by cab from Broadway to a seafood house on Third Avenue. Rather than in one of the raffish slatterns, have your meal in a large, cool, clean place; a civilized restaurant, in short. Have the small, savory stuffed crabs *(jaibas rellenos), huachinango a la parilla* (grilled red snapper), or, if there are fresh shrimps from Alvarado, don't miss them. If radios and jukeboxes permit, a discreet group of harp and guitars may play intermittently and not too many little boys pester you to buy shell necklaces.

A bit farther on (cross the bridge, bear left, and follow the MOCAMBO SIX KILOMETERS sign) is Mandinga, where one once could fish shrimp right out of the river and have them cooked at one of the local stalls.

Mandinga is now, in its limited way, "big business." The hamlet still is clusters of thatched roof over boxes of wood or adobe and flowers straying out of minute gardens onto the walks of earth and garbage and layers of sea shells. Across the narrow section of inlet, a stand of mangroves shelters fishermen pulling in the local small flat fish *(mojarras).* Nearer, men are mending nets or lining their dugouts with fresh palmetto. It is all quite picturesque and the efforts to sell and sell aggressive—or desperate. To get into an enormous eating shed that sits on the water, one must run the gauntlet of sellers of "típico" dresses and blouses (many of them adapted to what is called "jipi" style), beads, earrings. Once seated, there are itinerant vendors to cope with and children who hang on the backs of chairs, staring into the faces and plates of foreigners. Four groups of musicians vie with each other, at least two at a time, and they usually have with them a girl who taps out the fast, complicated *huapango* steps.

The fresh *mojarra* is delicious, the shrimp exceedingly good, the lagoon lovely, but be prepared for stultifying confusion and noise, especially if you go on a Sunday or holiday.

About three-quarters of an hour out by car, or a little longer by bus, off the road to Jalapa, there is a pleasant country hotel, **Puente Nacional.** It is a good place to rest from the rigors of Mardi Gras, or any one of several possible trips in the state of Veracruz, and has full hotel facilities, pools, bridle paths, and Totonac ruins to show. (Crowded some weekends, rarely on weekdays. Reservations: call 28-53-99 in Mexico City, or write Hotel Puente Nacional, Carretera Jalapa-Veracruz, Veracruz, Mexico.)

ZEMPOALA

The trip described below is best negotiated by car over decent roads that serve the local sugar mills and refineries. Traverse the Jalapa-Veracruz highway until you reach Tamarindo, about halfway between the two cities. A road sign or local citizen should point you northward to Cardel, and beyond it, Ursulo Galván, from where a usable road goes westward a few miles to Zempoala.

Even more than most ruins, Zempoala is a tragic place. The once immense and brilliant Totonac city which had reputedly a population of 250,000 (although this may be an exaggeration of local pride) is now three buildings constructed of round smooth stones, the decorations erased except for scattered spots of color on patches of the white stucco which once covered the buildings; the upper temples are gone, and of the walls which retained threatening floods, only the curious battlements are left. Far into the immense lush fields of sugar cane, morning glories, and corn spread jungle-covered mounds of other buildings. What is left of life and people is a minute, sleepy village of thatch, wood, and tin alongside a small canal (also made of smooth round stones in the local antique style) which is the village laundry and a guide or two who shelter in the small museum. This was once the seat of the Totonac king who undoubtedly had a name but was immortalized by Bernal Díaz as the "Fat Cacique," who sent emissaries to bring Cortés to him because "as he was a very stout and heavy man, he could not come out to receive himself."

It brightens the sad stones of Zempoala to imagine the "Fat One" standing in the court of his palace (probably the largest of the uncovered buildings) surrounded by an entourage of chieftains in magnificent robes and gold ornaments. He hands over presents of gold, jewels, and cloth to Cortés, but knowing (via the remarkable Indian grapevine that still exists) that Moctezuma's agents had brought infinitely more costly gifts to the *conquistador,* apologizes with "Accept this in good part: if I had more I would give it to you." He "complains bitterly of the great Moctezuma and his governors saying that he had recently been brought under his yoke; that all his golden jewels had been carried off, and he and his people were so grievously oppressed, that they dared do nothing without Moctezuma's orders, for he was the Lord over many cities and countries and ruled over countless vassals and armies of warriors."

It was at Zempoala that Cortés gathered his first party of Indian, anti-Aztec cohorts—and he went on gathering them in vast numbers, belying the simplified, romantic picture of a small, valiant "handful" of men miraculously conquering fierce hordes of bloodthirsty Indians. The Conquest was certainly initiated by Spain and the church and carried through by Cortés, religious fervor, and greed, but there were formidable numbers of Indians very eager to destroy Moctezuma and his empire. It was at Zempoala that the conquerors were given their first brace of Totonac princesses, among them the niece of the "Fat Cacique," as unattractive as her uncle. And it was at Zempoala that Cortés and the church first made a public demonstration of idol smashing, against the terrified protests of the local caciques. Pressed between fear of the Aztecs and fear of the Spaniards, poor "Gordo" could do nothing but retreat further into helplessness, and so sped the conquerors, now riper in confidence, on their way.

And it was there that Pánfilo de Narváez, sent by the Governor of Cuba to stop, arrest, or kill Cortés and his soldiers, established his camp. At the time of Narváez' landing, Cortés was in Tenochtitlán seeing to the welfare and pleasure of Moctezuma, who was under house arrest, holding polite, sympathetic conversations with the royal captive while plundering his palaces. Moctezuma appeared quiescent and easy, but when he heard of the arrival of troops inimical to Cortés, lost no time in sending them gifts and ordering local caciques to see that the men were generously fed. Also, yearning for defeat, he told Cortés of his danger. Cortés fled back to Zempoala and won over Narváez' men by the sure expedient of handing out blinding nuggets of Aztec gold, not only as bribes but also as promise of greater things to come if they joined his forces.

To recover from the dry taste of ruins and weight of conquests, you might go on to La Mancha (watch out for trucks laden with sugar cane and, maybe, a young black puma strayed from his wilderness), possibly the first "Villa Rica de la Vera Cruz." It is not easy, unless you have some Spanish and intrepidity. Continue northward and westward (as you have been going) and keep asking everyone you meet for La Mancha. You will be directed by farmers and children along a minor road. You should, within a few miles of Zempoala, be in sight of the sea, and in back of the dunes, small huts which are *cantina,* restaurant, and household of listless women, assortments of children, and sturdy husbands, whose job is to order them around.

The interiors contain a few bottles of cheap, hard liquor and a case or two of beer, often surprisingly cold, and nets, coils of rope, and the dark clutter that hides in tropical corners. The shaded porches are for guests, dogs, chickens, and small children. The restaurants stock little but keep replenishing the two or three fresh-caught fish on hand as soon as they are eaten—a matter of sending a couple of the boys out beyond the low, treed dunes to the sea. While mama fixes the fish by gashing and larding it and wrapping it in paper before it is placed over the coals in the small stove, the guests may swim in the warm, silken sea or walk or sun on the endless, empty beach. Or, ask that the cooking be delayed and take a launch into a nearby lagoon—a *lanchero* will find you, via the grapevine—full of water plants and frail white herons and egrets.

The fish, either *huachinango* or *róbalo* (haddock), is served with salt and lime; nothing else. But mama will make a stack of tortillas if you and papa insist, and the boys will bring beers. If there are no utensils available this might be a good time to explore the versatility of the tortilla, or to learn to use your fingers as elegantly and precisely as an Indian child does. A bottle of beer, a good-sized fish, and a pile of tortillas should cost much less than a fast-food hamburger back home.

If La Mancha seems too remote, skip it, and return to Ursulo Galván, a pleasant, ripe town in which to spend an hour. You will notice, if you haven't before, the strong Negroid strain that makes the curly hair and the curvilinear faces of the coastal areas. A river which divides the town from its neighbor was crossed by a swinging plank bridge whose walls seem to be made of paper clips. To anyone accustomed to the firmness of cement or steel underfoot, it provided quite a sensation, something akin to being in a mild earthquake. The chances are, however, that building and improving fevers have, by this time, created a firmer bridge and one less exciting to cross.

On the side from which you started—assuming you've walked across the bridge and back—look in at the soft-drinks stand nearest the bridge. Unless ownership has changed, its proprietor should have a gold tooth, a red eye, and a glorious repertoire of gestures. If your Spanish is up to it, ask him how things are in his part of the world. He will tell you, at considerable length. With joy, with fervor, he will make the speech he has been making to his less enlightened compatriots, the rural workers who have to be taught about progress—how to make it, how to keep it going. (In this he displays a marked Veracruzano attitude, which is often forward-looking, ambitious, with a strong community sense, contradicting the stereotype of the torpid man of the tropics.)

"We have," he says, "achieved electricity, a medical center, sons who are doctors, sons who are engineers, sons who are army colonels. Fruits we have: oranges, bananas, pineapples, mangoes, *guanábana;* we have corn and grain; we have radishes, cucumbers, chiles, tomatoes, carrots; we have fish and meat and eggs. We need, firstly, clean drinking water, and secondly we need night classes to teach our peasants about it. We don't have any more malaria now nor the White Pest [T.B.] but we must teach the people about the tiny animals in the water, that they will kill the best-fed child. And they must learn not to use human excreta in their fields; that the terrible small animals grow in it and grow up in the trees and plants of those fields and make sick anyone who eats of them. We must have latrines and farmers must use them and must learn to wash their hands after using them. We are a flourishing community which has come a long way and we don't want to stop here."

The ceaseless Mexican pendulum swings us violently back in time at Antigua (southward, through Cardel, and nine kilometers beyond, following the road that parallels the coast), the second "Villa Rica de la Vera Cruz," which preceded the present, and third, port city by some sixty years. It is a quiet town, drowsing in contented tropical somnolence alongside a slow river ambling toward the sea. The light breezes of the sea touch the pale green of the rice fields and rustle the disordered fringes of the banana palms. It seems hardly the setting for the plotting and counter-plotting which created a near-mutiny before the actual Conquest began. Getting wind of it (Cortés, besides his audacity, his courage, his quick insights, his indomitable rage for riches and glory, also had, quite naturally, great appeal for informers), Cortés immediately ordered two leaders hanged, others punished, and the ships destroyed, to prevent the return of anyone to Cuba, from where the expedition had started. But, being a man of foresight, he first had brought on shore all the anchors, cables, sails, and everything else on board which might be useful. This move also gave him several dozen young seamen to add as soldiers to his 500, and older sailors to fish for food.

Existent records have not actually pinpointed the site of these events, but they probably took place very close to the village which still bears conspicuous reminders of the Spaniards. The Franciscan church and convent which has since been enlarged and somewhat revised was founded by royal order in 1529 with the suggestion that its cost be defrayed by the gold in the small idols and ornaments somehow found by a Franciscan friar. Around the corner and linked to it by ruins of thick gray wall is the building which is believed to have been that of Cortés, either as house or seat of government. Sinuous heavy vines have draped themselves around the stones and thrown coiling branches and leaves across the windows, the matted knots seeping small spots of blue sky inside the bitter archways. The doors are gone and there is no roof, the little lizards flicker nervously across the stones; the Totonac tropics in their patient, noiseless, Indian way avenged themselves on the conquerors by slow strangulation.

JALAPA: THE ATHENS OF VERACRUZ

Jalapa can be reached easily from Veracruz or by bus or car out of Mexico City via Texcoco, Apizaco, Huamantla, and Perote, beginning with a dramatic mountainous ascent with fine views of the snow-capped volcanoes, Iztaccíhuatl and Popocatépetl. The road climbs into maguey fields and pine forests, into pastoral ranch country with wide fields and clear cool air, and continues to climb into chalky hills surrounding icy little lakes bordered by field flowers. Then it descends into towns again and views of ice-crested Pico de Orizaba, the brutal shape of the Cofre de Perote, and through the hills that crown Jalapa.

Jalapa suffers from, profits by, and delights the visitor with its common Mexican characteristic of contrast and contradiction, which makes each town many places with multiple meanings.

The town has, for instance, several lively faculties of the University of the State of Veracruz, and a devotion to theater, books, music, and archaeology. Its beautifully designed museum and crafts center was planned with an eye to a great future as archaeological treasury, preserver of old skills and folkways, and teaching institution.

The town has topped one of its lovely hills with a monument to a group of agrarian revolutionaries whose tomb carries the atheism of a carved hammer and sickle. A few miles below, in the center of the town, small jewelry shops sell silver arms, legs, hearts, and lungs to pin on the skirt of a favored saint. Fine new airy industrial and academic schools grow out of broad avenues fed by twisting, narrow alleys hung with old iron lanterns. The railroad workers have a sizable sports center—basketball, swimming, jai alai—enclosed in well-planned gardens, but milk is sometimes carried on a burro's back in tall tin containers. The newest big market is light, spacious, and handsomely muraled in tiles, and frequented by smoothly dressed women who follow European and U.S. fashion as closely as they can. But their maids will open the door to barefoot, wide-skirted Indian women with fauve faces, offering magnificent orchids.

Jalapa's lively main streets are cluttered with young people who are poets, painters, and philosophers when they are not students, great discoursers often more serious about their avocations than the vocation papa decided on (one of the reasons there are so many *licenciados* in Mexico is that a law degree is as common as our B.A., and often the easiest choice settled on by middle-class boys before they can indulge themselves in the arts).

Start at the Parque Juárez, on one of the middle layers of the many-layered town. The top of the park (very little in Jalapa stays long at one level) is sedate and mildly classic, formal walks under a wide, spreading gesture of immense shade trees. (Parks in Mexico, incidentally, are not necessarily for children, as they are elsewhere; Mexican children can find sun, trees, and dirt to dig in, and the companionship of their contemporaries, almost anywhere. Mexican parks are for courting, reading, chess playing, discussing, and—in a studious, intellectual town like Jalapa—for study: a student makes notes out of several texts he has spread around him; in front of him, a student-actor paces furiously, gesticulating with verve and passion; watching both sits a solemn boy sucking a stick of purple ice.)

The surrounding hills are mossy and melting behind the fogs that rise from the valleys, or sharp and luminous in clear sunlight. Closer and below are the curves and cuts of weaving streets, held in their flight by deep earth-red of tile roofs.

Downward, the park becomes a small-scale model of what a park should have and be: a miniature aquarium, a duck pond of three ducks in three heaping spoonfuls of water, gardens the size of boutonnieres.

To the right of the park (as one faces the cathedral) is the Calle de Miguel Barragán, which slips from the traffic-ridden square in steep, precipitate haste. Its roadway is cobbled, its muted, soft façades silenced and shadowed by deep overhanging eaves and the taciturnity of long, iron-grated windows. At the first cross street, one has the choice of climbing up or stumbling down another. Up is mainly blue and green, down is yellow and terra-cotta; and both streets are likely to be emblazoned with little girls and plants hanging over grillwork balconies in a folk-Goya effect.

Left on Calle Morelos brings one to the same composition on a smaller, poorer scale, with the smell of a meager life—rancid cooking oil, charcoal, a breeze of urine. Turn on Sebastian Camacho, which seems to be a thoroughfare of country people looking for customers or work, banging at each door with the market call, *"Marchante"* (merchant). Around the corner, to the right, is Zaragoza, which leads to the **Hotel Salmones,** where you might have a drink or a sturdy *comida* (a little more than $3 for a long string of dishes), or the soda fountain near it for a cup of coffee. You might then follow Primo Verdad and go into the alley of Enrique González Aparicio, at whose entrance there is often a vendor of oranges and limes which hang in cascading sacks from the patient sides of his burro. The alley is lovely blocks of light and dark and a fountain of sky. Return to Primo Verdad, which will take you into Enrique Zamora, one of the main streets leading to the center and back to the park.

With a map obtained at the tourist office in the square, you can follow Jalapa's lantern-hung alleys, secluded from the bustling, argumentative town. The Avenue of the Revolution starts, at the left of the cathedral, as a narrow alley, forced by the buttressed side of the cathedral. Before it becomes busy, it gives room to the old **Hotel Limón,** founded in 1894, painted in bright colors to mask its years. (Look into its courtyard if you don't yet know what an old provincial Mexican hotel looks like.) Across from the park is the lovely curve of the Callejón Rosas. Not far from the cathedral, to the right off Enríquez, you can climb up the Callejón de Lic. Off Enríquez again, a few blocks beyond the alley of the Diamond, search out the Callejón de Jesús Te Ampare (May Jesus Help You Alley), as naïve and Old World as its name. Or follow Lucio upward, to the bridge which links up two heights of the town and looks down on an ancient, ornate public wash place.

The museum (out on Avila Camacho) sits in a vast meadow ringed by green and blue hills. The complex consists of several buildings designed for housing classrooms, the museum proper, and a folklore center. Having taken a leaf from the Museum of Villahermosa, Veracruz has given its largest (and some of its greatest) treasures the drama of the outdoors for setting. Olmec heads of immense size and prodigious weight peer out of the grass. The huge faces with curled-back thick lips, broad noses, and round chins weighed down by sets of head bands, often have the petulant expressions of annoyed children. Elsewhere, the smaller Olmec heads show conspicuous fangs, linking them with the extensive jaguar culture of southern Veracruz and the surrounding Isthmus area. Some of the figures of the same culture are round and dwarflike—a manlike beast or almost obscenely distorted human, markedly phallic.

Under the portico of the front building and on the lawn beyond it are a widely varied group of Olmec and Huastec figures: crude and rough, cut like Easter Island monoliths, some of finer-worked bodies and heads, some serene, others in open-mouthed misery or tortured death. A few are fatly smug; a few appear immune to pain or pleasure. And there is a masterly group of early classic Olmec figures, almost life-size, in calm, natural poses, fleshly and plastic, like archaic Greek figures in their simplicity and controlled dynamism.

Two figures of Huastec (northern Veracruz) culture are Egyptian in mood, stiff, hieratic, a reduction of the human to flat design, and at the same time, an elevation to the impersonal, abstract, godlike. Less remote is a Huastec goddess of the earth, sun, love, and crops, rescued from the don't-touch-me of the archaic by a pair of frank breasts, a phenomenon in Mexican archaic art which often obscures the overtly sexual. Veracruzanos' love of music and dancing and laughter have obviously been nurtured by their laughing Totonac goddess, a figure of buoyant, bubbling pleasure with thrown-back head, eyes tightened in laughter, cheeks dancing in gay curves, the tip of her tongue pointed in glee and light malice.

Out of Jalapa you may take the twenty-minute bus ride through a tunnel of tropical greens southward to Coatepec, which is the richest town per capita in Veracruz and possibly Mexico; its coffee is of an especially valuable kind, the joiner and catalyst which makes other coffees blend well together. The best time to go is on Sundays, when family groups have the leisure to stroll to the plaza for little cakes and a dish of ice (nut, lemon, tamarind, *guanábana,* strawberry, and *mantecado,* made of corn) served by an ample waitress who herself looks like a sundae heaped with whipped cream. The radios blare with the same assertiveness as the bright paint on the houses (unlike Jalapa, Coatepec plays it straight; no muted tones or dulled colors here; red, plenty of red) and to add to the blasting noise, the church pipes out overtures by Rossini, while you have your picture taken against a background of piety, a painting of a desperately ornate cathedral gate under a patchy, poisonous sky. For this pious photograph, women may borrow, as part of the deal, a tired *"típico"* costume with lusterless sequins; and men, a *charro* hat which has lost its pride.

Or you might go on a short distance to Xico, to see its falls, or a short distance north to Banderilla, with its thousands of orchids, or to Cerro Macuiltepec, the site of the monument to the agrarian revolutionaries. The monument is, like many monuments, bad-tempered, but the ride through pine woods and forests opens magnificent views of the city. (Find out if the road is fully paved and has protective barriers; otherwise, don't venture, especially in the rainy season.)

HOTELS

The oldest and largest is the **Salmones,** with large flaky-walled rooms. Its immense dining room, in Tyrolean style, is generous, and the tablecloths usually clean. Modest. The **Pardo** is small and modern, well cared for, with an encouragingly overwhelming odor of insect repellent and soap. Modest; no meals. The **Hotel Mexico** is the most economical—clean, very respectable, and not inviting, but a few dollars gets a large room and bath and four words from the black-swathed Spanish proprietress, a correct and formidable woman. The restaurant, on the other hand, is quite good (try the steaks) and conducted by warm and engaging Spaniards—from a happier province, no doubt.

Lighter and cheaper eating exists in several places, as one might expect of a university town. Inquire or look around on the main streets.

REMEMBER: Carry sweaters, or topcoat and raincoat, if you go in the wintertime. Jalapa suffers a fine needle-like rain called, onomatopoetically, *chipi-chipi,* which penetrates like surgery if you're not well protected.

TECOLUTLA, POZA RICA, PAPANTLA, TAJÍN, CASTILLO DE TEAYO, PACHUCA, SAN MIGUEL REGLA

Unless you choose the fast superhighway from Mexico City and thereby lose a good deal, the following trip will take two, three, or more days through flatlands of coconuts wading into the sea, hill towns whose air is as crisp as their apples, through fields of oil and sulfur, through strangely Oriental ruins unlike anything else in Mexico, through a jazzy oil town. Most of it can be done by bus (and taxis for short distances), but a car opens the curtain on the drama of getting directions. No one person ever instructs you alone. From the houses and shops a group will gather and argue, because any Mexican knows better than any other Mexican. The verbal argument gives way to arm gestures, vivid, graceful, incomprehensible, and too many. Say thank you and restudy the map given you at a large gas station or bought in Mexico City.

Starting from Jalapa on Highway 140, the ride affords views of Pico de Orizaba, like Fuji, and the odd, sepulchral Cofre de Perote—unless a curtain of fog and clouds hangs over them. Up in the mountains, watch for La Joya, which is hardly anything but a shell of small houses crammed into a notch of hill, their façades dripping immense begonias. At Perote take the branch road leading northward (make sure by asking, "A Teziutlán?"), which leads up into broad plains and apple orchards, a startlingly North American landscape, washed by brisk air, to the lovely town of Teziutlán. It is a hushed town, its color shaded and discreet, its mood reticent, except for a science-fiction steam wagon of a vendor of candied bananas and sweet potatoes. Under the deep old trees is a good market which has some nice pottery, and once in a while, the dashing, large wool *rebozos* made in the area. These are usually of black or white wool, brightly embroidered in a large cross-stitch. If they are not available at the market, they can be found in one or two of the shops on the plaza.

If it's time for lunch, you might want to try a typical country *comida*. On the plaza, near the row of shops, is a restaurant like a converted pool parlor and as basic—but one hardly looks for elegant décor outside of Mexico City; that way lies starvation. The *comida corrida* (the meal of the day and the only foods in generous supply) costs about $2 in U.S. currency and usually consists of soup with pasta, a rice dish, lentils topped with fried bananas, a meat course (ask for the pork in raisin sauce, *puerco con pasas*), rice pudding, and of course, a plate of tortillas and a glass of beer. All of it will be rushed at you as if it were blood for a transfusion—a hungry tourist is a fearsome thing in Mexico. Each course is served separately, and if you want to hold on to your rice to eat with the meat, you'll have to lay hands on it forcibly. Leisureliness sets in with check time. Whether it is a unique form of hospitality, or the notion that only ease should come after eating, or a noblesse that considers money a low thing, or uncertain literacy, rural Mexican waiters have great difficulty handing out checks. You may have to ask for the *cuenta* several times, make gestures of writing in a check pad, wave, call. Each word and gesture will be politely answered with *"ahorita"* or *"un ratitito"* (here a finger gesture that measures a quarter inch of time) and nothing more. Stand up and prepare to leave. The check will fly to you.

Fed and *rebozoed,* take the road that leads to Martínez de la Torre, on Route 125 (an unambitious enclave that consists of a couple of *refresco* stands, a few pregnant women of all possible ages, and naked babies crawling among the banana and orange peels). It corkscrews down into valleys of thicker and more brilliant green. The air turns warm, banana and coconut palms appear; in one hour's long slide, you will have dropped into the tropics. From Martínez de la Torre go on to Nautla, and from there northward (on Route 131) toward the beach of Tecolutla. One has to ferry across the Tecolutla River to get to the town, a matter of bumping out of and crashing into slips, but no more inept or dangerous than our Staten Island ferries.

Tecolutla has several hotels, all gathered in a small stretch of beach area, so it is easy to look around, inspect rooms, and make your choice. Choices may be limited during Christmas and Easter weeks, and sometimes on weekends, but usually there is ample space. The **Marsol** (moderate) is prone to casual maintenance and has small rooms. The better-maintained **Hotel Balneario Tecolutla** has a largish dining room, whose waiters and cook run an erratic gamut.

The beach is immense and often empty. Early in the morning and in the evening, it ripples like the sea itself, with the demented, scuttling movement of millions of tiny crabs. There is no strong current at this point, but be aware of the fact that tropical waters belong to sharks as well as other fish and that these beaches have no lifeguards to watch out for the triangle of fin. (Dabbling close to shore may be child's play but swimming out in these unguarded waters is the play of fools.)

Fresh fish is, of course, available in hotels (the small **Hotel Playa** runs, they say, a good dining room), but you might enjoy one of the simple, almost rudimentary, fish restaurants that line the beach. They are large lean-tos that often accompany lockers and showers for a day of swimming and sunning, and usually family enterprises, like that of Dona Rafa, for instance. The affable son is the waiter, mama cooks and takes care of the counter that holds fruit-flavored (almost) chewing gum in appalling colors, Alka-Seltzer, Band-Aids, and amusing provincial postcards. She is also cashier. Grandma patiently sorts out handful after handful of grains of rice to take out and discard the unpolished few. While you have the excellent seafood, women will come by to sell you attractive, but not durable, hats woven of fresh green palm and their children will dangle before you shell and bead necklaces at one peso each. The ferry slip is surrounded by eating places, as you will have noticed, and the vendors of hats and necklaces, with one addition. Young men from Papantla (page 300), dressed in their regional white, sell vanilla pods which have been semidried and bent into the shapes of crosses or scorpions whose eyes are shining green beads; even through the plastic sacks the odor is heavenly, like the delicate sweet breezes that float through Papantla in the quiet of dusk.

Tecolutla is the reasonable place to spend the night; a day or two on the beach, and then on to Poza Rica, which is 40 miles inland, a trip best made in the evening. The first town you will reach is Gutiérrez Camora, where the road divides; take the right to Boca de Lima, about seven miles beyond. Here find a place to park your car, lock it tight, or hire a *"guachacarro"* (if you remember that *"g"* is often just breathed, and then pronounce the word, you will have its meaning and country of origin), who will appear before you have a chance to search for him, and take a walk through the town—not because it is distinguished but because it is not. It is typical of hundreds of night-blooming tropical towns which hide from the daylight heat and sun. The streetlamps are dim; light comes through the long windows and from the restless lamps on the small eating *puestos.* The long windows of the houses are open now, revealing mulberry and pink satin bedcovers. The middle-aged and elderly bring out boxes and folding chairs and gossip in front of their houses as they do in

Italian and French villages and the foreign villages of New York City. Radios pour the rhythms of *huapangos* and *bambas* into the soft, slow air, to mix with the sounds of voices and guitars and the sizzle of frying tacos. The *zócalo*, whose angular, modern fountain rarely gushes, neighbors a café, where the fathers of the local households drink beer and play dominoes. The bolder bloods are in the pool parlors, where naked light bulbs eye murderously the poison green of the pool tables. (Maybe all small-town pool halls are full of menace or, possibly, one can never escape Van Gogh's definitive statement.)

Farther along, in the flat dark that links the towns, and especially near Poza Rica, the earth spits flames out of its oil deposits. The hellish light and shadows they cast burn out the color of night and the shapes of wooded hills: the trunks of trees become bare, mustard-colored rock, and the leaves low puffs of yellow-gray cloud, sulfur-yellow glows into the distance and sends its rotting smell into the Inferno landscape.

Poza Rica is a boom town, pulled out of malarial marshes and slapped together for the workers in the local oil field. It is a harried, bewildered town, the oil and money pouring too fast (when they poured) for calm planning: it has neither the uniform, contented respectability of a well-planned company town nor the slow, sloppy charm of a tropical village. It was enriched and crazed by lines of oil tanks, immense complexes of fat and thin tubing, gas stations, auto agencies, and huge beer and Coca-Cola (and Pepsi) signs. You might use it for an overnight stop in one of its air-conditioned hotels and as a departure point for El Tajín, the very beautiful old city of the Totonacs.

Or is it the Huastec? Or was it partly Toltec or Mayan? There is neither sureness nor unanimity among the scholars on the question of who, exclusively, built Tajín. It can be reached by taking the Coatzintla road out of Poza Rica, on the western edge of town, then left at the circle, following the Coatzintla sign on a good broad road. After about a half hour, start watching for signs that guide, off the left of the road, to the archaeological zone. (Always check roads in this fast-changing area.)

The more interesting and shorter way is to go via Papantla, by a road which may be hard on your car and a boon to your eyes. It lies in a stretch of landscapes which hold the colors of Gauguin in the excesses of Rousseau. The flow of the green hills is stopped by flowering fences (nothing that was once wood here ever gives up; if it isn't burned, it flowers), the vines fly like restless green birds through branches of the immense trees whose green armpits enfold disorderly clumps of orchids. Bamboo plumes, like great ferns rising to a height of twenty feet or more, are breathed out of the earth in graceful, feathery sprays. Roadside weeds, pinker, more orange, thicker, taller, and more confident than weeds should be, mass around the houses.

Papantla is the town of the dance and flight of the *voladores* on Corpus Christi day, in June, and occasionally at other times of the year. A group of spare-bodied Totonacs climb an impressively tall pole, and while one turns and drums on the very top of it, the others, held to the pole by ropes, fling themselves out, flying around it like deft insects hovering around a weed. This was a Totonac ceremonial which the church converted to Catholicism by the common and efficient means of assigning to it the date of a church holiday. For days before, white-clad Totonacs used to march out of their villages, some of them carrying images of their patron saint, to converge in Papantla. One group of especially honored citizens searched through the hills for the tall tree which was to be honored and sacrificed. Before and after it was cut down, the forest was soothed and the tree paid for by offerings left on the cut roots. Religiosity is becoming rarer; through the years a running of the bulls has been added, sometimes horse racing, and more recently a large agricultural fair has been built around the flyers and their sacred pole, which is no longer changed from year to year but stands waiting near the upper end of the marketplace for the glory day.

When Papantla isn't steamy with visitors and fiesta it is a pretty, undulating town, the shopping center of the exquisitely dressed country people of the area. They are dark people, sparsely built, with narrow faces and large noses. The men walk along remote roads in wide white bloomers gathered tightly at the ankles and white shirts that fall wide and full from gathers at the yoke. A plain broad straw hat, often adorned with one red flower, and bare feet complete the cool, roomy costume. The women often wear lacy white satin skirts and white lace shawls (imported from England as a rule) over white blouses embroidered with strips of color. They look like brides and move with the shy solemnity of brides. The costume has a dignified quiet romanticism and the girls have to let themselves go with jaunty hair arrangements: the ends of braids pinned back over the ears with bright flowers or cockades of red ribbon, or one braid pinned up back, center—like a bullfighter's queue—while the other climbs up over the right ear, both ending in spurts of color. (Be warned: blue jeans and T-shirts are making effective invasions, as in other areas.)

These frail, starched people, like well-bred children in a confirmation procession, are supposedly the keepers of poisonous snakes as pets, and their domestic lives a source of salacious, admiring incredulity among the anthropologists and archaeologists who work in the area. Like a number of Indian groups, the Totonacs maintain their traditional polygamy, cannily arranged for profit and pleasure. One of these meager little men may have four or five wives (only one of whom he has married in church—possibly); one of them takes care of the children, another cooks, another washes. All live in adjoining shacks or under one roof, depending on the energy and enterprise of the king of the household, or the placidity of the women. Since a couple of the women are likely to be in advanced stages of pregnancy at almost any time, there are always spares for comfortable nocturnal pleasure and, of course, the prospect of more pregnancies, which will become more children who will work as papa tells them to until they make or join other households. In addition to his harem, the Totonac, like the Arab, often keeps a boy to whet his oversated appetite (which induced the Spaniards to speak of him as the *puta*—whore— of the Indians). This way of life, along with his consumption of alcohol and carelessness of infection, makes him listless, sleepy, and dead at thirty-five. But at eighteen he is beguiling, a lovely doll-like figure in his clean pajama suit, as pure and bland and deceptive as a white rabbit.

Almost single-handedly one anthropologist kept pulling Tajín out of the jungle for thirty-five years. Professor Payón was a Mexican who looked German, was educated in France, and consequently spoke Spanish and English with a French accent. He had a witty, playful face which matched the witty, playful mind under the completely bald head. He lived for long periods in a settlement adjoining the ruins and was godfather to many of the children who swarmed around it; consequently he was addressed by and addressed his helpers as *compa'*, the familiar for *compadre,* a term expressing the relationship between the father and the godfather of a child.

As you enter the ancient area you will notice mound after uncovered mound, as in Monte Albán and elsewhere, making almost a hundred buildings still to be explored. So far, scholars have discerned four periods of building and decoration: the first is of the fifth and sixth centuries; the next went into the seventh century; the third, richest, and most inventive lasted into the thirteenth century, when Toltec influences began to make their very marked appearance. By the time of the Spaniards, Tajín had already been abandoned, possibly because of the fires and destruction of war, which were a contributing cause to the abandonment of many magnificent cities. (The foregoing is informed conjecture; there is still too much to be excavated, studied, evaluated, and compared to the artifacts of other cultures, for a finished, immutable frame of time and development to have been reached.)

One of the first buildings you will probably come to is the southern ball court, whose top panel represents the sky, with the signs of the moon and Venus interwoven in a running band of designs and possibly hieroglyphs not yet deciphered; they may be symbols for clouds, lightning, and rain—phenomena to be courted in the hot countries. The large center panel depicts a human sacrifice by throat slitting, considered by Totonacophiles much more humane than the Aztec system of cutting the heart out of the living victim. That might be, but the distinction is an elusive one, particularly since all that the young man did was lose a ball game, sacred and deeply ceremonious though it may have been. At the left of the highly decorative bloodletting stands the god of death, his bare spinal column and skeletal arm quite ready for the victim. The coiled designs below him symbolize an inverted bowl of water from which he traditionally arises. (Why? As in much mythology and religion—because.) The lowest horizontal panel consists of various earth symbols, in a serene interlacing of broad ribbons that might be Mayan or Chinese.

The most extraordinary of the buildings is the Pyramid of the Niches (used very effectively as the setting of one of the episodes in the Mexican film *The Roots*). As in so many pyramids, what appears now was built on an earlier structure, which in turn had been built over rubble, clay, and heaps of rocks. The present building, obviously an edifice of ritual whose stairs led to a shrine at its very top, is characterized by a means of decoration quite unlike any other in Mexico. Each stage of the building, as it rises and narrows, spreads cornices which overhang successive rows of niches, creating dramatic plays of chiaroscuro with the differing positions of the sun. These niches were not frames for statuary nor had they any function but to be decorative, an effect enhanced in early years by painting the frames around the niches a bright blue against the red interior. The stairs flanked by panels with serpentine designs were applied against the side of the building, so that the bands of niches are uninterrupted—even where they cannot be seen—and the important number of 365, one for each day of the year, undiminished.

Other buildings, many of them suggesting once magnificent dimensions, carry the decoration of chiaroscuro as deep-cut Greek keys and crosses, or bars joined and crossed in repeated geometric patterns of strict modernity, or the angular waves and meanders of Mitla. Some buildings repeat the Oriental tone of the Palace of the Niches, other are vaguely classic in the Greco-Roman sense, while still others are characterized by the presence of the Mayan arch and roofs of extraordinary, wide, thick, one-piece slabs.

If you haven't found him before, look for Modesto, the old watchman who can't possibly be dead yet: his time for being called is long past, and now he has become immortal. He has no teeth to impede the meeting of chin and nose and no flesh to encumber his dry bones. He wears old-fashioned wrapped white pants, a loose Totonac shirt, and a very dirty old hat, and always carries the large guest book whose names he cannot read but treasures, showing it eagerly, with the toothless grin and gleeful slit-eye of a Totonac fire god. He has been among the ruins for fifty years, knows nothing about them but their location and that people from improbable places come to see them and to sign his book, but he will not stay away from the buildings even when he is quite sick, and if he ever does die, it will be among the ageless stones.

Return to Poza Rica, and if both you and your car are still sturdy, go to Castillo de Teayo, less significant than El Tajín, but something of a Huastec curio, and an opportunity to see the back country. Again on the western end of town, ask for the road marked "Tiahuan." It will be about fourteen miles to a gas station, where, after checking, you turn left, and left again at the fork in the road about a kilometer away. The road may still carry a Coca-Cola sign which displays above the familiar lettering a crude painting of the *castillo* and an arrow directing you to it, about ten miles beyond. Here and there you may find a thatched house with rounded sides very much like the Mayan houses in the Yucatán whose appearance locally, plus linguistic roots and some craft objects, suggests strong links between the Mayan and the Huastec cultures.

The small insubstantial pyramid dignified with the name of *"cas-tillo"* stands in the center of the small town. Its outlines are soft and wavy and it looks about ready to dissolve into the greenery. The pyramid is of red-brown stone, held together by mortar of sand and limestone, called *mescla,* and quite new, having been built very shortly before the time of the Conquest. At its top is the "temple," a thatched hut of local style, housing a group of church bells, a witness to the practice of the church which, when it didn't destroy or build over pagan temples, tried to put them to holier purposes.

Around the temple are the white, very white, concrete benches—unkind to the eye and seat—which stand in many small-town plazas. Here they have the additional function of inhibiting views of the archaic figures placed in the grass. Most of the figures are believed to be Toltec, with one or two Aztec and Huastec specimens among them—in the opinion of the physician-caretaker, whose knowledge may not match his devotion. A number of them are extraordinarily effective effigies of gods and goddesses, flat and roughly hewn except for their carefully cut, elaborate headdresses. The spring god, Xipe, appears a number of times. A warrior triumphant over cold and death, he appears in the flayed skin of the enemy, the stitching and the knots by which it is attached clearly visible, the flayed hand hanging disjointed and limp from a dangle of skin. One of these young spring gods stands in an attitude quite unlike the aristocratic others; one of his legs is crossed tightly over the other like those of a desperate little boy; on his face is that restless worried look, and on his chest dangles a medallion of flayed and stitched-on male genitalia. From the look on his face and his tense, crossed leg, he doesn't seem quite ready for the responsibility of manhood, much less godhood.

Back at Poza Rica, there is the possibility of flying back to Mexico City, or finding the superhighway, or taking the unforgettable ride through quite other kinds of terrain—high Swiss valleys, Dutch plains, Mexican tropics, fern forests, bamboo, and banana and pa-paya plantations—to Pachuca and Mexico City. (Have a sweater handy.) In the course of the 50 miles to Villa Juárez, the flat landscape creases into mountains and valleys; the elephants' ears and free-form trees give way to the neatness of cultivation and pine forests. Mountain laurel and apple trees are washed by mountain fog and the houses tend to be tall and narrow, backed against a protecting hill and crammed against their neighbors for warmth, a style and arrangement reminiscent of Italian hill towns. Around Necaxa and Huauchinango, the road winds among magnificent views of blue-green Lake Necaxa. Toward Tulancingo the country changes again, flowing into Pachuca in wide, flat bands of tan wheat and green corn bordered by the dark gray-green of maguey, encircling houses of low brick and tile which hug the earth for refuge in the windy plains.

Pachuca is a large, lively town which still makes its living out of mining, with comfortable hotels, rough saloons, and several places worth visiting in its environs. North of the city, a few turning miles away (there is a bus that leaves from the center of town), is the old mining town of Real del Monte, a poor, shapeless multileveled splash of tin roofs in verdant, steep hills that once yielded great riches of silver. It drinks a good deal of pulque to keep warm and to feel not quite so poor and, for its *amour propre,* gazes at a monument of a miner and his drill in the big town square. A few miles north of Real del Monte a side road takes one (four miles) to **San Miguel Regla,** a hacienda built in the seventeenth century and now a resort hotel where one can at robust prices swim, ride, walk, live, among pretty lakes and woods. (See note below.)

Not too far out of Pachuca there is a town of so-called Indian Jews. No one, least of all themselves, is certain of their origin; one theory holds that they are Seventh-Day Adventists who went the whole course, ultimately; others, that they are fairly recent converts affected by one powerful personality; the most colorful position—no more sure than the others—is that these people are the descendants of Jews who came to Mexico shortly after the Conquest, seemingly converted to Catholicism as was ordered by the Inquisition but actually practicing Judaism secretly, and indoctrinating successive generations while they continued to intermarry with Indians and *mestizos.* Whatever the historical truth, the group does maintain a Jewish cemetery, a simple prayer house, and traditional symbols.

The road back to Mexico City is more corn and maguey, until it slips into the endless, mottled backyard of the city.

NOTE: As mentioned, this is not a trip for hurrying through, particularly now that pleasant inns of several sorts have nestled into the hills overlooking long, green valleys. There is a small hotel and restaurant, quite modern, at the western end of Huauchinango, and some miles northeast, in a town called Xicotepec de Juárez, you will find **Mi**

Ranchito, a group of neat houses in gardens, supported by a pleasing restaurant and ringed by endless views.

There is a road from Real del Monte to Huasca and its market, which is also a stop for the little rusty bus that leaps through the farther hills dangling legs, turkeys, and chickens. You are on a high mountain plain, ranch country where the girls, unlike most Mexican women, ride very well and enhance the road. Six kilometers before you reach San Miguel Regla, you should see a sign that indicates the **Hacienda San Juan Hueyapan.** Six more kilometers through intensive rice cultivations, horsemen, red irrigated earth, and silos like Italian *trulli,* should bring you to the hacienda, the real thing, as Mexican as Juárez and infinitely less serious. The rooms are tall and sparsely furnished, the windows and doors leak drafts, but if you should find yourself there in wintertime, wood for the fireplace (it usually smokes) will be brought and arranged for you by several intelligent, courtly youngsters. The meals are carefully served in a huge dining room by these same adolescents, and they are extraordinarily varied and well prepared, of homegrown produce and meats. The grounds are endless, some of it overgrown, with clearings for a large pool and frontón courts, some used as fields, all of it fine for wandering through if you have a good sense of direction. Birds and orchids hang in the courtyard and the long hallways are decorated with colored photographs of Venice, Switzerland, and tropical beaches all taste- fully bound in bright paper strips. If the proprietor is not too busy he will show you the dining room of the original owners, great overlords of mines and properties before the Revolution. One side of the table is laid with a lace tablecloth, fine silver, and decanters, arranged as it used to be; "a sign of respect," says the present owner, who uses the other end of the table, covered by a plain cloth and a simple setting.

The total experience is most engaging and costs preposterously little, but check first in Real del Monte. Newer Mexico is destroying older Mexico rapidly.

PAPALOAPAN TO CATEMACO

Back on the Córdoba-Veracruz highway, at La Tinaja, a southward road leads to the Papaloapan Dam, which remade a vast stretch of land, harnessed the numerous rivers which flow into the Papaloapan, and rebuilt—not always with willing cooperation—many lives in Oaxaca, Veracruz, and Puebla. Reclamation of the land meant the education, coercing, and even forcing of large groups of depressed, primitive peoples into a newer world of fertile green, of teachers and agricultural experts, of roads, sugar refineries, canning plants, schools for the children, and classes for adults whose backgrounds had given them no preparation for the more abundant bewildering life.

From here, if you are avid for adventure, try the hard road into and over the mountains to Oaxaca. Or, you might view the reclaimed lands from launches which go from Papaloapan to Ixcatlán on the Tonto River, or along the Santo Domingo to Tuxtepec.

For Lake Catemaco, take the highway that runs along the river through bananas, coconuts, and sugar cane, through the pretty village of Cosamaloapan and north to the prettier town of Tlacotalpan, an important shipping center years ago and now fallen into picturesque disuse, its present renown limited to the charm and colors of its old houses and gardens, and skill in making turtle soup (the real thing, called *sopa de tortuga*) and fat tortillas called, naturally, *gorditas* (little fatties). Shortly out of Tlacotalpan the road connects with Route 180, which goes through green, flowered hills, to Santiago Tuxtla. This Tuxtla is a good hunting and fishing town and near the archaeological zone of Tres Zapotes, reachable with some effort and negotiation. It also has, on the highway above the town, a roadside restaurant, what we might call a truckdriver's place, open night and day and inexpensive. The great plus is its remarkable position far above the sprawling town and the views of mossy, velvety hills. A short distance southeast is the larger Tuxtla, San Andrés, a hunter's town, a tobacco grower's town, with a roomy modernistic plaza, a cool, large, empty church, an odd modern one, the symbol of riches represented by new hotels, and, in the square, the ugliest objects and most violently colored candies in all of Mexico.

A more direct way to Catemaco (skipping Papaloapan et al.) is a reverie of smooth new road, almost unused, through country that is Gauguin, a bit Chinese painting and African plain. Recross the ferry at Tecolutla and hug the river and sea inlets. Thatched huts and tawny zebus shelter in the multigreens of coconut palms; low jungle looped with flower vines opens to an endless carpet of green savanna at one side and green-blue waters on the other. A few attractive houses, all breezeway and fresh paint—apparently the homes of ranch owners—sit at the edges of the many rivers one crosses. It has been expensive to wrest the land from jungle and morass and it is now treated with great respect. The corrals are large and kept in fine repair, the swimming holes neat, and some of them have inviting little thatch and latticework restaurants. Should you decide to stay—and the quiet gold and green landscape is very tempting—look at the small **Hotel Palmar,** 18 kilometers south of the ferry landing, and, at about 21 kilometers, the **Hotel Playa Paraiso.**

As you cross the Puente Nautla, look down at the slender dugouts in the river and the zebus, now unprotected by palm trees, lolling together like harem ladies. Beyond, dunes and palmetto at the sides of wild lagoons lead into a view of hills folded on each other as in Oriental landscapes and a few isolated tall trees as regal and singular as giraffes. The road should soon indicate directions toward Santiago Tuxtla and San Andrés Tuxtla.

Sometimes the road southward to Lake Catemaco leaps up to peer down into valleys of coconuts, into a plot of elephants' ears sheltering three cows, ten children, and a horse, into cornfields rolling up into the hills. The thatched huts sit roof-deep in banana palms and the feathery dusty flowers of cane, foggy lavender in the morning, gold in full sunlight, and gray at dusk. Coffee grows here, and cocoa, and occasionally the papaya, a primitive fertility goddess who wears swirls of broad leaves as a headdress, and a cluster of long African breasts of fruit supported by one grotesquely thin leg of trunk—absurd and excessive, like the hot countries.

The town that hangs on the fringes of Lake Catemaco reflects the optimism and prosperity that once seized Mexico south. Where there had been little ease or charm, there are at least two hotels, the **Catemaco** and the **Berthangel,** an inviting restaurant, the **Suiza,** and children sufficiently well educated to yell, "Hello, good-by, you are a pretty girl" with an amiable lack of discrimination to all strangers.

The **Hotel Playa Azul** is still the most sensible place to stay. Right on the lake, it offers a pool, swimming in the lake, fishing, and adequate food (moderate). The most satisfactory item on the menu is the local small fish, *mojarra,* fresh and quick-fried, superb with or without lime juice. With it have a plateful of *pellizcadas,* or "gorditas," which are fat tortillas punched, scraped, and doused with oil—hardly the dieter's friend, but then the coastal tropics is for plump people; almost everyone there is. By the time you reach the Playa Azul, earlier loud and busy building may be finished, and the new project of many many rooms in a tight squeeze rather than in scattered bungalows may have come to fruition. It might be less than idyllic, but the lake is exquisite, spotted with round, verdant mounds of islands, one or two of which are covered pyramids. (In spite of their busy domestic lives and the climate, the Totonacs were energetic builders.) Thirty minutes by motorboat takes one to the mouth of a *Green Mansions* river, narrow and shallow, its edges bordered with water hyacinths and the tails of bright fish. Overhead the jungle makes a bower laced by hanging lianas, swings for small tropical birds with red crests and yellow wings. (The area is famous as an ornithologist's paradise.) The end of the ride is a turn in the river, where the current becomes very strong and forms a lovely, cool swimming basin. Go early and take a picnic along; there is room to sit near the bend of the river, and the boat boys don't at all mind staying the day. If the sky is not clear, don't go, or return quickly: the lake can become choppy quite suddenly and winter rainstorms are vigorous. Take a walk, instead, along the lakefront to see the enormous trees that stand in the water, ribboned with cactus, hung with bromelia, and still sufficiently vigorous to sustain avocado blossoms, and birds that chirp, birds that bark.

CATEMACO TO VILLAHERMOSA

If the southward journey is to be made by bus, return to San Andrés by local bus or taxi. In your own car you simply pick up 180 just where you left it, stopping to look down on the lake, its islands, and the mountains it uses for backdrop and to examine the curtains of tobacco on bamboo rods that cover barnlike buildings.

At Acayucan, there is the choice of traveling into the country of the Tehuanas directly south (see pages 251–253), or due east into Villahermosa and on to Yucatán. A decision can be made in Acayucan, while nibbling at the banana chips sold in the bus station. They are as thin as potato chips, wrapped like them, and taste a bit the same except for the missing flavor of salt. You might, in the meantime, also examine the string bags and hammocks made by the prisoners, who carry a brisk trade through the bars of the prison across the street from the bus station, and then take a walk in the town. Look in at the lively market, stroll through the inviting town square, observe again the large, ripe, sweet tropical smile, buy some fruit and continue on your journey.

Assuming you have decided on Villahermosa, you will now be traveling east on 180, through a landscape of purple morning glories, yellow-flowered vines, and thatched terra-cotta houses, disturbed by a sulfur plant, to Minatitlán, the airline stop which links Mérida to Oaxaca and has the frantic, raw look of being no town at all, simply a collection of industrial plants that produce by-products of oil.

A short distance across the River of Shoes (a stretch of swamp and marsh where hundreds of herons, cranes, egrets, and many other species of water birds once lived; some still visit) is Coatzacoalcos, which experiences the same efflorescence as its neighbor on a larger and gaudier style; quite operatic. Its square was refurbished and its buildings dazzled with fresh paint. The big, shining hotels were new, the money and the expensive boots were new; it all had the mood of gold-rush country (here the finds are oil), including the drunken Saturday night enjoyed by the men who came in from the distant, oily marshes. Should you want to stay in this town whose oil fortunes are now diminished, the tone less ebullient, try the serviceable **Lemarroy** or the **Valgrande.** The neatly functioning bus station hasn't altogether divested itself of the old-style peddlers; one elderly artist, with a significant mustache, may insist that you admire his idiotic geometric drawings; an artisan tries to sell a multiple rat catcher of his own devising, which can trap three rats at a time, or a smaller model for the wholesale catching of mice. Among the fanciful vendors, one begins to see Tehuanas from the south come to dominate the market of Coatzacoalcos, as they do those of Tehuantepec.

Out of Coatzacoalcos ("the place where the serpent died," probably a reference to the wandering king-god, the plumed serpent Quetzalcoatl), the road, a spine pulled out of the marsh, continues through clots of shapeless bush and vines. White herons stand on the shrub and watch, as children might, the Pemex (Mexican government oil monopoly) trucks roar by. If you are doing the driving, be careful; the road is straight, flat, and hypnotic, particularly when it blazes white and seemingly endless under the tropical sun.

Then there is the smell of cocoa from the processing plant in Cárdenas, a town whose small population rattles around in its ambitious plaza. Here one can stop for a soft drink and sandwich or the *empanadas* (meat pies juiced up by the chile that the salesboys carry in jars) sold at the bus station on the plaza or a meal in a toylike motel done in rich blues and reds at the side of the highway. And on, toward mounting hills and groves of deep-shadowed banana trees, grazing land, and lagoons, eastward to Villahermosa.

NOTE: Coatzacoalcos has a long gray-silk beach complete with vendors, food stalls, hammocks, families being photographed, boys playing ball, and children digging in the sand. It is not a South Seas treasure, but likable, and the water is usually fairly clean in spite of passing tankers. About La Venta, the site of the fabulous Olmec heads: Don't go. There is a road, Coca-Cola stands, a skyful of machinery, a closed-off small pyramid, and not much else.

"HONGOS MÁGICOS"

The following section abandons the travel-book point of view because the experience described was thoroughly subjective, limited to the reactions of a group of four persons, and more particularly, to the responses of one of that small group. Within the general effects the mushroom drugs produce on everyone who takes them, specific reactions vary considerably, depending on an individual's emotional state, his willingness to lend himself to an uncharted journey, his levels of vulnerability, his aesthetic development—in short, on his whole personality and biography as well as his body.

In its externals the experience is a "Mexican" one and belongs among Mexico's uncommon possibilities, but it is definitely not recommended. Borders of physical and mental safety have not been clearly defined, nor is the dose prescribed by an Indian woman who has been taking them all her life necessarily the optimum amount—if there is such a thing—for the unaccustomed body and psyche. Perhaps other reporters of the effects of hallucinogenic mushrooms have been luckier or sturdier; they seem to have experienced only the glorious visions. Our group suffered inordinate anguish, each in his own way, as abysmally black and suffocating as the earlier, perfect happiness had been supremely, vaultingly beautiful. It is not a thing to do alone or lightly or without some recognition of what one's own body and mind can tolerate.

The road out of Mexico City takes us into the mountains and then pours into Puebla, a city gathered tight on itself, as seclusive as a bitter man. On to Cholula, blistered with churches, and through scraped hills to Tehuacán, a spa of shaded streets and family hotels whose dining-room shelves hold arrays of vitamin pills and digestive aids. Shortly out of Tehuacán the road becomes rough rock and dusty pits; the vistas of dry scrub flow into the dark maw of the encircling mountains; the bump and sway of the car, the taut, hunched back of the driver, impose silence on the party of six. Everyone seems to be alone with his anticipation—curiosity, fear, hope—of the effect of the hallucinogenic mushrooms.

The dry, scratched plain dips behind us as the road narrows and coils upward into hill on hill, threading its loops and curves through the heaps of green-velvet mountain. For four of five mesmerized hours we climb and turn on the narrow dirt road, without guardrails, or even a warning rock. Twice we meet trucks and have to back to a curve in the sheltering rock from where we watch them swing along the outer, loose-edged curve of the road, their wheels scooping stones and earth into the gorge three thousand feet below. Once or twice we skid on a patch of mud which is, happily, the cover of a large hole and holds the car; a smooth patch might have made a ski jump into the clear, murderous air. (Obviously, the road would be unusable through most of the summer rainy season except for the valiant drivers of heavy trucks. Certain exotic supplies, like mushroom fanciers and anthropologists, are then flown in by chartered plane.) The mountains are endless, melting into each other in a hypnotic succession, and, except for a fleeting glimpse of a shepherd with a small flock of skinny goats and the minute white dot of an Indian working a distant, perpendicular scrap of cornfield, are as empty as the end of the world.

It is night when we reach the village, shapeless and anonymous in the dark, lit by just enough street lights to indicate the unpaved main street which leads to the hotel. The hotel is in the one stubborn mold of most Mexican rural hotels: large, bare, white-washed rooms, two or three hooks forced into the wall to hold clothing, one bare uncovered light bulb, weak and half blind, hanging from the center of the ceiling, two or three or five tired beds, and one thick tumbler on the windowsill. The toilet and shower are in a separate little shack, reached by flat rocks placed in a moist path. The dining room, directly open to the clatter, the sizzling, the odors, and the emotions of the kitchen, is painted red and contains three or four oilcloth-covered tables on which stand cracked enamel basins crammed full of gardenias and camellias. After a supper which starts with good soup and trails from indifferent rice to scarcely edible meat, we go to our rustling beds.

After breakfast the next morning, we explore the village. It is fairly large, and though the evidence may not be apparent to U.S. eyes, it is quite prosperous, the center of coffee-growing in the surrounding hills. The shopkeepers—some of them bake, shoe horses, and mend shoes under one low-pitched roof—and the growers are *mestizos,* while much of the labor is Mazateco. The latter are small, neatly designed people, golden-skinned and, for mountain Indians, extraordinarily affable. Their speech is quite unlike the Aztec tongue spoken in most of the area; it sounds rather like Chinese, running a scale of nasal sounds and glottal stops. Like a number of Indian groups they are polygamous in a casual system of picking up, dropping, and changing women. The men wear blue jeans or chino pants and cotton shirts, like workers elsewhere, but the women are beautifully showy. They spend much of their time embroidering bright designs of birds, flowers, and vines on rectangles of coarse white cotton. These pieces are then sewn together into a loose, knee-length blouse, and the sections marked off with ribbons of red or magenta or turquoise blue. A broad frill of ribbon of the same color at the elbow is the final flourish. Under the blouse they wear dark homespun woolen skirts, tightly wrapped and falling to the ankle.

The village is voluble and hospitable, very different from the usual closed, guarded mountain village. (It was suggested by one of the party that this extraordinary mood was a result of a light, constant diet of "happy" mushrooms. A less exotic reason may be that coffee is a good crop and the village eats fairly well, not depending on sparse stands of mountain corn.) It is a lovely place. The wooden, steep-roofed houses and the winding green-lined paths lurch and roll into each other in appealing illogic; gardenias and hibiscus well over the earthen steam-bath cribs which stand at the sides of the road; bird of paradise shafts flame through beds of broad, green-gray elephant ears; roses spill into the paths, and gaudy vines sing across the houses. The large town square holds an uninteresting church whose interior is dominated by a plump Italianate Christ very unlike the gaunt, tormented figure of Indian churches. From another side of the square, the metal park benches give a slow, wide view of a sea of hills streaked with the white of distant villages. The market nearby is of the usual open wooden stands, shaded by crude eaves of wood and dominated by the tall rectangle of the town hall. From its wall dangles a loudspeaker which alternates music and announcements in Mazateco—except for times of the day and days of the week, for which Spanish is used. Mazatecan thinking seems not to include time concepts, and it may be more than a coincidence that timelessness is one of the prime ingredients of mushroom intoxication.

Strolling through the village, our eyes fixed on its vividness, our minds and vague emotions moving around the prospect and mystery of the mushrooms, we were approached two or three times by men who, in the voices of stolen goods or prohibition liquor, offered us mushrooms. "Strong, fresh magic mushrooms, picked this morning. Meet me at my house in an hour and I'll have them for you." (There was no reason for the conspiratorial tone since the mushrooms are neither prohibited nor very rare; it was a detail of seduction.)

We visited the house of one of the men, who told us something about the mushrooms. They could be taken anywhere, there was no ritual place; one could sit up or lie down, it didn't matter. The mushroom dream seemed to answer a number of purposes: it would discover the seat of an undiagnosed disease or malaise, it would reveal beautiful places, bring one close to distant people, disclose the whereabouts of lost or strayed objects. Usually, when the "secret" disease is found, one goes to a "curer" for alleviation; the mushroom savant is merely a diagnostician, a primitive psychiatrist who makes the "journey" with his patients as companion and guide, warding off evil, helping and encouraging along the way. However, our host, better educated than most Mazatecos, a man of considerable though untrained scientific curiosity and an independent thinker (he believed strongly in monogamy, for instance), had tried the mushrooms for curative purposes. His wife had been suffering from T.B. of the bone, he said (but never said who made the diagnosis). He had cut her arm to the tubercular bone, poured bits of mushroom into the open wound, and bound it. She displayed the scar proudly. It was large but smoothly healed, and she seemed fine and hale, smiling happily at us with all her gold-rimmed teeth—a symbol of her husband's love and prosperity. The man had also treated other members of his family with the mushrooms and the whole large, attractive brood survived, seemingly robust and contented. He assured us that he used the mushrooms sparingly, only when the illness was grave, and always, he added, he took the mushrooms along with his patient. He then showed us the four varieties of local magic mushrooms which grew in the area. They looked like ordinary, putty-colored mushrooms, but there trembled an aura of magic around them: folk tales still felt but not remembered, witches' brews, toadstools, Alice's shrinking-and-growing mushrooms. They melted together with the sudden strangeness of standing in a Mazateco house ruled over by a grinning old cigarette-cadging grandmother in a beribboned *huipil*, babies with black cherry eyes staring out of hammock cradles, the soft singsong of the women's speech, the flat, impenetrable stares of the children clustered at the doorway, the being very far from our accustomed language and safeties. We said nothing but were already preparing fear.

Our intermediary for negotiations with the *sacerdotisa* (the gatherer and priestess of our mushrooms) was the proprietress of the hotel, a stout alert *mestiza* matron who was singularly knowing about Americans and dollars. The first asking price was outrageous, as usual, the test for determining the degree of gullibility or eagerness of the buyer. We made a counter offer, which was rejected (supposedly by a messenger from the priestess herself) on the shrewd ground that we didn't need the mushrooms, but were simply taking them for *"gusto,"* or kicks; therefore, the price to us should be high. Toward evening, we arrived at a sum which was the equivalent of $6 for each of us; probably at least half stayed with our landlady. We were told to be ready at about ten or eleven o'clock that night.

We are called for and enter the big, bare dining room of our hotel. All the tables but one have been pushed to a far side, the one arranged as a crude altar near the entrance to the kitchen. The proprietress, her daughter, her sister, and two of our group who had refused the mushrooms are seated on chairs across the room from a long straw mat stretched along a wall. The only light comes from a candle on the improvised altar which also holds a brazier of burning carbon and four half gourds which obviously contain our portions of mushrooms. The Indian woman kneels near the door, the girl who will later guide her home kneels behind her, both in the posture of the patient, endless waiting of the Indian women. The old woman has the face of an aged monkey with deep-set blank eyes under high-curved prominent brows. Two black wings of hair wipe across her low forehead. She is dressed in a dirty white *huipil* which hangs loosely from her meager shoulders. Her thin dark hands float like disembodied claws in the misty white of her lap. It is impossible to guess her age, but she is old, even for a society where women age rapidly. As one stares at her, trying to see more than the dim light permits, she becomes all her female ancestors kneeling and waiting, impassive, neither alive nor dead, not quite flesh, not quite stone.

Not knowing what to expect or what is expected of us we move rather aimlessly, like children in a new class, waiting to be directed by some authority. We are told that the two men are to place themselves at a distance from the two women, but on finding out that we know each other only two days or so, the priestess says (in Mazateco translated into Spanish by the landlady) that we might all lie on a long straw mat, decent space between us. While we arrange ourselves, making nervous little jokes, the old woman prepares the mushrooms—a matter of pouring some sugar water over them, we are told, to help reverse or slow up reactions. She then pours some copal (incense) over the carbon in the brazier, and as the sweet smell and smoke come toward us, one remembers Bernal Díaz' description of Indian emissaries passing braziers of copal over Cortés' clothing, and the sight of saints' images in Indian churches being caressed by the same incense from the same kind of brazier. The act is pleasing; it has a certain antique authenticity, an overture to mysteries.

The copal brazier is soon brought to us and we each make ceremonial gestures of washing and warming our hands in the smoke. Each bowl is then held over the brazier for a moment and is handed to us. We are ready to take the "journey."

We stare into the bowl prepared by the woman we had begun to think of as the *bruja*—witch. In the semidark we can't see the color of the fluid surrounding the mushrooms but we recoil from the imagined dirt in it and the memory of the dark little claws which handled the mushrooms. Each bowl holds four mushrooms (we check with each other), possibly of the four different types, although the two small mushrooms look alike, as do the two large ones. While we eat the mushrooms, gagging with disgust and fear all the way, the *bruja* eats hers slowly, ruminatively. We can get ours down only by swallowing sips of the gritty water with large pieces of mushroom; not chewing, not biting, just tearing off chunks and swallowing them whole. The rubbery, slimy stems are the most difficult and the stomach keeps rising like a large fist to push them out. We lie down on the mat to wait for effects. The room is now totally dark and quiet.

The *bruja* begins to make the slow, inhaling whistle sounds of a shaman drawing disease out of a body. The whistles change to a chant in low and high voices in swift alternation, almost close enough to be a duet. The low voice alone emerges, an inhuman grunting, rooting sound, then the duet again. In a mixture of Mazateco and Spanish, the woman invokes Christ, the Virgin Mary, and a long list of saints (Saint Eulalia and Saint Euphronia figure prominently) and asks them to protect us from ill or evil. Her chant is, for a while, quite simple and pretty, and then changes to a high nasal Oriental plaint. Now the low grunts again, back to the simple folk song, back again to the high and low voices. This goes on for fifteen minutes or so while we watch for the beginnings of hallucination. They come: lights, lines of glacial blue passing in a constant shift and flow of designs; line drawings made by illuminated icicles on a deep, blue field, changing in slow, stately motion. Our limbs and heads are becoming heavy, our jaws feel anesthetized, we have the stiff, tingling lips that follow novocaine injection. Disgust and apprehension are gone. The large, noble tempo carries richer and richer patterns and tonalities, colors glow like the depths of gems or layers of stained glass—perfectly lit, always in harmonious, beautifully balanced combinations. The colors and patterns begin to arrange themselves in series: one group combines with utmost felicity variations of cream, orange, lemon yellow, and ocher; another, deep red and purples around small areas of deepest emerald green. Sometimes the patterns appear as light cluster, sometimes as mosaics, and for a long, luxurious period, there move before us the most opulent pieces of jewelry, whose designs we desperately try to remember, but there are too many. We contain the colors and lights and are contained by them; a thousand years have passed and are passing. Our universe is moving designs in endless space and time and yet outside of space and time.

It seems simultaneous, as a number of our reactions do (possibly in response to time spans dictated by the drugs in the mushrooms, or maybe one of us triggers off reactions ripening in the others), but at some point, without saying so directly, we all find that we don't like being alone in the immense, strange beauty. We begin to call each other—"Where are you?"—trying not to say, "Where am I?" We reach for each other's hands, offered and taken with gratitude, a gift of kindness for kindness needed. The sexual impulses which had concerned the *bruja* do not seem to exist. We are too young for adult sex, swimming in an amniotic prenatal world, and at the same time, aware of its fantastic unsuitability for the adults we also are—gentle, very old, and lost.

Someone speaks of feeling entirely weightless, bodiless, yet the drunken body insists on being felt. Someone complains of intense nausea, which the *bruja* says she will cure. The nausea does leave in time, but reappears, and again disappears, and continues in intermittent waves (a common result of mushroom eating, we discover later). One woman complains of a terrible, clamping pain in her head, her usual response, she explains, to uncertainty and fear. The Indian woman, who seems to be taking the "journey" particularly with her, says that the headache is symptomatic of a secret disease, which she will unearth. We have the impression that she continues to chant for a while, but we are too much interested in each other to listen. (Is this a response to fear or is it a return to innocence, to a purity unstained by disappointment and mistrust?) We reassure each other, hold each other's hands. As the designs roll on, in inexorable large harmonies, we pull toward each other with words of almost maternal concern, having to break out of the splendid isolation in which we are drifting. If we are good, kind children and considerate of each other, nothing will happen, we will not be lost.

Someone calls out, "Evil seems so far away." He is answered, "I don't know what evil is." For one of us, the subject is so remote that it deserves neither thought nor words. Another *is* in the hideous presence of imminent evil, and she turns and twists trying to escape it.

The woman who had had the headache now insists that her bladder will not be denied relief any longer; this anchor, her body, reminds her that she is earth-bound and must stay earth-bound. The other three, with great patience and in gentle tones, as if to a very young child, explain why she can't go to the bathroom: the light coming in the door will break into the visions; the sensation is false, only the effect of the mushrooms; wouldn't it be better to concentrate on the colors instead? They would all love to help, but they are much too drunk, they say. The sufferer insists, laughingly, that their observations are reasonable but make no difference to the basic fact. And they all laugh and continue to laugh in radiant full voices, lovely children dancing in a summer shower. The laughter is a river of gold and they ride it wittily, charmed with each other, enchanted with themselves, radiant with all gifts and beauties.

The old woman makes herself heard, saying that she and her chosen companion are in a most beautiful country. Relief is expressed among the spectators; the American's headache and nausea followed by fever had frightened them. They begin to reassure each other—"She'll be all right; she'll be fine"—and go on to explain that they had seen people leap and shriek and run in uncontrollable flights from anguish. The American woman seemed for a while to be headed that way.

One of the men, still laughing, breaks in to say that nightclub comics might do well to distribute mushrooms to their audiences, and we embroider on this theme, glittering, inventive, audacious.

Between bouts of laughter and love, we *know* that we are coming into full control of our situation, that we can move in and out between reality and the color world at will, by the simple act of concentrating with open eyes on what *is.* It is a little surprising, but of no significance, that a man coming toward us is eight feet tall and moving from a very high place sharply downward. We are still in control, invincible, flowers of grace, shining with affection, laughing shimmering music, incandescent. A woman calls out, "I feel all-powerful, but what's much better, I don't want to use any of my power," a kindlier god than any yet devised. A shadow moves over the gleaming world which is oneself; the small, cold sliver of judgment which pierces the visions warns: this is an echo of infantile omnipotence suddenly returned, too magnificent and mad.

There has been enough of glory for two of us. One retreats to nausea, is taken out and put to bed; one woman, muttering that she can't bear any more, please, please, take her to bed, is led out. One woman and one man, still rolling in the waves of laughter, stay on. By this time, the candle has been relit and the pair are lying on the mat talking and laughing luminously, swinging in great arcs from the bright, loving conversation to rhythmic seas of jewels and lights. The woman asks to be conducted to the bathroom, and assuring the man that he is not to worry or feel alone and she will be back, she floats and stumbles out of the room, supported on either side by the two spectators. When she returns to the big room, her partner is still lying on the mat, roaring over a private joke. He is aware of her return, opens his eyes to greet her, and shuts them quickly with a grimace of pain. The red of the wall is too red, the color has changed, its brilliance is insupportable. Her assurance that the wall has not changed makes him easier. He opens his eyes, asks her to sit down: "Let's talk." She is afraid to sit down, it was so difficult getting up before. She tries to persuade him to go to bed and offers him her hand to help him up. She can't pull hard enough, loses her balance, and almost falls on him. They break into laughter again, making exquisite jokes about each other's drunkenness. She turns to her gracious audience and explains in extraordinarily fluent Spanish that they are playing a classic drunk scene. She translates carefully: "You're drunk." "You're drunker." "No. I know I'm drunk but you don't, which shows that you are drunker"; then turns to her partner, who is enjoying the act inordinately. Between bursts of laughter he tells her that they would have made a great vaudeville team. Inspired by this judgment, the laughter of the audience, and the spotlight that the candle casts on her shadow weaving against the blood-red wall, the woman turns to the spectators again and tells them that they are witnessing a rare performance, a fine demonstration of ancient, universal vaudeville, older than Dionysius. Her Spanish is flawlessly supple, her accent classic, of the academy. The audience is beautiful soft shadows floating in exquisite arabesque designs like the music of flutes.

Suddenly, she is drowning in nausea and drunkenness. She makes one more effort to get the man up; she doesn't want to leave him alone, the red wall may frighten him again, but he is invulnerably cocooned in his laughter and can't be reached. She asks to be taken to the bathroom, where she vomits eagerly and lustily, knowing that getting rid of the mushrooms will take her out of her awesome private universe. (Some idea flashes by about the Hebrews fearing to use the name of God, something about Moses not wanting to see God, or was that Krishna? Something about religious revelations which were too large and blinding.)

Eagerly, she awaits the return to the familiar. It doesn't come, though; surely the visions and unsteadiness should go now that she is rid of the mushrooms. Standing on the balcony outside her room, the goddess cloak slipping from her shoulders, she looks up at the sky. The stars are heads of glowing pearl, linked by dancing paths of sparkling diamonds pulsing against deep-blue velvet. The woman describes the sky to the girl who helped her. The girl says that the stars are very dim and few and asks the woman to describe some nearby leaves. They look completely natural. Out, away, up, are the directions of magic.

As she looks at the sky, her chest becomes constricted; she cannot breathe and knows she is going to die. It must be done with dignity, no hysterics, but can't quite be managed alone. She asks the girl to stay with her a little longer, saying only that she is having difficulty breathing and apologizes for keeping her up so late. She waits for death, knowing that the witch has put a curse on her, had given her poisoned mushrooms to eat. Her invocations were false, she had really called down evil, like the uninvited fairy at the happy feast.

Death is slow in coming. She tells the girl that it must have been a long, cold night for her, probably frightening, and suggests she go to bed. The girl leaves and the woman is alone. The others have been in bed for some unmeasurable time, the "witch" had been conducted out and up the road by the Indian girl, the landlady and her relatives have retired to their houses. She is alone with a hideously gorgeous sky, the witch's poison in her chest, the poison of Sleeping Beauty's spindle in her heavy arms, the wicked stepmother's poisoned apple in her throat. Now she is no longer so much afraid of dying as of meeting the dead. Her mind opens a little dark tree-covered path at the end of which stand two small figures, shrouded, shapeless. She quickly closes them off, but knows they're waiting and who they are. They hate her because she couldn't keep them alive, because they have no one to take care of them in the black quiet place since she abandoned them. They will be unbearable. From their desiccated, frightful heads will come reproaches and loathing and she will have to see and hear them forever.

Out of the unbearableness rises the voice of the woman: "This is silly. I'm reliving fairy tales and Bela Lugosi movies. I am a fairly sane adult bothered by the altitude, drugged and drunk, nothing more." She comforts herself with the common answer to agony: "It will pass." But the little girl is stronger. She clings, strangles; like a huge amoeba, she engulfs and swallows the woman. "I *am* poisoned and cursed, the dead are coming for me. If I don't go to bed," she thinks slyly, "they won't catch me. If I stay awake and alert I'll be able to run away from them." The grotesque sky beats down; terror tightens around her. She wants her mother with every sinew; every pore is begging, every bone is stretched in supplication. Somewhere in her chest she hears a deep wail and feels a thick emptiness of desperation and loss.

The woman takes over and convinces the little girl to go to bed, but the little girl won't let her undress. "In case I have to run from death it's better to be fully dressed, sweater, shoes and all." She turns, sits up, lies down in bed, violently hyperactive, afraid of sleep and death. The woman in the next bed is awake, and they talk in frantic explosions of remembering, conjecturing, evaluating experiences. Between attempts at rational speech the other woman moans that she is wrapped in anguish, she cannot move, and during occasional lapses into sleep, screams, "No, no! Don't! Don't! Please don't!" When awakened (and movingly grateful for her partner's presence), she cannot describe or explain what she is experiencing but keeps repeating that she is trapped in anguish and insupportable guilt. She has been somewhere she shouldn't have been, has seen things she shouldn't have seen, lived with something abysmally evil. She is sure they might have died or gone mad and cannot understand how they escaped.

She falls into a quiet sleep finally and her partner realizes that her own fear of the dead and death are gone: she can undress and get under the covers, and does. She looks around her. The chair standing in the faint dawn light coming through the open door (the other woman had insisted that she leave it open, her escape hatch, though she couldn't move if she wanted to) is throwing off fast-moving swirls of color whose rhythm is audible. The skirt hanging from the bedpost makes a downward, swishing sound as her eyes move along it. The sleeping woman's muttering voice makes color patterns. Everything seen is heard in a parallel rhythm, everything heard is translated into vision. An old anesthetic dream, never entirely forgotten, confronts her again; sounds arrange themselves in a ring of lights moving in a tormenting circle, blinking on and off in a steady rhythm of sickening blows. As she frantically searches for a way out, a great voice comes from all directions, embedding her in a black nest of sound, and says, "You are thinking that this must end, if only in madness. That's not necessarily so. And now you're thinking if not in madness, it must end in death. How do you know that death is an end? That it isn't interminable torture like this? How do you know that 'an end,' with which you console yourself, means anything at all? It doesn't." She is convinced, as before, that the voice is right. It must be; it is the voice of the God of childhood, Who sees everything and forgives nothing, the God Who makes you collect all your fingernails and bits of hair—no matter where they may have been discarded and forgotten—when you die. It is the God of the eternal purgatory promised Joyce as a schoolboy.

Hanging like loathsome rags on this dream are other experiences of tangled sight and sound, and terror: the deafness of high fever; watching a schoolmate anesthetize a cat which they had both caught; Poe's cat screaming from its wall tomb; mashed, decaying bodies of cats in street lots. Recoiling from the murky well of remembering, unable to sleep, she stares and listens intensely, trying to dispel the noise of the closet angles and the patterns of color made by the early-working voices outside. The fears and guilts gather into a strangling knot. Is this tangling of the senses the promised punishment for the forbidden titillations and explorations of childhood? Is this what they meant when they said you were an odd child? Painfully bright are the beautiful designs which now sing whether the eyes are open or shut, suffocating, inescapable, rushing through the body as if it were a sieve.

Do something practical and helpful. There hasn't been a sound from the room above, where the men are staying—not a stumble, the creak of a bed, a shoe dropped. The woman begins to worry about them and finds it a great pleasure. She reaches for her clothing, examines each piece with drunken care, puts her slip on over her pajamas, her brassiere on top of that and, very proud to have thought of it, a large sweater. The woman in the next bed awakens and dissuades her from going upstairs: "They're all right. The stairs are slippery and you'll fall and break your neck and I won't be able to help you. I can't move." She does not want to be alone, the rest is rationalization. The woman in the peculiar costume returns to bed and they talk, the other repeating periodically, like the refrain of a ballad, "I'm so glad you're here. I couldn't have borne it alone."

Gradually, terror ebbs, washed away by short periods of sleep with insignificant dreams. The sight-sounds well back, but with less frequency, and the woman is lost in admiration of the crude, now silent chair and the band of daylight standing mute in the doorway, plain, cold, and thin. She runs out to look at the world from the balcony. The sky is dull and heavy, gray mist drags along the gray-green hills, the elephant ears in the corner of the garden lie flat and gray, the boards of the balcony and the bathhouse are a wet gray, the rocks in the path are gray. The air is cold, like gray steel. She goes back into the room and her friend asks, "How does the world look?" She sings, from her toes: "Like its old, ordinary, dull, beautiful self." She is still drunk, still assailed by chills and fever, but nothing bothers her. She lies on the bed, wallowing in the pleasure of being back;

her blood sings and dances; she is in love with the whitewashed walls, the hooks in the walls, with the creeping cold and the lumpy bed, with her moaning companion, with her untangled self, and with the troublesome, imperfect world she knows.

NOTE: The village has been "discovered" by those who couldn't quite make it to Nepal. Communications, therefore, must inevitably improve and the lovely village deteriorate.

Villahermosa

Villahermosa was once upon a time a city of exaggerations, excesses, paradoxes, extremes, a little frantic with leaping between the old and the new and back, from gamin charm to reposed, civic dignity. While every town had one *paseo,* Villahermosa had two. Saturday night was the time of the tight-dress *paseo.* In dresses that seemed painted on rather than fitted, with zipper closings that clung to the curve of the buttocks and the backs of the thighs, hair carefully arranged in the bedroom casualness of French and Italian movies, hobbled by narrow skirts and wire-thin heels, the high-style girls tottered arm in arm around and around the plaza, talking and laughing in a busy show of satisfaction with themselves and each other while their eyes raced like mice, seeking attention. By some mysterious, prearranged timing, they suddenly broke off their animated circuit of the plaza to enter the **Café de Portal,** a large dance hall and restaurant on one side of the plaza, slinking past the groups of men seated at the tables outside. They emerged soon, to resume their determined march around the plaza jabbering lightly, gaily, always searching, always evaluating their effect.

The Sunday-night *paseo* featured the wide, gathered skirts of the younger girls, the tulles and rosebuds of saints' days and confirmations. The young children danced to the band music, played gentle games, and kept their starched white clothing pristine. Now and then two five-year-olds imitated the courtly round of the *paseo,* practicing the invitation of ten years hence. Around them circled small groups of adolescent boys in one direction, girls in similar bands of mutual protection and respectability in the counter direction, learning to eye each other in swift, sliding glances. On both nights, the *paseo* of walkers was ringed by a steady stream of small trucks, jeeps, and work cars of various kinds, carefully polished and brought into town from outlying ranches to do the *paseo* in mechanized style. Among them there appeared an occasional, large American car whose passengers were several sophisticated young women, carefully made up and dressed as if for a party; all the party there was for them was the endless circling of a small space in too large a car. (They might easily have been a Mexican translation of the Chekhov "Sisters" wearing out their hearts and wardrobes in the provinces, while they yearn for the big city.)

Five minutes' walk from the formal pavanes of the *paseo* plaza was the haphazard life of the Grijalva River, easy, half naked, and slow. The best place to observe it was from the balconies of the raffish **San Rafael Hotel**, which sat over the river. Early in the morning the eastern, rural shore still lay in deep shade, gray and cool, somnolent except for the sounds of irritable dogs and early-morning children. On the near, the town side, the *zopilotes* with dusty wings and wrinkled, naked necks, resembling the garbage they eat, sat in black ominous rows, waiting to swoop on the discards deposited at the river's edge. The sluggish brown river slowly carried long, narrow dugouts neatly fitted with soft-drink bottles, their tops shining like jewel studs in the morning sun. Some dugouts were huge flat fruit trays carrying golden mangoes and green bananas to the markets of the town; some of the larger craft were of the *African Queen* school of shipbuilding: old boats made of relics of older boats; clumsy sailing vessels too tired for the challenges of swifter waters and stormier air; barges which never had pressing appointments, loading and unloading their cargoes of lumpy sacks and weathered crates in slow motion, with a minimum of fuss or efficiency.

Toward evening, the last rays of sun burnished the peeling paint on the shacks across the river to satiny bronze, the thatch shed its prickly skin and turned to deep moss, the fronds of the tall palms lifted and fell in the evening air, russet patches of cow wandered through the smoky distance, a horseman on a red horse floated through the gold-streaked shade of the trees which leaned over the bronze river. The shadow of the hotel fell across the river and onto an opposite gray-green slope to make a sharp, cubist patch of dark, deep green. Two men poled a high-sterned ferry-dugout like a huge wooden spoon, their upright bodies and the seated bodies of the four passengers silhouetted still and sharp, against the dark-shining river. Evening sounds began to drift across the water: the lowing of cows, the anxious bark of the nervous dogs, boys drumming on tin cans.

The dark-green shadows turned purple, the river light washed out to soft gray, and webs of smoke rose from the cooking vents of the shacks to fade into the night. The *zopilotes* folded their crepe wings and floated down like bits of burnt paper to roost on the housetops.

The market began near the river, and like it, oozed straight through the waterfront section—through arcades piled with bright tin trunks, gaudy toys, crude alligator bags, plastic pails, yard goods, canoe-shaped tubs of clay and wood, cigarettes and painted candy, spools of thread and hide pocketbooks. Past the arcades it spilled onto the street its heaps of fruits: green *guanábana* whose skin is a hundred closely set thumb prints; *pitahaya,* unreal and florid, a rococo artichoke; monumental pineapples with fronds like palm trees; brown tamarind seeds; coconuts hairy or denuded; bananas small enough to use as beads on a necklace and large enough to inflict a blow; *huilicuila,* giant peas whose sweet cottony pod can be eaten raw, while the bean—an inch or longer—is eaten as a cooked vegetable; mangoes; piles of banana leaves to be used as wrapping paper; bouquets of parsley, bouquets of precisely matched stringbeans. Right on the river were the refreshment stands and the handful of cooked-shrimp stands and several tailors' stalls equipped with old-fashioned foot-treadle machines or only a chair on which the tailor sat bent in deep concentration, his body immobile except for the swift whipping hand deftly edging a buttonhole.

Gone, gone, almost all gone. An infusion of energy that becomes ambition, the promise of oil finds nearby, hundreds of tons of concrete (bought, it is said, as elsewhere in Mexico, from foreign capital invested by uncertain Europe), a feverish sense of competition among the southern cities, have created of the erstwhile appealing dump heap a respectable, though still gay, city. The river has been cleared of its laden wobbly barges, their produce removed to trucks that ply the broad new roads, and passengers are taken across the river on a regular schedule of brightly colored ferry boats. The market has been swept off the waterfront and organized in a new, closed area. The places where the buzzards fed and played have been covered by a riverfront road.

The market is, as it should be, jostling and reasonably noisy, but it has been modernized to include pedestrian malls, which hold some of the better shops, a dental office or two, and silvered fountains. Nice, but not the old roaring thing it once was. Nor does an evening walk—except maybe in some remote areas of the thriving city—reveal the once immutable middle-class arrangements of piano or refrigerator in the center of the room, wax flowers on top, a heavy carved settee and two equally heavy, dead chairs, a table which holds more wax flowers, and beyond, a large-flowered cretonne curtain that conceals bedrooms.

The prime reason for staying in Villahermosa, other than its irrepressible vivacity, is the orderly, beautifully arranged museums, among the finest archaeological museums anywhere. They were originally developed and arranged by Carlos Pellicer, one of Mexico's leading intellectuals and poets and a local son. The museums are a distillate of his knowledge, his devotion, and his impeccable taste and are recently redesigned to meet the oil city's need for modernity. One section is part of a large park at the edge of town, toward the airfield. Footprints in rough terra-cotta cement patches thrown down on the leafy paths lead from a La Venta head of a giant baby in a football helmet set in a lush tropical bower (to approximate the setting in which it was originally found) to a magnificent frieze pressed into the earth as if it had been embedded there for centuries, to an odd stone teddy-bear figure with a bellicose crest on his head, like the helmet of a Roman centurion, and on to other Olmec artifacts. There are benches to rest on, under the deep wide shade of mango trees, which in season shed their fruit with generous abandon, offering food as well as shelter from the sun. The paths are lined with splotched Jackson Pollock leaves which must, one thinks, be artificial. They are not; simply a part of the careful, detailed planning that sought the loveliest tropical vegetation to surround the remarkable objects.

The indoor section of this extensive Parque-Museo de la Venta (once a prison that held many intellectuals at the time of Porfirio Díaz) is as beautifully planned as the park. In the dim coolness of the first floor, you will find several more of the large somber Olmec figures—the football-helmeted heads, the omnipresent jaguar-headed body somewhere between human and animal, and the torsos seated in eternal Buddhistic calm. The upper floors, salons interspersed with attractive, small terrace gardens, hold a great variety and quantity of objects, stemming from pre-Cortés cultures. However, much of what the museum contains is not to be seen elsewhere. Look, for instance, for a female Totonac clay torso wearing a wonderfully designed necklace, strangely pre-Hellenic in its flattened, simplified anatomic lines and its serene poise. And the Jaina figures—perfect, small, monumentally calm funerary sculptures which had been buried with Mayan priests and nobles on the small island of Jaina, off the coast of Campeche. Or the magnificent polychrome vase painted with the bold plumed figures of the Bonampak murals, the Indian codices folded like old Oriental books, exquisite small heads, and life-size death masks, with simplified, flattened contours as if death were a hand that straightened and smoothed.

Look for the group portraits of little squat figures eating and drinking and dancing in ritual costumes, busy and appealingly giddy, like children cavorting in party hats.

Here, too, are the little, round-thighed Tlatilco figures, flirtatious and fleshly and eminently suitable for fertility symbolism. And a couple from Nayarit sitting in sodden, suburban dullness, like the day after New Year's in Bronxville. Sharing the mood of their neighbors are clay figurines from Colima, whose eyes, slit disks of clay, make them too look miserably hung over. And, that *is* actually a jaguar scratching on the bars just outside your window, as unbelievable as the small tropical animals you saw gamboling among the Olmec gods in the park an hour before.

About an hour out of Villahermosa by a good road, one reached the Gulf beach of Miramar. The road, running almost due north (toward Frontera, with a turnoff to Miramar), went through numerous inlets of the river and the sea, their silvery surfaces clotted with purple water hyacinths brushing the backs of munching cows. Hummingbirds of iridescent greens and blues darted across the heads of horsemen disappearing into clusters of low trees, while high above them the aloof palms looked into the distance. The deep-emerald mango trees were heavy with the jade drops of ripening fruit, and the ground below jeweled by the confetti of yellow, yellow-orange, orange-red fallen fruit.

The beach had a few amenities—lockers and showers, shaded eating and drinking places, and palm trees to support hammocks. Were it better developed, little pink-dressed girls couldn't whip along the beach on russet horses, nor could one drive to the water, using a car in which to dress and undress. The sand was smooth, the water tranquil, and the various treatments of shrimp and *mojarra* delicious.

On the ride back to the town toward evening, the twilight turned the countryside a silver gray. The birds sang and the herons gathered like bouquets of white flowers on and near the zebu cattle. Food odors emerged from the thatched shacks in front of which the local people sat and talked while the children poled dugouts in the lagoons behind the houses. (We had no courage to check, afraid it might have turned into a minor Coney Island as these places often do.)

When oil began to glitter in promising bounty, Villahermosa, as suited her new promisingly rich status, thrust highways through her cities, which makes walking, for one who is unaccustomed to the geography of the city (or worse still, listens to enthusiastic, vague instructions) quite difficult. The raised highways, held, it seems, by a million tacks of orange pins, offer too few crossings, so one walks and walks, seeing signs that should be a block or two away move back into the distance. That which sits in the distance beyond the ordinary streets is "the new city." It is a large enclave of leading shops, the three fine, not much used hotels—the **Hyatt,** the **Cencali,** the **Maya Tabasco Hotel**—plus an upper- and middle-class mass of housing, rather like Mayan stone in color and cluster in the distance, a splendid dark marble government palace and nearby, a generously spaced, handsomely detailed exhibition hall. One hopes it flourishes well, this ambitious new city of noble distances and bold design, planned for a distinguished future.

HOTELS

The **Holiday Inn** on the Paseo Tabasco and the **Hotel Hyatt** on Juarez are both well-kept with reliably air-conditioned rooms. The **Hotel Cencali** and the **Maya Tabasco,** the former in a slightly rural setting, the latter right in the midst of all sorts of things—mainly traffic—are somewhat less expensive and equally satisfactory.

RESTAURANTS

The **Meson de Castillo** carries nostalgia for old Spain in its décor, in the manners of its waiters, in the three-hour lunches enjoyed by a group of steadies. Women, though a surprise, are courteously welcomed, and everyone is well fed for comparatively little money. The compound that embraces the museums and adjoining cultural activities also holds a popular restaurant, **Los Guayacanes,** consistently trustworthy for its seafood especially. The **Maya Tabasco** has amiable waiters who serve amiable dishes. For a snack downtown in the pedestrian mall area, try any of the variety offered by the **Cafeteria La Alianza** (Aldama 612), which wears an apron of outdoor café.

Palenque

The Tabasqueña Airlines once flew—and probably still does, but, one hopes, with considerably greater calm—motored kites out of Villahermosa to Palenque on a daily schedule. One can make the trip by car on a glossy road that leaves the highway about 115 kilometers east of Villahermosa; then it is about 35 to 40 kilometers to the small trailer camp—hippy and aged—that is shaping up outside the archaeological zone. There are also buses from Villahermosa that make the distance in fair time and return the same day for a few dollars. If you are driving and can choose your time, remember that the zone opens at 6:30 A.M. and stays open to 5:30 P.M. but the museum is open only from 10 to 11 A.M. and 3 to 4 P.M. and the remarkable tomb from 11 A.M. to noon and 4 to 5 P.M. Take a picnic lunch (it is five miles back to the village); there is only a drinks stand immediately outside the entrance.

There is at least one new hotel in town and by the time you get there, there should be two or three more plus restaurants and snack bars, which should change the desultory mood of the village. It already undergoes considerable enlivening now and then when a bus disgorges a load of high school girls from Campeche, dressed in their current national costumes of tight pants and shirts that cling to the plump thighs and bellies and behinds like those of the innumerable little fertility goddesses shaped by ancient cultures whose artists observed more acutely than we often imagine. And look and talk to, if you have a few words of Spanish (they usually manage a bit of English), the gentle, fine-featured Mayan faces. These girls are neither aggressive nor shy; the Mayan is a singularly poised human, at whatever age.

There is little to match the disdainful beauty of this Mayan city placed in rhythmic hills of closed jungle, a setting for epic and tragedy. The low throbbing of the jungle counterpoints the waiting silence of the small temples whose dynamic design is a play of opposed movements; the roofs reach heavily downward while their stone-lace crests cut boldly upward, in the counterpulls of light and dark, life and death. Some of the pyramid mounds are half covered by jungle vines, the stones of others have been hacked bare, and still others, their temples destroyed or never built, are green roundnesses retreating into the jungle, awaiting disclosure, to make, again, the view Stephens had of the palace over one hundred years ago: "Through openings in the trees we saw the front of a large building richly ornamented with stuccoed figures on the pilasters, curious and elegant, with trees growing close against it, their branches entering the doors; in style and effect it was unique, extraordinary, and mournfully beautiful."

The mournful beauty has been found, lost, and rediscovered several times, first by a group of Spaniards who penetrated the area in the middle of the eighteenth century, although Cortés quite probably passed close to it in his progress into the Mayan country. The presence of the ancient ceremonial city which had already lost its Indian name (and was called, unimaginatively, Casas de Piedras) was casually received by the Spanish Throne, and it wasn't until thirty years later that a Captain Antonio del Río was sent out to explore the city. He hacked and burned his way through the jungle to a few buildings and made some reports which, through the hazards of distance and Colonial lassitude, were left to molder in archives in Guatemala. According to Stephens, Charles IV of Spain ordered another expedition, which reached Palenque in 1807. The reports of the French head of the expedition, Dupaix, traveled a tortuous route to Europe and back, then were left to languish in the "Cabinet" of Natural History in Mexico City. In 1828, an Englishman with fanciful theories reawakened an interest in Palenque, and later Count Jean Frédéric Waldeck wrested a subsidy from the Mexican government to make intensive studies. He was soon followed—in 1840—by the American John Lloyd Stephens and the English artist Frederick Catherwood. Since that time, the city has been visited, explored, and mapped by a variety of viewers and savants, but it was not until the twentieth century that intensive, more scientific searches of the ruins were made.

The extent of Palenque, covered for centuries by the slow, steady march of jungle, has been variously estimated. It "covers a space of sixty miles; in a series of well-written articles in our own country they have been set down as ten times larger than New York; and lately I have seen an article which represents this city as having been three times as large as London." This is Stephens at a time when ancient cities were being rediscovered and reinvented by imaginative reporters, resulting in exoticisms rather like Elizabethan "voyages." More recent estimates of the city have it reduced to about four or five miles from north to south, and are vague about its other dimension.

The visible, explored center is small in area, a center plaza on an artificially constructed terrace, and a few scattered buildings, circled by the impenetrable green, all that is left to see of one of the most magnificent and important cities of the Old Mayan Empire in its Late Classic Period (A.D. 500 to 800). It probably housed the priest-astronomer-mathematicians who controlled the elaborate ceremonial life, who calculated and foretold propitious dates—when the divinities would smile—to sow a crop and harvest it. It may have housed the magnificently plumed, bejeweled, and sandaled nobles and warriors who ruled and protected the city's secular life, and the artists who carved the bas-reliefs and sculptures of the most graceful and sophisticated stucco-work decoration in all of the cultures of the Americas. The look and connotations of the city must have been awesome: numerous pyramids and beautifully proportioned, richly carved temples surmounting fecund hills; the knowledge that this was the abode of the mysteries that controlled life and death, that it was a fount of learning, science, and art, a place of noble burials, a bastion of an Empire supported by a large and formidable populace.

The most conspicuous complex of buildings now reachable is the central plaza, the "Palace," which consists of a number of buildings of several periods, placed around interior courts and connected by galleries and subterranean chambers. From their center rises a four-storied tower, unusually rectilinear and narrow for this part of the world—more like an Italian campanile touched by the Orient—and believed to have been used for astronomical observations and as a watchtower. Some of the masterful decorations of the "Palace" have been removed to the National Museum in Mexico City and to the local museum, as well as to other parts of the world. All the surfaces were probably once covered with carvings and stucco molds, much of them gone, but what remains still indicates consummate skill. The slender, overbred figures of the stuccos move in the restrained hieratic gestures of religious dance, the gestures, headdress, jewels,

aristocratic curves of the profiles balanced by a few sculptural ornaments, a few hieroglyphs, to make of a tablet a beautifully composed
whole.

On a terraced rise a short distance from the "Palace" are the group
of buildings called the Temple of the Sun, the Temple of the Cross,
and the Temple of the Foliated Cross. Although they are of similar
structural design and the latter two have lost much of their shape and
decoration, all three are worth looking at even though it may mean
scrambling over slippery rock in one of Palenque's torrential rainstorms. A number of the most remarkable tablets have been removed,
mainly for the safety of museums (not always altogether burglar-
proof, however), but the still-undisturbed carvings are also fine examples of the local art. Some have an odd history: for a number of
years they ornamented the façade of the church in the village, and
before that one of them was the property of a lady whom Stephens
considered marrying so that, as the husband of a Mexican citizen, he
could buy, legally, the ruins of Palenque.

The name panel of the third building is carved with ceremonial
figures and a floral offering—probably a stylized cornstalk—which
makes an ornate cruciform shape. This symbol has given some enthusiasts cause to claim that Mayans, as early Christians, were converted by daring, legendary missionaries. However, the cross is a
simple, eminently usable symbol and appears often in early times and
cultures. (Díaz, describing a Mayan altar at Campeche, said, "On the
other side of the Idols were symbols like crosses. . . .")

The Temple of the Inscriptions, set upon the tallest pyramid, has
the most startling history of all the buildings. For one thing, its
tablets of numerous hieroglyphs establish a date close to that of the
construction of the building—A.D. 692—and, more important, it was
this building which reversed the assumption that pyramids in the
New World were simply supports of temples and not, like Egyptian
pyramids, housing for royal tombs. In the late 1940s the archaeologist
Alberto Ruz began excavations into the body of the pyramid, encouraged by the fact that the walls of one of the temple rooms obviously
did not stop at the floor but continued downward, leading past stone-
and earth-filled stairways. The work went slowly because of weather
and the masses of obstruction, clearly intended to discourage intru-
sion. After some years of interrupted work, the excavators reached
the bottom of the stairs, which led to a corridor, also closed off.
Cleared and followed, it revealed a wall near which was a box con-

taining jade ornaments, a pearl, ceramic plates, and shells painted red—apparently an offering. Behind the thick wall there was another stone box, which carried a more macabre treasure, five or six skeletons of young men, presumably sacrifices, guardians for a dead personage whose actual tomb was still to be found. And it *was*, behind a large heavy stone cut to cover an entrance. The walls of the tomb were covered with stucco figures, the nine gods of the nine underworlds watching over the crypt protected by a wonderfully carved stone slab. The crypt itself, additionally covered with heavy stone under the ceremonial tablet, held the remains, finally, of the entombed personage.

Although probably a man of advanced years, who he was isn't known, because many centuries of decay, the destruction of records during the Conquest, the uncertain and incomplete knowledge of the inscriptions now extant make such knowledge impossible at present. He was undoubtedly awesome, as awesome alive in the seventh century as he was to the men who found him dead in the twentieth, and awesome in the effigy which now lies in the National Museum in Mexico City. In death, as in life, he was surrounded by exquisite care and rarities—a carefully shaped sarcophagus whose interior was painted cinnabar red, wrapped in a red shroud which left its color on his bones, and jade, pounds of it, as bracelets, as earplugs, as rings for each finger, as immense collar, as scattered idols and symbols, as pieces to hold in each hand and in his mouth, as a death mask. Among the riches of jade there was a huge pearl, actually made of bits of carefully joined nacre, and on the floor of the crypt, ceramic containers and two heads of stucco. (One of them is incomparably beautiful and has taken to its aristocratic self the role of being *the* "Mayan" symbol that appears on postage stamps and travel-folder covers.)

The so-called Temple of the Count, that in which Count Waldeck lived for two or three years, also revealed, as have other explored buildings, tombs containing funerary offerings of jade and clay vessels but no human remains.

As further testimony to the building skill of the Mayans, a skillfully constructed aqueduct runs through the grounds, probably connected with one of the most delightful of swimming holes. At the side of the small local museum, a grassy incline runs down to the shade of several huge trees which stretch over a gentle, shallow fall of water, a silvery-gray piece of silk rippling over a bed of flat rocks.

Unless Palenque has become inundated with tourists (hardly likely for a number of years), it is perfectly all right to go in your underwear, or the fast-drying magic clothing you will undoubtedly be wearing; or change into a suit in any clump of bushes. The slide down the rocks is easy and lands one in a lightly swirling, fresh pool, deeply shaded and blissfully cool after the clinging steam of the open, sun-cooked places.

Refreshed, you might wander around some of the smaller, less complete buildings (don't go too far from the center; this is snake and wild-animal jungle) to find subterranean chambers with altars and precise carving or, in a roofless court, a set of figures something like the *Danzantes* of Oaxaca (p. 245)—one of them obviously the Priapus of Mayan mythology.

For a longer stay in this complex and beautiful Mayan city, try the hotel **Chan Kah**, the **Nutatun Viva**, the **Hotel de las Ruinas** or the **Mision**, seemingly becoming part of a "ruins" chain of small hotels.

Bonampak, of the famous murals, and Yaxchilán, reputedly as beautiful as Palenque, are less difficult to reach than they were until recently. A number of small, almost impromptu, plane companies serve them, but it still may mean uncertain waiting and primitive accommodations. Inquire of tourist agencies in Yucatán, of airlines in Villahermosa, of the desks of local hotels.

Hard words for a "ruin," but as Palenque enhances the environs of Villahermosa, Comalcalco diminishes them. It is a set of mounds and platforms, dating from the seventh century, extending its communications as far as Uxmal and Tikal in Guatemala two centuries later and beyond that in time with the northern Nahuas and Totonacs, when the heavy grasses began to cover them. There are almost three hundred buildings, none of immense size, spread over and under the damp grasses of Comalcalco and, since there were none of the stones that made the other Mayan and Toltec buildings rough, sun-yellow and awesome, these made of burned shell (oyster), sand, and water are of ash-dark brick not very well designed (the top of the Palacio looks now like an unfurnished factory) and adorned with bizarre melted images, one of them like a big Alice-in-Wonderland sleeping dormouse.

There is more amusement in reaching the town through a number of alert villages: Nacajuca, for instance, has a children's zoo, children's animal figures painted on its walls, houses of unabashed color and a strange, appealing toy-like nineteenth-century church, dripping all sorts of decoration. The village of Jalpa has not only a Casa of Cultura but, announced by a large old photo of Juárez, the Museo of Coronel Gregorio Mendez who owned this house and the cannon guns and photos in it. Opened as a museum in 1984 it commemorates the triumph of the revolutions, the Indian Juárez over the effete French Maximilian, and for lagniappe has treated itself to a miniature Mayan temple.

One of the surprises of the countryside, after you pass Jalpa de Mendez, is the slow laziness of the zebu cattle always embroidered by white herons, the gourds carved by some of the local craftsmen and, if you've never seen it, the heavy green gourd of cocoa seed that waits to drop from the slender tree and be turned into several kinds of cocoa and coffee. You will notice that their cultivators, a tribe called Chontales, cover their houses with thatch and paint the sides and the children's schools with merry designs.

If hunger catches you on the way back, stop in at **Mary's**, who fries big fish in huge vats along with heavy local tortillas. Subtleties of cuisine lack but it's fresh, wholesome fish as primitively cooked as you might ever get it.

Isla del Carmen

The trip from Villahermosa to the Isla del Carmen can be made by car or bus or plane but cannot be negotiated on a very tight schedule because of *nortes.* There is, purportedly, a *norte* season, but it is an elusive thing; the *norte* season is when it comes, with heavy winds and rains, often covering the whole Gulf area. The large port of Veracruz is closed, fishing boats in the lower part of the Gulf scuttle like water bugs to sheltered bays, the women run from house to well with tin basins on their heads as umbrellas, the wind-driven clouds have the explosive shape of clouds in old maps, the rain is a dirty, torn curtain over the world. This may last in varying degrees of violence and intermittently for three or four days. Practically, for the traveler by bus or car (four to five hours) it means that the ferries which connect the island with the mainland may be held up for an hour or two, or a day or two. The planes which run on a daily schedule usually manage to slip through the clouds and maintain something like regular service.

The waiting time need not be dull. Some Mexican, local or a traveler, will adopt you, find you shelter, show you where to eat the local seafood, watch the waterfront life with you, exchange Spanish-English lessons with you, and teach you the patience of Mexico.

Some of the bus service is second class, which means that neither seats nor springs are too amiable and odd cargo may clog sections of the aisle. Departure points are from the center of town but have been known to change because of street reconstruction. If your Spanish is not reliable, have someone in the hotel buy your tickets and take you to the proper place.

Ferry runs are usually vaguely coordinated to give you time for crossing an isolated strip of land and staying for a short time at each stop. Ask at each arrival when the ferry at the next point leaves.

If you are traveling by car, don't let the possibilities of *nortes*—they don't always blow—discourage you. It shortens the ride from Villahermosa (via Frontera, Carmen, Aguada) to Campeche to take the variety of miles of narrow beach and green vaults of coconut groves, alternating with slow, tropical rivers and lagoons, the ferries full of people leaving their own seafood to eat the same dishes near a neighboring ferry dock for a change of scene and a chance to show their children the gleeful, showoff dolphins that follow the boats.

Ciudad del Carmen, the main city of the island, is a perfect place to stay for a day or two, or a long time; it hasn't enough to offer in variety for a week's visit but is fine as a not-too-primitive retreat in which to write that book or paint those pictures, or for a shorter rest to break up the long bus or auto journey from Veracruz to Mérida.

It is surprisingly worldly and almost stylish for an island which lived in semi-isolation until fairly recently. A pleased and placid life is lived in well-maintained bodies and houses; there are no beggars; bicycles—hundreds of them—are left unchained in the central plaza. The honesty and trust, along with the well-packed look of most of the citizenry and the clean respectability of their clothing, is a reflection of the rather high economy the island enjoys because of the unbelievable shrimp—both in size and quantity—that the local waters produce. These are the immense prawns that are sold at the price of rubies in the States. (Consequently, there may not be any of the giant shrimp available on Carmen when you're there; it's all been shipped to more profitable places.)

The island gives no indication of having been a pirates' lair for many years; the distractions are few and as wholesome as good bread. In the morning, for instance, you might walk down to the waterfront. The many fishing smacks may be busily loading or unloading, or just cradled in the small harbor, their winches, masts, and nets shaping geometric mobiles against the sky. Then you might wander through the market, not remarkable but no Mexican market is ever colorless. Turn in off the waterfront, and where streets 22 and 25A meet (it's easy to find your way; streets are numbered, the odd crossing the even) you'll find a once-pretty old church in a bright green and red plaza which bears, of course, a statue of Juárez. On the plaza are some impressive Colonial-style houses with good grillwork and pleasant, subdued colors. Around the corner, on Street 22, there is a house completely covered in tiles of muted colors. A block or two away (ask for the *Preparatoria*) is the senior high-and-normal school, housed in an airy, graceful old building, recently renovated with taste and skill. At the far end of town, the cool, fresh buildings of Carmen's university and a huge monument to The Shrimp, odd and appealing after all the outsized heroes that usually greet one dourly.

For lunch you might walk back to the main square, past the too frequently redone church, for platefuls of fresh shrimp at the **Restaurant Cantamar.** The proprietress, born in British Honduras, speaks English quite well and prides herself on the large menu, which includes Corn Flakes and fruit shakes, but you should stay with the fresh local product.

Having fed, take a close look at the bandstand erected in 1886, with its gate ornaments of fleur-de-lis, and the carved wood which is replaced, in exact reproduction, whenever sea and sun have eaten into it. Thursday and Sunday evenings there is music and dancing in this faintly chinoiserie pavilion.

After lunch the town folds its arms and closes its eyes, and you might too, particularly since the night may be noisy. (Axiom for Mexico: the smaller the town, the nosier the night.) The crowds bounce out of the two movie houses at about midnight stimulated to loud conversation no matter what the bill. A few hours later the early risers clank, call, and whistle their way to the boats, trucks thunder to and from the wharves, and the sturdy-voiced radios bellow in concert.

Sit in the square and watch the local traffic: housewives skillfully and atypically speeding by on bicycles, their generous flanks billowing over the small seats and their faces set in the determination of six-day bike riders; motorbikes holding papa, mama, and baby, in the French style; the two-wheeled carts drawn by mules which carry anything the trucks scorn—a mattress, a few chickens sitting in a basin, a small catch of fish, a collapsed bicycle, a delicate lady sitting enthroned like a Mayan goddess. Or, go to one of the local beach places. **Laguna Azul** is large and well kept, with bath houses and a cool open area for dancing, eating, or just sitting in the shade. **La Puntilla** is a little lower in the social scale. It has a few simple little beach shelters and not much else for a visitor's comfort, but the thatched huts and strings of small fishing boats bordered by sea on one side and palms on another are eminently photogenic and/or paintable. (Both places, however, may be turning into big jolly beach resorts.)

A longer stay affords trips on the local ferries to little-known fishing and jungle villages, one on the river Agua Dulce, for instance. This is not advisable unless you have a great deal of time and can live on fish and bananas and sleep in a borrowed hammock if you're held up by any of a number of possibilities or impossibilities. (Inquire at hotels or the Cantamar.)

Evenings are spent at the side of the square. For men there are the numerous pool parlors which serve as local clubs, and new, airy cafés. One café seems to be the chess-domino center and affords the interesting spectacle of chessmen, set in place on the board, being transported on a tin tray, along with the beer and soft drinks. Some of the rest of the cluster are devoted to eating and drinking, and one might eat supper in the style of a "progressive dinner": soup at one café, *panuchos*—the local tortilla plus a bit of meat, a bit of onion, etc., either fried soft (Carmen style) or crisp (Yucatán style)—at another, *tortas*—minor hero sandwiches of turkey on *bolillos*—and coffee at still another.

HOTELS

There are two, which are clean, usable, furnished in no style at all, and modest in price. Since there is rarely a flood of tourists you will probably be able to inspect and choose between the **Hotel Fernandes** (about 60 pesos for two), and the **Zacarías** (about 40 pesos for two).

Gullible tarpon thicken the waters off Isla Aguada, northeast of Carmen, served by one of the ferries. There are some motels near the dock. Both provide boats, guides, etc. (Inquire at agencies in Mexico City.)

FIESTAS

The "Come to the Land of the Fiesta" ads sport seductive girls with ribbons in their shining braids and sequins on their whirling skirts, accompanied by beautiful boys in gleaming white, against a background of gay waters and the suggestion of plangent voices caressing romantic guitars. This is the fiesta of the movies, of tourist galas, of a well-organized civic project in a big town.

The country fiesta is quite another thing—a somewhat thing, a sometimes thing. And the more remote and difficult to get to—via second-class bus, truck, and foot—the more attractive it appears to many tourists, who hope to taste the pure pleasures of the simple life: indigenous, naïve dances in beautiful costumes, happy peasants happily dancing in a happy circle (as they used to in old-fashioned musicals), strange primitive practices to be observed. In actuality, a country fiesta is often an opportunity to see people from neighboring towns, a chance to sell a few tacos and ornaments, an excuse for getting drunk without waiting for Saturday night; in short, a chance to enliven a monotonous existence. The visitor who lives with radios, television, movies, cars, and his own literacy may find it an odd means of "changing life" (as they call it in Mexico), but it is the best available to a peasant. Even the most shapeless fiesta, however, limited to cheap liquor, a few firecrackers, and directionless milling, may produce a particular mood, an unexpected flash of charm and humor. And there are the exoticisms of costume and language, the beauty of facial structure, the curious repose of passive people waiting to be quickened, the erratic tempo—a series of false starts, unexplained bursts of activity, long empty waits, and the constant, aimless walking around. (It might be a comprehensive symbol of rural life: interminable waits after interminable walks.)

Rural fiestas are rarely gay, except in the tropical, coastal towns. A fiesta can have humor, but it is rarely good-humored or consciously funny; it can be dramatic but the drama is unplanned, accidental; the ceremonies are rarely understood by the participants, who do what they did the year before and years before that. It can be planned and raggedly arranged, but at least one of the arrangers too quickly becomes too happy or too sad to carry on and a bewildered substitute is pressed into service. A banner has been mislaid and must be found. Where are the musicians? Where are the fireworks? The priest doesn't like the way things are going and lengthily says so. Tourists must be placed in the inner circle or eased out of it. It all takes time, fascinating time hard on the feet until one consents, like the sensible locals, to sit on the ground.

The above is not at all meant to discourage, but simply to warn that a fiesta is not always a big, gorgeous block party—although it can be; and it can be superbly irrational, mysterious, and moving, or a child's dream of fireworks and flowers. Unless there is too much trouble involved getting there, try any fiesta you might hear of, dressed in your most modest clothes, most comfortable shoes, and best brand of patient curiosity. In general, the state of Oaxaca stages beautiful fiestas compounded of sound pride, lovely regional costumes, tasteful flower arrangements and tall *castillos* (towers) of ingenious fireworks. Chiapas ceremonies are pagan, alluring, and frightening; some regions simplify to eating, singing, dancing, and drinking, leaving church meanings in a misty background (especially true of the irreverent tropics, which are devoted to present laughter—and who cares about the rest). Religious pilgrimages, shows of horsemanship, of hilariously inept bullfighting, of giant papier-mâché caricatures, of floats of religious or historical figures can be fiestas. Any gathering of Mexicans not specifically a paying audience can be a fiesta.

No matter what its basic design, the party holds the seeds of indelible possibilities: An improvised bull ring made of criss-crossed beams and branches holds on its narrow, top ledge a load of audience perched like sparrows on telephone wires. A domesticated, peaceable bull just whipped into the enclosure looks around with mild interest, decides he wants out, and goes directly for a piece of fence already occupied by dangling legs. The legs lift, scramble, fall to the other side, and try to find a perch again, unsteadied by tequila and laughter. One of the fallen, a toothless little man weighing one hundred pounds—including his heroic absorption of mescal and beer—decides to fight the bull. Waving his tattered shirt, he dances, sidesteps, slips, roars, stamps, and lurches before the bull, who looks on blandly, a monument of calm. The man, in a frenzy of frustration and *machismo,* teases and taunts the bull, taps it, pokes at it. The bull looks at the audience for confirmation of his disdain. Maddened by the bull's contempt, the man darts behind it, lifts and pulls its tail, then bites it hard. The animal, feet still stubbornly planted, turns his head languidly, stares for an aristocratic moment at the frantic man, and goes back to surveying his public.

Or, you might see a drunken man charging another with a limp, tattered banana frond as if in serious, murderous jousting. He is amazed and infuriated that repeated charges produce not blood, but the impotent, musical rustle of frayed leaf.

Or, you might watch the fine, painstaking building of a high fireworks tower and later see it explode in dazzling stages: the first ring a burst of flowers, the next a clump of Mexican flags flickering and waving, the next a show of bulls and *toreros* teasing each other, then upward and upward to thunderous rockets and showers of gold.

Or, you might participate in the tourist game of how chummy can you get without courting trouble? Should an American drink, and how much, with the dim-eyed splutterer hanging amorously from his shoulder? What happens if he refuses to drink to moist Yanqui-American friendships? That couple being offered sugared water, the drink of saints-washing-and-dressing day, delicately tainted with fresh flowers, picked where? Should they drink it and its uncertainties? How little can they drink and still stay safe internally as well as socially? Can they spurn it altogether and hurt the feelings of the pleasant old lady and the saints she washed and dressed today? The possibilities are worrisome and infinitely varied.

There is hardly a day when there isn't some sort of fiesta going on. Hagiography makes a crowded calendar; commemorative celebrations of an eventful history crowd it further. Every village has its saint's day, and the *barrios* of larger towns each have theirs. There are the miracle saints and Virgins who call forth long pilgrimages; Carnival, which is celebrated in one gaudy way or another everywhere, and especially full of bibulous affection and music in the coastal towns; the numerous sets of fiestas which flow into each other from early in December through Epiphany; the dance fiestas of Oaxaca during the latter part of July; the remarkable flight of *voladores* from the tall pole of Papantla on Corpus Christi Day; Huauchinango's beautiful flower festival, which takes place the third week in Lent. Holy Week frequently expresses itself in penitential pilgrimages and in reenactments of the Passion, but the borders of solemnity often turn into *fiestacitas,* and where a town is not too worried about the law which forbids it, Judas (more Mephistopheles than Hebrew) is strung up and exploded on Holy Saturday. The Tehuantepec area often holds its weddings on Sunday. For a peso one gets a drink, a cigarette, a paper flag, and the right to watch the ritual processions—the groom and men to the bride's house, women bringing food and drink to the groom's house—the confetti-throwing, the dancing, and the magnificence of Tehuanas on show.

Following, you will find a sampling of a few fiestas of different regions and moods. For fiesta dates that especially suit your schedule, pick up a copy of *Esta Semana, Mexico This Month,* the *Mexico City News,* the *Bulletin,* and any of the free pamphlets on hotel desks or at Pemex, Juárez 89, in Mexico City.

SANTA MARÍA DEL TULE

Having put aside the flags, the broad white, green, and red banners, taken out and stored the millions of light bulbs that pearled buildings and plazas, reduced the splash of fountains to a trickle, taken down the portraits of Father Hidalgo, muted the rococo oratory which trumpeted through September to celebrate its independence, Mexico eases into simpler pleasures in October. This is the time of agricultural fairs and harvest fiestas; one of the loveliest takes place early in October in Santa María del Tule of the famous tree, a few miles from Oaxaca.

The town is ordinarily seclusive; the only visible life is that of little girls in top-heavy *rebozo* turbans who sell fruits in season and offer to escort tourists around the great *ahuehuete* tree, pointing out various limb configurations—the lion, the elephant, the alligator. On fiesta days the girls have other things to do and one finds one's own zoo in the twisted bark.

Mexican towns wake early but on fiesta days they wake up earlier and more noisily. Excited, babbling girls dash back and forth with water to fill the tubs standing outside the doors, then help scrub the younger children, not yet quite awake and outraged at the damp, vigorous assault. Arches of cane and bamboo, prepared days before, are placed across the paths and studded, laced, and looped with pink and yellow roses, white and peach-colored gladiolas, bronze, copper, and purple dahlias, giant daisies, grasses, and fruits. Slow oxen, garlanded in leaves, are hitched to broad, two-wheeled carts, and the carts heaped with corn, melons, white onions, peppers, tomatoes, quince, pineapples, and girls. The girls echo the fruit-and-flower theme: ripe dusky peaches in the heavily embroidered, white-edged skirts and *huipiles* of Tehuantepec, in the long, loose white dress of Yalalag, or in their best pink city dresses.

As the day lengthens, the *cantina* becomes an orchestra of popping beer bottles, the rolling of kegs of pulque, the gurgle of tequila, the voices of pleased men ambling in a field of friendship and beer. The narrow lanes fill with people from the surrounding villages and the city, lured by the smell of barbecued kid—crisp, brown, hot, basted with a spicy sauce, eaten off fingers and tortillas, and sluiced down by Mexican beer. (This might be as good a place as any to advise that every menu which carries English or near-English translations backs away, in concern for American delicacy, from translating *cabrito* as "kid"; it always appears, unexplained, as *cabrito* again.)

In the afternoon, a small orchestra starts up in the ample atrium of the church, and everyone, except the shy mountain Indians, the bartenders, and the barbecue tenders, dances under and around the great, hoary cypress tree. Bottles are passed from mouth to mouth; tourists are flirted with, plied with liquor, whirled, pulled, and shaken to the high-paced music, taught Spanish, and wrapped in boozy skeins of *amistad.*

As night falls, the music stops, the fires are put out, the carcasses are thrown to the waiting dogs. The slightly tipsy crowd, replete with good will and roast kid, starts to disperse. The lanterns of the hill people flicker like fireflies in the distance, the valley people answer the blinking summonses of the swollen old country buses, the cars of the city people slide into the sober night. Only the *cantina* keeps going for the two die-hards who can still lift a glass and direct it to their mouths, unconcerned that the lantern on the bar is running out of fuel, and the bartender too.

SAN JUAN'S DAY OR SAN PEDRO'S *(Chamula)*

The day of San Juan is celebrated on June 24; since it is also, tacitly, the Day of the Rain God (San Pedro shares responsibility), festivities start at noon of the twenty-third, in accordance with the pre-Cortesan calculation of hours. On the other hand, fiestas wind up slowly, and it is just as well to follow the Christian calendar.

San Juan Chamula is about twenty minutes out of Las Casas, through a bucolic arrangement of greenery, sheep, and thatched houses leading into a large pasture-plaza surrounded by crosses set up in groups of twos and threes. (Like the crosses of Yalalag and Palenque, these are thought by some scholars to be pre-Christian.) At ten in the morning the field is crowded with masses of Chamulas and Zinacantecans in the handsome costumes of the region, wandering, drinking, greeting each other, while the women and children sit quietly, in whispering dark clusters, nursing babies, feeding older children, and themselves eating small bits constantly and delicately, like young animals grazing. Some of the women, particularly the Zinacantecans, are attractively dressed in clean pin-striped white and many lengths of necklace made of beads and ribbons. Others are unkempt, ragged, and seem frightened, clinging to children who have the savage appeal of bear cubs. Under the dirt one can discern the lovely, dark, rich skin color and the beautiful design of their faces—if they don't turn away or bend downward to avoid a stranger's eye.

At the wide, arched entrance to the church, the major-domos of the fiesta, wearing straw hats laden with coiled ribbons and bearing staffs (some tipped with silver), consult with each other, direct, shout orders, with no visible results. The shapeless, dense movement flows in its accustomed fiesta way to and from the plaza and in and out of the church. The large church is almost bare—no pews other than a crude, high set of stepped benches, no church art other than a stone set of saints—dour, primitive, and forceful, like early medieval sculpture. Garlands of palm fronds stuck with paper flowers hang from the walls and the front of the altar, and a few paper flowers decorate a corner of the church railed off for the rapid baptism—out of a round washbasin—of insulted, squalling babies.

All over the vast pine-strewn floor family groups set up clusters of slender white candles and kneel, weep, and pray before them in Mayan and Spanish. Later they leave the candles—a field of white and flickering yellow—to continue the prayers for them. Deep in the church, a group is busy dressing San Juan, the Virgin, and another saint or two in their new clothes, vivid rectangles of flowered cloth. Those of the years before are not removed, and the accumulated shapeless wrappings below the meaningless white doll faces give the saints a diseased, obscene look, more totem than Christian. The newly dressed saints are brushed with bunches of herbs and greens (a fertility gesture?), and urns of *copal,* an Indian incense used long before the Conquest, are passed along the folds of their clothing.

The excited sartorial discussions around the saints, the murmur of hundreds of private prayers, the louder prayers of a standing delegation of beautifully dressed men sent to talk with God and San Juan (probably about the need for rain) by a neighboring community, the crying of babies, the yelp of a dog being kicked out of the church, the running back and forth of little boys, the busyness of the priest and his acolytes, the commands of the major-domos, the color of the costumes add up to our picture of market rather than church, and yet there is mystery under the confusion.

Outside the church, toward noon, fireworks are set going, the fireworks bulls chased and lassoed by men in tall, bushy hats of fur. A group of young men in white, wearing beribboned hats, their graceful legs bare, wander through the busy yard strumming their homemade guitars and accordions. On a rise outside the church, men in striped cotton tailcoats and fur busbies dance in the small-spaced walk-stomp-hop of Indian dances, waving banners of bright printed cotton, topped by great streamers of green-blue, red, and yellow ribbon. Behind them stands the painted box in which banners and saints' clothes are kept. (Don't try to make your way too near the box; it is sacred, you unknown, and the keepers of the box are ecstatic with religion and drink. Stay on the sidelines throughout the fiesta, hug the walls of the church as you go in and out, take your pictures as unobtrusively as possible—or not at all.)

The dancing, the praying, the drinking, the male restlessness, and the female patience continue and continue, until the collapse of most of the dancers and musicians, who sleep the drink off wherever they might drop. Only the older women—and few of them—have the courage to wake the men; the others wait with their sleeping children until the master gives the signal. (Long before that, though, you should have left for Las Casas.)

DAY OF SAN MIGUEL *(San Miguel de Allende)*

Saint Michael's Day falls on September 29 and is expanded to the whole weekend—and longer—nearest that day in San Miguel de Allende. On Friday afternoon, the carefully clipped trees in the *zócalo* sprout paper roses of pink, aqua, and purple, the face of the clock in the parochial church takes on the colors of the national flag, and later the churches are especially lit for a duet between the deep declivities and heavy encrustations of pseudo-Gothic and Mexican baroque.

Early on Saturday morning (about four o'clock) a procession with music, banners, and lanterns makes its way to the cathedral, to bombard the church with fireworks. Since the church remains undamaged it is clear that the assault by Lucifer and his band of bad angels could not withstand the might of the protector, San Miguel. Having triumphed, San Miguel must now be honored. At about 10:30 A.M. the town's population of schoolchildren, all tailored, starched, and white-gloved, accompanied by their teachers, with umbrellas against the sun, march through the town followed by soldiers, bands, a girls' fife-and-drum corps, all orderly and pleasantly lacking in military snap.

Saturday afternoon is drowsy. The town's schoolchildren are resting at home, the women and children who trudged in early for the bombardment are lying or sitting out of the sun under the *portales,* sunk in sleep or Indian waiting, distant and yet sharply, immediately aware. Around them rise the smells of chicken cooking (one of the delicacies used to be head, beak, eyes, and all), tacos sizzling, soups, barbecued meats. In a café on the corner blond tourists are trying to appear untouched by a plate of *huevos rancheros picante.* Near them, unconscious of fiesta, travelers, Indians, churches, and San Miguel, sit a pair of chess players wearing the look of contained fury indigenous to chess players.

Outside the town near the railroad station, groups of *concheros* begin to gather. These "shell people" are an association, particularly active in Guanajuato and Querétaro, said to stem from fraternities which existed before the Conquest. They take vows of ethical conduct and religion, observe a few pagan-Christian rites, and, most especially, preserve the old dances in the noble, ancient costumes— wide flourishing capes, embroidered shields, tall, plumed head-dresses, sequined robes, spangles, beads, mirrored platelets, worn with monumental dignity. As they march to town they carry with them the *suchiles,* structures of carefully arranged flowers and pearly cactus to be set up near the entrance to the cathedral. Then, accompanied by the music of their armadillo-backed lutes and the dried shell on their ankles, they dance tirelessly through most of the hours of the fiesta. There is considerable intricacy in their steps and variety in the dance patterns and, once in a while, two virtuosi dance a pantomime of combat which is marvelously graphic and artful. Even if you can't get close enough to see the steps, four groups of *concheros*—capes swirling, plumes waving, beads and mirrors flashing to the rhythm of two hundred lutes and ankle bells—are a mesmerizing sight.

On Saturday night, the universal Saturday night takes over. While the *cantinas* shout conviviality and *mariachi* music, some of the visitors settle themselves to sleep on the grass and benches of the *zócalo.* Several little boys in new, too-large blue jeans and stiff caps of straw droop on their fathers' shoulders. Three dark, small wands of girls, all dressed alike in shapeless new rayon dresses, too obviously home-made and salmon-pink, walk silently around and around the plaza absorbing every glittering, strange detail of the great day in the city. On Sunday, the school parade is repeated in identical detail except that, this time, it stops at the corner near the church, to be addressed by the principal of the school. The band obliges with excerpts from

Aïda and then gives way to the *concheros,* who are ready to begin again after a few hours' rest. Some of the crowd drifts toward the market, which has become a fair, with games and rides and a fat, young, tough lady snake handler in tight pants. She is her own barker and her own cashier, making change, biting into doubtful coins, while she watches her tarantulas climb along the walls of the pit and slaps off the snake in her hair. As always, the country crowd stands transfixed, but lets no sound or expression escape its face.

At the same time the bull ring, a short distance out from the center, begins to swallow up the *aficionados.* The card usually lists good names—fiesta crowds assure an audience and a good take—but the luminaries may not feel like working too hard or the bulls may be unworkable; it might be ridiculous or it might be glorious.

Back in the plaza, the texture thickens. The sun is strong and the dust heavy, vendors of plastic toys and oranges bawl above the sounds of the band and the tinkle of *conchero* lutes; religion, awe, sweat, drink, and the importunities of beggars seep through the quiet, quiet masses of Indians and their utterly silent children. As night falls, four large, valiant groups of dancers are still turning and stepping before the church, ultimately giving way to a fall of fireworks which covers the church in shimmering cloaks of color. Great paper globes, wafted by the heat from the candles attached to them, blaze up in the night air or disappear among the stars.

The plaza empties, the sleepers sleep, the tired children trot homeward, the vendors close their stalls, the soup lady wraps her pot in a cloth and ties it over her shoulder, the bottles are taken off the stands and clinked back into boxes. In the corner café the *toreros* are dividing the day's earnings, and near them and worlds away sit the chess players, bent, intent, belligerent.

DAY OF GUADALUPE

Juan Diego saw the Virgin of Guadalupe, according to the legend, several times early in December, but the specific day dedicated to her is December 12, reaching back into the evening and night of the eleventh and even earlier, when bands of pilgrims begin to gather for their long walks to the Sanctuary in Mexico City.

It has long been poor and holy, this area of the city which is called La Villa. According to locals there was here a burial ground for penitents (one still sees them in brown robes or flagellating themselves during Easter processions in the country or buying scourges at Atotonilco, not far from San Miguel de Allende). Near the burial ground, vestiges of a subterranean nunnery whose inhabitants came out only at night to pray in a small church attached to the basilica.

On the broad street below, Misterios, a dense market, the kind that has surrounded especially holy places, here and elsewhere, for centuries. Among the holy medals and chromos of holy figures are found tacos and soups, toys and toothpaste, cheap pocketbooks and tinselly jewelry; beggar girls with babies, little boys in penitents' gowns. On the tangential big street, Fray Juan de Zumaraga, stiff, colorful jelled sweets, gaudy balloon-balls, and souvenir booklets about the basilica. Among the bright jollities are the crawling supplicants hoping for miracle cures. A man spreads a blanket for his very old mother to make her slow, twisted progress and then spreads it again, and again as she inches up the stairs and into the vast atrium. A woman wearing homemade shoes of goat fur pulls her body along with a stick keeping pace with her daughter, who is moving along on her knees. Babies in arms seem extraordinarily quiet, solemn-faced, held in the arms of their creeping parents.

The perilously slanting old church buildings appear much more appropriate to this primitive devoutness and pain than does the new Basilica of Guadalupe. It is a large circle topped with a slanted cone, laced with rather pedestrian stained glass and enamel plaques that repeat the traditional fish-and-wheat-with-grapes designs. Above the polished wooden pews, immense clusters of modern lamps hang from a wooden ceiling arranged in drapery folds which shelter several balloons loosed by young hands. A stray dog sleeps through a sermon. Somehow this acute modernism appears especially startling on December 12, when crawling lines reach far into Misterios, as far as the markers which look like small Roman arches that point the way to miracles.

A happier way to spend December 12 is to go to the bullfight at Tlalnepantla, a northern suburb of the city. (Check with the hotel desk to make sure it's on.) The ring is small and festive, garlanded with loops of green, and frequently dedicated on Guadalupe's Day to a benefit *corrida* for aged and injured bullfighters. The performing *toreros* are retired bullfighters who managed to elude successfully the ravages of horns, of obscurity, and, less successfully, of time. Their own glittering *trajes* won't fit over small pot bellies any more, but they still look like demigods as they strut out in arrogant hard black hats, tight trousers, and short jackets. The bulls are usually small but good, the style is courtly, the mood lightly aristocratic. Now and then, one of the distinguished *hidalgos* forgets the weight of years and performs a slow, close turn with the bull dancing with him the great duet, but the general effect is of a pretty, tasteful travesty of the high, serious art and a very engaging way to spend a holiday afternoon.

NIGHT OF THE DEAD *(Janitzio)*

Animecha-kejtsitaku, the Tarascan term for the offerings to the dead, takes place on the nights of November 1 and 2. It is a ceremony of reconciliation, of mutual consolation and propitiation (one never quite knows what the dead might do). The fishermen of the communities bordering Lake Pátzcuaro go out on November 1 to bring down ducks, the day's delicacy, to be cooked and placed on the graves of the dead. Traditionally, the ducks were killed with lances which, properly hurled, could catch them in full flight; more recently, the sound of guns marks the hunt.

Back at home on Janitzio, the women are cooking other dishes favored by their dead, ironing the embroidered cloths on which the food will be served, brushing out their wide, long skirts of homespun wool, washing the children, and spreading out their best clothes. They put the final touches to the grave decorations of marigolds (the flower of the dead), autumn fruits, sugar angels, and death's heads, arranged on structures which might suggest a gravestone, a cross, an arched doorway of a house. At about ten o'clock that night, they will take their food offerings to the church and place them for blessing on a long table especially set up and decorated; some of the food will be left for those souls who have no family to feed and console them. Between midnight and one o'clock, the women and children will then bring their food and flower-fruit headstones to the graves, set them up carefully, light their numerous small candles among the dishes and flowers, and settle down for the vigil through the night.

In Tzintzuntzan, the men accompany the women to the graves, or, at least, visit with them and, becoming cold and restless at about three in the morning, build big, warm bonfires, cook up strong hot brews of coffee and tequila, sing, laugh, and chase each other around the graves. Outside of Mexico City, a village church is hung with pictures made by the local children in commemoration of the day and prizes given for the best. It is much more solemn on Janitzio—possibly because of the dignified and taciturn Tarascan character, possibly because of the somber drama of the setting of its graveyard high on the steep island, the village and lake below, a stand of tall rock above. Quite possibly, the thousands of tourists—women who wear pants and men who wear unlikely sweaters—staring at them, crowding them, nipping on bottles to fight the cold, and, above all, the constant lightning of flash bulbs, disturbs them and makes them self-conscious and silent.

Neither the cold, nor the organized entertainment of regional dances and speeches held—after interminable delays—in the open, stone-seated school stadium, nor the camera-eyed crowds in carnival mood can erase entirely the beauties of the island or the vigil of still, hieratic figures.

Unlike the rest of the crowd, go early, just before sunset, as the sun pours streamers of colors over the lake, And watch as the shore and the mounds of green island slip into the night, and pale house lights begin to glow under the tiled roofs. Groups of two and three women mount the steep paths to the church, their full skirts brushing the lanterns held by the children who accompany them. The church bells ring slowly and softly, a few voices sing out in unison from the brightly lit church. The paths become increasingly crowded soon after and the mood changes, to change back again at twelve o'clock, when the graves are set with the feast for the dead.

NOTE: Wear warm stockings, extra socks, and sweaters, and take a blanket along. A flask of brandy is a good idea, but don't flourish it and don't try to stay all night (there is no profit in it and the earlier the better for getting a place in a boat back to Pátzcuaro).

In other communities the ritual time is broader: for some days the bakeshops have been selling *pan dulces* shaped like a man, rivulets of red-dyed sugar running down his body for blood and heavier drops of clear sugar as tears.

For a couple of days before the vigil night families walk with flowers and wreathes, a loose procession, to decorate their graves. First, many dig lightly at the earth on the graves, freeing the passage of new air to the dead man and destroying weeds that might strangle him. One man covers a grave with a carpet of many-colored stones; a woman covers her child's grave with purple flowers and marigolds. An old woman, heavy and lame, lies at the side of her son's grave, scraping at the earth with her hands while her grandson digs with a child's shovel. Then everyone gathers on a broad path, early in the afternoon, to sing hymns, most of them with the lilt of old sentimental waltz tunes. Some go home to return at night; many stay through the day, prepared with bundles of food, and into the night until dawn.

CHRISTMAS IN THE TROPICS

The sun burns out the serious intent of Christmas and leaves it a limp Carnival. It fades and shrinks the balloons hung on papaya trees and dulls the red of a jolly Coca-Cola Santa Claus who shouts from shop windows, *"Feliz Navidad y Próspero Año Nuevo,"* and stretches the poinsettia in front of thatched houses to lanky, tropical heights. No one knows fir trees and snow, so the incomprehensible northern symbols are translated into beards of Spanish moss dotted with absorbent cotton. No one thinks it peculiar to set up a crèche sprinkled with cotton snow under a tree heavy with ripe oranges.

From the yellow, blue, and ocher churches comes the sound of recordings of "Holy Night" and "Noel" in English, competing with the squalling babies being baptized—Christmas Eve is a lucky time for baptisms—and from the *cantinas*, "Jingle Bells" sung as *"Navidad, Navidad"* in hot Afro-Cuban rhythm. Under the holy sounds, like a constant wash of waters, is the slap and shuffle of the Japanese rubber sandal worn by all the women and children, at all times except confirmations and weddings.

The big, big Christmas tree here becomes the big, big crèche as crowded as village fairs and taking up all the space of the *sala* from which the customary furniture and the white, unconnected, unfunctioning refrigerator have been removed. (The *sala* almost always fronts on the street, and its shutters are closed against the sun during the day; nighttime is the time for crèche-viewing.)

Since it dances at the drop of a tune all year round, almost any town will have a *"Gran Baile"* on Christmas Eve or Night, or both, with considerable chic in Mérida and much more flavor in San Andrés or Catemaco, where it will be held on the upper floor of the town hall decorated with crisscrossed paper streamers dripping Spanish moss and slack balloons. Mamas and Indian ladies from nearby sugar plantations sit stolidly on the backless benches which ring the dance floor. The light is neither gay nor romantically dim, simply meager.

The marimba, two horns, and one drum keep a vigorous, sure beat while the tunes wander listlessly. Like a country fiesta, a country dance takes a leisured pace toward liveliness; the first two hours or so is a dance of wooden puppets: awkward, self-conscious boys and frozen-faced girls tramping tight squares. Much later, the feet become light and the hips juicier, the guarded faces break into smiles and conversation, the floor becomes more crowded with late arrivals, and the stamp of high life is set with the entrance of the town "bad woman" and her man. No matter how densely packed the floor is, a barrier of space is set between the good girls and evil. The large buttocks in a short, tight satin skirt have plenty of room in which to weave and bounce and the slick black-suited man with slick black hair over the smooth anonymity of dark glasses has space to thrust her and pull her back while he admires the deep cut of her clinging red blouse. The mamas don't give them a glance. The maternal lips fold tighter, the eyes grow smaller and sharper, the arms clasp each other more firmly across the matronly chests; suddenly, they all look like statues of Juárez.

Campeche

The Mayan village of Ah Kim Pech, later hispanicized to Campeche, had the distinction of being subject to a foreign visit even before the years of the Conquest proper. Córdoba and his party landed in 1517, but weakened by recent battle and feeling menaced by the large crowds of Indians gathering around blood-stained altars, withdrew in dignified haste.

In the course of the next twenty-three years the locals, worn with struggles among Mayan groups, lost some of their talent for formidability and the town was conquered by Montejo in 1540 after years of bitter fighting, no gentlemen's rules on either side. Having subdued the town with immense loss of life and usefulness, Spain stamped it with the royal seal of Charles III, calling it the "City of San Francisco of Campeche," in the usual manner of combining a saint's name with an approximation of the pagan name . . . and then neglected it.

Pirates found it worth concentrated attention, however; in 1597, Campeche was taken by William Parck; in 1631, by Diego the Mulatto; thirteen years later, by Jacob Jackson, the English corsair; the Dutch pirate Laurent de Graff burned a good part of the city and its ships in 1672 and was permitted to return for an encore in 1685. It was not until a year after "Lorencillo" made his second visit, almost a hundred years after the first pirate assault, that the authorities decided to make Campeche a walled city, which it remained for two hundred years.

It is an exhausting history and Campeche is tired—not too tired to be polite and pleasant to the visitor but not yet too energetic in the seductions and posturings of a tourist city. For instance, it comes as a surprise to discover that four well-known antique Mayan cities—Uxmal, Kabah, Labná, and Sayil (and a few obscure ones)—are about midway between Mérida and Campeche. Campeche hardly mentions them—probably because they are on the border with Yucatán or altogether in that rival state—Mérida wears them as crown jewels. Campeche fishes extraordinarily flavorful small shrimp and weaves fine Panama-style straws in its damp caves. Who knows about them? The local tortoiseshell is plentiful and well worked, Veracruz sells much more of it, often inferior. Tourism is served mainly by a slab of hotel, boxlike and busy. It rose out of a meeting of two strong forces: a Campechano who refused to pay his enormous tax bill and a governor who wanted to attract tourism via kidney-shaped pool and terraced seaside hotel. The deal: the reluctant non-taxpayer built the hotel, turning from robber baron to public benefactor.

Cement, the symbol of progress, has been poured as plazas, as tall spines of giant concrete cactus, as flying saucers. And, adjoining an *avant* government building and ancient section of fortress, as coiled, white, large concrete things emerging from curious pools. Also, there may be a large trailer camp along the sea and practically in town by this time, still another invasion, this time by the gentle elderly traveling in long trails of self-sufficient aluminum boxes on wheels. Yet, Campeche still buys its water from two-wheeled carts.

Campeche is a good twenty-four-hour town; an undemanding city, easily attained. On the waterfront there is the sea to stare at and at the southwestern end of town (Lerma), nets and fishing boats, strong sea smells, and small ships in the making. The recently restored old fortress arches along the sea wall give meaning to the ruined heaps of stone which once protected the city. The Archaeological Museum, a short distance east of the big **Hotel Baluartes,** occupies a section of the old fortifications, its hoary walls circling a small garden and a neat, modest display of artifacts—copies and originals—of a number of Indian cultures, mainly Mayan. The pièce is the Jaina room, which has a reproduction of the burial arrangements found on the island of Jaina (two hours away by launch from Campeche), where the skeleton was placed in a fetal position and surrounded by lovely figurines now sufficiently costly and rare to be expensively faked.

A block or two westward, also part of the sea-wall structure, is the Museo de las Armas, filled with embattled disuse—silenced harquebuses, muskets, and pistols in dim cases; Dutch, French, and Oriental powder caskets now as impotent as powder puffs; great swords, daggers, hatchets, sabers, lances, their lightning extinguished. On the walls hang some interesting etchings of old pirate ships and portraits of the pirates, including John Hawkins (here spelled "Jhon") and Henry Morgan, both in ruffs and curls, looking very much like Spanish grandees or English nobles or successful pirates. An upper ramp leads to a row of old cannons sitting like grotesque brood hens among the yield of rusty cannonballs, and beyond them stretch the unbusy road, the long mute shore, and the shrimp boats riding the green sea.

To the right, as one faces the sea, the broad sea-front avenue stops at a set of arches and becomes, a few streets inland, market alleys with the usual, meticulously arranged small tomatoes and giant radishes. In the geometric shine of red-brown bags of dried roe, of snapper and pompano placed head to tail, the fishwives in white embroidered Mayan *huipiles* stand peeling with infinite patience and care thousands of the minuscule local shrimp, or cooking portions of fresh-caught fish, served on a piece of paper or a banana leaf. (Some of it will be small shark; if you're squeamish, ask which is *cazón* and avoid it.) Among the stalls that stray from the central food sections it is possible to find the brilliant wooden toys—dotted, flowered, striped, wildly colored—which are becoming rare, crude wooden chocolate churns which serve attractively as spice mortar and pestle, and woven baskets whose charm is coarse, but *auténtico;* also, begemmed live beetles.

The university (and secondary school) is a skillfully rebuilt structure. The free, broad sweep of the entrance arches is echoed by inner arches which give onto a big inner court whose severity is softened by open patterns cut into the concrete walls. Off to one side is a small, well-arranged art gallery of Mexican paintings, not always the best, but there are few exhibitions in this part of Mexico and the very existence of a gallery with changing shows is cherished here. Whether your interest is art or not, the building is the experience—the whole yellow and white, cool, intelligent structure.

Campeche at night is quiet and more secretive—more respectable—than other tropical towns: the thrusting open of street-level windows revealing décor and humanity is not a habitual gesture, but here and there a blown curtain reveals a lawyer's Dickensian office in a covering of learned dust, cracked old tomes reaching to the ceiling, and an old-fashioned rotating octagonal bookcase in the exact middle of the room. A *sala* comes into view. The angry, heavy furniture stands stiffly, immortally, where it was placed sixty years ago. Ornate vases thrust spiky wax flowers through the dead air. High on the walls are family photographs, in dark, thick frames like tombs. In an honored necropolis corner is a huge portrait of a mustached pre-Revolution gentleman flanked by a funerary wreath of black and white beads on one side, and on the other by mama in a rocking chair, all in black, her face an old fortress, staring into time. She is almost as terrifying as the immense Mayan torso holding a torch (electric light inside) in his tensed gigantic hand who greets you on the highway. (One often wishes that Mexico will altogether recover from the Olympics and the flood of execrable art it loosened.)

HOTELS

The **Hotel Baluartes,** balconied and well kept, has a pool. The rooms on the sea side are more expensive, but the view from the cheaper rooms of the old scarred sea walls is pleasant in the early afternoon light. Moderate. There is a big restaurant at the side of the pool, moderate but not as cheap as some others, and service, in the tourist season, is slow and forgetful. Order *lisa* (a local fish), pompano, snapper, shrimps.

The **López** is in from the waterfront, 198 on Calle 12; has solicitous service, a large cool bar and restaurant. Moderate.

The **Hotel Colonial,** Calle 14, near 55, is usable and modest in price.

RESTAURANTS

The **Miramar** restaurant, on the waterfront, offers quite satisfactory seafood. Try the tiny local shrimp in a cocktail and any of the fish on the menu.

See what the **Baluartes** or the **López** are offering or try the *panuchos* in one of the places near the market.

NOTE: The tortoiseshell in the market is sometimes fairly expensive and not always authentic. If you are seriously interested, go to a workshop on Calle 57, number 10.

A trip to Jaina, where there are still some ruins which produced the superb figurines, is a fair distance by boat. It will cost about 400 pesos for the day and from all reports is not worth it to most travelers.

ENVIRONS

Lerma offers swimming, and farther south and west is the beach at Champotón, where the Spaniards were badly beaten on their first foray into this coast. There are simple dressing rooms and refreshments available and not too many clients ordinarily. Watch for the enchanting thatched hamlets that meander in the river at Puente Chumpan and Puente Candelaria. And notice (this is true of the south in general) how much of jungle is being and was cleared for grazing. As busily, some beaches are preparing for resort hotels like **Sihoplaya,** between Champotón and Campeche.

One can take a blind stab at almost any point in coastal Yucatán and be sure of hitting an archaeological zone, jungle-covered or stripped to its Mayan shape.

About 15 miles from Campeche you should begin to see the oval adobe and thatched huts which mean Yucatán, and in stretches of ranch country, cowherders on horses who use red traffic flags to protect their cattle at crossings. Masterful riders, serious and alert, they look like medieval knights leading troops: one red banner at the front of the line, one in back, and two or three at the sides to keep the troops in tight formation. You might pass a considerable number of boys riding bareback, imitating the haughty gaucho style or a picture of young marriage, rural style. He is on a horse shaded by an umbrella; she walks in front wearing his stiff, curly hat.

Forty to forty-five kilometers out of Campeche, traveling eastward, you should come to a highway sign that indicates "Edzna," at the end of a road that is still rough but fortunately not very long, and in repair. The village is an insignificant hollow of oval huts and women in shabby cheap *huipiles,* lost in the thick matting of low jungle. The rest is a landscape of covered ruin mounds and piles of rock, most of it already numbered to rebuild the temples of the Old Mayan Empire that stood here. Rebuilding is as laborious as the original building: each man carrying one marked stone up narrow steps under a hot, moist tropical sun. Several temples should be complete soon; one is already an imposing white temple with short columns and flat at the top, rather Greek; another shows the decorative roof lace of Palenque although not as delicate. As you climb around still-unfinished areas, watch out for tumbling rocks, uncertain in their places or discarded as wrong fits. There is, by the way, a second-class bus that comes here from Campeche; ask for the schedule in the tourist office there. And don't try to slip any carved or painted sherds into your pocket; there are very alert and zealous young archaeologists always on the grounds.

These are fine fishing waters—as the market and restaurants will attest to—but organized sports fishing is rare (people who live by fishing hardly ever find it sport). To size the situation up you might ask at the desk, *"Dónde se puede pescar por aquí?"* and see what that brings.

CAMPECHE TO MÉRIDA

The road from Campeche to Mérida runs smoothly over a flat countryside of brush and henequen and white Mayan villages, rising once to a small hill, a phenomenal thing in this sea-level country.

The ride can be made in three and a half hours, but there is no point in rushing. Stop at Hopelchén, 56 miles out, and walk around the gaunt old Franciscan church and, if it's open, in its cloistered walk, and stare at the startling blue concrete plaza. In the square someone will be selling *arepas,* hot flat cookies baked on paper; thirty centavos for the very thin one, fifty centavos for thicker ones, and *suspiros,* a variation at thirty centavos. About 20 miles beyond, the road goes through Bolonchenticul, which is a collection of fat, round, whitewashed Mayan houses (in contour and color, enlarged shadows of the Mayan housewife) topped with deep palmetto thatch. Near Bolonchenticul is the cave of the Nine Wells which has, inevitably, its legend of an unhappy Mayan girl—beautiful, of course—who hid from a forbidden or unrequited love here. The descent is dramatic, stalactite-hung, and the fish that swim in the wells purportedly blind cave fish.

About two hours out of Campeche, the road passes Kabah and Uxmal, and soon reveals a vista of ranches, a few windmills, and stretches of henequen in long scrubby rows like green toothbrush bristles; and a procession of white villages inhabited by Mayans with high-bridged noses and thin jaws like those of the nobles of Palenque, and fat Mayans with fleshy faces and narrow eyes like Eskimos', all living in the shadow of enormous little-used churches.

THE LIGHT AND THE DARK

Like all human beings, Mexicans are a swamp of contradictions, which you may notice in *them* more sharply because you bring a fresh eye—or should.

The attitude toward death, as one example, has been marveled at for its insouciance, its playfulness. Don't they eat cakes and candies shaped like skulls on the Day of the Dead? Don't they make skeleton toys for the children, and big papier-mâché Deaths for decoration, and caricature their politicians as death's-heads? This bespeaks an acknowledgment and even intimacy that we avoid, but it doesn't necessarily mean fearlessness; it might mean a fear which calls for elaborate propitiation.

A young child's burial is a fairly calm, even pretty act because the child has been spared the agonies of this world and its own sin and goes directly to heaven to become an angel. Other deaths can be ringed with fear and superstition, in spite of the solace offered by the church, if it is understood. The servant in a household which has had a death will be shunned by others who don't want to be touched by the bad luck; a delayed burial is frightening because the body wants to go into the earth and suffers in the air of the living. For days after the death the women will go back repeatedly to the sounds, the sights, the dreams which were all premonitions. Death is no less fearsome than it is to us; it knocks more often in Mexico and must more frequently be admitted.

Mexico has an old habit and history of violence (the fine, elegant princes of Palenque were warriors, Toltec artists were conquerors). Present-day Pablo might kill a man who insulted him but he could not conceive of the cool, impersonal crimes of Nazidom or building a shelter whose machine gun would keep out his neighbor's children. In view of the world's progress, his violence is fairly innocent, and when he is not stabbed in the frail ego, he is his brother's keeper. The poorest has five centavos for a blind beggar and the time to help him across the street. He will share his house, his food, and his energies with a friend. A Mexican train ride can be a delight in spite of all sorts of oddities because of the food and child-sharing, the easy companionability.

Some of us are appalled at the cruelty to dogs in Mexico, though they are skinny, yellow curs, poison-colored, and the shape of death. Mexicans are appalled at the harsh, piercing voices we sometimes use with our children. To them, *this* is the great cruelty. Comparatively few Mexicans have the scientific enlightenments of our young, but they are infinitely more sophisticated about the human condition than we are. If you are traveling alone (and are not excessively Anglo-Saxonly forbidding), someone will join you and, although you may valiantly deny it, commiserate with you on how sad it is to travel alone. Should you find yourself in a Mexican hospital, some neighbor will lend you a part of his family to visit with you frequently, with pots of *frijoles* and flowers. Ask a Mexican woman why she broke a date: was she sick? Yes, quite sick; she was suffering from *bilis,* an excess of bile, which means outrage, fury, and self-pity. Her husband had been more conspicuously unfaithful than usual so she became ill and went to bed. Her mother and sisters and aunts came to soothe and pet her for a couple of days and now her attack was over. It has taken us centuries—and we don't totally accept it yet—to see that so much pain and emotion *is* being "sick"; Mexicans have known it a long time.

Inevitably, several of the numerous faces of Mexican nationalism shine forth. A U.S. traveler may be accused of drowning Mexico in his native corruptions of television, punk, porno, and spongy white packaged bread, of sullying "pure" Mexico. (A couple of workable answers: Mexico is a prime example of the benefits derived from mixtures and "impurities"; in the case of television and boy crooners, it takes two to make a seduction, and Mexico, like most of the complaining world, couldn't wait to fall to the blandishments of our peculiar arts.) There is, of course, the common form of nationalism which states that all things Mexican are biggest and best, for which there is no rejoinder. Then there is the nationalism which is a deep attachment and sense of responsibility for one's compatriots. A university education must, in many cases, be government-subsidized; very few students can afford much tuition and, often, have a difficult, hungry time of making ends meet while they go to school. In a light *quid pro quo* arrangement—and because it is an enormously enlightening experience—medical students put in a year of work as physicians in remote areas before they receive diplomas. There may be young men who resent the arrangement, but one rarely hears a complaint, rather expressions of enormous interest and eagerness to serve. No Mexican has been reported reluctant to go home after training abroad; he loves his *tierra* and wants to offer it his knowledge and skills.

The Mexican's smile is broad and full; it seems to hold back nothing. He may not be happier to see you than anyone else, but, at the moment, you will appear to be the most pleasurable person in his life and, considering the Mexican talent for high-dive concentration—deep and fleeting—you might very well be, at the moment. He will tell you his house is your house but you will rarely get a glimpse of it. For some reason, North Americans are disappointed and even shocked by such "insincerity," choosing to forget that our hearty handshakes and big health-club smiles are *our* means of being polite and uncommitted. In short, the Mexican shares the silliness and burdens of the human condition; only the idiom is different.

Yucatán

The Mayans, in Antonio de Herrera's account of the "Indies," published in 1615:

> The whole country is divided into 18 districts, and in all of them were so many and such stately stone buildings that it was amazing and the greatest wonder is, that having no use of any metal, they were able to raise such structures, which seem to have been temples, for their houses were always of timber and thatched.
>
> For the space of twenty years there was such plenty through the country, and the people multiplied so much, that old men said the whole province looked like one town, and then they applied themselves to build more temples. . . .
>
> They flattened their heads and foreheads, their ears bored with rings in them. Their faces were generally good, and not very brown, but without beards, for they scorched them when young, that they might not grow. Their hair was long like women, and in tresses, with which they made a garland about the head, and a little tail hung behind. The prime men wore a rowler eight fingers broad round them instead of breeches, and going several times round the waist, so that one end of it hung before and the other behind, with fine featherwork, and had large square mantles knotted on their shoulders, and sandals or buskins made of deer's skins.

The abundance of questions and conjecture which mists a clear view of Mexican origins also hangs over the Mayans. A quick glimpse at any archaeological map of the peninsula will reveal a crowding of sites already discovered, and there are probably some yet to be stumbled on. Where did the hordes of people come from to build and serve these cities, to haul the stone and carve it so lavishly, to shape the varieties of pottery, to perfect a calendar and imagine a concept of zero, to devise a style of writing, to model magnificent pieces of sculpture?

Theories of early settlement divide, unevenly, into the two most common for all Indian life on the continent. One states that nomadic hordes wandered from the Orient through the Bering Straits, spread southward and, after centuries, stopped here and there to establish rudimentary agricultural settlements. The less popular theory holds that some of the cultures made their way across the Pacific at a much later date; proof offered is the presence and importance of jade (reduced to the status of "jadeite" by some opponents of the theory), the marked epicanthic fold of the Mayan eyelid, the common appearance of the Mongolian spot on spines of Mayan babies, and especially, resemblances in art forms. In that case, say the Bering Straits men, why didn't they bring the tools of the Orient or, more important, the wheel?

The argument seesaws and is further frenzied by later complications. Pottery characteristics, decorative building elements, the hieroglyphs of the Olmecs, and the people of the early Oaxacan periods show up in early Mayan art. How did this come about? Why were the great Mayan cities abandoned? What was the relationship among them? Was there a "capital" among subject towns or were they city-states, balancing independence and interdependence? These unknowns are not the residue of neglect; the Mayans have been explored and studied for a long time by many scholars and from various points of view, but all the knowledge of this gifted civilization has not yet fallen into clear shape.

Evidence of a distinctly "Mayan" style begins to appear four or five centuries before the Christian era, with the construction of ceremonial buildings, refinements in pottery, and, quite likely, the development of the calendar. From A.D. 200 to 800 was the time of greatest flowering: the temple-palaces of Palenque in Chiapas, of Tikal in Guatemala, and Copan in Honduras were built; the pottery evolved in delicate shapes and color; mathematics, the calendar, and systems of recording (numerals and hieroglyphs) became more complex and efficient; the crescent arts produced the masterpieces of Palenque, Jaina, and Bonampak. Then, the vast centers were abandoned. The causes may have been crop failures of several years' running, exhaustion of the soil, catastrophic weather, plague, hit-and-run attacks by other peoples, or dire prophecies of the priests, which, as in the case of Moctezuma, made a climate of disaster and a bending toward it. Whatever the reason, it is believed that the peoples of these cities migrated northward and eastward to the Yucatán peninsula, where they built Uxmal and the centers that surround it (A.D. 800 to 1000). On the heels of these refugees came a tribe of invaders, possibly invited to help one of the warring cities against another, who called themselves the Itzás. Whatever *their* backgrounds, they brought with them the full complement of Toltec matters: the worship of Quetzal-coatl (here called Kukulcán), feathered-serpent columns, and the architectural concepts whose flowering was their city, Chichén Itzá. It was this period (the twelfth and thirteenth centuries) that saw a coalition government of the three important centers, Uxmal, Chichén Itzá, and Mayapan, followed by a century or two of truce, and again a period of warfare during which intellectual and artistic achieve-ment came to a standstill. By the fifteenth century the Mayan-Toltec vitality was an extinguished candle.

In spite of Mayan apologists, it was not altogether the sweet, reasonable society they like to picture. In essence it was rather like the other Mexican cultures, a structure of priest-nobles and warriors at the apex of a social pyramid that broadened downward from merchants and artisans to something very near slaves, a vast popula-tion bedeviled by an elaborate pantheon of gods and subgods who could blow hot or cold for their own arcane reasons. These gods, like the others, had to be fed; the favored method was to throw virgins into the sacred wells *(cenotes)*, which are Yucatán's only sources of fresh water and, consequently, the abode of powerful and greedy spirits.

The Mayan may or may not have been as enthusiastic for blood as the Aztec; he was a valiant and stubborn fighter and would not be conquered by the Conquest. In battle and in guerrilla warfare, May-ans killed more Spaniards than did any other group. Some committed suicide rather than submit, while others fled into remote areas to hold out against the Spaniards for over a hundred years after the rest of the country was subjugated. Sporadic rebellions against white rule went on into the beginning of the twentieth century. One of the most violent of these uprisings, which brought the Indians short-term control of practically all of the peninsula, occurred in 1847. It was inspired and aided by the corruptions of Mexican politics of the time and by conditions described by Stephens only a short while earlier:

In consideration of their drinking the *water* of the hacienda the workers are obliged to work for the master without pay on Monday. When they marry and have families, and of course need more water, in addition to their work on Mondays they are obliged to clear, sow and gather twenty *mecates* of maize for the master, each *mecate* being 24 square yards. . . . The authority of the master or his delegate over them is absolute. He settles all disputes between the Indians themselves, and punishes for offences, acting both as judge and executioner. . . . There is no obligation upon him (the Indian) to remain at the hacienda unless he is in debt to the master, but practically, this binds him hand and foot. . . . A dishonest master may always bring them in debt, and generally they are really so. If he is not able to pay off his debt, and the Indian wants to leave, the master must give him a paper to the effect that "Whatever señor wishes to receive the Indian named ——, can take him, provided he pays me the debt he owes me." When he has obtained it, he goes round to the different haciendas until he finds a proprietor who is willing to purchase the debt, with a mortgage upon him until it is paid.

Like most subject people the Mayan continued as stubbornly as he could to hold on to his language and his customs. His isolation from the rest of Mexico—early explorers called the Yucatán an island—helped the peasant cling to his indigenous image as it helped the rich to achieve a rare cosmopolitanism. Until slow chicle and mahogany trains were drawn through swamps and jungle and, later, highways, the only way to get to and from Mérida was by boat via the port of Progreso. It was easier to go to Havana and on to Europe for education or pleasure than to Mexico City. One still finds elderly physicians with degrees from Leipzig, and matrons whose old-fashioned china was bought in Limoges. Add to this a mild disdain for the Johnny-come-lately, imperfect peoples of the north, and the lack of impassioned nationalism becomes understandable. Yucatán is to Mexico what Sicily is to Italy, without the bitterness; what Brittany is to France, without the tight-lipped shrewdness.

MÉRIDA

At first glance a good portion of the populace of Mérida seems to be divided into white masses of internes, hospital technicians, and dentists, balanced by female pillows and puffs in embroidered cases. The crackling white of men's *guayaberas* and women's *"ipiles"* (the local version of *huipil*) sparks the city on sunless days and lifts the spirit of some of the too-tight commercial streets. We speak of the conservative and the poor rural visitors; the rest is blue jeans and well-cut cotton dresses.

Mérida is a contented city, mildly gay and mildly eccentric, rather "un-Mexican" in a number of ways. It drinks as much as other cities, but more discreetly; it is as voluble as Veracruz, with less abandon; it is ringed by national historical treasures but less awed and sombered by them than Puebla is by hers. The gentle Mayan indulges in open displays of affection unthinkable to a mountain Indian. The Náhuatl-speaking highlander rides his burro, sometimes with his young son aboard too, while his woman walks behind, as laden as the burro; all are silent, inward. The young Mayan will caress his wife's face while they are riding the bus, induce her to nap on his shoulder, and stuff the children with candy to keep them from molesting mama. His old country uncle, dressed in the loose white shirt and trousers, the sandals and straw hat of the village, will stroll through the market hand in hand with his billowy comforter of a wife, chattering softly.

The Mayans' substitute for Mexicanism is intense Mayanism. The city people pride themselves on some knowledge of Mayan, if only a few symbols. The Mayaphilia extends among intellectuals to the point where, although they know better, they categorically deny that Mayans were capable of human sacrifice; it was, they say, the fault of those barbaric Toltecs who came from the north. A rare few have gone as far as to absorb the vague mystique of the Mayans as religion. The less rarefied citizen will prove his love by searching out opportunities to extol everything Mayan—the cleanliness, the gentleness of the country Mayan, the sophisticated and varied cuisine of the Yucatecan, the game, the fish, the splendid history and arts of the peninsula. As lagniappe and for his own pleasure, he will try to teach a visitor—Mexican or foreign—a few words of what he thinks is Mayan. It isn't, but pick up some of the graphic words to carry home. "Tzootz," for instance, means both smoking and kissing. Try it in front of a mirror.

Mérida's shops are crowded, its main streets congested with bustling citizens; the atmosphere is one of enterprise and purposefulness, yet the coffee breaks are interminable. At almost any time during the day the cafés on the plaza and the main streets are full of gesticulating men who have bought the rights to two hours of chair and table by ordering a *greco* (a demitasse of strong coffee and a glass of water).

As if the day were not long enough for talk, they also sit in groups of twos and threes in the small parks and plazas, discussing far into the night. They must work, if only to keep themselves in the linen pants and shirts, but *when,* if a day is overlapping coffee breaks and a long siesta, and the night for more talk? There are fewer women around; they lead separate, hard-working, enclosed lives, moving in the restricted gamut of market, stove, children, and female relatives. A husband sometimes stays at home, but those times are decidedly of his own choosing, as in most Mediterranean cultures.

Although the great hobnailed boots of progress march inexorably on, Mérida still clings to its older color. A housewife laden with market baskets picks up a horse and carriage just outside the web of market alleys and is driven home in leisured, if rickety, style for a few pesos. Oddly enough, some Méridanos—probably the owners of overbig cars—would like to see the carriages, fast dwindling in number, off the streets altogether and dislike having them photographed; it displays to the world, they say, a picture of backwardness, undeserved. Another city phenomenon which they feel the city might do without are the *confidenciales,* S-curved concrete benches, the perfect seating arrangements (if they weren't quite so hard) for quiet tête-à-têtes, safely public and eminently respectable.

Divesting itself of the problems and interminable discussions concerning whose favorite patriot deserves what street, Mérida has numbered them, the odds running east-west, crossing the evens. Sixtieth is the Broadway, running past the **Hotel Mérida,** the cafés, the plaza of carriages, the souvenir shops, forming one side of the main plaza and continuing with shops that run into the market area. In any direction off the main streets—particularly toward the upper sixties and seventies—one can still see some of the tall red-brown, heavily carved wooden doors, the decorated shutters and twisted grillwork of houses in late Victorian-Díaz style: one of these—possibly that of a henequen *hacendado*—is at 498 on 59th Street and bears almost all the decoration a house can bear without collapsing. It is white and aqua, pillared and urned, broad-stairwayed, garlanded with stone fruit and leaves, its doorway encrusted with leaves banded by *fasces* in the style of Rome triumphant, the roof surmounted by gargoyles spitting out of medieval mouths.

Mérida has few treasures of architecture but still holds on to a few curios. A carriage ride on the Paseo Montejo, and beyond, brings to view the more lordly residences. The Paseo has a number of cool, intelligently designed, modern houses, but here and there one finds an omnivorously perioded house with carved wooden doors, little French gardens ringed by neo-classic colonnades; graceful Moorish arches—reflecting the nostalgia of the many Levantines *(los arabes)* in the area—framing views of rigidly cut topiary gardens. But a number of the gardens have relaxed and the buildings have been simplified to be used as schools and other institutions.

The end of the Paseo is marked by one of the most astounding monuments in Mexico. In a style compounded of decayed Mayan, furious Toltec, and ambition, the begetter of the structure has carved a subway crush of all of Mexico's heroes frantically crowding each other in a crazed ring around an enormous eagle pouncing on a thick snake, all marked in heavy black incisions. Viewing is best in the evening: it is too challenging for the eye and understanding in full sunlight.

Though Mérida is the hub of a wheel of important ancient cities, its newer antiquities are worth a look also: the university (at 57th and 60th), established as a Jesuit College early in the seventeenth century, with an inner patio shaped by tiers of Moresque arches; the sixteenth-century palace of the founder of the city, Francisco de Montejo, on the main plaza, whose plateresque façade is a dignified balance of coat of arms, symbols of conquest, and ornamental detail, strongly and naturally reminiscent of the entrances to old palaces in Seville; the cool, high-vaulted churches of cream-colored stone; the market, a great splash of colors spreading around the main post office; the neat regional museum in the Palacio del Gobierno on the Paseo Montejo; the big sturdily sports-minded Parque de los Americas in the fashionable part of town, past the Paseo.

The museum (check hours) was housed in the basement of an unused mansion whose history is especially Latin American. It was built in the late nineteenth century by a general, a helpful friend of the dictator Díaz, or the friend of a helpful friend. All the rooms were of ballroom size, and into them he put crystal chandeliers, solid gold hardware, porcelain bathtubs, and rare woods. He had planned too nobly, however, and ran out of money, or favor, before his dream of the perfect life was fully furnished. The house became government property, to be used as the palace of Yucatán's governors, a succession of gentlemen who, experienced in the mutability of political sentiment and guarantees, and convinced that there is no point in being a victor without grabbing the spoils, took out the gold faucets, the dazzling fixtures (even the tubs), and left nothing but superb emptiness surrounding a few insignificant bits of furniture and an immense (immovable) upper-floor terrace which gives a lovely view of local gardens and some of Mérida's light, insubstantial windmills. (The mansion is not officially open to public view, but the caretaker may let you in if you are accompanied by a guide.)

The museum, now in calm, formal quarters of the Palacio Canton, is of neat human scale and just generous enough not to tax the attention span of a nonexpert; it is reasonably arranged within an area easy to traverse, the objects chronologically placed according to the logic of the chart on the wall just inside the entrance. The emphases are, of course, Mayan, with enough groups and examples of other cultures to demonstrate links and influences. Look for a set of deformed crania with diagrams of the instruments used to produce the long backsweep of forehead and exaggeratedly high nose bridge that characterize Mayan figures, for the fine pieces of Tepeuh pottery, among them a golden calabash incised with delicate glyphs, for little golden animals rather like those of Central America and quite possibly brought from that area in some distant time, for a recently found wooden figure which seems more African than Mayan, and, most important, for the remarkable Mayan calendar.

The most direct way to find the market is to follow 60th to 65th and turn left, assuming you've come from the hotel area and passed the main plaza and the cathedral. Street stalls sway under weights of heaped toys, eyeglass frames, plastic hair curlers, sections of searchlights, and machete handles. The narrow sidewalks fronting dry-goods stores are heaped with multicolored hammocks and the ubiquitous stands of sizzling *papadzules* and *panuchos* add their smell to the fresh, slightly acrid odor of oranges freshly peeled on an old apple peeler or under the skillful chipping of a large machete. The small square opposite the open market displays a good number of Levantine names, such as Rosa de Siria and Aladín. As in other parts of Mexico—and the world—Syrians and Lebanese control the retail selling of dry goods. Mérida has an unusually high percentage of such citizens, many of whom have married Yucatecan women, raised busy enterprising sons, and, as family tribal units, have flourished abundantly and in magnificent Moresque houses.

Before turning into the open market proper, continue on 65th to the wholesale grain shops, sack-heaped dimnesses whose outer walls are pastoral scenes of life-size horses, pigs, and chickens gamboling under very blue skies on very green grass. On 65th, too, are the small wholesale dealers who sell to country vendors—one sack of potatoes, one of onions, five cartons of cheap cigarettes, a row of minute packages of spice, tiny boxes of detergent, and a pound of hard candies.

It takes talent to lose the open market, but if you should, look for the post office *(correo)*, a dignified building held in the tight network of shaded alleys which house the usual skillfully arranged florets of purple garlic, tomatoes green and red, fat, bumpy white *jicamas* (edible roots), pyramids of oranges, and pools of green limes. Mérida's market is different from others in that here one may still see craftsmen at work—a fast-fading section of the Mexican canvas. With luck one might find a tinker, people twisting henequen cord and sewing sacks. On an outer edge of the market you might see a box of a repair shop: a jumble of four workers, pots of paint and glue, bits of cloth and ribbon, dolls with heads, dolls without heads, naked baby dolls. The dolls, repaired, dressed, and washed with coats of new paint as you watch, will be the saints of home altars and small village churches.

Another distinction of Mérida's market is the presence of several indigenous products: objects made of sisal (fiber of the henequen, which bristles through the countryside), filigreed gold jewelry (growing scarcer), and the local *ipil* (elsewhere *huipil*). The price one pays for an *ipil* (other than the primary consideration of bargaining talent) depends on size—guest towel to mattress cover is the range—and the method of embroidering. (Machine embroidery can be so complicatedly patterned and sewn that its cost will equal that of hand embroidery.) One of the culturally confused, expensive types (called, justly, a *mestiza*) is of shiny white rayon, heavily machine-embroidered and dripping white machine-lace, a confection much favored by poster painters and the local belles, whom it suits beautifully, especially with a thin loop of silk *rebozo* gracefully slung around it.

The silver dealers are at the back of the market and nearby streets. Their equipment is a set of glass-enclosed shelves, a small scale, a box of weights, and an uncanny capacity to size up the thickness of your wallet as it hides in your pocket. Comparison shopping here is entertaining but futile; there is a gentlemen's agreement among the stall-keepers which keeps prices inflexible.

Sisal sits back of the silver, made up into shoes, wallets, pocketbooks, hats, and carrying baskets. None of it is distinguished in design, but the smaller objects make light, inexpensive presents and the large baskets will carry a sizable load of impedimenta.

The pleasantest product of the Mérida market is its village ladies. The more prosperous, wearing dangling, long filigreed earrings, black thin silky hair peeled back from their high foreheads and gathered under a stiff red bow, a slim *rebozo* draped across their shoulders, and enveloped in local pride, make their dignified way through the market like banks of white cloud. The poorer vendors, set in compositions of red, yellow, brown-red, and green-white vegetables, or screened by a fan of apricot gladiolas, are just as appealing, especially the older women, whose faces have the significant mellowness of their antique cities.

For more formal, better-organized shopping follow the streets (have your hotel provide a map) that will take you to beads, *huipiles,* some handicrafts in shops near the cathedral and the choice Panama hats and hammocks made in the area. (Ask your concierge for the best places to find these. The quality varies widely.)

RESTAURANTS

There are no four-star restaurants, but unlike the other Mexican provinces, Mérida has a separate, sophisticated cuisine, well mixed with Levantine specialties. Compared, for instance, to Guanajuato or Oaxaca, the variety and number of satisfactory eating places is extraordinary. You will meet everywhere the usual tropical favorites, *pastel de cazón* (shark pie), *panuchos* (tortilla sandwiches of meat or chicken), the shrimps, *gambas en gabardina,* and the many fruits of the tropics. More strictly Yucatecan are *papadzules,* a treatment of the tortilla with eggs, calabash seeds, and things; *huevos motuleños,* a small pyramid of *frijoles* and toasted tortilla topped by fried eggs, those topped by bits of ham and sausage, those topped by crumbled cheese, and around the structure a sauce, peas, fried bananas, and anything else the chef can find room for; *pollo pibil* is chicken in *pipian* (a red spice which looks hotter than it is) and a bit of oil, steamed in a banana leaf; *relleno negro* is chicken or turkey, stuffed with pork and cooked in a black, black sauce with oregano and other spices; *queso relleno* is a ring of bland cheese cooked around ground pork and covered with a tomato sauce. *Cochinito* is suckling pig and usually well handled; turtle steak *(tortuga)* is common, so are venison *(venado)* and a variety of seafood. The local beers, particularly the light, fruity Carta Clara, are good.

Four-star restaurants, sometimes an arbitrary designation, are actually rare in provincial cities, although Mérida does better than most, its repertory still rich in the ancient "Pibil" dishes, dressed in a fairly hot native sauce. There is still venison—not as much as there once was—around, and the Yucatecan thick tortilla, the *papadzule.* These and their variations are available at the big, clean, amiable **El Expresso** across from Hidalgo Park and among the generous servings at **Los Almendros,** less free-form and a bit more expensive—about five dollars for a full meal. The price, but not the quality, drops for the good lunch at the **Portico de Peregrino** near the Casa de Belem.

The current reputation for prime excellence sits on the head of Alberto's **Continental** which will, for several courses and a substantial number of drinks, ask about twenty-five dollars for a full repast for two. **Le Gourmet,** which concentrates on a sort of Frenchified service, asks similar prices for similar generosity. A very small sum—two or three dollars—will still, at this writing, buy you a good lunch at the **Portico de Pellegrino,** near the Casa de Belem. (Incidentally, many restaurants are closed during Carnival; phone to make sure, and remember to ask your host to get you a taxi back; they do not prowl the streets).

The leading hotel and the largest—and not as expensive as you might think—is the **Holiday Inn** on one of the edges of town—not too distant an edge. It supports a handsome pool, but, unfortunately, not quite such appealing restaurants. A new, extremely attractive hotel, several months old, is the **Calinda Pan Americana,** part of a growing chain that introduces you to not three but four plump nude graces and the open light of an old courtyard, which may have been part of the house to which this entity once belonged, as did the dark doors marked "Tabaque" and "Curiosites," vestiges of a period when there was attempt at other types of trade. Pristine, neat, polite, hardworking, fronting a pool and good local entertainment (mostly local dances), it is worth a long look, particularly at the modest rate. Since most of Mérida is inexpensive you might want to look in at one of several others: the venerable and respected **Montejo Palace,** the **Pasea de Montejo** and the modern, stylish **Hotel El Castellano** and the simpler **Hotel Colon.** Check on air-conditioning in the older hotels.

Long filled with the pride of shining white houses, Mérida also sports a grandiloquent Paseo named for the main progenitor of the town, the "Montejo" of almost everywhere in Mérida. Besides its essential allure, Mérida seems to be adding more and more greenery to become a pretty stutter of parks. Look, for instance, at Park Hidalgo (the statue in the center does not pertain to him; some mistake) and observe it nestled behind good bookshops and sheltered in the huge yellow and red leaves of almendra trees. Next door a movie house and, if you'd like to investigate, a couple of doorways that will lead you to accommodations for as little as five dollars per night. There are less basic rooms at the edge of the park that will house you for eight dollars, with two dollars added for air-conditioning.

Having settled in, one usually heads for the center of town, the Zócalo, where, in many instances, the main pagan temple once stood. Here it is the smooth yellow-stoned cathedral and the belligerent, challenging Montejo Palace (named after the founder of the city), established in 1549, a couple of years before its neighbor, the largest cathedral in the Yucatán. One of the central cluster is the local governor's palace, like all of Mérida seemingly freshly painted and showing the usual proud symbols and historical insignia.

WARNING: Although Mérida itself has sufficient allure for several winter weeks, it is becoming increasingly a jumping-off point for Cozumel and the more stylish and expensive Cancun and the large—and growing larger—hotels that line its sands. Mérida is frantic with agents trying to find space—at $150 and, one hears, $200 a room for clients who think that Mérida is an easy moving-on point and some of them incredulous as to the cost. Sophisticated agents will tell you in all seriousness—they mean it—that you must make winter reservations, for Cancun especially, six months ahead of time, preferably with a large group which cannot suddenly be denied its reservations (as has happened). All costs for transportation, room, possibly a minimum of meals, and a string of extra charges must be what is called "guaranteed"; that is, totally prepaid. What may surprise you is not so much the symptoms of American prosperity but the considerable number of Germans and French driven to such expense by the spur of icy Februaries. (Recent threats to the world's economy may reduce the crowding and the greed.)

There are a few hotels, in the main elderly, in the center of Cancun: the eccentric **Kin Ha**, near the vulnerable **Presidente** hotel; the **Plaza del Sol** and the **Hotel America,** which runs a shuttle to the beach. Even these, in season, are "iffy" and may not afford you too much pleasure, particularly after you have wandered through the magnificent beach ziggurats.

MÉRIDA ENVIRONS—MAYAN CITIES

Although they seem to lie very near one another, the going among Mayan sites can be rough. Some of the edifices are still shrouded in heavy jungle, others were too thoroughly destroyed by time and warfare to make much structural or aesthetic sense. For the visitor who comes equipped with a normal amount of time (five to seven days in Yucatán) and interest, the twin splendors of Uxmal and Chichén, both easily accessible, plus the less-known Kabah, Labná, and Sayil, should suffice for a good view of "Mayan" architecture and art. (Keep in mind that Uxmal and Kabah can be visited on your way from Campeche to Mérida—and possibly the others as well—particularly easy if you are driving.)

One doesn't necessarily have to be taken by the hand to Uxmal and Chichén. They have been described and photographed almost as much as the splendors of Egypt and their looks become familiar to most of the civilized world. Pamphlet in hand—available in town and at the sites—one can wander through the ruins on a do-it-yourself basis. Buses run to both cities frequently; the trip to Chichén takes about two hours, to Uxmal it is about an hour and a half. A taxi needn't be wildly expensive and the drivers are usually well informed or will put you in the hands of a local guide if you like. *His* fee will be little but he may suffer from a common form of Mayaphilia: he may insist that everything you look at is "pure" Mayan, whatever that may mean.

Like Uxmal, Kabah sits close to the road, but the wait for a bus to take you there from Uxmal or back may be hot and time-consuming. Guide services usually make Uxmal-Kabah one trip and Sayil-

Labná another. For those with prodigious stamina, Uxmal, Kabah, and Sayil can be arranged as a long one-day trip.

Kabah is a bitter structure, with the inelegant proportions of a squat fortress. It sits on a height of terraces and platforms as befits a fortress but its most imposing building has been given a singularly nonbelligerent name, the Palace of the Rolled Mat (Codz-Pop). This refers to the "nose" of the stylized masks of the rain god, Chac, a characteristic of local ornamentation valued by adherents of the trans-Pacific theory of Mayan origin as proof that the migrants brought with them a memory of the elephant's trunk. Opponents consider it phallic, or an ornamental step device which facilitated scrambling up and down the building.

Tour cars or jeeps continue on to Sayil; check at Uxmal or Kabah to find out if the road is ready for your car. The Palacio at Sayil (the guides like to expound on it salaciously as a fertility center) is, next to Palenque, the most dramatically placed of the structures now visible. High and alone, long, horizontal planes surrounded by a silent, motionless sea of green, it echoes the isolated Greek temple at Segesta in Sicily. The three-layered building bears sections of Mayan frieze, including the mask motif, and a preponderance of small columns as architectural and ornamental elements. Tight clusters of columns like pipers of Pan (Puuc style) flank the doorways, then change to sets of thicker, peculiarly shaped columns; one of each pair is straight, the other softly indented—rather like a waist—suggesting a primitive female figure. Other than these details, there is not much on or in the Palacio to surprise or enchant: it is the total effect—the ride through the brush, the stillness, the sudden sight of the isolated, regal building. There are ruined buildings of which one says, "I would love to have seen it before it fell apart," but not of Sayil. Like the Greek temples, it must have been covered with much more ornament and brilliant color and, like the Greek temples now, has achieved a new beauty in decay.

One of the best places from which to get a distant view of the building in its setting is at the "observatory," a few minutes away by car. From here one walks a short distance to suggestions of other buildings, and on to a grove in which lies a huge figure of a priapic god who may have fallen from a set of columns nearby. In another direction from the Palacio, a short ride and short walk again, there is a cave on which is clearly carved a figure of a woman in a froglike squatting position, and just below her, on a ledge farther back in the curve of the wall, the figure of what might be another woman, or more possibly, a baby; it has no breasts, its shape is rounder and less clearly defined than the other figure—more evidence of fertility rites, the guide eagerly points out.

The road to Labná should be usable in dry weather. Labná, again judging from jungle-choked mounds, must have been a very large city, and to judge from what is left, an ornately beautiful one. It has some of the clustered, banded columns of Sayil, the elaborated rain-god masks of the whole area, the open work, and the geometric ornaments of stone mosaic which adorn Uxmal. The famous arch of Labná, of itself strikingly large and tall, offers a clear demonstration of how near the Mayans were to the keystone arch, and also how much they could do without it—as they did without the wheel and without metal until late in their history.

With more time and the proper passion for Mayan you might investigate (always checking the condition of roads) the Cave of Balancanche, less than three miles from Chichén, which revealed, some years ago, a good number of pottery objects still to be dated. Chacmultun gives evidences of once having been a large center and its frescoes are not altogether gone. It is reached via Muna and Ticul, a town which embroiders *ipiles* and whose inhabitants are purport-edly the descendants of the Xius, kings of Uxmal.

Or try either the ruins of Dzibalchen or Xtampak (savoring the pleasure of rolling these names out when you get home).

Much less demanding is Dzibilchultun, off the Progreso road, now being excavated and potentially an enormous, important site. At the present writing it shows a few structures, including remains of an ancient church, one tall pyramid, and a platform holding a plump column. The rest is a small museum, the first stirrings of a university, and a few distinguished statuettes that were found in the Temple of the Seven Dolls (now in the museum). One wonders how long it will take Tulane University and the National Geographic Society to re-build the large city, which was, it is said, in continuous use from 1000 B.C. until the arrival of the Spaniards. It is not a particularly rewarding site at present except for the young picnickers who play their porta-ble phonographs and swim at the edge of the *cenote*. Or go by bus to Progreso, an unprepossessing port town whose beaches are steadily coming out of a long slump. At the end of a road shortly before one reaches Progreso, there are two beaches equipped with cabins and snack bars and numerous of the local young: Chelen and Yucapeten. From Progreso one turns left for the white sands of Sisal, and right to Chixulub, whose fine sand holds interesting shells and a respected seafood restaurant. Should you be in Mérida in mid-August—a daring time—find out the precise dates of the Chixulub fiesta, which includes regional dancing, lots of seafood, and often a bullfight. If you have the energy, take a walk along the avenue which parallels the beachfront for a glimpse of some of the wildest domestic architecture extant, and some very good modern. On your return, get to the bus station early. For one thing, this obviates waiting through the filling and departure of two buses before you get a seat, but more important, the bus station is the pulse of the town and to sit on one of its benches is to be the spectator of an eloquent pageant. A bus from Mérida delivers a covey of old ladies in white, their thin hair pulled back tightly into the clublike knot which has been the fashion for centuries; a few wear shoes. Two younger women glowing in white rayon heavy with bright embroidery and lace, hung with gold chains and earrings, with stiff new sandals on their feet, step down solemnly, like young priestesses. The general factotum of the bus— not yet of the aristocracy of drivers—helps an old man lift down a cake of ice wrapped in cloth and rope which, somehow, survived the hour's trip of many stops. A sack of dried kernels of corn to be soaked and made into tortilla mash is the next bundle down, and the assistant arranges it as a great deep hat on the head of a Mayan woman who is also carrying a large, ugly doll dressed in a man's hat and a cloth whose embroidered banner names it Saint Michael.

At the entrance to the station, a timeless tableau goes on: A young man, red-eyed, weaving, his gestures watery, is trying to placate a girl of fifteen, an unkempt, savage little beauty, who answers him in snarls and grunts. He had taken her to the beach for the night, rather than the hotel room he had promised, and drank up the fare money which was to take them back to Mérida. They approach the factotum-collector of the bus, who assures them in a reasonable manner that he cannot take them to Mérida without fares. They start to walk down the dusty road, separate and morose.

An insistent drunk who has been gently urged off two buses now boards yours. The man of all work of the bus, resigned to his company, helps him curl up under some seats and at each stop, when the bewildered head rises to look around blindly, pats him back to sleep in a mixture of Spanish and Mayan. When his charge is asleep and all the fares collected, the young man fixes a doll, adjusts a slipping bundle, and dandles one of a pair of babies while the mother attends to the second.

The return from this second-class bus ride might be just the time to leave Yucatán, carrying the savor of its pretty, generous people whose sophisticated lineage shows in their profiles, in their open, trusting manner, their easy smiling, and complete lack of xenophobia. You interest them, they assume they interest you, and they make it clear that the encounter is a mutual pleasure.

HOTELS

The rates for **Hotel Mayaland** at Chichén Itzá and **Hacienda Uxmal**—pools, tropical gardens, meals, gift shop, music, immense charm, and *norteamericano* tour groups—will run to high moderate.

Hacienda Chichén, the **Posada Uxmal,** the **Villas Arqueologicas,** and the **Misiones** are somewhat less expensive: several inns provide dinners for day tour groups.

NOTE: Carry a raincoat, check the condition of roads before you venture out, and make no attempt to get to any but the easily accessible ruins without a guide. And always wear old clothes and a hat or scarf for bumping through the dusty *mata.*

There is—was?—in the Hacienda Uxmal a young assistant cook who hand-embroidered *huipiles.* If he is there (the name is Manuel Jesús Dzi-Chuy, the common Spanish-Indian combination), have him take you to his village, Santa Elena, to see what he and the women of his family have made. It may not be cheaper than a bargain you can drive in the Mérida market but it will be entry into a Mayan hamlet and a house of thatch surrounding a few hammocks, several pots and dishes and strings across the corners for the hanging of clothing and *huipiles* to sell. The father of the house will walk out in a show of disdain for women and a son who cooks and embroiders. Young cousins, fifteen to eighteen, all carrying babies and dressed in nothing but ragged cotton shifts will come to visit, look, and giggle. And if they are the same cousins, you will see under the grime three or four exceedingly beautiful girls. Bathed, dressed attractively, the black falls of hair coiled on their heads, they could compare well with whatever your paragons are, Nefertiti or Sophia Loren.

NOTE: The second-class bus, which waits at Mérida's tourist bureau on the square, offers a "Ruta Puuc" ride that takes you to Sayil, Labna, Uxmal, the grottoes of Loetun and touches on other ruins, giving you about a half hour to explore each; an inexpensive method of sightseeing, but exhausting and sometimes noisy with the protest of chickens being taken to market by a couple of the local citizens.

Cozumel-Cancun

Not too long ago Cozumel was served by two or three flights a week (sometimes held up by *nortes,* when they didn't fly at all) from Mérida, and Isla Mujeres was connected to Mérida by a ferry and a long bus ride. Except for the imports in the duty-free shops most people couldn't afford and the occasional vegetables and meats brought in from Mérida, the eating was turtle steak in several—usually inedible—styles, venison, lobster, which can become a bore too, fish, and bananas. Now there are constant flights from almost everywhere, including directly from Miami. (These planes are purported to carry vast weights of American canned and boxed foods.) San Miguel was a sloppy, slow, affable town that danced, sang, drank, fished, dried copra, and slept away the rainy season in its capacious hammocks. There were pleasant breezy beach cottages at San Juan, a few scallops of rock and sand that edged clear blue-green waters full of sportive little fish and an occasional shark. Now San Juan beach is the playground for a government housing project on the other side of the road. The one hotel, rows of thatched houses run by gifted, mischievous, troublemaking fantasists, served some of the best music and food in Mexico. Now large hotels line the beaches on the edges of town, at the sides of fresh roads which once were paths for iguanas.

The assembled hotel cars pick out their cargoes at the airport and start their journey to the metropolis of San Miguel. The Caribbean pours into the sky at the left, spotted by a few boats clustered around the town dock. On the right is a papery little town of colored cardboard, cut out with crude scissors. The side streets rise a bit, fall a bit, and disappear into the deep-green stain of distant palmetto and coconut.

Someone, in the course of the ride, will point out that one family owns every other house on the waterfront street, half the island, and the bank; it controls the airline office; it owns a hotel in town, one on the beach, and a number of well-stocked shops. Like an impressive number of Méridanos, the family is of Syrian descent, stemming from the classic peddler who dragged a pack of threads, shiny ornaments, and dazzling tapestries of Turkish earth goddesses with improbable breasts and watermelon thighs. Peso by peso, the ancestor amassed a good deal of money and the family, now mixed with other bloods, is reputed to be flagrantly rich. How rich depends on the envy, imagination, and tequila consumption of one's informant; it varies from dollar millions to peso millions.

The next domain in order of conspicuousness is that of the travel-agency groups based in Mérida, which are busily luring, soothing, arranging, and carrying visitors from Mérida and points north—on their laps, if necessary.

The third dominion worked more quietly. Except in the tangential ways of property, leases, and debts, its strength lay in tracts of coconut plantation and the copra processed and sold from them. In the jealous concern of the three kings that one not gain a handful of sand over the other (and there are stories about property fences moved three feet in a dark of night to encroach on enemy territory), the development of Cozumel as a resort island moved very slowly for a time and then raced ahead breathlessly and is still racing—more shops, more hotels, more tour groups, more derricks digging out roads. The advantages to the village have been considerable. The sea wall, at one side an endlessly long bench, is new, and one no longer enjoys the indigenous view of rocks, dried weed, and garbage. There is a public library, the church has been propped up and repainted, the hotels have created many jobs, once marginal shops with nothing much to show have been buying imported cheeses, liquors, and English biscuits, enterprising young men and women from other parts of the country have opened boutiques of crafts and near-crafts to replace the scabrous little houses that sloped on each other on the seafront, the pile of stone and cement that was the dock is a substantial pier.

What's to do in Cozumel other than escape the northern winter? Pretty much as before, in more luxurious circumstances and at increased cost. About seven miles from the center one can share a pretty lagoon (Chankanab) with startled and startling fish. There is no beach, but there are one or two places where sliding into a shallow place is easy. After a swim and the triumph of frightening a ton of fish, go back for your snorkel and propel yourself smoothly toward the end of the lagoon away from the road.

The lace wall of coral is close and threatening—a world of blistered mountains and deep caverns, of a dark liquid sky with its own aurora borealis of fleeting lights, a world of silence except for the soft, whistling suck of fish feeding off the coral walls. Reach for an edge of coral (which will not be quite where you think it is), hold on, and lie as motionless as you can, a shadow among shadows. The fish glide in and out of their coral grottoes: snub-nosed and thick-sided vul-garians with outraged faces, fish thin and elegant as flute solos, small silvery fish with foolish eager mouths making way for a deep blue dowager wearing a glory of red behind her gills. Like a tropical sunset or a field of flowers, the fish cast a gaudy confusion of colors suspect in art, perfect in nature.

Once upon a time and, with luck, occasionally now, serviceable boats, available through the hotels, take one to long strips of yellow-white, empty beaches. The crew will be an assortment of slender, brown amphibians whose command of English varies from one phrase: "Goddem sawn a beech!" to surprising fluency. (Beware of fluency; it often carries misinformation.) They can tell you within a half hour when an enemy wind will turn benign, pick the exact spot on the vast blue anonymity of sea where the lobsters lurk, and spear two at a time for your lunch. They are friendly with rum; they fix good drinks and often manage to put away a respectable amount without losing track of gear, ropes, lobsters, clients, or schools of fish.

During the holiday seasons, a beach picnic party rarely stays iso-lated. Several boats spill lobsters, rum, soft drinks, assorted packages, and tanned torsos onto a favorite beach—and a party is on. A huge palmetto fire is built and a platform of twigs over it. The dozens of lobsters (Caribbean crayfish, all thick tail with no nonsense about emptying claws with tiny forks) and the large fish are placed over the fire, broiled and smoked, protected from sand and high flame by palmetto fences and covers. While the lobsters and flames crackle, the drinks are poured: someone's rum, another's tequila, someone's En-glish gin. Because Cozumel is a free port, the assortment of liquors and hors d'oeuvres can be quite stylish. There one stands in a drip-ping bathing suit, or seated on a prickly piece of driftwood, drinking the best British gin with local lime juice, fingers folded around a Danish sausage, or Argentine pâté on U.S. crackers, or chunks of good Stilton cheese just arrived from Belize. No one says thank you, everyone is host and guest and a little high on liquor, sun, sea, and amiability.

The homeward ride is a race. The boats are cleared, the passengers stowed, the crews prepare the sails, and off! The late afternoon sun turns the sea to blue flame; at a distance the dolphins, fat ladies who dance so lightly, slip their round bulk through the air and through the sea, then through the air and through the sea, sewing the elements together. The workaday tub, dressed in her great plume of sail, skates across the sea at a flirtatious angle. The rum, lobster, and cheese sit in friendly consort. Who really cares about winning? The race is called and everyone goes snorkeling.

Small planes fly to Tulum, on the mainland of Quintana Roo, and there are local buses—on a sparse schedule—as well as excursion buses from Cancun. The most romantic way to do it is only a cherished memory of a time, two decades or so ago, when there was no Cancun development and few Cozumel roads. The way it was: Guests and the amphibians boarded at midnight after a series of forays to wake one of the boys, pick up the snorkels, return for the forgotten sweaters, dash back for the soda. (No one ever forgot the rum.) The sky lowered its net of stars and the lustrous veil swung gently with the motion of the boat. The deck was too narrow for sleeping; one stretched out below with the rhythm of the engine.

The dawn light revealed a new, early world, just molded, just painted, its shapes sharp, distinct, its colors moist and fresh. The boat had been docked for some time at a pier leading to a clearing of houses and machinery, the center of an immense coconut plantation which stretched for tall, fringed miles along the coast.

Here, if you had arranged it, a jeep would have been waiting to take you through a coconut grove at the edge of a jungle on this tropical morning adorned with green arcs, green fronds, spirals of green; green dancing, green singing, smelling of the essence of young fresh green. The luminous moist world, like the inside of a fresh pea pod, melted away in the gray harshness of the ruins of Tulum.

Its remaining walls with their tight, narrow entrances, and the fortress-castle dominating a vastness of sea, speak of a fierce, late time in Mayan life. The datings of Tulum are vague and much disputed; a Mayan date glyph on a stele found at the site was interpreted by one scholar as A.D. 304 and by another as A.D. 564. Either would place the city in a fairly early period of Mayan development. However, although the buildings show the imposition of structure on structure over stretches of time and style, the earliest extant seems to be of a much later time. Like Chichén Itzá, it shows Toltec influences (carvings of plumed serpents, for instance); the wall paintings indicate Mixtec influence, which would also be a late development; the total picture seems to point to the twelfth or thirteenth century A.D. The early stele? Someone has suggested that it was brought in, possibly after a raid, from an earlier ceremonial center.

Tulum's later history is better documented. In 1518, the then governor of Cuba, stimulated by stories of treasure brought back from Yucatán and Isla Mujeres the year before, sent an expedition under Juan de Grijalva southward along the coast of what is now Quintana Roo. Its report mentioned three large towns on the coast, among them one "town so large, that Seville would not have seemed more considerable nor better: one saw there a very large tower. . . . The same day we came to a beach near which was the highest tower we had seen." The town was probably Tulum, much more extensive than it is now and apparently densely populated, and the "highest tower" was the Castillo, which stands like a huge fist of rock thrust up from the sea.

In the latter half of the nineteenth century, when the coast was bloodied by rebellions against the Mexican government, the walls of the ruins were used as a fortress by government troops. In a sporadic, vestigial way, the Castillo must have been used as a ceremonial center and may still be, by the not quite Mexicanized Mayans. Morley reports that copal, the traditional Indian incense, was still ceremonially burned in the Castillo as late as the 1940s.

The site is piles of worked rock over small, tight openings (this gave rise to the legend that the early inhabitants were a race of dwarfs), with walls running inward as they came down in a gesture of protection and seclusion, their decoration roughly erased and battered by time, storms, sun, and soldiers. The site has none of the reasonable, cool perfection of Sayil or the controlled exuberance of Uxmal or the matter-of-fact big-business look of Chichén Itzá. It is bitter and dramatic, sunbaked and barren, an old, abandoned battlefield which now houses only a frightened iguana or snake.

Fronting the Castillo, in what might be considered the center of a courtyard, is the Temple of the Frescoes. Like the Castillo, it had a columned base which was filled in, built upon, and rebuilt upon.

Its remaining frescoes are finely drawn in controlled skillful black lines and filled with the rich blue-green frequently seen in this area. Priests in overwhelming headdresses seem to be making offerings— bouquets of flowers, sheafs of corn, twists of serpents, and what looks like a human hand. The lower façade is richly decorated with stucco bas-reliefs still touched with color. A center niche holds a descendent god (better realized in another building), priestly personages in plumed headdresses; a set of solitary Laocoöns, each man (or god, or priest) struggling in the coils of a serpent; on the corners, two distorted masks of an old god.

To the right of the Castillo, as one faces away from the sea, stands the temple of the Descending God, a tightly designed little building whose upper walls slant inward and seem to totter under a heavy, three-ply cornice. Its Descending God, in the niche above the temple entrance, is the best preserved: head downward, legs spread and flying, he might be the god of the setting sun, or the god of rain (probably the more important deity here, since rain is in scarce supply, not sunlight) or he might be a fertility-birth figure. Since no one can say surely—he has even been called a flying bee—the choice is the spectator's.

Unless unprotected heights disturb you, edge yourself around on one of the lower platforms of the Castillo and face the sea, her rush at the rocks too far away for sound. The sun films the senses; the spectator becomes a column, a figure on a frieze, absorbed into the gray stones.

If you've come by boat, getting back can be a damp matter, but wet, sun-dried, then wet, then sun-dried is the natural alternation of this life, its reptilian theme. No sooner are you dry than one of the boys may remember the beautiful grottoes of Xel-Ha on the way back. On goes the bathing suit and the boat slips into one of the better versions of Paradise. The thick multitoned green calls out in the clatter of tropical birds; rococo coral islands float like fancy meringues across the water now a billion diamonds of stained glass shimmering over a satin banner of creamy sand. (See page 400.)

Celarain, the lighthouse at the southernmost tip of the island was, and one hopes it still is, reached by boat slowly, easily, with stops for lobster spearing and snorkeling among thousands of slender striped fish, black and silver darts painted on the luminous canvas of the water. The flying fish, aching to be birds, soar, skitter, and skim along the water for a breathtaking moment, then drop, exhausted by their vaulting ambition. The boat gently rocks, the rum gurgles, the fresh lobster is sizzling in the best and most honeyed of all possible worlds.

After a few hours, the boat docks at a strip of beach and scrub, disgorges hammocks, blankets, rum, Spam, passengers, rum, Nescafé, soda, bread, and rum. From a path back of the beach comes an assortment of shy men who pick up the bundles and bags and trot back down the path, followed by unencumbered kingly you.

Near the lighthouse there was the dormitory, a large square building of high whitewashed empty rooms, studded with heavy hooks for hammocks. Set in wild scratchy creepers above a wide curve of beach, it contained a bathroom—literally a room to take a bath in; no toilet. For men this presented no problem—miles of beach and brush and the protection and company of other men. A woman could march conspicuously and resolutely to a small abandoned building near the main palace. The *toujours l'audace* manner and frequency established the house as hers. She could, of course, take another woman along, but then she missed the pleasure of being the queen of her domain: one man polishing improbably colored conch shells with hair oil, to present to her; another making heaps of thick *gorditas,* a lusty version of the attenuated, pale tortilla, for her; another whispering little compliments when no one else was around. And being carried piggyback into a jungle swamp is a romantic, adventuresome thing when it involves one woman; a line-up of two or three makes a foolish routine.

With the fall of night came the preparations for the alligator hunt. The equipment was relatively simple: a rowboat, a pistol, a machete, a spear, a large head lamp, 6-12, sweaters, a swamp. After a five-minute walk along an obscure path, the brown, overripe smell of swamp begins to thicken the cool air, and the path ends in a clump of bushes rising out of a narrow pool of noisy, viscous muck. For a few yards one progressed over two planks, successively placed one before the other. When the planks no longer resisted the sucking mud, men proceeded as best they could (mud only to the ankles and inside the sneakers) and women were carried.

The rowboat is, as always, heavy with water. One of the bearers bails it out with an old tomato can while the guide checks his pistol, lays his spear down in a handy position, stows the machete out of harm's way, and adjusts his headlight. The stars shine down faintly on the water, whose reluctant dark is cut and cut again by the long arcs of light from the head lamp. The lamp becomes the hunter, persistent, quiet, smooth, patiently and methodically searching the edges of the water, then darting to pin down a sudden sound. The sounds are bird sounds, the faint rustle of a pair of white herons soaring into flight; the creaking of a bough under a sleepy pelican rearranging his awkward bulk; a huge pink bird rustles in her nest, a wild duck cries his homesickness. The leader adds to the sounds his alligator call, a long, mournful "Wa-a-a, wa-a-a" through cupped hands followed by two slow, loud claps of the hand. He explains that this is the alligator mating call.

Suddenly, it all became silly: cramped humans in a little rowboat, buzzed by mosquitoes, shoes full of gelid mud, damp night air icing the bones, trying to think like an alligator, who has a notoriously small brain. Will he be lured by the fake lady alligator? Or is he lying at some edge of the lagoon, trying to think like a man, and outthink him? Sensing that the glamour of the night is fading with cold time and the absence of alligators, the guide directs the boat to another lagoon, a chaos of mangroves. The boat cannot be poled through; the thick interlacing of lower roots brakes it, the stiff dangling upper roots slash at faces and shoulders. All hands pull and push at the knotted woods which claw upward and pierce downward like grotesque teeth chewing up the space and air of a world without a sky.

A third, clear lagoon is even shallower than the others and gives off the loveliest of night sounds, the whisper of underwater grasses yielding to the passage of the boat, a delicate, brushing, passive sound. Listening to the murmur of the grasses one hardly notices now the constant flow of light, around and around the edges of the water until, suddenly, it stops. In the aura of its fixed glare sits a gray, craggy head, carved of the rock and mud of an ancient, unknown universe. Smoothly, smoothly, the guide poles toward his place. The alligator pulls down his primitive snout and tiny eyes and disappears. The guide searches the waters and all the shores of the lagoon. He "Wa-a-a, w-a-a-s" and claps his hands repeatedly. Nothing, except for the shocking change in the confirmed nonhunters, the people who had gone along for the ride. With the sight of the head, one was no longer a spectator. Perhaps it is the sudden meeting with a primeval enemy or the blood lust flowing in subterranean human swamps; maybe it is the long waiting and a need for action; one wants that alligator, close, in conflict, to spear him, to see him thrash, to drag his carcass through the swamp.

Back in the lighthouse dorm and cupping the solace of rum, the guide consoles with how it should have been and will be. In pigeon Spanish and lively pantomime, he enacts the kill. "We go, we go, close, close. Take spear. Make big stab. Zoom. 'Gator turn and turn and turn." (He makes spinning motions with his arms.) "Then take pistols—pam, pam, pam. Alligator still move. Take machete, chop, chop, chop. Wait. He dead. Put him in boat. Carry him out on shoulder. Heavy, heavy, plenty dollars." (Alligators were and may still be caught here, the bellies skinned, and the bodies left on the beach for the buzzards to eat. A good skin sells for $75 and more, a lordly sum in an area which lives off fishing and copra-chopping—and little of that, since hurricanes pull up miles of coconut—when the tourists are gone. Consequently, an alligator hunt is not essentially a tourist attraction; it is a deadly serious search for treasure.)

The table, a cave drawing of a table, has been pulled in under the portico, near the cavalier lean-to which houses the tin-plate-over-charcoal oven. It is now boiling coffee and baking the wet socks suspended from a string above it. The chickens are in their coops, the dogs bedded down in one of the empty rooms, the weapons have been cleaned and stored, another empty bottle thrown in the brush. It's time to get some sleep in the anti-*Yanqui* hammock.

Morning breaks. The chickens are aghast, as always, at the new day, at people, at the indignity of being a chicken. The dogs snarl, nip, roll, and bare their teeth at each other like adolescent boys. The guide courteously hands around water and everyone gravely brushes teeth, gargles, and spits into the dirt. After breakfast the inexhaustible guide drives his sleepy troops through a brisk walk along the dunes to a small Mayan ruin. An irrepressible liar and eager to give you your money's worth, he places the ruins in Babylonian times, though they were probably of the time of Tulum and are much destroyed. Some of the buildings, not large, are just barely visible slabs of rock. A small mound-shaped building to which he hacks a path with a machete is undecorated except for a ring of conch shells around the sides and top. It gives out a large, fearsome sound when one blows into the top, and it is easy to understand how storm winds rushing through the upper opening and forced out of the holes in the conch shells could have been the voices of gods bellowing dread at one time.

An antique fowling piece is introduced into the scenery in the afternoon, admired, carefully polished, and you are off to the lagoon again. The birds are noisier now, squeaking like rusty machinery or tropical birds, and obscure the sounds of the reeds whispering to the air. Torpid pelicans weigh down the light brush, herons flash by, and a whir of white birds tautly extend skinny red legs like a young ballet class. Sometimes there are ducks, sometimes there aren't. But always it is a birth-of-the-world experience to glide through the wild hidden lagoons.

With the means, time, and inclination for it, one finds bonefishing at Boca Paila, a good distance away, where whistling brings up the eager fish. And there are still untouched beaches, some of them small, shady coves and others open, glowing bands of pale gold. (Don't swim out too far. A shark's size, his rows of neat little efficient teeth, and his doughy belly are repellent company.)

Don't set your heart on these trips, rewarding as they once were. The fact that the waters around San Miguel are sleeping like good children does not mean a safe, peaceful voyage all the way. If you plan to spend some time on the island, tell your hotel people that you'd like to make this sort of excursion and keep reminding them. They just might be able to arrange it.

There are ruins on the island reachable by jeep or horseback, wrecked ships—quite thoroughly investigated—to view; great spreading stains of sunset to watch; local gossip to gather, which, like island gossip everywhere, is likely to be elaborate and apocryphal; unconfirmed rumors that descendants of the pirate Lafitte still live on the island.

There are shops to explore and vast quantities of imports, should you be yearning for Cadbury chocolates or Planters peanuts.

And then there are the village girls: four to eight years old, rarely above thirty-five pounds of talking weight. They stand in groups on the corners or walk arm in arm talking, talking, talking very seriously. When they reach a crucial point in the discussion, they fold their arms on their chests, stick out their small bellies and, standing exactly as their mothers do, thrash things out thoroughly and at length. Some of them are little hippos and there are a few giraffes, but the common design is gazelle, in spite of the market-woman stance.

Little-girl-watching is best on the streets near the school, but try to find the time also for a short walk in the streets where town turns to country, four or five blocks from the waterfront. Immense creepers tumble from the rickety fences, huge mango trees rise above the tattered banana palms, every yard is its own jungle, every vine has its own vines, and every flower is an overstatement.

Basic living can still be done cheaply in rooms rented out by some of the local householders, plus meals in one of the town's restaurants, or cheese and crackers bought from the local grocers. The meals won't be varied or stimulating, nor will they be remarkably cheap. Unless one wants to settle (and it can grow stultifyingly dull after a while), there is hardly any point in coming here on a shoestring. The fare from the States to Cozumel is a respectable expenditure and, once one has arrived, to deny oneself fishing trips, boat rides, ruin explorations, lagoon snorkeling, is to divest the cost and the place of meaning.

HOTELS

The current favorites are the **Sol Caribe** and **El Presidente.** Then there are the reputable **Cabañas del Caribe,** attractively planned and decorated, the **Cozumel Caribe,** the chic **Mayan Plaza,** and the **Hotel Mara,** which practically sits in the sea.

The above are air-conditioned, of course, and the beaches rather limited in size, since they had to be built up out of little curves of sand and rock. To encourage family trade, an extra bed for a youngster and his board will cost about one-half to two-thirds of the single rate.

The most splendid hotel, **El Presidente,** is south of the village, a thing of bold stretches of orange, purple, and yellow in a style of architecture that encourages inside and out to flow into each other. A row of glass-walled rooms is reached from the main building by a shelter that uses the lovely, complex thatch weaving that is singularly Cozumel. The beach is vast (and swept with brooms) and its sections of shelters arranged like conversation sections in a huge living room. As you might expect, its shop has some of the most appealing "artes populares" on the island. (In spite of the calming effects of sea and sun, the little sea scooters may drive you wild.)

In town and inexpensive: the **Isleño,** which has a restaurant and a pool, **Captain Candela's,** an old-time institution which looks like nothing from the street, has gardens and a pool and plain rooms, the **López,** on the square, keeps its office-desk between two shops. The rooms, some with bath, are meticulously clean and a few give on an enormous mamey tree loaded with fruit in February and March. If the **López** has no more room, try the **Yoli,** on the square, or the **Hotel Pepita,** all three modest in price.

RESTAURANTS

There are a number of showy places on the seafront and less showy near the square. Some have live music, some jukeboxes. Take a short walk and see what appeals to you. One waterfront café, **Pepe's,** sits near the dock and is a sophisticated and efficient—for Cozumel—place. Pepe hangs a sign that says, "Ask me anything," and you can and he answers, in perfect English. Ask about Denis, a relic of the modest, motorbikeless, somnolent days, with a wife who cooked wonderfully well. They lived a few houses off the square, near the post office. If she felt like cooking, if he could get his children to serve, if you let him know a day or two in advance, he would send forth a lengthy parade of platters. If he and she are still at it, gather a convivial group, bring your own rum or tequila and a bottle of insect repellent if the mosquitoes are in full vigor. Denis served in his backyard under a fine old tree which bore one fruit, a large red paper Christmas bell. Maybe it still does. (The latest information is that **Chez Denis** now requires advance booking and has much higher prices than before.) **Morgan's Bar** is less aristocratic but fine nevertheless.

ENTERTAINMENT

There is no lack of bars and you can play pool, dominoes, or chess or go to one of the frequent dances held by local organizations. The salon is a large backyard ringed by tables at which drinks are served, with one long bench for mamas and girls not quite fifteen years old—not old enough for public dancing, yet old enough to be displayed. The deadpan swivel-hipped style may be beyond your Arthur Murray lessons but if you do dance, limit yourself to partners in your own group. The hotels provide entertainment evenings and music almost all day long.

From time to time some adventurer decides to take a boat from Cozumel (or Cancun) to Isla Mujeres, a smaller "Escape Island" to the north and lovely. There are cargo tubs which ply between the islands, with accommodations consisting of whatever space is left on the deck after coils of rope, lengths of pipe, sacks of salt, and vats of water have been stored. The schedule is flighty and often means waiting out day after day. Better to take the Aeronaves de Mayab, which also makes the Mérida–Isla Mujeres flight. Or you can bus from Mérida and then ferry. (This ferry terminal was to have linked Mexican roads with Cuba and, by another ferry, with Florida, a feasible plan for expanded tourism were it not for a Cuban revolution, sugar quotas, oil tankers, and tangents of the cold war.)

The ferry ride should take about an hour, but one doesn't set one's watch by Mexican schedules. Isla Mujeres (the name probably derives from fertility goddesses found by the explorer Grijalva) is a smaller, cruder version of Cozumel: coconut palms and smooth white beaches, thatched huts and blue-green waters, snorkeling, swimming, and a diet of fish, lobster, and turtle. The **Hotel El Presidente Caribe** is, by comparative standards, fairly expensive; the **Rocas del Caribe** somewhat less; and **Maria's,** small, serves extraordinarily good food. There are several inexpensive pensions which are cheaper. Between Isla Mujeres and Contoy there is superb fishing, as there is off Cancun. Entertainment at Isla Mujeres is limited, cuisine basic; one needs no wardrobe and just a little Spanish. For total flight from a nervous world, the island does well, and if it does too well, there are always the jazzier worlds of Cozumel and Cancun.

NOTES: Jeeps and motorbikes are hireable through hotels and on the square and they make Cozumel sound like an annex of Florence. Their advantage, other than speed (and why the rush? to where?), is to make the elderly feel young and jaunty.

There are daily boats that leave at 9 A.M. (go earlier to see fishermen lay out the fish, turtle flesh, conch meat, and lobster on the ledge of the waterfront) to go to Puerto Morelos on the mainland, passing

Tulum on the way. Barring *nortes,* it should take about five or six hours there and back.

Unless you are addicted to your own, don't bother to bring snorkeling masks, flippers, etc.; they are available for hire everywhere.

No matter where you stay, you can use any beach; it is the law in Mexico. The beach boys in the luxury hotels know this and, for a tip, will bring you a beach mat and umbrella and you can, for a while, live it up.

Too bad that Cancun, the beach resort on the coast of Quintana Roo, got rid of the mangrove trees and the tropical birds, the alligators and plump thatched huts to create an entity that is a fury of building going on all along the sea road, from the careless tropical village to the spit between lagoons and sea that holds the large, blazing white hotels and a Club Méditerranée.

Many of the small hotel-motel-condominium buildings of attractive fantasy-colonial with splashes of tropical design are launched by experienced managers who establish the necessary systems and then abandon them to the control of young men who speak English but know nothing about service and cuisine. The erratic service or lack of it, the *"qué me importa"* attitude of the handsome, indifferent young man at the desk, create an atmosphere that is less than amiable. Spend extra money for the good-looking, smooth, and knowing **Camino Real** or the **Aristos** or the ornate, sybaritic charms of the new **Exelaris Hilton** or the **Krystal Cancun** and its startling decor. Or any new costly wonder that has sprung up since this writing. Or stay with the trustworthy **Cancun Sheraton.**

Part of the vaulting ambition of Cancun has fostered fine new roads that lead to interesting places. Car hire is easy, but go to a responsible agency and insist on checking all essential functions: there are few garages and fewer mechanics in the low jungle that borders the road once you leave Cancun. The map of the general area (maps, by the way, are given away profligately by every establishment) will indicate, to the southwest, the farthest point of a one-day excursion, Cobà, 47 straight hypnotic miles inland from Tulum. Cobà is a vast Mayan zone, a center of prime importance once, and now a deep endless tangle of green and toppled stones that, experts say, may have been hundreds of pyramids and other ceremonial buildings. One may not enter without a guide, nor are there vehicles to take one through the mile and a half into the jungle and then out. The stone paths are irregular and slick after rains; not too bad, but they require more solid shoes than sandals. And the insects, from invisible pests to hulking mosquitoes, make slacks essential. Following the guide into the path that leads to the Conjunto las Pinturas, you may become aware of a faintly familiar sensation and odor, the moist, close atmosphere of the reptile house in a zoo, an artificial replica of the damp heat that steams from close, tropical woods.

The Conjunto las Pinturas presents a building that has lost its outer shell and decorations that might have been very much like those at Uxmal and quite possibly Palenque. It is now reduced to basic, rough stone with a suggestion of a pyramid shape, strips of surviving color—blue and dark red—protected by thatch near its truncated top and fronting it, remains of small round and square structures that had, like altars, ritualistic uses. From the Conjunto one can see a high building heap sprouting heavy green fringes of trees and another very tall building (Nohoch Mul, "tall house" in Mayan), cleared, isolated, distorted, and infinitely sad. Many centuries ago, the guide says, this and other buildings of priests and warrior-kings were carefully repaired and redecorated every fifty-two years (a terrifyingly significant time span, as it was among the Aztecs) but have since been left to destruction by conquerors, lashing rains, and merciless sun. Nearby sits the thatched hut of the caretaker with its complement of plum-eyed infant, one piglet, one chicken, and a cat. Overhead the long curly tail of a monkey is seen disappearing into the trees. Inside a dense grove rests a stele (one of forty found in this zone) that shows a priest or warrior in full plumage and armor and, as well, the chisel marks of a thief who tried to cut the figure away from his heavy stone. The symbols on the stele bear the date 780, a time of the High Classic period that produced the most elegant of Mayan art and architecture.

Heading back, the guide points to a low pyramid that was a marker on the ancient road to Chichén Itzá, one of several roads to various Mayan cities, and then he points to a stand of slender trees that resemble birches. From these, he said, the sap is extracted and fermented to make the intoxicating *"balche,"* the same liquor mentioned in Spanish reports of the customs and habits of the Mayans written three centuries ago. Not too far away, another Mexican immortal, bushes hung with minute chile peppers that, for all their toylike innocent size, bite like scorpions. Through the brush can be glimpsed the blue shine of a lake, one of the five hidden in the jungle, and near the entrance and along the outer road, is a lake studded with water lilies. Suddenly, from a bend in the road, emerge the voices of children and a streak of neat, white-clad little bodies trailing bags of books. More surprising than the pyramids and the stele and the durability of *balche* is the unseen presence of a schoolhouse that teaches more than a dozen children. Where do they live, where do they play in this brooding green silence? Should you want to learn more of this mesmerizing area, settle in at the **Hotel Villa Arqueologica**, impressive and informative.

The first stop on the way back is Tulum, once isolated and hard to reach, now bordered by a parking lot full of cars and excursion buses, an arc of thatched stands that sell oranges, drinks, coconut milk, coral T-shirts, and undistinguished examples of Mexican crafts, none of them of the Maya who has no present crafts except his skillful roof thatching. The best in the hectic display is the Mayan face of the vendors and the lively spiel of an English-speaking guide who keeps calling, "What you gonna really see if you don't let me tell you about the Mayan civilization?" (For the historical background and actual presence of Tulum, see page 388.)

Continuing northward, stop at Xel-Ha. A pre-auto road description on page 390 gives the general flavor of this beguiling place. Most of the birds disappear when excursion-bus hordes of swimmers and snorkelers disturb their terrain. In compensation, though, you can walk through delightful, light-streaked groves in the company of multitudes of fish that swim among the shallow ledges of rock near the path. There's compensation also in a place to change into a bathing suit, a few pleasant thatched circles for refreshments, and, on the rocks from which one enters the snorkling hole, fossil marks of coral and big shells, reminders of a time when the little green islands and outcroppings of rock were under water.

Akumal confronts the road with a dining room for its beach bungalows and a small museum of ships' wreckage. The charge for visiting here includes a beach fee (not absolutely legitimate because, as mentioned, all beaches are free). The charge is not large, though, and affords a swim in the luminous blue-green waters of a graceful bay, almost pristine except for a few houses neatly hidden among the palms, but to judge from the advertising, eager to be as crowded as Acapulco. There are already three hotels: the largish **Akumal Caribe**,

Las Casitas Akumal with fine cottages, and the simpler **Villas Maya**—and more undoubtedly to come.

With a ticket available in any hotel or travel office one meets a capacious excursion boat across from the Hotel El Presidente to slip—and when the wind rises, to rock—through the pale greens and the deep blues of the Caribbean. There is intermittent music, but you can't hear it well because of the thrum of the motor. There are glass-bottomed boxes in the hold that show nothing but the rush of bubbled waters except when the boat slows for a mysteriously beautiful scene of gently waving fronds of rust-brown coral fringed with very white sand and fish darting around and under the waving brown fans. The goal of the trip, an edge of Isla Mujeres, affords a half hour to swim in a scallop of beach and a view of several big local turtles oozing around each other in a box on the pier.

The ride back takes its route through one or two narrow lagoons in meshed mangroves and the faint shine of inner lagoons from which, now and then, a cormorant sails out to do his fishing over the open waters. Now depleted of their richer wildlife, the low, tight tangles of jungle and slender, still waters yet give some idea of the remote, undisturbed mood of the area as it was a few short years ago.

As one approaches the shock of tall and wide buildings on the Cancun shore comes the question, where to eat?, assuming that your hotel serves one immutable, unsatisfactory menu. At this writing, the **Camino Real** and the **Aristos** offer satisfying variety and quality at no higher prices than do the unreliables. Or a snack at the **Convention Center,** or seviche of conch and a lobster at **Augustus Caesar.** For a similar list at similar prices, investigate **Carrillo's** in the village. If your impulse runs to Oriental food, try the lower restaurant in the elaborately Polynesian house of **Moana Loa,** at a price, and you may have to reserve in advance. What one rarely sees in tourist restaurants is any hint of local cooking or the distinguished cuisine of Yucatán, a close and sophisticated neighbor. This can be remedied at low cost at **El Bocadito,** in the village a short distance from the bus station. It is a cheerfully ugly and generous place, the service of old-time amiability. Have a shrimp cocktail or conch seviche and the Yucatecan *pollo pibil,* chicken in a reddish spice that gives a warm, pleasant flavor, served as it should be, on a banana leaf. With it, just-baked tender tortillas and a beer. You might choose broiled or fried fish or, if it is Sunday, the local "Pochero," a stew of meat and vegetables, or, for the pleasure of saying its name, "Poc Chuc," which is Mayan for grilled pork. **Los Almendros,** more formal, offers the same Yucatecan cuisine as it does in Mérida.

NOTES: Taxis are expensive, but the frequent bus service between the village and the hotels costs only a few pesos and is much more entertaining.

Mexicana Airlines flies you from Mexico City to Mérida, to Cancun, to Cozumel, on a seven-day, six-night tour. The price was recently something under 6000 pesos, which included everything except a few meals, beers, and Coca-Colas. The competition has been, and is, avid. Inquire about other tours through your travel agent.

MEXICAN HOURS

8:30 P.M. *A red light at a corner of Avenida Juárez in Mexico City. A boy thrusts a newspaper into the window of a waiting taxi. No, he doesn't want it, says the passenger. Lottery ticket? No. Maybe a toy? No. Well, maybe a belt? And he thrusts a ringful of dangling strips of leather into the cab. No. Paper fan from Japan? No. The light changes.*

9:00 *The University of Campeche has organized a small celebration for the opening of its art show. After greetings and a view of the paintings, the guests seat themselves in several rows of chairs and listen attentively to a local poet read from his works. His hair is longish, he wears the flowing black tie of* La Bohéme *and the authentically starved look of romantic tradition. No one in the audience thinks he is strange, of the wrong place and century; they applaud him enthusiastically and show him every sign of high respect.*

9:30 *The fiesta at Tenango is over. Going away from it, the massed shadows of women and children move over the night road like dark clouds; their bare feet make no sound; they hardly speak. The only light comes from their lanterns, which illuminate swinging triangles of long skirts and the children's flashing legs.*

9:45 *A group of travelers orders dinner in a seafood restaurant not ordinarily frequented by foreigners. The opening order is for mussel soup all around, with one exception—shrimp cocktail. The rolls arrive, then the soup; they are slowly consumed. No shrimp cocktail. The waiter comes back, stares at* the shrimp fancier and disappears. He returns with the chef, points out the eccentric, and they both disappear. Hungry eons pass before the waiter triumphantly ushers in a shrimp cocktail. One half of the shallow goblet contains the expected red sauce supporting several shrimp, the other half, kept separate by the miracle of surface tension, is a Manhattan cocktail. The kitchen, having discussed, inspected, reinspected, finally identified the customer as a Yanqui; any Yanqui ordering a "cocktail" must have it laced with alcohol.

10:00 In Pátzcuaro the fiesta goes on. Several men are meticulously concerned with a large heap of painted papers and small wooden boxes. With breathless care they open the folds of delicate paper, attach a box to strings that emerge from one fold, put a lit candle in the box and slowly, slowly release the immense paper balloon which they have been cutting, pasting, and painting for a week. The white globe rises, sways, turns, and is caught by the flames, which consume it. The men start raising another, which burns, too, and another and another. There is no sign of impatience or disappointment; this is the way things are. On the fifth try, one balloon rises straight and full into the dark sky and holds until it becomes a star. The fine-strung crowd breathes a deep, long "Ah-h-h" in unison, the balloon craftsmen permit themselves to smile, and everyone goes off for another drink.

A Grab Bag of Information

Airlines Service is frequent and increasingly widespread—from U.S. cities, Canada, other Latin American countries. Aeromexico, Eastern Airlines, and Pan Am make nonstop flights from New York to Mexico City; American and Compañía Mexicana fly Chicago–Mexico City; Western and Mexicana fly the Los Angeles–Mexico City route. There are direct New York–Acapulco flights and Miami–Mérida, for instance, to indicate the growing meshwork of plane service. Increasingly, package tours carry visitors from several U.S. destinations directly to popular resorts.

Train service, as in the States, is not what it was. There are changes to make, uncertainty about dining services, etc. But if you have the time and curiosity, try.

Your tourist card permits you a discount on restaurant taxes but not on hotel tax. Remember to carry it with you—for possible discounts not related to eating.

Bargains The currently depressed peso causes the dollar to buy a gratifying amount, especially outside of tourist centers.

Travel by plane, train, bus is cheap in Mexico. Another bargain area is repair. Shoe repairs, for instance, are skillfully done, and no pair of shoes is too run-down to rescue. Jewelers do fine, inexpensive jobs, as do seamstresses and tailors. Since labor is cheap, services in general are low in cost.

"The Bite" As it does everywhere else, money talks in Mexico, but rather more simply and openly than in other places. Salaries are so low (a traffic policeman earns about $4 a day) that bribes are generally counted on as part of a salary, comparable to a waiter's tips.

Going to Acapulco by plane in season can be arranged by sweetening a hand (the more realistic Mexican calls it the bite, *la mordida*). Customs men can be moved, so can policemen, so can people in government offices. A *mordida* can whistle misplaced papers out of their hiding place and act as a magic wand when words, gestures, and the attrition of passing time have no effect. The above isn't *always* true; more and more, the government is trying to improve salaries and is instilling a sense of shame and national pride in its employees, but the great day of absolute rectitude still sits far over the horizon. The present situation has its clear uses to the traveler, however. For a little money, he can save himself hours and days of time and the services of an interpreter and, in addition, feel considerably more powerful than he might in the same situation at home.

Bus Travel Bus drivers in the bigger cities and towns despise the sober, full stop; it lacks style. If you are going to use public vehicles be prepared to sharpen your reflexes.

Although buses and trains have time-honored reputations for starting late, don't count on it; except for Toonerville trolleys in unrushed hamlets, they make an effort at keeping set schedules. The "Pullmans," fairly luxurious buses that have toilets and connect major towns, leave near the precise minute.

Remember that there is practically no place in Mexico to which some bus or other doesn't trundle. It sometimes takes time, patience, and a suspension of fastidiousness, but it will be very cheap and, one way or another, stimulating. (There are very few vacuums of dullness in Mexico.)

Greyhound Lines, and one or two similar companies, connect with Mexican border towns for transfer to other buses. It will be inexpensive, undoubtedly interesting, and probably backbreaking unless you stop for a day or two along the route.

Car Rental American car-rental services have branches at major airports, in the large cities, and there are some Mexican agencies. Inquire at the AMA (the Mexican equivalent of AAA) or your hotel. A car plus driver may cost about $25 a day (one can bargain) plus the driver's keep. If you are doing your own driving, be aware of the fact that new roads are being cut through many areas and old roads steadily repaired. Inquire at AMA if you can and at gas stations about what lies ahead. Also, watch out for dogs, goats, and burros who choose to cross roads at the most frightening moments and for signs that say *"libre"* (free), *"cuota"* (toll), usually for newer roads. If you can possibly avoid it, don't drive at night and keep your car in good repair.

Children About taking children to Mexico: Milk is no serious problem; one can find evaporated milk anywhere and powdered milk in most large towns. Mixed with water boiled by the small, traveling heater one brings from the States, it should be satisfactory to any but the most recalcitrant child (who hardly deserves to be taken on a trip, anyhow). Babysitters—chambermaids or houseboys or their sisters— are in good, happy supply and their patience, affection, and gentleness will ruin your child for all other babysitters.

The problem is mainly that of interest and attention span, which only an individual parent can judge. Can he be absorbed by the shapeless milling which takes hours of fiesta time? Will he be interested in Villahermosa's fascinating museum, or the charms of Oaxaca's market, or Orozco's searing murals? In other words, will he spoil *your* fun?

Documents If you are driving you will, of course, be carrying all your car papers, plus an auto permit issued at the border. Consult the AAA about the validity of your car insurance in Mexico, most easily obtained in border cities. The Mexican government gives you a visitor's permit at no charge valid for 90 or 180 days (*not* six months, a wispy difference which can make trouble) and obtainable within a few hours at government tourist bureaus, consulates, and some airports on presentation of proof of citizenship. (Always carry it with you.) There are other visitors' papers—for students, employees of American firms, honored guests of the government—and if you are in one of these categories, find out what the most recent regulations call for. A passport, new or obsolete, is not required, but comes in very handy for cashing express checks in suspicious towns and to show at inspection points along the road where an inverse ratio of more-papers-equals-less-delay usually works.

Fauna Tropical Mexico breeds bugs like its fruit, fantasies of shape and size which often lack character. It is understandable that you be impressed and even shocked, but there is little to worry about. The real nuisances are almost invisible, little flecks of dust that leave itching torments felt several hours later, usually during the time of deepest sleep. "Cutter's" or 6-12, as stick or liquid, will keep these and mosquitoes away. For *garrapatas,* a particularly tenacious tick, try lavings of liquid before venturing into their brush. Should they pierce the oily film, do as they do in Yucatán: soak tobacco in alcohol (used butts in rum will do) and, having dipped a match end into the mixture, touch it to the tick. When it begins to emerge, help it along with tweezers or your fingernails.

Guide Service   Don't count on organized tourism in any but popular places; you're on your inefficient and stimulating own in the hinterland, except for the ubiquitous little boy who will attach himself. Trust him and his knowledge. For being led by the hand, consult with Aguirre Guest Tours, Cook's, Mexican Travel Advisors, Garza, and your hotel desk. Your travel agent and newspaper advertisements will advise you that package tours—some of them fairly inexpensive—to resort areas are proliferating rapidly.

Liquor   You may bring one bottle into Mexico, but the taking out is a question of local regulations at home, anywhere from a gallon to a depressing nothing. (Cigarettes? One carton.)

Unless you choose to get potted, watch the drinking in the altitudes. Something magical and scientific happens to alcohol and the human body; the latter becomes weaker, the former stronger. Even the light, maidenly Carta Blanca beer can make a fuzzy eye and a wayward tongue.

Lottery   Lottery tickets are, obviously, legal or they wouldn't be the leis of Mexicans, blind and crippled, who sell them. As these things go, it is remarkably honest and the Mexican Commonwealth Fund for many of Mexico's hospitals and public institutions. A ticket costs little, and if you win nothing, the chances are still good for a *reintegro,* which means that you get your money back for another try. The newspapers list winning numbers—a great many of them, for small to immense sums—the many lottery stalls carry lists which go back some days. Drawing is on Wednesday nights at the National Lottery Building (at the juncture of Rosales and Juárez in Mexico City) with much ceremony and excitement, and open to the public.

Mail Never mail a card or letter to the States, or anywhere out of Mexico, via ordinary mail. If it arrives at all, it will get to its destination weeks after you can evoke pleasure or envy. Only the air-mail stamp is considered a serious symbol of communication, sufficiently commanding for postal employees to bother about. *Except* in towns that have railroads which go to the U.S. border; then ordinary mail, bypassing sorting in Mexico City, is usually faster.

Minor Aids Before you venture out anywhere in the country, buy a supply of Kleenex, and a couple of plastic bags, the latter for fruit ripe from country market stalls and wet bathing suits, the former for a hundred uses, depending on the necessities which turn up and your ingenuity.

Carry a flashlight. Short, dramatic storms frequently demolish power lines, and although every household and hotel keeps a good store of candles on hand, it sometimes takes a period of scurried searching to find them. For travelers who are readers in bed, it (plus extra batteries) is essential; the one weak unreachable bulb in very rural inns is not for bookworms.

If you are going into fairly remote places, supply yourself with canned food, a can opener, and a pocketknife in the nearest large town. You won't starve without canned meat or tuna fish (*atún*, comparable in quality to ours), because there are always bananas, breads, tortillas, eggs, *frijoles*, and soups, but they make a more varied diet.

Mexican baskets, as everyone knows, are a world of varied shapes, weave, decoration, and color. For trudging through jungle paths or climbing pyramids the best are those with shoulder straps, like the Oaxacan bags or the *morral* carried by farmers. Just as useful is an army knapsack or a lightweight camera bag.

Although effulgent gas stations are blossoming on even minor roads, should you be planning a long drive through fairly empty country, put in a supply of extra gas, water, and snacks.

A traveling alarm clock is important to have. Although you leave word to be called in the morning, the *portero* or desk clerk may sleep through your hour or, in some rural instances, not understand why anyone asleep should *want* to be awakened, for any reason. On the other hand, some zealous youngster who is also night watchman and eager to show his efficiency will start waking you at four in the morning for a six o'clock call.

Moctezuma's Revenge, or the Aztec Trot Many residents carry Lomotil as preventive and cure for intestinal bugs. It is available in Mexican drugstores, without a prescription, and taken one tablet a day, except when the attack has set in. This calls for two to begin with and one at four-hour intervals thereafter. Most malarial regions have been cleaned out or remain inaccessible to visitors, but if you are concerned, get some Paludrina at Sanborn's and ask them how to take it. If you must drink water, doctor it with Halozone tablets. (New anti-bug magics keep appearing; check.)

Mural Glut The traveler often has the sinking, uncomfortable feeling that Mexico City has too many murals to see and that he really doesn't want to see them all and that he should. Their huge strophes are intense, often angry, sometimes incomprehensible to those who know little of Mexico's history and revolutionary agonies. They have the large, portentous weight of Wagner's music, and like Wagner, a moderate amount can sometimes go a long enough way. Take what you can and let the rest go.

Museum Glut As indicated elsewhere, Mexico is beginning to bloom with interesting regional museums. Considering the multiplicity of artifacts each of the old cultures produced, you may have a sense of repetition, and often cry, "Hold, enough!" Unless you are passionately interested and knowledgeable, don't try to examine every object, but do keep a sharp eye out for the two or three (or more) objects in each museum which soar out of their times and context to become great art.

Prices Acapulco, Cancun, Ixtapa, Las Hadas, and the fashionable fishing resorts of Baja are at the top of the money tree, then Cuernavaca, Taxco, Mexico City; and then a steep slide to inconsequential costs in smaller towns and villages. The designations—modest, moderate, and expensive—used in this book are based on Mexican prices with a recognition of the differences between the scale in Mexico City and that of Oaxaca, for example. It is safe to figure 20 percent less than Mexico City for the rest of the country, except for one or two remarkable and deserving nests of luxury.

One can expect a "modest" dinner to cost up to $4 (without drinks); up to $6 is "moderate," and beyond that is living high off the hog except in the big city. But remember that prices keep rising as the peso falls.

Reading A lifetime of concentrated reading would just about skim the depth and breadth of material available on Mexico, a multitudinousness which is a mark of the country's fascinations and problems. For the traveler who likes to go intellectually newborn, there is no indispensable reading except the sentences in a phrasebook. Near-indispensable are Flandrau's *Viva Mexico*, an account written over fifty years ago and still valid, by a writer of talent, humor, and affection; Madame Calderón de la Barca's *Life in Mexico*, a series of keen-eyed, keen-witted letters written by the wife of the Spanish Minister to Mexico early in the 1840s, and in many ways, not dated at all. Bernal Díaz del Castillo, a soldier with Cortés in his youth, did not get around to writing his version of the Conquest until he was quite an old man settled on the Guatemalan land grant given him by the grateful mother country. How absolutely accurate his report was no one can say—there are few others extant—but his flatfooted prose, completely devoid of ornament or gestures of imagination, lends his *Discovery and Conquest of Mexico* a plainness which impresses as verity. Here and there a disgruntled scholar crops up with a sneering allusion to Miguel Covarrubias as an "inventor" of Mexican archaeology. Pay no attention: his *Indian Art of Mexico and Central America* is an invaluable collection of text and pictures, which provides a sturdy thread for wandering through the maze of Mexican pre-Conquest art. History? Henry B. Parkes' *History of Mexico* is a brisk, vividly written account. Architecture? Trent E. Sanford's *History of Mexican Architecture*. The people? *Idols Behind Altars* by Anita Brenner, *Little Mexico* by William Spratling, *Labyrinth of Solitude* by Octavio Paz, and Mexican fiction in translation: *The Underdogs* by Mariano Azuela, *Pedro Páramo* by Juan Rulfo, the novels of Carlos Fuentes, *The Nine Guardians* by Rosario Castellanos, and those of Luis Spota's novels available in English. Travel, sociology, archaeology, and pioneering of the nineteenth century? Stephens' *Incidents of Travel in Central America, Chiapas and Yucatán*. Readable anthropology? Robert Redfield's *Tepoztlán,* and Oscar Lewis' *Five Families* and *The Children of Sanchez.* And these are only a beginning.

Refinements It is good form to say you are a "norteamericano"; Mexicans, Guatemalans, etc., consider themselves American, too.

Eggs as printed on menus are *huevos,* as voiced in many areas they are *blanquillos* (little white ones), circumventing a common and almost universal obscenity. (There are still places in the world where two eggs are bought as "those of which one is too little and three are too much.")

If you want griddlecakes, flapjacks, or pancakes—whatever they call them in your part of the country—ask for "hawtkeks" (hot cakes). "Pancake" (pronounced "ponkek" and sometimes spelled that way) means "pound-cake," of which it may be a corruption. Or, it may be a combination of English "cake" and Spanish "bread" *(pan),* thus effectively describing itself.

Schools A fruitful way to broaden the horizons of an adolescent (not too young) is to send him to a summer school for dabbling in Spanish, Mexican history, crafts, archaeology, anthropology, guitar-playing, and folk-dancing. It costs little; with a few exceptions, the courses are undemanding and the English-speaking authorities will usually place him with Mexican families who, because he is so far from home and mother, will pamper the *pobrecito* and teach him—by osmosis—some of the gestures of the civilized man. Mexico City's university has a summer program, and Mexico City College (American-run) also. School life in the smaller cities is easier, more companionable, and often more flavorful. Inquire of Jalapa and Cuernavaca, which have lively, full programs, as does Guanajuato. Morelia recognizes the outside world; inquire of the university. San Miguel de Allende has its art-plus-culture schools and a respected writing center. Taxco has an art school, Mexico City has several. Morelia's is well known and Guanajuato has been talking about one, possibly a firm fact by this time.

Shopping In the happy days of $500-duty-free foreign spending, one could sprinkle a homecoming with a shower of Mexican silver, belt buckles, money clasps, tie clips, and cuff links for men, and a great variety of ornaments for the ladies. Now that the allowance has been reduced to $300 the buying must be a bit circumspect. (It is possible to send "unsolicited" gifts, clearly marked as such and not exceeding $10 in value, in endless numbers, but the packing, marking, and mailing can chew up a huge chunk of vacation time.) Consider some other possibilities variously amenable to packing and carrying, and described more fully in the appropriate sections:

Baskets and embroidered bags.

Wallets and coin purses.

Blouses embroidered, blouses beaded, blouses tucked, blouses belaced; primitive, demure, sporty, or sexy. And skirts to go with them.

Old silver coins, in imitation or authentic.

Bulky sweaters, smooth or scratchy.

Drugs, cheaper than ours, some available without prescriptions, and price-controlled. (Make sure you know what you want and keep the quantities reasonable.)

Sandals, indigenous or East Village style. (Bring along footprints to measure by.) For dancer friends you might buy flamenco shoes.

Magic paper figures.

Semiprecious stones.

Medicinal herbs, amulets, and armadillo skin for hypochondriacal friends.

Animals, of straw, papier-mâché, clay, tin, glass.

Dressed fleas and jewel-studded beetles.

Walnut shells surrounding minuscule weddings or bullfights.

Coconut shells surrounding the same, larger and more elaborate.

Rosaries of wool, seeds, and tin, which make attractive necklaces.

Pottery sirens.

Papier-mâché skeletons jauntily dressed.

Papier-mâché Judases.

Paintings on paper or bark.

Matches, wax. Classicos boxes carry reproductions of great paintings. Talismanos bear horoscopes and advice: Scorpio is told to give his family more attention and love because they need it; Sagittarius is given more demanding advice—he is told to increase his self-esteem and ego, and not to be egotistical.

Toy kitchens, old style, with charmingly arranged little casseroles hung on the walls, the way you might see them in the Pátzcuaro museum.

Clay whistles, an ancient toy.

Knives engraved "I die for love," or "Death before shame."

Scarves, black-and-white-checked, pink-tasseled, worn by the Beau Brummels around Las Casas.

Boxes of tin, glass, wood.

Trays of wood or tin.

Colonial furniture, copies.

Colonial portraits, copies.

Pre-Columbian masterpieces, copies.

Heads and headless torsos of small figurines in authentically antique style and not necessarily authentic.

Huipiles or *ipiles,* the square blouses worn in the tropics.

Rebozos.

Serapes.

Mats and napkins, hotly colored, beaded, embroidered.

Morelianas, flat, chewy disks of caramel.

Ates, fruit candies.

Cajeta, a syrup, like melted caramels.

Rum—try Ron Castillo.

Tequila.

Silver—as jewelry or elaborate coffee services or flatware.

Brandy—taste some first; they vary; try Madero.

Onyx beads.

Pottery. The crude things made for home consumption are often the most appealing and the most usable.

The Mexican counterpart of *TV Guide* will tell you where to get a device that will give you "a new nose in thirty seconds; no surgery." It is a bent wire, which, inserted in the nostrils, makes the nose appear shorter. Guaranteed painless unless you sneeze.

Taxis The taxi situation is a tune with endless variations. In most towns taxis are unmetered and it is essential to make a flat rate beforehand and arrange to be picked up for the return trip. Except in the large cities—Mexico City, Monterrey, Guadalajara, Puebla— no trip within town limits should cost much. Resort areas cling to the universal resort practice of overcharging, and there is nothing much you can do about it. Mexico City's metered cabs ring up pathetically low fares, as mentioned elsewhere, but the driver will ask for several pesos more. He doesn't expect a tip beyond this, but it does come in handy to a man who has too many children and too little money. Cabs are not easy to find on the street (nor will they necessarily go where you want to go), especially when you need them most, at going-to-the-restaurant times and bullfight time. Have your hotel call a radio or *sitio* cab which should charge something extra and increases that charge at night. The airport and bus terminals sell taxi chits at fair, flat rates, no tip expected. To go to the terminals your hotel may put you into a luxurious car that asks twice the price of a taxi. Fight or resign yourself, depending on your degree of rush. If you're traveling light and have the time and confidence, try the subway (Metro) which has a branch to the airport (Aeropuerto Station) and another to the terminal of southbound buses (Taxquena Station).

Except for the buses, the *pesero* of Mexico City offers the cheapest and most companionable ride. These are gallant, beat-up cabs, with well-marked stops which show a man leaping into a car, that ply Madero, Cinco de Mayo, Juárez, and Reforma at small fees, depending on the length of the ride. Some of them can be found on main avenues leading from the center, but the common run is between the Zócalo and several points on Reforma. (It's best to ask what the terminal point is before you board.) Characteristically, the stuffing isn't quite contained by the plastic of the seat covers and one door handle doesn't work—decrepitude that calls for all the symbols of luck the drivers hang over the front windows: baby shoes, bright-colored saints, horseshoes, fringed banners of the Virgin of Guadalupe. Women are not to expect courtesy in boarding a *pesero;* they must run, jostle, and push with the rest.

Taxis seem to shun the city streets after eleven o'clock at night. If you are in the hotel belt, ask a doorman (for a decent tip) to get you a radio cab; or he will find you a guide car, whose charge will be astronomic by local standards but still less than you'd pay at home. Having a Mexican friend who belongs to a call-taxi service helps enormously.

Telephone   If you are phoning friends in Mexico City and the number is some years old, dial 5 and then the other digits.

To call the States is usually much easier than to connect with another town in Mexico. Have the hotel operator take care of the latter for you. To call the States directly, dial 95, the area code, and the number. If you have difficulty, dial 09, the international service with a good command of English. It might be well to remember that calls are expensive: a high tax, a hotel charge, etcetera. It is cheaper to call after 7 P.M. and cheaper still after 10 P.M. and on Sundays.

Tickets   Whenever possible, have the hotel get you train and air tickets and seats for the bullfight. The surcharge will usually be negligible and worth it for the time and energy it saves.

Tipping   The self-conscious field of tipping needn't be. The 15 percent rule works everywhere, and slightly smaller percentages are perfectly acceptable outside big cities and lavish establishments. The money added to a metered taxi fare in Mexico City is a tip, but if you want to offer more, no one will turn it down. The sinks of public bathrooms always display a show of pesos as shill for others. On your dollar you can afford to be generous.

Toilets   A country toilet, particularly in the dry season in a dry area—Yucatán, for instance—can be a shock to one who considers a flush toilet with ever-running water one of the natural rights of man. You are not being victimized by sloth or backwardness; there is no water. The only thing to do is forget your antiseptic upbringing and hurry. Where there is water, and flush mechanisms that work, there may be some difficulty in finding the activating button. Look for it on the floor or in the wall or as a set of dials like the controls of a toy airplane, or a hand pull which enlivens a web of chains. The signs you are to look for are "Damas," "Caballeros," and "Sanitorios."

Travel   Make reservations only in big cities and resorts; small towns go into a panic and so will you.

Trouble   Confused reservations, overcharging, immediately new-born "regulations" (in actuality a request for a bribe)? In spite of the fact that the official envelope of the Department of Tourism bears, in red, the legend "Tourism is an inexhaustible fountain of economic resources for Mexico: LET US GUARD IT!", there is little you can do except waste exasperated hours seeking justice. If the transgression is high, try the local police with the understanding that you will probably get nowhere. In Mexico City, call the U.S. Embassy or look for one of the bilingual policemen (the uniform bears a conspicuous badge), who will undoubtedly try to help you until *he* meets a wall of musical, courtly double talk. Best forget the whole thing.

If your trouble is physical and you need a physician or dentist, take your pick from the Anglo-American Directory in Mexico City. If you're in the country, head for the nearest town and ask at the police station *(policía)* for a doctor—a good number of Mexican doctors take their postgraduate training in the States and speak English— or ask to be guided to a *médico* or *dentista*. The most elementary Spanish will get the idea across; point to yourself and say *"enfermo"* or *"enferma,"* as your sex dictates, and then repeat *"médico."* In the general area of medicine: carry rubber sandals to wear in bathrooms and under showers of tropical hotels.

Unburied Treasures   Remember that Mexico's archaeological treasures belong to her; the days of openly carrying off Elgin marbles and Moctezuma's cape of feathers are over. Serious consequences trail from trying to smuggle out a rare Jaina figure or Zapotec funerary urn—a very illegal act. However, no one objects to your carrying one of the copies becoming increasingly available or a small, common object like the hundreds of figurines or parts of them which turn up at practically every site. It was the practice of many cultures to throw handfuls in with the buried dead; two or three more or less is hardly national depletion.

Unless you are an expert, resign yourself to the possibility of buying a fake. Mexican boys are awesomely clever at any kind of imitation and patient enough to go through the laborious process of making a figure look old and long-buried. (Sometimes, they scratch an authentically old piece because it appears too clean.) If you don't spend much, a fake is not necessarily to be scorned: they are often beautiful pieces of sculpture and sometimes look more "handmade" than the artifacts which were made in molds when the demand of the great ceremonial cities outran the artisans' capacity to make them individually.

In addition to spending little, expect little. How it happens is not open information, but the big cities in the States are well stocked with "primitive" and "pre-Columbian" Mexican art, some fakes, others the real article. It is also known but never acknowledged that road workers, ditch diggers, gravediggers, and farmers in rich zones (and it is said of Mexico with considerable truth that you can dig almost anywhere and soon hit archaeology) are kept on stipends by dealers to whom they are obliged to bring whatever they find. What, then, are a tourist's chances for a great find?

Understanding   The Mexican nodding under a tree at midday was not born drowsy, nor is he posing for the souvenir book end of *artes típicos.* He has been up since early dawn and, on little food and against the airlessness of high altitudes, has been digging in an arid, discouraged field or trotting for miles, bent double, under a load twice as heavy as himself. Soon he'll wake to another six or eight hours of the same. He may not always be enterprising—particularly in areas where there is nothing to be enterprising about or with—but he's not lazy.

Weather *Always* include a lightweight raincoat in your luggage (not the kind that creates its own steam bath). The rainy season runs to various stretches of time between early June and late September. The rains may be short torrential storms, a light moist dusting, or a slow listless slide of waters. A distinct "rainy season" is not dictated by immutable law; the fall typhoon season can drown roads and Gulf ports and make itself felt in milder rains in mountain country. (In spite of these irregularities the Mexican sun *does* shine effulgently most of the time.)

For Women Especially The first question women traveling alone ask, and properly, is "Can I go out alone at night?" Hemming and hawing and exceptions can provide encouragement but basically the answer is "No." This is very much a man's world, where only the most enlightened couples go out together at night, except for big family celebrations. The woman stays at home while the man meets his friends for outings which he needn't explain or lie about. A well-brought-up girl is rarely alone on the streets at night and only rather recently permitted out alone with her young man. In spite of this advance (mainly visible in Mexico City, where the "new woman" is vibrantly making herself felt) the provincial custom is for a spinster of thirty-five, earning her own and the family's keep, to ask papa's permission to go out, and then not alone. A young widow of a good provincial family, whose husband was killed in a drunken crash, along with his tinseled dance-hall girlfriend, may not be seen anywhere with a man. The father and brothers of the deceased control the purse strings and the future of her children; if they say she may not go out, as they almost invariably do, she stays.

It is not difficult to see the picture; a woman out alone is not a good woman and therefore searching for sex as trade or pleasure and open to molestation. She may, of course, go to a restaurant in the tourist centers with perfect ease, but she must not wander too far off. The solution is to join tours, pick up another lonely soul, or, if possible, travel with a friend; or to fly to smaller towns where there is absolutely nothing to do at night but go to bed and start life early in the clear, washed Mexican morning.

Mexicans flatter and flatter opulently. You may be called "My Queen," "My dream," and a thousand other endearments. Your hand may be grabbed and pressed significantly while you're reaching for your key; a hotel official may ask you for a date while your husband is upstairs shaving. You will be delighted to be called *"señorita"* although salesgirls at home stopped calling you "Miss" many years ago—until you notice that every woman is called *"señorita"* until she is ready for embalming. If a valet or taxi driver asks whether you like to dance, weigh your answer carefully; in Mexico one thing leads very quickly to another. Should you go to a public dance hall, *never* dance with anyone but your escort and never engage in light banter with anyone outside your party. Don't wear naked dresses, don't wear much jewelry, don't carry furs, don't flash insulting stacks of money, and don't sit in front with a cab driver when you are alone, no matter how much he beams and glitters at you.

Should you become involved with a Mexican, remember that along with the immortal passion and the flowers and the serenades, he is a busy man trying to support a large family and a smaller one (the *casa chica*) on the side, that he *must* spend hours talking with his friends, that he *must* visit his sainted mother frequently, that cars always break down under him, and that trains dash past him at railroad stations. To paraphrase the old saw about New York: he is fine for a visit but you wouldn't want to live there.

Outside of Mexico City, which has real elegance in a few places and provincial elegance in others, the simpler your clothing the better. You cut yourself off from many people by being too well and perfectly dressed, particularly in small towns and villages. Having a run in your stockings (if you wear them at all) or creases in your skirt or a stain on your blouse is of no moment; many have them. And, although the nylon-dacron-acrilon wonders have all sorts of virtues, take some cottons for the tropics; the others feel like viscous metal in the high sun.

Don't let a maid or laundress wash stockings or frail underclothes. For centuries her predecessors and her family and friends in the village have been beating clothing with sticks over rocks or stone slabs, fine for removing grime and soil, to her mind the only reason for washing clothing. The notion of lightly swishing something in water to freshen it has come to some country girls. Others have still to learn. Until that time do your own.

It might interest you that gold jewelry (in addition to the famous silver) is comparatively cheap in Mexico and often beautifully designed; and that with enough time to make the necessary contacts, you can have a simple (not inspired) dress made, several hems raised, two zippers replaced, and a bit of hand mending done, all in one day, by a seamstress who will charge about $3 to $5 for the day plus the cost of two simple meals.

One of the great bargains and sources of entertainment for women in Mexico is a session at a small neighborhood beauty salon. (Those on the big avenues are politer versions of their counterparts in the States and offer no novelty.) The cost is little—three or four American dollars will buy almost all repairs, short of plastic surgery or dentistry—and the girls are skillful. It may take as much as an hour to be manicured, a slow, painstaking process—like painting miniatures, and done with the same breathless concentration. Combing out the hair takes time, too, not only because the hairdresser is inventive as well as meticulous, but because he understands the sybaritic wallowing that upper- and middle-class Mexican women indulge in to fill their days and please their imminently wandering husbands; it is part of their harem life of children, maids, hairdressers, and teas.

To compensate for the loss of time, there are extraordinary experiences with temperamental water pressure: water may trickle playfully or shoot out with the force of a fire hose, turning from burning hot to congealing cold, and back, in seconds. And the novelty of having hair lacquer sprayed at you from a Flit gun, your face protected by a Mexican comic book. There can be nothing hazardous, however, in these adventures, because the Virgin of Guadalupe stands in a shrine over the water taps and she, notoriously democratic, protects the foreign infidel as well as the faithful.

Index

Tuxtla Gutiérrez, 254–55
Tzintzuntzan, 229
  pottery, 77
  Night of the Dead, 354

Umbrias, Joaquin Hernandez, 258
United States:
  invasion at Veracruz, 275
  and Mexican rebellions, 185, 186–87
  and Mexican War of Independence,
    181
  war with Mexico, 134, 183
Universities:
  Campeche, 402
  Jalapa, 292
  Mérida, 373
  Morelia, 213
University City, 44, 121, 135
Upset stomachs, 55, 57, 409
Ursulo Galván, 290–91
Uruapan, 224–25
  crafts, 78
Uxmal, 358–59, 363, 369, 379–80, 384
  hacienda, 383

Valencia, Fray Martín de, 147
Valladolid, 213
  See also Morelia
Valle del Bravo, 151
Vanilla pods, 299
Vegetables, in Merced market, 24–25
Vegetarian restaurants, Mexico City,
    72
Vendors:
  Cathedral village, 31
  Coatzacoalcos, 311
  Cuernavaca, 159
  Mandinga, 287
  Mérida, 376
  Mexico City, 8, 9, 12, 35, 68, 402
  of rebozos, 234–35
    Mitla, 248
  of serapes, 235–36
  Tecolutla, 299
  on trains, 4–5, 95, 156
  Veracruz Carnival, 282
Venison, 377
Veracruz, 2, 14, 114, 184, 274–86, 340
  dances, 102
  environs, 286–87
  Huastec art, 139
Villa, Francisco (Pancho), 185–87
La Villa, Mexico City, 352–53

Villages, 174
Villahermosa, 326–32
  museum, 170
  route to, 310–12
Villa Obergón, 134–35
Violence, 364
Virgen de La Soledad, 38
Virgin of Guadalupe, 12, 177–78,
    352
Visitor's permits, 406
Voladores, 301, 346
Volcanoes, Paricutín, 225
Von Humboldt, Alexander, 125

Wake-up calls, 408–9
Waldeck, Jean Frédéric, 334, 337
Walks, 21–22
  Mexico City, 23–47
  See also names of cities
Walnut-shell souvenirs, 209
Wanderers, 10–13
War of Independence (1810), 178,
    180–81, 202
Washington, George, statue of, 286
Watchmen, 13
Water:
  for drinking, 56, 409
  faucets, 145–46
Waterfall, Cuernavaca, 162
Watermelon, 25
Wax museum, Mexico City, 36
Weather, 417
  Jalapa, 296
  nortes, 340
Weavings, 86, 143
  Mitla, 248–49
  Oaxaca, 244
  See also Crafts; Textiles
Weddings, rural, 346
Whitefish, 223–24
Williams, Tennessee, Night of the
    Iguana, 270
Wines, 56, 141
Women, 227–28, 417–19
  clothes shopping, 88
  Mexican, 2, 37
    Las Casas, 256
    machismo and, 52–53
    Mérida, 372, 376
    mothers, 225–27
    Oaxacan, 238
    photography of, 252
    Tehuanas, 251–52